DISC Encyclopedia

Behavioral flexibility is the key to your success.

CHAMELEON
ON A RAINBOW™

DISC Encyclopedia
Published by Indaba Press

Indaba Global, Inc.
5050 1st Avenue North
Saint Petersburg, FL 33710
727-327-8777

www.DISCflex.com
www.Indaba1.com

Written by Hellen Davis

Co-Authors
Derrick Brown
Cale Owen
Tyssa Garner

Editors
Lindsey Davis
Jack D. Davis
Justin Davis

ISBN: 978-1-58570-250-1

Printed in the United States of America

DISCflex™

DISC Encyclopedia

Behavioral flexibility is the key to your success

CHAMELEON ON A RAINBOW™

"Learn the critical skill set to become 'a chameleon on a rainbow'™ no matter what situation you face."

Hellen Davis

DISCflex™

Table of Contents

Foreword

When the Indaba Global Team began this undertaking, we had no idea the amount of time, energy, resources, or effort it would take. Had I known, I probably would not have made the decision to embark on this project. But, this experience has truly been one of the most rewarding of my career, I am very proud of the results - the DISCflex™ assessment, the DISC encyclopedia and the DISCflex™ eLearning suite. Throughout my life I have always strived to understand people's behavior, their motivation and most important, their willingness or unwillingness to adapt to the situations they face. When I was in my late teens, I memorized this quote from Norman Vincent Peale when my mother died.

As I looked at how each family member dealt with our loss, I began my quest into analyzing behavior.

> *"Understanding can overcome any situation, however mysterious or insurmountable it may appear to be."*
>
> *~ Norman Vincent Peale*

About the same time, I stumbled upon Viktor E. Frankl's book, Man's Search for Meaning. This book was written in response to Doctor Frankl's experiences as a World War II concentration camp prisoner. His words resonated and I carried a binder of thought-provoking quotes for several years to inspire me to make the best of any situation I might face. Dr. Frankl's words are the perfect introduction to the DISC Encyclopedia:

"Between stimulus and response there is a space. In that space is our power to choose our response. In our response lies our growth and our freedom."

"A human being is a deciding being."

"When we are no longer able to change a situation - we are challenged to change ourselves"

"For the meaning of life differs from man to man, from day to day and from hour to hour. What matters, therefore, is not the meaning of life in general but rather the specific meaning of a person's life at a given moment."

"Everyone has his own specific vocation or mission in life; everyone must carry out a concrete assignment that demands fulfillment. Therein he cannot be replaced, nor can his life be repeated, thus, everyone's task is unique as his specific opportunity to implement it."

Frankl's words made me consider the purpose of this offering. It is our goal - at Team Indaba Global - through the information in the DISC Encyclopedia - to provide you with knowledge so that you can choose to situationally flex or long term morph your behavior at will. By teaching you to use these skills to better the world, we will be rewarded for our efforts.

I wish you all the best in your own search for meaning.

Hellen Davis
CEO, Indaba Global, Inc.

Team Indaba Dedication

First and foremost the DISC Encyclopedia, DISCflex™ assessment, and eLearning are dedicated to the Indaba Global Team, our customers, and our distributors around the world. Everyone who worked on this project added their thoughts and concepts, stories and toil to create a marvelous end product. I couldn't decide the appropriate order for thanking you all so I will go with the old standard: alphabetical list.

Andrea Behn - The volume of work you produced in a short amount of time was stressful indeed! Thanks for always being a trouper with a sunny smile and great disposition.

Derrick Brown - Your persistence, research, insight, and push back along every stage of this mission were critical. This was an exceptional project precisely because you were the project manager. Not only did you steer the logistics of the assessment, you led the drive for accuracy, questioned the assessment industry and found it sorely needing an overhaul, and finally, together as a team we decided the best way to change an industry for the better. **WELL DONE! BRAVO!**

Lindsey Davis - You put together the video production and reference materials and kept us on schedule. To that end, you were awesome in herding tigers. As an author's note, Lindsey is not my daughter, or is she related to any of the Davis family at Indaba Global, but that doesn't make us any less proud of how far Lindsey has grown in the years she has been on the Indaba Global Team.

Jack D. Davis - We all handed the final chapters to you the vet because of your quick mind and amazing editing abilities. I don't think anyone turns around word documents quicker and without one word of complaint. No matter how tired you were you always came through for us! I will always be proud of your work ethic and high standards. Plus you are an amazing partner!

Justin Davis - I was rewarded beyond my wildest dreams when you became intrigued by the DISCflex™ product and the associated learning. When you said that you were learning a lot, I took that as a fabulous compliment. I could tell that you were enjoying the journey of taking in the materials, figuring out how to use them, and making decisions about how to influence the various situations that you find yourself in.

Tyssa Garner - Diligent, hardworking, and bright. Always thoughtful in your comments and input, you added a great deal to this body of work. The design you shepherded through is tremendous.

Cale Owen - You jumped in right in the middle of this and stepped up to the plate; writing, editing, adjusting whenever someone needed something done - you did it without complaint (even if it meant having to dramatically dial down your Dominance and severely increase your Compliance for many months ☺).

Brittany Russell - I have never seen you come into the office without a smile on your face! Every team should have the benefit of someone with your beautiful, sunny personality and quick laughter.

Debra Volpe - We can always count on you to get whatever we need done, in record time, with no errors. This level of professionalism is rarely seen and everyone - especially me - appreciates your time and efforts on this project.

 DISCflex™

Personal Dedication from Hellen Davis

I have been very fortunate. I have been inspired by many people. As this book goes to print, I have several people who are important to me that I would like to mention. All are dear to my heart. All are so different. All have taught me a great deal about Dominance, Influence, Steadiness, and Compliance; and how these Factors meld together in unique ways to underpin our personalities. Without our differences, what a boring world it would be!

The first is my Baba, never far from my thoughts, waking or sleeping, near or far apart. I don't know what happened when we met, but you rocked my world instantly - and you still do! You have a listening ear (even when you'd rather hear golden silence) because you know it makes me happy. You have a depth of thoughtfulness that I continually marvel at; and I have been privileged to see you excel in many situations where others without your skill level and behavioral aptitude would have floundered. One of the things that I admire most about you is your willingness to work hard, even when the odds are against you. There hasn't been a time that you haven't won out through persistence and sheer determination. Yes, we battle, as Elevated Ds do! But I have faith that we will always feel the love and get back on the same channel, no matter what life has in store for us. You are a great man. I am honored that you love me.

Fran Landolf, you have been a colleague and friend (tried and true) for many years. I count our friendship as a special blessing! You have that interesting mix of Steadiness (thoughtfulness) and Influence with a graceful, strong Dominance that pops up out of its hiding place - just when people don't expect it! You are constantly in motion, always moving yourself and others gently but firmly forward with quiet determination. If we could bottle this trait we'd make billions…

Rob Jennings, how many decades has it been? I can always count on you to be there for me with great advice, a joke, a soldier's honor and value system, the perseverance of a saint - all meshed together by a brilliant mind.

Marty Sasson has the kindest, biggest heart on the planet, the warmest soul ever, and is the 'go to' person when I want my cares to slip away. How fortunate am I to have a friend like you!

Jackie Hewitt: my sister and best friend, my traveling buddy, my laughing crony, companion, supporter, and cheerleader all wrapped up inside the most loyal, kindest person in the world! Lately, you've been through the wringer and as expected, you've come out stronger and even more capable. I admire you and love you more than words can say!

Theresa Cowie, you have always been a second mother to me, steadfast in your love and caring. Your laughter across the miles is beautiful to hear. My father will probably never know exactly how fortunate he was when you came into his life. He thinks he knows; but I can tell you, he doesn't even come close!

Richard Cowie: Well, Dad, another book under my belt. This project has been one of my favorites because of the complexity and research involved. Because of your influence, the many experiences, adventures you gave us, and through our travels, the cultures our family was fortunate to learn about, this body of work was made richer. Having the blend of experiences that I did made this book a possibility. Combine that with the ethic of hard work and can-do attitude you fostered in me, and ultimately this project became a reality. An international viewpoint was vital in making sure the DISC Encyclopedia worked for people across the world. I thank you from the bottom of my heart for being such a great Dad and for always being proud of your children.

And finally, my daughter, Jazmin: My heart swells with pride when I think of the person you have become. There are no limits to what you can accomplish. You are a true 'chameleon on a rainbow'; morphing, adapting and flexing to every new adventure and each new challenge (most self-imposed!) with grace and ease. Your future is so bright it burns my eyes!

Introduction to the DISC Encyclopedia

"Everyone is capable of behavioral flexing, given knowledge, but they have to be willing to change. The missing piece required to complete the puzzle of reaching full potential is usually your willingness and practice."
Hellen Davis

For any manager or leader, this book is critically important. In performance management, there are only three areas where the law allows management to hold employees accountable:

1. Deliverables based on expectations for task assignments and responsibilities,

2. Attendance, and

3. Behavior.

Behavior is the most difficult aspect of management to regulate - whether adjusting your own behavior or communicating appropriate behavior expectations of others. Here is precisely the reason why this area is so essential in business.

> *"Behavior is what a man does, not what he thinks, feels, or believes."*
>
> *~Unknown Author*

Traditionally, managers are fairly well trained in telling employees what tasks need to be accomplished. They are also quite good at letting employees know when to come to work, what meetings they need to attend, and what customers they should call on. So all in all, most managers have the 1. deliverables and 2. attendance part of performance management down pat. But when it comes to the third point - behavior - there seems to be a huge gap when it comes to communicating to behavioral expectations.

Communicating Expectations Regarding Behavior

Managers typically stumble over topics like how an employee is expected to control their emotions, how assertive an employee should be, how an employee should balance paradoxes. Several of these paradoxical quandaries revolve around behavior tendencies. An example is being independent and self-motivated; but also being an exceptional team player. Another is the paradox of precisely how to behave when you are asked to be friendly, warm, and respectful to other employees; but are also told to be efficient and effective in getting tasks accomplished - even when team members consistently let you down. Or precisely what is the appropriate way to act when your team needs you to close a deal; but you know that it might be more prudent to have patience and not pressure your customer.

The DISC Encyclopedia addresses these points as well as how to recognize behavior that employees typically exhibit, how to teach managers and employees how to choose the appropriate behavior for the situations they face, how to assess (through the DISCflex™ Business Behaviors Report) their current behavioral patterns and DISC Sub-factors™, and finally how to communicate behavioral preferences. With the DISC Encyclopedia, managers can learn how to effectively express expectations and how to outline and communicate appropriate behavior guidelines to their employees no matter what situation they face.

Nowhere is behavior more important than in decision making. What specifically are the behaviors of a prudent decision maker? Does the decision maker wait until all the information is in, weighing every pro and con, stalling on making the final decision until all each and every part of the entire process is mapped out? Or does the decision maker move ahead self-confidently knowing that they are able to balance uncertainty with an assurance in their abilities to tackle any problems that might arise? The choices in behavior are abundant. The key in running a successful business is training employees to know how to pick the best behavior to get the best results. Equally important is training management to coach employees in this skill.

Benefits of the DISC Encyclopedia

With the DISC Encyclopedia, behavior is explained easily and is taught by using meaningful examples. The goal is for managers to use the 4 DISC Factors and 12 DISC Sub-factors™ as well as the 15 typical DISC Patterns to explain what behavior they expect and in what reasonable guidelines, boundaries, and limitations that behavior should be conveyed. Knowing how to explain a specific, expected behavior will lower frustrations that might pop up between managers and employees. It will save the organization from having to settle employee disputes associated with unclear behavioral guidelines. Ultimately this knowledge will help the enterprise thrive because employees throughout the ranks will know precisely what the behavioral norms and expectations are.

The DISC Encyclopedia is a 'how to' course that helps you change and adapt to any situation; giving you the skill sets necessary to achieve excellence; regardless of your desired goals or outcomes.

The DISC Encyclopedia is about personal development and accelerated learning. The DISC Encyclopedia gives you a method of discovering the behaviors that will propel you toward your goals in a way that will allow you to bring out the very best in yourself and others. You will truly be able to create the results you want while keeping in touch with your value system.

"People don't change their behavior unless it makes a difference for them to do so."

~Frank Tarkenton

Goals of the DISC Encyclopedia

The primary goal of DISCflex™ and the DISC Encyclopedia is to teach the necessity of short term or situational behavioral flexing and the potential for long term behavioral morphing. The secondary goal is for you to be armed with the knowledge for understanding other people's behavior with a view to adapting yourself in such a way that makes communication and understanding between the parties better. The DISC Encyclopedia will present you with a comprehensive understanding of the components of behavior as well as how to adjust them in yourself and recognize them in others.

For each Next Steps section, in each chapter, please log on to the eLearning platform to view the 'How To's' and more information.

DISCflex™

Changing Your Behavior

First let's talk about the primary goal: Changing your behavior. When you want to make changes in your behavior, you are faced with two choices:

1. Do you simply want to be more adaptable or flexible in the situations you face? We call this situational behavioral flexing.
2. Or will you make the decision to change how you behave in a fundamental way? We call this long term behavioral morphing.

In the DISC Encyclopedia, we discuss each in great depth. Regardless of which of the two options you choose, you must have the knowledge, capacity, and willingness to actually work on the skills associated with changing behavior.

If you utilize all three aspects:

1. knowledge,
2. capacity, and
3. willingness, you will be successful.

Without any of these, we admit that the knowledge we provide in the DISC Encyclopedia is just a tad above useless! Our motto at Indaba Global is 'Success Through Applied Knowledge' so it was extremely important to deliver a manual with tactics that can be applied most immediately for instant results.

It is also important to know the steps you will have to take to change behavior.

- Determine what the behavior is that you want to emulate. What is your goal?
- Take a cold hard look at your current behavior and determine precisely what needs adjusting.
- Understand and utilize the information given to you about precisely what it takes to change behavior to be successful.
- And finally, *you must be willing to make the change.*

Recognizing Other People's Behavioral Patterns

The word programming is borrowed from computer science but it is equally applicable when we discuss behavior. Behavioral patterns are predictable ways of how people react and respond. Our behavior is shaped or for want of a better word - programmed - through societal norms, modeling (parents, teachers, peer, etc.), and by being rewarded or punished for our actions. It suggests that our thoughts, feelings, and our actions are simply habitual programs that can be changed by upgrading or corrupting what we call our mental software. Programming refers to the way we organize thoughts and ideas into patterns. These patterns produce results or outcomes which we call actions and behavior.

Positive programming is a set order of events, a planned method or a system that is installed to achieve desired results. Corruption results in less than acceptable behavior. How we organize what we see, hear and feel; how we edit and filter information from the outside world; is a major component of behavior training techniques. Each human being is unique and so is their behavior but, because we live together and interact on so many levels, we have indeed been programmed to behave in certain ways.

Behavioral tendencies are to a large extent based on the underlying behavioral preferences that people have. These are called behavioral factors. To make is easier to dissect and break down behavior, we talk about DISC Factors and DISC Sub-factors™. It doesn't take a lot of common sense to understand how important it is to be able to recognize behavior patterns in others, to understand how behavior patterns might emerge, and how it might benefit an individual to be able to have a deep level of understanding about these topics. The information regarding how to recognize the 15 DISC Behavioral Patterns, the 4 DISC Factors, and 12 DISC Sub-factors™ is readily available in the DISC Encyclopedia. This is indeed a powerful skill set to acquire!

"To know what people really think, pay regard to what they do, rather than what they say."

~René Descartes

1 Introduction to DISC

After completing the DISC assessment, you were most likely amazed with your DISC report, since it could easily have been written by you, about you. In fact, you might have even asked, "How could they get all that information so quickly and accurately?" DISC profiles are one of the best (and most widely used) profiling vehicles to assess a person's behavioral tendencies. If you take some time to review your patterns – your peaks and valleys on the assessment graph – you will notice the fluctuations between the four Factors which measure your Dominance, Influence, Steadiness, and Compliance.

> *"The man of character, sensitive to the meaning of what he is doing, will know how to discover the ethical paths in the maze of possible behavior"*
>
> *~Earl Warren*

At this point you may be asking yourself, "Now what?" How can you use this information to improve your performance, and possibly change and develop behaviors? Based on your unique personal assessment's results, Indaba Global has developed online and blended learning (combination of e-learning, webinar, in classroom, and/or coaching) training programs to make sure you have the knowledge, tools, models, methodologies, theories, and ultimately the skills necessary so that you can easily adapt (dial up or dial down behavioral tendencies) in any given situation. In simple language, it means that after successful training you should be able to modify your behavior at will, according to the situation you are facing. You can then examine yourself, your personality, and your behaviors more accurately than ever. With this information, you will be ready to begin your training to learn how to develop and improve your behaviors.

For example, if a CEO's DISC indicates a highly Elevated Dominance Factor, associated with control, and a much lower Steadiness Factor, associated with thoughtfulness, this individual would most likely make choices that will insure immediate control or power over most situations. A CEO with this profile would not necessarily spend lots of time being thoughtful about the ramifications of authoritative power. To compound this, if the spread between Dominance and Steadiness is large, he/she might do so with very little patience for people who move at a difference pace than they find acceptable. With the proper training, this individual could adapt and purposefully make the factor spread less by bringing down the Dominance Factor and raising the Steadiness Factor. After appropriate training, this CEO might be a bit more thoughtful and a little less assertive or domineering when trying to accomplish goals in the situations that require different behavioral strategies.

Once you start to understand your behavioral patterns and train yourself to adapt and 'flex' your behavior muscles - making them stronger and more adaptable – you will be able to handle almost any situation with great ease. The bottom line: YOU can decide what you want to do with your own DISC profile, and Indaba Global will be here to help with e-Learning solutions.

A Cautionary Tale: Why Job Fit Doesn't Work

While considering how to use personality profiles or behavior assessments, some people wonder how they can use the results. Some experts say that you can (and possibly should) 'job fit' people into occupations, professions, or careers based on the results. They ascertain that assessment results uncover strengths and weaknesses; that patterns emerge leading to predictive analysis. While it is indeed true that behavioral and other preferences are uncovered by the assessment process, it is simply untrue that people should be forever 'put in a box' of 'job fit' or anything similar, based on the results of any form of assessment. In my opinion this type of assessment profiling or usage does a grave disservice to personal and professional growth.

In my world, behavioral flexibility is the key to growth. Knowing who you are today and deciding what you can flex or morph into in the future is your choice. Being able to adjust your behavior to the situations you find yourself in unlocks a world of opportunities. With this type of thinking, you can be anything you want to become - especially in the realm of performance and behavior. With the appropriate self awareness, knowledge, and willingness, you can uncover unlimited potential. So now that you know precisely how I view 'job fit' or similar ideology, let's look at specifically why this thinking might be dangerous in a practical application.

Diverse Behavior in an Engineering Team -- If you look at the table below, you will see that 'job fit' does not really explain how a team of engineers (below), who many 'job fit' proponents would surmise should be Elevated Ss and Cs, manage to be so diverse in their behavioral approaches and preferences as reflected in their DISC results. Let's look at the make-up of this highly successful, fully functioning engineering team:

	Pattern	D	I	S	C
Engineer 1 (Team Leader)	SC	D51	I30	S56	C68
Engineer 2	DS	D86	I39	S82	C10
Engineer 3	DIC	D63	I58	S15	C59
Engineer 4	DC	D79	I15	S44	C61
Engineer 5	D	D100	I30	S25	C33
Engineer 6	DI	D58	I86	S25	C33
Engineer 7	DI	D64	I74	S16	C51
Engineer 8	DC	D58	I18	S34	C68
Engineer 9	DI	D100	I86	D44	C4
Engineer 10	DC	D72	I18	S34	C68
Engineer 11	C	D58	I15	S34	C95
Engineer 12	DI	D72	I100	S25	C10
Engineer 13	DIC	D58	I52	S44	C51
Engineer 14	DIS	D64	I62	S69	C10
Engineer 15	SC	D23	I10	S93	C98
Engineer 16	SC	D43	I6	S100	C95
Engineer 17	IS	D51	I62	S69	C33
Ranges:		**23-100**	**6-100**	**15-100**	**4-98**

DISCflex™

Our advice (especially after viewing the prior table): Look at proven experience and future capabilities, as well as behavioral flexibility, when hiring. Please do not 'job fit'! We find that a vital component in making the appropriate hiring decision is the individual's willingness to grow and learn and change (including their desire to view feedback in as a gift). Very often, these types of traits completely override the person's natural tendencies as uncovered by an assessment. So, again, 'job fit' does not take this into account.

Now take a look at the patterns and look at the spread between the various factors. There are many different behavioral styles that all contribute to the same team and responsibilities. An engineer does not have to be an Elevated SC individual to dial up those traits. Whatever behavioral style an individual has is their natural strengths, which are fully capable of completing tasks and working to flex their behaviors. A word of warning, however, as you look at this chart, please note there is an abundance of Elevated D characteristics on this team. One of the complaints the leader had is that the team seemed to be in constant chaos with very little planning before they take action. By looking at all of the DISC patterns in a team, it is fairly easy to see where the strengths and weaknesses of the whole combine to make this team successful, or to make it fail.

	Pattern
Engineer 5	D
Engineer 11	C
Engineer 6	DI
Engineer 7	DI
Engineer 9	DI
Engineer 12	DI
Engineer 2	DS
Engineer 8	DC
Engineer 4	DC
Engineer 10	DC
Engineer 17	IS
Engineer 1 (Team Leader)	SC
Engineer 15	SC
Engineer 16	SC
Engineer 14	DIS
Engineer 3	DIC
Engineer 13	DIC

Something else to think about in a team environment: Does the person you are thinking about hiring or bringing into the team, bring diversity of approach and/or behavioral flexibility to the team? In other words, if you already have a team of Elevated Dominance individuals, it probably isn't a good idea to bring another, similar Elevated Dominance behavioral preference onto the team. Perhaps it might be prudent to look at the skills an Elevated Influence, Elevated Compliance, or Elevated Steadiness person (or other combination of behavioral pattern) might bring to the mix. Cognitive diversity is a crucial element in a high performance team.

Now let's take a deep dive and examine the prior table. As you can see, the results are distributed quite a bit amongst the DISC factors. Out of the results, there are only 3 Elevated Steadiness individuals, 4 Elevated Compliance individuals, and only 2 Elevated SC individuals. This blows proclamations like "Look for Elevated SC people when hiring engineers" out of the water.

"To place individuals in jobs based on their assessed patterns and personality profiles limits them and in turn constrains your company."

~Hellen Davis

From observing this team, I can tell you that all of the engineers in this group have a mix of DISC elevations and all have different traits and profiles, but all are successful in their jobs. And I can take just about any group of people in just about any profession and show the similar results - the range of DISC factors shows them to be spread across the board. Time and again, we have shown this behavioral preference diversity aspect to hold true in both high and low functioning teams. This proves that pigeonholing people into roles or jobs because of their profiles or patterns is just not appropriate or accurate. If that had occurred, all but two of the engineers could potentially have been advised to go into another profession or would not have been selected for this team.

Unlimited Potential

If you look at individual's patterns and fit them into a job based on it, it simply will not work. There is no mold that says what people will be good at or what they can do. Individuals are not limited by their behavior or their assessment pattern. Nor should they be pigeonholed or have to accept a specific profession because of their behavioral preferences. We believe you can be anything you want to be. You just have to learn behavioral flexibility and morphing - much like a chameleon on a rainbow.

Here's the bottom line: Behavior assessment tools measure not what people can do, but how the person approaches their responsibilities - the "How" not the "What".

Additionally, although they may not have the "ideal" pattern or preferences for a job, it does not mean that they can't learn to do it effectively. If they can flex their behavior to a mission, deliverables, purpose, job or a task, they can be highly successful. Keeping jobs and minds open to the different ways that different people might approach their responsibilities is extremely beneficial to an organization.

Thinking Critically About Job Fit and Patterns

Consider another example: an IT person. This specific IT person must write code for a new program. Because this task involves details and steady focus, does this mean that only a Compliance or Steadiness individual can be a successful IT person and write code? Absolutely not! Remember, it's not about what a person can do based on their behavior pattern, but about how they approach their responsibilities.

- A High D person might prefer to first start writing and driving down the path to finish the code before using their other DISC factor behaviors.
- A High I person might prefer to gather a team together, talk about the goals, and only having done so, then drive it forward (D).

- A High S person might prefer to spend 95% planning and 5% implementing the plan.
- A High C person might prefer to gather the rules and expectations before starting to ask other people's advice (I), think about how to move forward at the 30,000 foot level (S), or move forward into an action state (D).

As you can see, all these people CAN succeed in IT jobs and perform these tasks in an appropriate fashion. They are not limited by their pattern or behavioral preference, which upon first inspection - if you were in 'job fit' mode - may say that they are not the "ideal" candidate because they're not a C person, but they CAN accomplish their responsibilities by approaching them in vastly different ways.

Managing Behavior

I hope by now that I have given you something to think about with regard to 'job fit'. Besides 'job fit', another caution is when people impose their 'behavioral will' on an employee. Imagine the stress this might cause! This ultimately does not work either because employees over time will resent this imposition. When managers delegate tasks and responsibilities, they should be careful NOT to impose only one behavior 'how'. Rather focus on performance, results, and behavior guidelines while taking into account the different ways DISC preferences might approach their responsibilities.

Assessments Are A Snapshot In Time

Assessments are really simply a snapshot in time based on the answers to how a person reviews a series of questions based on what the individual is thinking about situationally and contextually as they take the test. For example, if the person is thinking about how they might handle a new uncooperative team versus managing a well-run department, the results might be vastly different for the same leader. If an employee is viewing the assessment from their role as a technical expert rather than from their management role, the results will be different.

The true value of assessments is holistic view of self-perception and personal preferences, as well as soliciting third party input (e.g. from work, family, social). By looking at the inputs we can easily determine whether the person has the ability to 'flex' their behavior to accomplish the deliverable. The question is: "Does this person we are assigning this to have the capability to get this done in an acceptable way?" Capability is the combination of ability, knowledge, and time. To get beyond the status quo you have to thrive - not just survive - in discharging your responsibilities. And in discharging those responsibilities, reading the situation and being able to adapt to it whenever appropriate is key. Think of being a chameleon on a rainbow!

2 Introduction to DISC Sub-factors™

If you recall from your initial introduction to DISC assessments, there are four primary Factors or measurement indicators used to assess an individual's personality and behavioral tendencies. The four primary DISC Factors are D (dominance), I (influence), S (steadiness), and C (compliance).

> *"Knowing yourself is the beginning of all wisdom."*
>
> *~Aristotle*

- D (dominance) relates to control, power, and assertiveness. It focuses on an individual's drive and need for authority. Dominance elevated individuals are driven to achieve, love getting results, and are determined to find success. They are compelled to change the status quo. These individuals can't help but drive forward and are often described as highly energetic.

- I (influence) is associated with social interactions, as well as the person's persuasiveness. It speaks to influencing flair, or the individual's tendency to be charming during interactions. Influence is also apparent in the person's confidence and a tendency to rely on their communication abilities to shape a situation.

- S (steadiness) denotes patience, persistence and thoughtfulness, as well as the person's need for spending adequate time in paying attention to detail. It is required, for action plans to be fleshed out and goals achieved at an optimum level of forethought.

- C (compliance) sometimes referred to as conscientiousness, correlates to a person's need for structure, order, and organization. It addresses the individual's desire to know and adhere to the policies, procedures, and rules of order governing the situation.

DISC Elevations

The extent to which these four primary DISC Factors are indicated in a person's emotional makeup can be measured in degrees of elevation on a scale from 0 to 100. The highs and lows of each of the four primary DISC Factors can be quantified by analysis. Then, these can be visually plotted on a graph. These measurements form the basis of a personalized DISC assessment.

While there are literally millions of variations for the pattern combinations created by the degrees of elevation of the four predominant factors, Indaba Global research has grouped the various pattern possibilities into 15 basic DISC patterns. These basic DISC patterns depict the peaks and valleys associated with the four primary DISC Factors. These basic 15 patterns, however, should only be used as guidelines for insight into how people with these types of peak and valley patterns behave. Most important is customized DISC analysis based on the precise elevations for each individual. This process is what is truly insightful. Your behavior depends on how you combine the factors. Having a low factor in one area is not necessarily a negative. All that the assessment measures is what YOUR preferences are as well as providing insight into your ability to 'flex' or adapt your preference to the circumstances you currently find yourself in. Knowing how you would prefer to make decisions or act, you can learn how to encourage all four of the factors to work cooperatively together for you. By using the customized elevations, an individual can determine how much 'situational flexing' they might have to do. They can also figure out what stress this might cause based on their current skill level at flexing.

Reviewing Your Assessment

When reviewing your assessment results, it is beneficial to look at the four principal DISC Factors (dominance, influence, steadiness, and compliance) as the regulators of our behavior. Since we have already described each factor and the associated behavioral tendencies in great detail for each, now we will move on to DISC Sub-factors™.

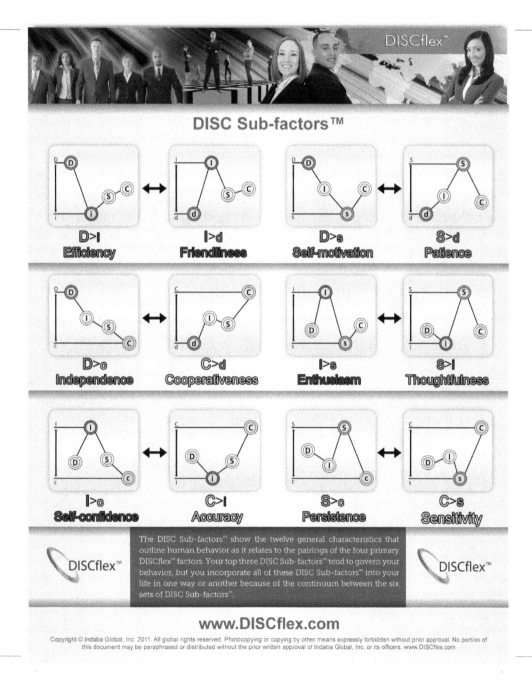

The DISC Sub-factors™ show the twelve general characteristics that outline human behavior as it relates to the pairings of the four primary DISCflex™ factors. Your top three DISC Sub-factors™ tend to govern your behavior, but you incorporate all of these DISC Sub-factors™ into your life in one way or another because of the continuum between the six sets of DISC Sub-factors™.

www.DISCflex.com

DISC Sub-factors™ are used when describing the relationship between only two DISC factors. When comparing the two factors, we refer to their pairing as a DISC Sub-factor™ and we can describe the typical behavior when one factor overpowers another. For example, a person's Dominance Factor scoring far higher than their Influence Factor, is called 'Efficiency'.

This Sub-factor descriptive word 'Efficiency' is logical if you think about the behavior of a person who wants to get things done by driving forward without thinking about how to best influence. They don't want to talk about it, they know how to do it and talk is wasting time.

There are twelve possible combinations or pairings which connect the four Factors on the DISC profile.

The 12 DISCflex™ Sub-factors are:

D>i Efficiency	I>d Friendliness
D>s Self-motivation	S>d Patience
D>c Independence	C>d Cooperativeness
I>s Enthusiasm	S>i Thoughtfulness
I>c Self-confidence	C>i Accuracy
S>c Persistence	C>s Sensitivity

The Sub-factor pairings that preside over an individual's behavioral tendencies can easily provide a deeper understanding of behavior preferences. Most important in a team, family, or group setting, these behavioral preferences can be mapped and compared to others within the group. Understanding of other people's Factors and Sub-factors opens dialogue and, most essential, can assist in building a foundation of respect and tolerance for how others communicate and operate.

It is vital to understand that Sub-factors are experience and perception based.

How someone defines the characteristics and behaviors associated with the DISC Factors and Sub-factors will form the basis of how they exhibit behavior and how they expect you to behave. Let's look at an example of how this might play out. If an individual has a highly Elevated Dominance with a much lower Compliance score, they will have a behavioral tendency to be regulated by the Sub-factor called Independence. If you think about it, Independence is the perfect descriptor for a behavior where a person would be governed by the need to be in control, rather than live according to someone else's rules. They are governed by an independent streak. But remember, being independent means different things to different people. It could mean that the person will forge a path on their own, never asking for assistance. It could be that they choose to be independent only from certain people - from their parents for example. Or it could mean that they equate independence solely with financial or decision

"Do not believe in anything simply because you have heard it. Do not believe in anything simply because it is spoken and rumored by many. Do not believe in anything simply because it is found written in your religious books. Do not believe in anything merely on the authority of your teachers and elders. Do not believe in traditions because they have been handed down for many generations. But after observation and analysis, when you find that anything agrees with reason and is conductive to the good and benefit of one and all, then accept it and live up to it."

~Buddha

DISCflex™

making independence. What you have to remember is that people will only exhibit that behavior which they equate with the DISC Sub-factors™ - AS THEY KNOW IT TO BE. Once you realize the importance perception and experience have on the Sub-factors, you can start to understand why there are so many different personalities in the world. The Independent Sub-factor literally holds a plethora of different personalities, as do all the other Sub-factors. Use the Sub-factors as a starting place to find out your behavioral preferences as well as those around you. You must know what your co-workers, friends, or family view Independence, Cooperativeness, and the rest of the Sub-factors to be.

Behavioral Authority

Even though the DISC assessment shows the behavioral tendencies of an individual at an exact measurable elevation, the amounts of D, I, S and C can move or adjust depending upon different situations or the particular place where the individual may be in their life. They really should be viewed as a 'snapshot in time'. The DISC Factors and their corresponding Sub-factors can also be highly dependent on the environment that the person is operating in. This is why some people behave vastly differently in a work, social, or family situation. This is precisely why we recommend completing a separate DISC assessment for each of these areas of your life as well as after significant life changes like: completing high school or college, beginning a new job, upon retirement, or when contemplating a change or when facing an uncertainty in your career. That said, DISC Factors and their corresponding numerical values can be fairly easily modified as circumstances require. People who score low on the Influence Factor can train themselves to become highly competent in this area. The same is true of the other Factors. When an individual chooses to allow one of the DISC Factors to become more or less governing, we describe it as dialing up or dialing down a particular trait or behavior. DISC's four prevailing Factors continually compete with each other for behavioral authority because most of us naturally adjust as the situation requires.

When you have to decide whether you will use one Factor's behavior rather than the other for the particular situation you are presently in, the Factors are what we call 'competing for authority'. One of the Factors has to win or dominate. Otherwise, the individual will not be able to move forward into action. As you learn to understand this in greater detail, you will learn how to 'fine tune' the frequency on your dial for each DISC Factor.

Negotiating Situations

As you can imagine, we will have situations where we need to bring out behavior associated with all of the DISC Factors and Sub-factors. The more versatile we are in various situations, the better we will be able to negotiate the numerous relationships we have in life. We just need to know how - the precise process and methodology - for adapting our thinking process so that we are able to call upon the appropriate behavior to benefit each situation. So keep in mind, when looking at the numeric values in a DISC assessment, that while the actual measurements can be plotted on a chart, they can change dramatically if the individual chooses to adapt their behavior to their present situation.

This ability to 'flex' your behavior - at will - by dialing up or down one or more of the DISC Factors is a highly desirable skill. Take for example the Sub-factor Enthusiasm. This Sub-factor is the trait of a high I and a low S. But by adjusting the I and S elevations, you can completely change your behavior. In fact, even though your primary behavioral DISC Sub-factor™ might be Enthusiasm, you can completely reverse the IS relationship to the point where you reverse the factor's governance. You can flex your S to go up and flex your I to go down during certain situations so that you are able to use the S over I Sub-factor, Thoughtfulness, when it helps you achieve a goal. Thoughtfulness is the opposing DISC Sub-factor™ to Enthusiasm. Bottom line: You must be able to flex your behavioral muscle to use all the Sub-factors to your advantage.

As you understand more and more about how the DISC Factors and Sub-factors affect behavioral choices and combine this knowledge with the lessons we are providing, you will learn how to shift gears in situations. You will consciously decide to use your DISC knowledge to get what you want accomplished most effectively. You will learn how to shift gears and decide which D, I, S or C Sub-factors will give you that Behavioral Authority to use as situations arise. By perfecting your ability to shift gears, you will have the ability to control your Sub-factor usage to your advantage.

DISC Factor Governance

Let's step back a moment and reiterate an important concept. The further apart the two DISC Factors are when measured in the original assessment - the greater the numerical difference in score, the stronger and more overbearing and forceful the governing Sub-factor will be. The greater the difference between the scores, the more stress it will cause you to override the behaviors associated with your governing Sub-factor.

It is easiest to change between Factors that are relatively the same because one is not completely overriding the other. It causes a lot of stress, however, to use a Factor that you are not comfortable using. If you tend not to like rules, you have a lower Compliance score, and if you also have a highly Elevated I Influence score, you will naturally ignore rules you don't like or will tend to try to change them through your influence. If you had less spread between the two, however, this lower difference might allow you to think about which one - Compliance or Influence type behavior - would be appropriate for the particular situation you are involved in. In other words, the two would compete equally waiting for your decision.

Bear in mind, we are multifaceted individuals who exhibit a plethora of different behaviors. You can embrace one or multiple Sub-factor behaviors at once. For example, you can most certainly be Independent and Efficient, or Cooperative and Patient, but the most prevalent Sub-factor - the one you will go to first - will tend to be the one with the greatest difference between two Factors. We call this your primary Sub-factor. For example, if a DISC profile indicates an extremely elevated D and on the opposite end an extremely low C, then this individual will naturally show Independence (D>c).

If the pairing spread results in the greatest difference between any two Factors of the four DISC Factors, then this Sub-factor will govern in your behavioral tendencies. This is important because it is extremely difficult to change your primary, governing, or overriding Sub-factors. You can change them for a certain situation, but it will cause a lot of stress to do so. As you look at your DISC information, focus on your most dominant Sub-factors and think about how these determine what types of careers, interests, hobbies, and jobs will work well for you. By understanding that your prevailing Sub-factors probably won't change too much over the course of your life, you

"People's behavior makes sense if you think about it in terms of their goals, needs, and motives."

~Thomas Mann

can take advantage of this information to create the life that best suits your natural behavioral tendencies. When you make this linkage, you'll find a fit you will undoubtedly be happy with.

Let's take a look at some of the Sub-factors and see how they are denoted in our materials. The first determinant in the pairing is which Factor is more highly elevated - or greater. For example: Let's examine a pairing of Dominance (D) and Influence (I). We have two potential Sub-factors. In the first case, we'll investigate when Dominance (D) is more elevated (higher) than Influence. In the second case we will flip the elevations and consider when Influence is greater than Dominance.

Think about this in terms of a situation. Imagine that you are in a position where you have a lot of experience and expertise. You are working on a team and time is of the essence. You have to choose between using Dominance or Influence type behaviors to accomplish the task. Are you going to tend to be more persuasive to encourage the team to work (I – Influence) or are you going to use the knowledge you have as a subject matter expert (D-Dominance) to get the goal accomplished? Well, the way you will most likely tend to go depends, to a large extent, on whether your Dominance or Influence Factor is more elevated. In the first case, Dominance (D) is more elevated (higher) than Influence, so this individual will most likely use his knowledge to simply power the project to the end goal. He chose Dominance type behavior over Influence type behavior.

We depict this symbolically as D>i. Notice that we use a capital letter 'D' for the more elevated Factor and lower case letters for the subordinate 'i'. Now let's reverse the relationship of the DISC Factors to see what might happen. If the Dominant (D) Factor is more elevated (higher) than the Influencing Factor (I), it creates the Sub-factor called 'efficiency'. In the second case where Influence is more elevated than Dominance, I>d, - we call this Sub-factor 'friendliness'. Here is the rub: You absolutely have behavioral choice in the actions you choose. Are you going to use 'friendliness' type behavior or its opposite, 'efficiency' type behavior, to accomplish your goal? You decide. Will you exert power or win the team over through communication and smiles? Again, you have to decide. In trying to figure this out, try to remember that the closer these two Factors are together in terms of elevation, the more conflicted you will be about which Sub-factor's behavior to use. This can be a good thing because you might vacillate between 1. Exerting power and 2. Being friendly and communicating well. In other words, you use them both equally effectively to get your way. You exert flexibility and use the behaviors inherent in both in equal measure.

The problem comes when the degree of separation is so great that you forget to flex your behavioral muscles and completely override one Sub-factor with another without thinking about what is best for the situation. You may naturally want to just tell them what to do - because your Dominance Factor is much more elevated than your Influence Factor. But, might there be negative consequences for this behavior? Shouldn't you think about what your natural tendency is and adapt to the situation if warranted and appropriate? Isn't it important to be conscious of making the appropriate behavior choices?

This is precisely why we study Sub-factors - to make it easier to differentiate what behaviors within our DISC pattern are causing us to behave in a certain manner.

Once we know about our Sub-factors, and their opposing Sub-factors, we can start to understand and re-train ourselves for many situations. We can learn about what we naturally gravitate

> *"Whatever is the natural propensity of a person is hard to overcome. If a dog were made a king, he would still gnaw at his shoe laces."*
>
> *~Hitopadesa*

to, and gain knowledge about skills that fall outside of what we might be comfortable doing. A good example of this is that people with a high degree of Cooperativeness, C>d, might be great team members, but have not yet flexed their behavioral muscle of Independence, D>c. They might be very uncomfortable using typical Elevated Dominance behaviors. But to be promoted, you have to step into a leadership role, and that requires D-type behavior. This doesn't mean that they have changed their natural tendencies; it just means that they know what the opposite behaviors of cooperativeness are and how to use these when appropriate. The reverse is also true, Elevated D-type people who are highly independent D>c might want to take a page out of the cooperativeness C>d book and learn what it takes to exhibit Elevated Compliance-type C>d behavior, when the situation calls for it. Especially since in order to get promoted, you also have to show that you can get along with your peers.

> *"The meeting of two personalities is like the contact of two chemical substances. If there is any reaction, both are transformed."*
>
> *~Carl Gustav Jung*

Unconscious Competence Model

Now, let's take a few moments to examine a simple 4-step model called the Unconscious Competence Model. The model describes how people discover areas that need work. It serves as a roadmap. This model will help you understand how you can dial up or dial down your Sub-factors to a point of using excellent situational behavioral flexing as a habit. It explains the process of going

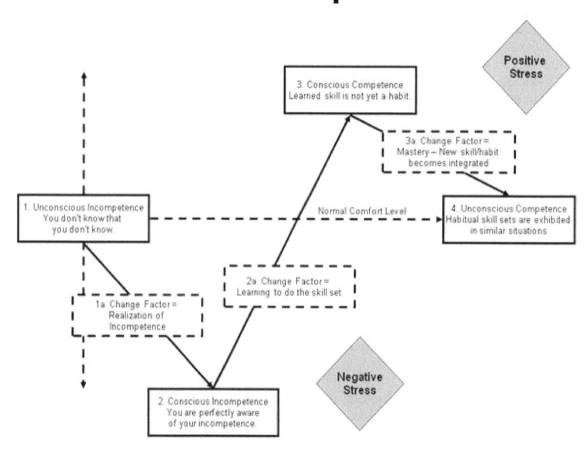

from Unconscious Incompetence, to being Consciously Incompetent. To move forward, you have to decide to learn how to become Consciously Competent. At last, if you make the effort by gaining adequate knowledge and applying focused practice, you can finally become a master. When you do, you are finally at the stage of Unconscious Competence.

A variation of an ancient proverb walks through the steps of our modern Unconscious Competence Model.

"He who knows not, and knows not that he knows not, is a fool - shun him.

He who knows not, and knows that he knows not and is willing - teach him.

He who knows, and knows that he knows not enough, is awakening - rouse him.

But he who knows is a wise man - follow him. "

The thinking behind this model starts with being 'blind' to decisions we are making every day. For example, people with the Patience Sub-factor may be putting off decisions that could affect their life, often without even realizing what they are doing and the effects this behavior might have. They are Unconsciously Incompetent at making important decisions. This person doesn't even know that they sideline the important decisions in their life. If they knew that their unconscious habit was holding them back from success, they might be horrified. This realization might be just the catalyst they need to cause them to think about changing. They might then work at seriously making those decisions and practicing making those types of decisions.

Unconscious Incompetence is something you should understand thoroughly because we do so many things unconsciously. You know how annoying some little habits can become, but the person who has the habit most likely is not even aware of it.

The next step is when this individual either hears about this habit or they actually realize they are avoiding important decisions. Besides being embarrassed, the individual must be willing to move forward. The opposite choice is deciding to ignore the problem. When people do this they stay in denial. They stay stuck in their ways. Doing nothing is a choice. If they choose to change, they will then move to the next phase: Conscious Incompetence. They are now consciously and painfully aware of their feelings. This pain is more intense when they now consciously recognized themselves avoiding important decisions. It becomes irritating and disturbing to them also; especially when they realize that they can't easily stop it. They are incompetent in their efforts to stop their habit. Upon examination, their current habit pattern is actually an unconscious decision that their mind makes every time they falter at making an important decision.

Hopefully, after their painful discovery, they consciously move toward the third phase called Conscious Competence. In this phase, they understand or are conscious of what they have to change even though they might not know precisely what they need to change or do to become competent. Trial and error, tacking into the wind, and making course adjustments, and consistently improving is the goal. In this phase, they must, however, work at changing themselves with concentrated focus.

This is where consciousness comes into the picture. They have to listen to themselves to become conscious of what other people hear. They make the decision to train their mind to analyze and make important decisions. Through this mental training, they begin to change. The ultimate goal is to get to the fourth and final part of this conscious awareness. In the next phase, they will hopefully eliminate the hesitation from their decision making. When they are consistently successful at eliminating their hesitation, they have reached the fourth phase - Unconscious Competence.

This is the final goal - to get to the point where they are making good decisions unconsciously and instinctively.

Much of what we do unconsciously, we have not planned. We haven't really thought enough about how we have formed our habit patterns. We forget to research and assess the best course of action. We don't seek council. If we are lucky, our unconscious habits are good habits, but what if they aren't? What if all the decisions that underpin our habits are hurting us? Wouldn't it make sense to examine our habits and unwind those that we don't like? Shouldn't we make the decision to systematically go through the Unconscious Competence Model for the habits that are important to our success?

"When a man learns to understand and control his own behavior as well as he is learning to understand and control the behavior of crop plans and domestic animals, he may be justified in believing that he has become civilized."

~E.G. Stakman

These four steps in the Unconscious Competence Model can occur anytime we do something over and over again. Until we become aware of what we are doing and are trained in the best way to do something, it will be difficult to make good decisions - or form great habits with regard to the behavior we choose - and have this become a natural part of our psyche. Our goal is to train our minds in the Unconscious Competence Model to achieve that final outcome – making good intuitive decisions about our actions and behaviors over and over again - by rote or habit. Unconscious Competence is where the right types of decisions -- ones we choose to make -- eventually become second nature and therefore become instinctual.

Sub-factors, Stressors, and Emotions

When you are going through the Unconscious Competence Model process, there will be stressors that will make your journey difficult. Let's go over the concept of stressors and emotions now.

As we examine the distinctive Sub-factors, we are going to focus primarily on two concepts:

1. There is a degree of separation or spread between the Factors we are comparing. Stressors occur internally in the individual because of the differentiation. Determining your unique Sub-factors in the DISC assessment is based on which Factor prevails over another in a pairing (unit).

2. Learning how to dial up the potential positives of the Sub-factor and dial down any potential negatives. This means that you adjust your attitude, emotions, and behavior at will depending on what is best for the situation. You shift gears using Behavioral Authority.

"Industrial society seems likely to be entering a period of severe stress, due in part to problems of human behavior and in part to economic and environmental problems."

~Unabomber Manifesto

Stressors

The best way to learn about Sub-factors is to examine yourself, your personality, and your behaviors. Study your DISC profile thoroughly to understand it – this will be easy since YOU know who YOU are. Then, after you get the hang of it, look at other people's DISC assessments and uncover their Sub-factors. The ultimate goal is to train yourself in understanding behavior,

DISCflex™

then procuring a sufficient level of behavioral flexibility and finally to acquire the skills necessary to adjust to any situation you might find yourself in. Having employees with greater flexibility and the ability to adjust their behavior depending on the environment or situation is invaluable to any organization.

As we said before - and it bears repeating - to first understand your own DISC Sub-factors™, you must realize the stressors caused by relationships between the four DISC Factors. There will either be one, two, or maybe even three Factors governing your behavior at any given time. It is important to understand that the most elevated DISC Factor you have is the one that governs your actions the most. For instance, if an individual has a 100% Dominance Factor, they are likely to be assertive in any situation they face. It will be very hard for a person with that Factor to dial down their Dominance because it is their main prevailing - or guiding - Factor. Plus, because it is so highly elevated, it is probably overriding the other three Factors. If this person can learn to dial their Dominance score down to even 90%, they can allow other Factors to come in and help them achieve more balance in their work life.

All the Factors mix together to form your personality, and that is precisely why the Sub-factors are so important. When you have a 100% Dominance score and a 7% Compliance score, you have the Independence Sub-factor. Because the D and the C Factors are so far apart, it is nearly impossible for this person to use the Cooperativeness Sub-factor (the opposing Sub-factor of Independence) without causing themselves high levels of stress.

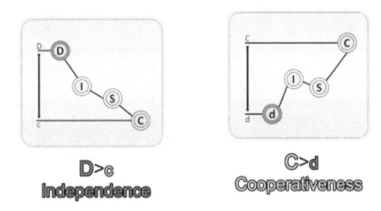

D>c
Independence

C>d
Cooperativeness

That is what stressors are. When you are trying to adapt your behavior to a certain situation, you will be stressed out if you are trying to use a Factor that you aren't comfortable using. As in the example before, you will always want to use the Factor or Factors that you are most comfortable with. The good news is that because of human nature, we have the ability to morph our behavior over time and flex our behavior in situations without stressing ourselves out.

There is another type of stressor as well. When we have Factors that are very close to each other on our DISC graph, such as a 78% I and an 80% S, we cause ourselves internal stress in determining which Factor should be used for the current situation.

There are three options with this combination, you can either combine the Influence and the Steadiness and use a blended pattern, use the Influence Factor, or use the Steadiness Factor.

The stress comes as a result of having to pick between these three options. In the first example, the 100% Dominance individual would have no internal stress about how to behave in different situations because they would always use the Dominance trait (even if combined with another trait it would still be the governing Factor).

Your goal as an individual should be to learn how to use the DISC Sub-factors™ to balance yourself throughout life. This does not mean using the Independence Sub-factor and the Cooperativeness Sub-factor equally, it means knowing when each works best in your life. It is critical to understand how to dial up and dial down each Sub-factor without stressing yourself out.

Dialing Up or Dialing Down Emotional Involvement and Behavioral Traits

As you learn about your personality Sub-factors, you need to learn how to dial them up and dial them down according to the situation you are in. Although the Sub-factors are based on your most positive traits, there are downsides to each Sub-factor as well. We will explain how to dial up and dial down the Sub-factor and how to look at the degrees of the Sub-factor as well. In order to fully understand this concept, please study the Feelings and Emotions session in the Life Skills course. This session and its associated exercises will provide invaluable insight and give you exactly the skills and knowledge you need to master this concept.

Blended Learning Using eLearning

Once you have looked at your Sub-factors, we encourage you take the time to do the exercises provided in the eLearning Suite for each Sub-factor that you have. You will first want to complete the Degrees of Sub-factors exercise where you will keep a log of whenever you displayed the Sub-factor during each day and write down whether it was positive or negative and why. The second exercise, the SWOT Analysis, focuses on your strengths and weaknesses, and your opportunities and threats for each Sub-factor. The SWOT Analysis is invaluable in enhancing your strengths or limiting your weaknesses in order to get the most out of opportunities and the mitigating threats. The third exercise deals with dialing up and dialing down your Sub-factors during certain situations. You will have to examine what the effects of dialing up your Sub-factor would be and what the effects of dialing down your Sub-factor would be. Complete these three exercises to understand how to apply your Sub-factors to improve your life, both professionally and personally.

The Continuum of Behavior

There are extremes in behavior. We call the space between polar opposite Sub-factors 'the continuum of behavior between Sub-factors'. Almost everybody is somewhere between independence and cooperativeness, never one or the other. An example of this is a person exhibiting extreme independence to the point of becoming a hermit - unable to interact with others. The opposing Sub-factor, Cooperativeness, also has extremes. A person might be so willing to go along with others that they lose their self-direction in the process.

The four Factors: Dominance, Influence, Steadiness, and Compliance, are how we get to our corresponding Sub-factors. So how do we temper a high level of Independence, for instance? Think about this from a logical standpoint. If we have a Dominance Factor that outweighs

Compliance, we can simply work on dialing down the D and dialing up the C behaviors. Doing so will automatically make us les independent.

As you continue to use the Sub-factors, make sure that you are using all of them in appropriate measure- at the appropriate point on the behavioral continuum- to give yourself the greatest strengths that each Sub-factor has to offer.

Conclusion

In conclusion, Sub-factors are important to your overall success. There is a time and a place for all of the Sub-factors, depending on your unique personality. Although you may be comfortable with using one or a few of the Sub-factors, you should learn how to use each of the Sub-factors situationally and at the appropriate degree of intensity.

"I believe that you control your destiny, that you can be what you want to be. You can also stop and say, 'No, I won't do it, I won't behave his way anymore. I am lonely and I need people around me, maybe I have to change my methods of behaving,' and then you do it."

~Leo F. Buscaglia

3 Behavioral Shifts Introduction

Welcome to the Introduction to Behavioral Shifts. Before you read this chapter, complete your DISCflex™ Business Behaviors Report.

As you have seen in your DISC Assessment Report, your DISC scores are measured by your own perception of your behavioral tendencies as well as the perceptions of others around you. The Differences in Perception graphics are important to understand because they show your behavioral flexibility in terms of how others see your behavior as different from what you perceive it to be. Others will perceive your behavior as either dialed up or dialed down from your self-perception or you could be perceived by others exactly the same as you view yourself. If you take a look at the bar graph, if you have a positive number, others view you as having dialed up your Factor. If the number is negative, others view you as having dialed it down. This is useful in understanding how your actions around others can change depending on the situations you find yourself in every day. Knowing this, you can learn to adapt your behavior where it needs to be for optimum performance in your work, family, or social life.

At any given moment, we make choices about how we will behave. Our behavior in particular situations and reactions to the messages we receive will depend upon a variety of things, but the prevailing consideration regarding how we may act or feel is our attitude. Our attitude and behavior are linked by expectations - our own and those of other people.

We all have our own perceptions of how we should behave at work, with our family, and in our social lives. Our self-perception of our behavior is important. It makes us feel that we have behaved well or poorly. We judge ourselves based on our core values and drivers. Most of us don't just react to a situation simply through our gut instincts and feelings, we actually think about the consequences of our behavior and try to make the right behavior choices.

However, we rarely take the time to minutely examine and pull apart our behavior through the eyes of other people. In fact, people do make ongoing judgments about our behavior. Unfortunately these are most often based on their perceptions of how we measure up to their behavior yardstick. And, from what you already know about perception, you must realize that perceptions can be dead wrong.

Can you remember a time when a friend, coworker, or family member thought you behaved poorly, but you didn't think you did? This behavior probably came from what we thought was acceptable, but they did not. After thinking about it, when faced with a similar set of circumstances, you have the choice to behave exactly the same way again or you can change - or shift -- your behavior to something they might find more acceptable.

Usually, the behavior we exhibit emanates from our most governing DISC Factors or Sub-factor pairings. In order to adapt to various situations we are put in, we have the innate ability to shift our most instinctive or natural tendencies to other behaviors during a specific situation. This is what we call our 'behavioral shift'. We use this shifting all the time. We are highly adaptable creatures. Most of us, especially those who have a varied life, have learned to do this in order to deal with the many varied situations we are faced with every day.

This adaptable self - the one that shows in our actions - is also the side of ourselves that others are basing their ongoing perceptions on. So, even if you are feeling one thing on the inside, you may be displaying something else on the outside. As an example, have you ever been seething and angry on the inside, but appear cool, calm and collected on the outside? This is how we control our behavior for different situations. We are able to shift it from what we might otherwise do if it was solely based on feelings and emotions rather than on expectations.

People love to see if the behavior they expect is what they get from others. Think back to a time when you watched a beauty pageant. As the winner was announced, didn't you watch to see how the winner and the runners-up would behave? People always watch. And they have expectations for the situations we are facing.

So to function, we learn how to 'shift' from our natural feelings and tendencies, to our adapted behavior, depending upon the current situation. As it applies to DISC Factors and Sub-factors, we need to be able to flex the individual Factors of the DISC profile to adapt to any given situation. We need to be able to elevate or suppress the Factors when we need to. This behavior shift is a flex, or a DISC stretch, from a natural behavior to the adapted behavior we want to show. For example, if your own perception of your C, Compliance, is at the midpoint at 50%, you can flex this number or shift it higher in an effort to adapt to a particular situation or job where you need to be more compliance conscious or when you need to follow the rules more tightly. You are shifting your preferred or more comfortable behavior in an effort to fit into your work environment. In a business sense, although it's recommended that you get a job that fits your own perception of your behavioral style, you will still need to be able to flex the Factors of the DISC profile for any job that you will ever have otherwise you run the risk of curtailing your potential or pigeon-holing yourself.

Stress may occur if your adapted style flexes or shifts away from your preferences by more than 15 points. If you adapt your behavior too much, you will cause yourself stress because your natural personality and behaviors will conflict with your adapted personality and behaviors. Understanding how to shift your behavior in certain situations, but keeping your overall core values and personality in step with your natural style, is the key to being successful in any business or life venture. You can adapt, but you must never lose yourself in doing so.

Behavioral stretching or flexing usually causes stress. It therefore cannot go too far away from who you are naturally, or carry on for too long because you will end up being 'out of your element' and feel uncomfortable and stressed. You can 'act' more compliant for a time, but you may begin to exhibit stress. As you get more comfortable with any situation, or you are in an environment where trust is high amongst the people in the group, whether in your work life or your personal life, your natural style will begin to take over again. You'll tend to revert back to the behavior you are comfortable with. There is a caveat to this, though. If you practice flexing your behavior, you can become very comfortable shifting it to fit any situation.

In fact, over time, this short-term behavioral flexing might become a habit. When it does, we say that your behavior has 'morphed'. We call this long-term behavioral morphing. During the DISC sessions, please always keep in mind that you choose your behavior. You also choose your core values. We want to make sure that you stay true to yourself and strive to live up to your behavioral potential and are able to adapt to different situations. Make sure that you continue to have others fill out your DISC with 3rd Party input so that you can get more reliability as to how others perceive you. This will allow you to know how much you have to work to adapt your behavioral flexibility.

"If we always do what we've always done, we will always get what we've always got."

~Adam Urbanski

4 Changing Your Behavior Introduction

The objective of learning about your behavioral patterns is to learn situational behavioral flexing as a primary objective. The secondary objective is to determine if long-term behavioral morphing is an appropriate goal and if so, create a plan to achieve this goal.

Core Values

Before we begin discussing situational behavioral flexing and long-term behavioral morphing, let's first set some guidelines. Whenever you examine your behavior, you must first consider your core values. Your value system governs your decision making, your actions, your perceptions of right and wrong, your conduct, and how you think of others. Most important, your value system determines how you judge yourself. The predominant question you will ask about your behavior, after the fact, is: Did I do the right thing? And, the judgment of what the 'right' thing is resides in your value system's core principles.

It is important that you make certain to take your core values into account prior to undergoing any change in behavior. If you do not do this, you run the risk of creating undue stress or anxiety. In the worst case scenario, you could very well unwittingly harm your core value system.

Value Hierarchy Exercise

If you haven't already done so, we suggest that you go through the value hierarchy exercise prior to undertaking any situational behavioral flexing or long-term behavioral morphing. This exercise will have you examine your core values, and having examined them, you will determine if they work for who you want to become. Be circumspect in your thinking - and remember, your core values can change over time. But, be consciously aware of how these are changing and always make certain that the changes you make in this area are well thought out and aligned with your life goals.

Another important element is that at no time do we recommend that you have to change who you are inside - your natural behavioral tendencies. In other words, the goal is to have you decide what behavior will be best for your goals. Undue outside influence to change your behavior is not recommended. If you decide that either situational behavioral flexing or long-term behavioral morphing is something that will help you - you have to make sure this is something you really want - that this is something that will enhance your life and the lives of those you care about.

Now that we have established parameters for looking critically at our behavior and what you need to adjust either to help you get through a current situation - a short-term fix - or over the long haul, you can look at what we mean by situational behavioral flexing.

Situational Behavioral Flexing

To influence a situation effectively, you should have the skill to be able to adapt your behavior and influencing tactics ideally to what the situation requires of you. This is common sense. And again, it doesn't mean that you have to change who you are and what you believe.

Studies show that in order for a person to be successful in various situations they should be able to display a variety of behaviors and actions depending on several criteria including:

- The communication style of the people they are interacting with,
- The tempo or pace that the circumstances necessitate,
- The gravity of the state of affairs they find themselves in,
- The tension levels between the individuals,
- The stress levels that are occurring.

Situational behavioral flexing requires you to find the best solution in any given situation. For this method you have to be willing to get out of your comfort zone. Flexing your behavioral muscle is quite hard for most people. Your DISC profile typically defines you as either an introvert (elevated Steadiness and Compliance Factor) or an extrovert (elevated Dominance or Influence Factor).

Although there can be combinations, it is trying to adapt to a Factor that you are not comfortable with. Take the Influence Factor for instance: Having a low Influence Factor means that you are typically an introvert. When you attend a networking event, however, you risk missing opportunities if you do not adapt your persona at the time to elevate your Influence Factor. The Influence Factor itself determines the amount of social contact and person-oriented tasks you prefer. Most people believe that introverts are socially awkward, but this is simply not true. It is surprising to find CEOs and CFOs that are natural introverts, but are great at flexing their behaviors to what the situation requires. Although it is generally harder for introverts to get themselves to be more comfortable with being outgoing, it is not hard once they push themselves to do it.

How to Flex Your Behavioral Muscle

There are a few key areas that you have to improve your understanding and implementation of in order to effectively flex your behavior muscles when the situation demands it:

1. Understand the Range of Possible Behavior Choices on the Behavioral Continuum
2. Choose the Appropriate Behavior
3. Self-talk
4. Read and React to the Situation as It Unfolds
5. Expect the Unexpected – Have a contingency plan

1. **Understand the Range of Possible Behavior Choices on the Behavioral Continuum. That Is, The Range Between the Dominant Sub-factor and Its Opposing Sub-factors.**

   For every Sub-factor that you display, there is an opposing Sub-factor that is equally as important in determining how flexible you are in your behavioral patterns. Your Sub-factors run on a continuum which is discussed in the whitepaper 'The Continuum on the Degrees of Behavior'. Depending on all four of your DISC Factors, you will be displaying a behavior on that continuum for every single Sub-factor pair. Although the Sub-factors themselves seem to be simple and descriptive, there is much more to the puzzle of your behavioral preferences and patterns.

Let's take the example of D>c Independence and C>d Cooperativeness. These Sub-factors are on opposite ends of the spectrum, but people rarely operate at the extremes.

Whether in a meeting, giving feedback, working with teams, or any other work-related task, the twelve Sub-factors can bring more success to your life if you use them at the appropriate degree of intensity for the situation you are in.

> *"Behavior is the mirror in which everyone shows their image."*
> **~Johann Wolfgang Von Goethe**

2. Choose the Appropriate Behavior for the Situation You Are In.

Every situation and every personality type interact in a different way. In your career, you may rarely need to use some of the Sub-factors, and that is perfectly acceptable.

> *"A man is but the product of his thoughts what he thinks, he becomes."*
> **~Mahatma Ghandi**

How do you know when you should use a certain Sub-factor? You'll need to make a goal setting chart to mark what goals are important to you in each area of your work life. These should align with your values and the organization's policies. For more instruction on how to create a goal setting chart, watch the video introduction to learn 'How to Dial Down' and 'How to Dial Up' each Sub-factor.

3. Examine Your Self-Talk to Flex Your Behavioral Muscle.

The push or the drive to adapt your behavior is your only real obstacle after you know the basics of behavioral change and have a plan to accomplish the change that you desire, either for situations you are facing or for long term alterations in how you act. Self-talk is especially important. You are only as limited as your self-talk. The biggest change in many people's lives is when they change their self-talk from negative to positive. It's very easy to focus on the negative aspects of your life, of work, and anything else in the world. Unfortunately, many people view their world through a negative scope rather than a positive one. Learning positive self-talk will help in any situation by giving you the proper frame of mind to find a viable solution. Let's again look at the networking example and how self-talk can help to prepare you to find solutions to the appropriate behavior.

> *"We Barbie dolls are not supposed to behave the way I do."*
> **~Sharon Stone**

Some quips that you might tell your subconscious mind are:

• "I'm a great communicator of my ideas and for my business."

• "I know the solutions that my business can provide like the back of my hand."

• "I have great conversations with people that have the same interests as me."

You can even cater your self-talk to your specific Sub-factors.

Still looking at the networking example, let's look at the self-talk for someone that has a low D, a low I, an elevated S, and an elevated C:

- "When it comes to influencing others based on thoughtfulness and logic, there is no one better than me."

- "I am great at starting small talk at networking events and make good impressions because of it."

- "I am highly aware of my surroundings and can change my behavior to get positive reactions because of it."

Self-talk allows your subconscious mind to come up with solutions to what you are asking it. You will be surprised by all of the solutions and affirmations that your subconscious mind comes up with if you ask it the right type of questions. Self-talk is not about lying to yourself to be someone you are not; it's about finding the hidden potential in you. Claiming that you don't have the skills to be a successful influencer is nonsense. Everyone is capable of it because any of the four DISC Factors can be used to influence others. In fact, different people require the use of different Factor's inherent behaviors in order to be influenced.

4. Read And React To The Situation As It Unfolds.

Learning how to read a situation and reacting to the situation as it unfolds is imperative in situational behavioral flexing. The Steadiness Factor is the most important Factor in becoming aware of your environment.

Those with the C>s Sensitivity Sub-factor tend to fair instinctively well at reading the situation compared to the other Sub-factors. Extroverts who tend to have elevated and are stuck with the generalization that they don't think things through. Although this is true of some extroverts, it is not characteristic of what an extrovert means. Just like how the introvert is able to situationally adapt to influence, the extrovert can situationally adapt to read a situation and influence effectively as well. The core message of the Sub-factors is to understand that every Factor of the DISC profile is relevant to your behavioral patterns and your ability to adapt.

5. Expect the Unexpected – That is – Have a Contingency Plan.

Make it a habit to continually prepare for life's uncertainties. Self-talk can help you with this by telling yourself, "I am prepared for any obstacles that may meet me on the way to my goal." The goal is the light at the end of the tunnel that you are working towards. Always remember that every individual circumstance is part of a larger goal. If your goal is to write a book and you quit on that goal because you got writer's block one day; this would be illogical. Goals can be accomplished in a matter of minutes or a matter of decades.

> *"For many people, one of the most frustrating aspects of life is not being able to understand other people's behavior"*
>
> *~Unknown*

For situational behavior flexing, you have to focus on short-term goals while always remembering what your long-term goals are. At a networking event, your short-term goal is to make a great first impression and gain a new contact. At the same time, you must remember that your long-term goal is to get a better job or improve your sales for the coming year. Therefore, it wouldn't be in your interest to spend time the entire short time available at the event on influencing someone that wouldn't be able to help you meet those long-term goals. Your short-term goals must be weaved into your long-term goals so that you don't waste your time or resources.

"Studies indicate that the one quality all successful people have is persistence. They're willing to spend more time accomplishing a task and to persevere in the face of many difficult odds. There's a very positive relationship between people's ability to accomplish any task and the time they're willing to spend on it.

~Dr. Joyce Brothers

Expecting the unexpected is difficult to prepare for because it is unexpected. What to learn from expecting the unexpected is making sure that you don't let obstacles get in the way of your overall goal. Also, you need to learn how to make the most of unexpected opportunities. One way of preparing your mind for finding opportunities and identifying threats is to do a SWOT Analysis. A SWOT Analysis identifies your strengths, weaknesses, opportunities, and threats and outlines effective strategies for capturing opportunities and mitigating weaknesses. First, you have to list your strengths. Make sure that you are honest so that the strategies you put together are effective. When you list your weaknesses, remember that they aren't necessarily a bad thing. Some weaknesses you simply can't help and others just aren't your personal interest, such as not being good at drawing or computer graphics. Being good at artistic endeavors requires motivation and practice.

Depending on the situation that you may encounter, you have to list the opportunities that may present themselves or the threats that may come up. Going back to the previous example, if you are at a networking event, your main opportunity should be to create new business. The threats you may encounter are giving a bad impression to a new acquaintance.

Preparing for obstacles that you encounter falls back on your self-talk. Telling yourself that everything is going to work out for the better will force your sub-conscious mind to continually work on making those beliefs come true. Then you can take steps to think through and plan for opportunities and threats.

Long-Term Behavioral Morphing

Now let's discuss what long-term behavioral morphing is. It is important to consider whether or not your current behavior patterns fit your long-term goals. Do your actions and the way you handle situations work well with the goals you want to achieve? If they don't, you may want to morph your long-term behavior to match that behavior best suited to who you want to become in the long-term. By practicing and modeling the behaviors that are more suited to your objectives and the goals of how you want to conduct yourself, you can achieve consistency in the type of behavior and that would be exhibited by the future person that you want to become.

"What got you to your current level of success is not necessarily what will get you to the next level or ensure your future success."

~Hellen Davis

If you determine that you want to morph your behavior and create new behavior habits, you should learn how to improve your behavioral competency to the point that you are proficient in three important areas:

1. Choose the appropriate behavior for the recurring similar situations you find yourself facing.
2. Practice that new behavior on a consistent basis.
3. Make sure that the old unwanted behavior is curtailed and be able to exhibit that new behavior at an optimum level so that it becomes second nature.

The first thing to remember with long-term behavioral morphing is that you are not necessarily changing your overall value hierarchy. There are a lot of people who fear change in their behaviors because they believe they will change their value hierarchy or core values. This is generally an excuse that the sub-conscious comes up with for not having to put any effort into improving yourself. You have to know when your sub-conscious tells you this and remind yourself that you aren't changing your core values, but rather improving the value hierarchy you already have.

Let's look at the Patience Sub-factor (S>d). If you have a low Steadiness Factor, you are much more likely to be impatient. Making it your goal to improve your patience is not changing your value hierarchy. Viewing it through the SWOT Analysis is the most effective way of learning how to improve your weaknesses. Improving your weaknesses in no way has to change your value hierarchy. If you improve your patience, you still might not be viewed as a highly patient person, but rather you won't be viewed anymore as an impatient person. That is the overall goal. You want to make sure, especially in the business world, that you have very few incompetencies in the critical areas. Some of the best business people in the world aren't known for any great strengths, but simply don't have any incompetencies.

"You cannot tailor-make situations in life, but you can tailor-make the attitudes to fit those situations."

~Zig Ziglar

Changing your behavior in the long-term requires a lot of work, continuous self-talk, and open awareness. You cannot expect to improve your weaknesses if you let your negative self-talk stand in the way.

Long-term behavioral morphing requires:

1. First, that you have Positive Self-Talk (Asking why you want to change and visualization).
2. Second, you need to have Open and Direct Awareness of your behaviors.
3. Finally, you should complete the Exercises provided to help achieve your goal.

Positive Self-Talk

Just like situational behavioral flexing, long-term behavioral morphing requires the use of positive self-talk to motivate your subconscious mind to find solutions. Remember that you are only as limited as your self-talk.

Whenever you have a block in your thinking about what to say to yourself, go back to why you want to change your behavior in the first place. Letting your subconscious mind visualize the behavior is incredibly important to the success you will have in changing your current behavior. If you want to be more patient, why do you want to be more patient? What would the benefits be? Would you act differently? You have to set yourself in the state of being the behavior that you want to be. For self-talk to work, you have to use it in the present tense. Instead of saying, "I'm going to be more patient," you need to say, "I'm a patient person." You have to be what you want to be. Consider self-talk as making the change right then and there. From now on, you ARE a patient person, you ARE thoughtful, you ARE efficient, etc. There's no time to wait for the future, you have to be what you want to be right now.

> *"It is not your aptitude, but you attitude, that determines your altitude."*
>
> *~Zig Ziglar*

Positive self-talk requires that you leave the word 'not' out of your sentences. Instead of saying, "I'm not impatient," say, "I'm patient." As humans, we have a general tendency to focus on the negative. We must make our conscious minds continually remind our subconscious mind that it is positive and needs to look through a positive lens at the situation at hand. Positivity is one of the essential elements of making a change and also of being happy. You can continually improve yourself simply by thinking positively.

If you are already an efficient person, positive self-talk revolving around that fact could be, "I'm creative when dealing with situations so that I can adapt my efficiency to fit the needs of any situation." Making your behavioral strengths even stronger is another benefit of positive self-talk.

Open and Direct Awareness

Long-term behavioral morphing depends on your ability to be aware of how you use your Sub-factors and when you use them. You must be equally aware of your opposing Sub-factors. Your opposing Sub-factors determine your behavior as much as your Dominant Sub-factors do. You can be both independent and independent's opposite, cooperative, at the same time. Although it seems like a contradiction, making yourself bring independent ideas to the table and yet match those ideas with others is demonstrating both of those Sub-factors. Knowing how to balance your dominant Sub-factor and your opposing Sub-factor will help you achieve success in any situation. In the long-term, you want to be able to be seen as both independent and cooperative. The key is balance. Knowing when to be independent and when to be cooperative is essential to morphing your long-term behavior to incorporate both of those qualities into your overall behavioral patterns.

Awareness is how you accomplish this feat. Being honest with yourself comes first because you won't be able to change if you tell yourself you don't need to change. Then you have to be constantly aware of your actions. Notice the trends of how you act in certain situations and whether they are beneficial to you or not. If they are beneficial, applaud yourself and keep at it. If they are hurtful, then be aware of how you can change the outcome of the next situation you face into a benefit.

Remember that Noble Intent is always the best policy when looking at the situations you have faced and that you will face. You have to understand that people are generally not trying to sabotage you or get the best of you. Acting on Noble Intent will help you make sure that you do not make the mistake of assuming someone is purposely acting against you. There could be many reasons why a person is acting the way they are.

The two whitepapers you must look at are the Transitional Time Line and the Perceptual Positions. The Transitional Time Line highlights the negative and positive phases people go through when making any change. The Perceptual Positions are important in understanding the situation from your perspective, the other people involved in the situation's perspectives, and the perspective of a 'fly-on-the-wall' or an observer to the situation that has no emotional involvement in it. Knowing all of these different perspectives will help you understand the real impact of your overall behavior.

"An individual's self-concept is the core of his personality. It affects every aspect of human behavior: the ability to learn, the capacity to grow and change. A strong, positive self-image is the best possible preparation for success in life."

~Dr. Joyce Brothers

Exercises to Hone Your Behavior Skills

Long-term behavioral morphing requires you to hold yourself accountable to the behavior you want to display on a continuous basis. There are a few exercises that are extremely useful in helping to morph to any long-term behavioral pattern.

"If you want to be enthusiastic, act enthusiastic."

~Dale Carnegie

The four exercises are:

1. SWOT Analysis
2. Degrees of Attitude activity
3. Escalation of Emotional Involvement activity
4. Future Pacing activity

1. SWOT Analysis

The 'SWOT Analysis' outlines your strengths, weaknesses, opportunities, and threats and puts them together to form strategies. The four strategies are strengths + opportunities (SO), weaknesses + opportunities (WO), strengths + threats (ST), and weaknesses + threats (WT). These strategies fall into opportunity capture and threat mitigation.

Opportunity capture involves SO and WO strategies:
- WO strategies should only be used when needed to downplay or get past an obstacle or issue.
- SO strategies are when you use your strengths to take advantage of opportunities. For instance, if you are a good artist, you would be using an assessed strength in taking the opportunity to design a new logo for an organization.
- WO strategies are when you get past your weaknesses to reach opportunities. Weaknesses are usually current deficiencies in capabilities. They are new skills or something that you need to update for the circumstances you find yourself in. When weaknesses appear as obstacles, such as the price of something you are selling, you have to downplay it and get past it. When the question of price comes up, tell them your price, and then tell them the reason why the price is what it is.

Threat mitigation uses ST and WT strategies:
- WT strategies are typically defensive plans to make sure that your weaknesses don't allow external threats to affect you.
- ST strategies are when you use your strengths to mitigate threats. Companies use this strategy most of the time in their commercials. A company will tell you that their prices are lower (strength) than their competitors (their threats) in order to get you to buy from their company. Establishing value is the best way to use ST strategies.
- WT strategies are when you downplay or get past weaknesses in order to mitigate threats. You never want to bring up weaknesses when threats are present, but you must be able to use these strategies if you are caught in a situation where you have to.

The SWOT Analysis can be closely related to your Sub-factors. Typically your strengths fall in line with your dominant Sub-factors and your weaknesses are their opposing Sub-factors. When you have a window of opportunity to get something accomplished, you have to balance your Sub-factors using SWOT strategies and then find the right measurement to capture that opportunity. The same is true of threats. You must find the right strategies to use to mitigate the threats.

"Act the way you'd like to be and soon you'll be the way you act."

~George W. Crane

2. Degrees of Attitude

The next exercise is called the 'Degrees of Attitude'. This exercise is particularly beneficial because it allows you to be more aware of how you use your Sub-factors in the various situations you find yourself in. This is basically a journal entry of the situations you were in each day, how you responded, what Sub-factor you responded with, whether the reaction was positive or negative, and the degree of maturity of your response. Seeing how you react on paper and judging yourself through the third perceptual position will help you understand the steps that you need to take in order to morph your long-term behavioral patterns.

3. Escalation of Emotional Involvement

The third exercise that you should do is the 'Escalation of Emotional Involvement'. This exercise is important in your understanding of how to dial up and dial down your Sub-factors. Although this exercise is generally more useful in situational behavioral flexing, there is a strong correlation between your ability to adapt situationally and your overall long-term behavioral patterns.

Behavioral shifts can cause stress whenever they are more than 15 points away from each other. As you teach yourself how to situationally adapt, however, you will build up your tolerance to stress because you will be creating a new comfort zone and will be able to change your long-term behavior as a result.

4. Future Pacing

The final exercise you must do to help with long-term behavioral morphing is called 'Future Pacing'. Future pacing is a method of planning for the future and taking steps to achieve your goals. Future pacing is critical in giving your subconscious mind a good reason to change your behavior. The subconscious ideally needs a logical base to formulate solutions. Also, future pacing helps you create a commitment to yourself, which tells your subconscious mind that this is a priority. Making it a priority helps your subconscious mind to come up with solutions faster because it will view it as a necessity.

Be consistent with completing your exercises, as they will help your self-talk and your awareness. Long-term behavioral morphing requires commitment and consistency in order to occur. Visualize yourself behaving the way you want to every day and before every decision. Eventually your subconscious will follow the path and continue to act in that manner without you having to think about it. The power of the subconscious is substantial. The ability to consciously influence your subconscious is one of the best abilities you can have.

Conclusion

Both situational behavioral flexing and long-term behavioral morphing are important. Situational behavioral flexing is needed for every situation that you find yourself in. You should constantly adjust and be flexible. In professional situations especially, you have to balance your Sub-factors according to the demands of the situation. The key to making people see your overall persona and choosing how you want others to view you happens through displaying consistent behavior. You can use the strategies for long-term behavioral morphing to improve or show your existing Sub-factors more.

The bottom line: Use situational behavioral flexing to adapt to every situation while still keeping a view on consistently displaying behaviors over the long-term. In this way, you choose attributes that fit into a strategy of behavioral morphing. This will result in what you want your behavior to ultimately look like.

"A mission could be defined as an image of a desired state that you want to get to. Once fully seen, it will inspire you to act, fuel your imagination, and determine your behavior."

~Charles A. Garfield

5 How to Dial Up Dominance

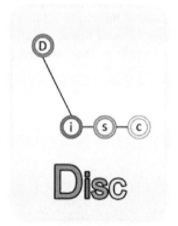

In certain situations, we must learn how to dial up our Dominance Factor. These situations may come in group settings or individual scenarios. You may need to dial up your Dominance to get something done or to get your point across. Remember that Dominance does not just mean controlling situations; this Factor can help you expand your opportunities and develop your creativity. The Dominance Factor can give you the tools to get results and find success because of the driving characteristics that it represents. Upping your Dominance means tapping into your drive and motivation; this can really help you persevere and give you the energy to sustain long-term inspiration.

Being able to dial up your Dominance levels can help you insurmountably, while not changing your overall personality. Remember that people governed by any of the other primary Factors have some level of Dominance. In fact, you must have some level of Dominance in order to function and get goals accomplished. To ramp up your Dominance is a critical component in assertiveness, risk-taking, and decision-making abilities. Otherwise, you might get caught up in helping other people reach their goals and never actually achieve yours.

We've found a few steps for you to take to become more dominant and learn how to increase your Dominance in the situations you need to. In the following section, we have two parts: the immediate steps and the secondary steps. Both of these are important in learning how to dial up your Dominance.

Immediate Steps:

The immediate steps in dialing up your Dominance will help you practice how to become more effective at displaying dominant type behaviors. These

"If you don't run your own life, somebody else will."

~John Atkinson

behaviors involve decision-making, assertiveness, self-motivation, independence, efficiency, and other similar behaviors. Let's take a look at some of these steps:

1. Do, Not Say.

We usually say we want to do something or we wish things were a different way. Stop just talking about it and make a plan; then do something about it. Dominance demands actions. As soon as you start to take action, things start moving. This impetus will give you the drive to finish them through to a successful conclusion. Many of us think or wish things were different, but do little to change the situation. The difference in Elevated Dominant people is that they consistently propel themselves into action states to make it happen.

> *"We are what we repeatedly do."*
>
> *~Aristotle*

If you need to dial up your Dominance for any situation, it is imperative that you overcome hesitation and essentially do something; especially if you are in a leadership position. Hesitation will almost always be seen as a weakness in a leader. People look to leaders to lead - not to just sit there and wait. That does not mean that you act quickly without thinking. Making decisions in a prudent manner before acting is vital. You need to practice this by going through the Rational Decision Making Process. This will prepare you to be ready to make decisions whenever the situation calls for action. The same is true in family and social situations. If you mull over decisions thoroughly, you will have less hesitation when you actually have to take action on that decision.

> *"You can have anything you want- if you want it badly enough. You can be anything you want to be, do anything you set out to accomplish if you hold to that desire with singleness of purpose*
>
> *~Robert E. Lee*

The bottom line: It is difficult to make a decision if you don't have a solid process for making decisions.

If you need help with this, visit Indaba Global's Decision Making course as well as the Life Skills course. In the Life Skills course, the information is contained in the sessions entitled 'Overcome Hesitation and Do Something' and 'Creative Visualization'.

There is a lot of truth in Abraham Lincoln's statement that "All things come to those who wait, but only what's left over by those who hustle." Stick-to-itiveness and a commitment to finish what we start will determine our satisfaction and success with projects we embark on.

2. Set Your Goals in a Smart Format to Increase Your Chances That You Will Achieve Them.

SMART is an acronym that encompasses five critical points of goal setting.

* S stands for Specific;
* M - Measurable;
* A - Attainable;
* R - Realistic;
* T is Time.

> *"The greatest discovery of my generation is that a human can alter his life by altering his attitude."*
> ~William James

This methodical way of working on your goals and setting down SMART components will certainly elevate your Dominance Factor because you are propelling yourself into goal setting and achievement mode with specifics. When you write a goal list or task list for the day, make the list detailed and write down precisely how you will achieve everything. If you write down that 'eventually' you desire a promotion, it may never actually happen. You have no deadline, no specifications, and no guidelines, nothing precise when you think about how to accomplish the goal. You should write down something like this: "I want to be promoted to executive sales manager by April by contributing more in meetings, recruiting three salespeople by August, and increasing my personal sales revenue by 25% by year-end by asking my top 20 clients for five referrals each." This says exactly what you want to achieve, when you will do it, and how. The most important part about setting goals is to make them as specific as you can.

3. Use Your Subconscious Mind as a Driver in Ramping Up Your Dominance.

Most people fail to realize the simplicity and effectiveness of writing down your goals in a SMART format as it relates to employing your subconscious mind. When you start thinking about your goals and how to achieve them, your subconscious kicks into gear. It starts thinking about how to achieve your goals in the way that you stipulate, so the more precise and specific you are with what you want, the better it will be at delivering ideas and suggestions - as well as motivation - to achieve them. This creates a form of visualization in your mind and sends signals to your subconscious mind to start working on achieving that goal or goals that you write down.

The subconscious mind is your best ally in helping you to figure out ways to achieve your goals. A highly effective technique in making sure your subconscious is working at its optimum is to ask the right sorts of questions of yourself. You would be surprised at how asking the right questions can propel your subconscious to answer those questions effectively. It will provide suggestions, ideas, alternatives, and will continue working to achieve a perfect answer until you are satisfied with the results. Your subconscious mind is an amazing tool. Knowing how to make use of it effectively is an amazing skill.

> *"People with clear, written goals, accomplish far more in a shorter period of time than people without them could ever imagine."*
> ~Brian Tracy

If you want to learn more about the subconscious, review the Subconscious session of Indaba's Life Skills Course as well as the associated recommended reading.

4. Try Something New.

As you learn to become more dominant, you'll inevitably be trying new things. The Dominance Factor needs change and new environments to continue to motivate it. If this is uncomfortable for you, start very small and try something new that won't dramatically affect your life. This may be a minor thing such as taking a new route to work or going to a new place for breakfast or lunch. Being adventurous is a great way to enhance your Dominance Factor as you get yourself out of your comfort zone. The Dominance Factor is known for bringing people to try things that would typically make them uncomfortable, many times involving risk-taking. The more you try new things, the more comfortable you'll become trying new approaches or taking on new opportunities.

5. Watch The Leaders.

When you're in a group setting, watch to see who emerges as the leader. Watch how they establish themselves and lead a group. If you need to, take notes. Practice these actions at home and whenever you can. One of the biggest things to watch when you are studying leaders is their body language. Leaders usually carry themselves a different way. They appear more confident, more comfortable and in control. If you can copy that non-verbal communication, you can greatly enhance your career. Also, you'll learn how to use appropriate body language to take control of conversations in your family and with your social groups. This may be necessary at times so that you don't get dominated by other people. This can help you make sure that your ideas are considered, that others don't ignore your suggestions, or that team mates refuse to debate the alternatives or negotiate with you. Having the ability to situationally amplify your Dominance Factor will go a long way in making sure incidents like this do not happen to you.

There are some secondary steps that you can take to further dial up your Dominance Factor. These may take longer to put into action and to practice but they are equally as important as the immediate steps. Note, these are also critical to your overall success in business and life because they can give you tools necessary to boost the drive you need to achieve your goals.

Secondary Steps:

1. Act Quickly.

In order to act quickly to new situations, you must prepare to see them and have an idea of what you will do if that event presents itself. You don't need to have a thorough plan; you just need to know what you would do in the event that happens. While preparing for something or while making choices, always consider the opposite outcome than the one you want. You need to prepare yourself to tackle the undesirable option if it comes up.

Try to start with small tasks to get prepared to act without spending too much time in the analysis stage. Eventually, you have to learn to implement decisions. The Dominance Factor will help you increase your implementation skills and give you more proficiency in your life.

2. Take Risks.

In acting quickly, you may be taking a huge risk. You may feel uncomfortable doing this, but the more you do it, and the more results you see from it, the more comfortable you'll become. Risks are an important part of life, and we actually make them every day. Even if you decide NOT to act, you are taking a risk. If you decide not to go for a promotion when the opportunity is there, you risk never moving ahead in your career. Understand that risks are important for our lives and that knowing how to take calculated risks will give you much success. Learning how to effectively use the SWOT Analysis and the Assumption Matrix will help you to uncover the ability to make great decisions relating to risk. You will find more information in the 'SWOT Analysis Sessions' of the Life Skills Course and the 'Analyze Options Session' of the Decision Making Course, respectively.

> *"Teachers provide the door, but you must enter by yourself."*
>
> *~Chinese Proverb*

DISCflex™

3. Change Your Pace.

Look for new opportunities and take them. Take on as many new things as you can. The more you tackle, the more everyone else will see and take notice. This will make you feel confident and capable in your workplace. Become the person 'too valuable and too versatile' to replace. For example, think of a baseball player who can play many positions compared to the player who is limited to just one position.

It is very noticeable to your managers or your employees how much effort you put into your work. The Dominance Factor is a characterization of action. If you are able to show your employees or your managers that you are willing to take on new opportunities, they will consequently view you as more dominant and 'go-getting'. Becoming a person that says, "Yes!" to new opportunities will give you a better perception of your job and what you can do to accomplish more.

> *"What you do today can improve all your tomorrows."*
>
> *~Ralph Marston*

4. Take On Opportunities To Be The Leader.

If you're in a group, be the leader. You may feel unqualified and uncomfortable initially, however, you will grow into the role. It is normal to feel uncomfortable initially. Deliberate practice makes perfect. The more you practice, the more you'll feel confident taking the leadership position and dialing up your Dominance.

If you can take this philosophy to something that you want to achieve, you will understand the importance of continually taking on opportunities to practice your developing skills and techniques. And to be practical, even if you don't have 10,000 hours to devote to increasing your Dominance Factor, any amount of sustained practice will make your abilities better in this arena.

In his book Outliers, Malcolm Gladwell explains the 10,000 hour rule to become a world-class expert. He claims that those who become the best in the world at what they do have had an enormous amount of practice leading up to their accomplishments. Some examples include: Bill Gates founder of Microsoft, NBA superstar Karl Malone, Baseball Hall of Famer Cal Ripken, theoretical physicist Stephen Hawking, master cellist Yo-Yo Ma, and Bill Joy -- the founder of Sun Microsystems (now part of Oracle).

6 How to Dial Down Dominance

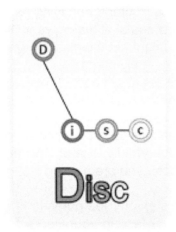

Since everyone has a bit of each of the four primary Factors, it is important to understand that the mix of levels or elevations determines how much governance these four Factors will have over your behavior. In this session we are going to talk in depth about the Dominance Factor's potential negative impact and when it is appropriate to dial it down. A word of caution regarding ethics: By situationally adjusting your Dominance Factor, you must make certain that you are using it to make the situation better. Never plan to use it in a scheming calculating way and always think of Noble Intent.

The Dominance Factor's influence will give you the motivation to get where you need to go and the momentum to accomplish great things in your life. But your Dominance Factor can sometimes put you on the bumpiest of roads because the nature of Dominance is to be powerful perhaps to the off-putting set of circumstances where it tips the scale to being forceful. The Dominance Factor is the hammer that has the potential to oppress, coerce, tyrannize, and afflict harm.

In one of the lessons, we told you that Dominance can be viewed as steamrolling over others when it is at the far negative end of the highly Elevated Dominance spectrum. In extreme cases, highly elevated domineering people have been known to take license to torment, browbeat, or bully others. In these cases they must learn the consequences of their Domineering behavior. A person's Dominance Factor can be driving - leading them to become controlling and authoritative in extreme instances. Your Dominance Factor can be assertive and sometimes move on to being highly aggressive. Although it can be commanding it can also sometimes be the Factor that imposes your will on others even against their wishes. And although your Dominance Factor is the mechanism that makes you strong and able to realize your goals, it might lead

"The key to success is often the ability to adapt."

~Anthony Brandt

some with very highly elevated levels to think they are superior to those less dominant in nature - especially those who are unwilling, unable, disinclined to stand up to them. Learning how to dial down your Dominance to the appropriate level for the situation will help you protect yourself from the profound weaknesses of the Factor, while hopefully still retaining the positive attributes it can present to your life.

Dominance can sometimes get in the way of rational decision making. An Elevated Dominance Factor puts a focus on results, not necessarily on the method or procedures of getting there. This may be during a team meeting or while working on a project, or it could be when you are out to dinner relaxing with friends and family. In any case, if you do have a natural tendency to unleash your Elevated Dominance Factor's behavior, you must learn how to dial it down for various situations. When you are successful at dialing your Dominance down you'll find that you'll have better balanced relationships, might get things done smoothly, and you might not stress out those around you as much as you normally might.

Although your first instinct may be to take control and dominate, or to make sure that your opinions are heard; step back and let things happen without jumping in right away. When you do this you might be surprised at how often people step up without you having to do so first. By simply waiting, you give other people the opportunity to lead. This might be one of the best gifts you can give to those you care about and those you are helping along in life.

Remember that you can use these steps for the purpose of situational behavioral flexing, which means adapting to situations that you face in your life, or for long term behavioral morphing, if you feel that you want to change your habit pattern of behavior. Figure out which works best for your current life situation and your values and then make a determination to approach these steps either situationally or over the long term. Either way, you will be giving yourself a skill set that most people never learn in their lives.

These are a few steps that will help you to learn how to dial down your Dominance. Let's look at the immediate steps you can take to dial down your Dominance.

Immediate Steps:

1. Take A Time Out.

If you are in an Elevated Dominance state, you need to recognize it and curtail it. The key is to recognize your triggers. For more information on this I suggest you review the activity in the Dial Up your Patience session. Then decide if the Dominance level your behavior is operating at is appropriate for the situation. Good questions would be something like: "Am I reacting like I should be?" or "Would I want my boss to see me acting like this?" or "Would I be proud tomorrow of what I am doing today?" or "If someone else were doing the same thing and I was coaching them, would I be suggesting behavior changes?" If your Elevated Dominance behaviors aren't acceptable, here are some pointed suggestions: Just be quiet. Count to 10. Refrain from charging out of the gate. Hit the pause button. JUST STOP YOURSELF!!!!! Impose a time out on yourself. Do whatever works to stop your Elevated Dominance. You might want to have a few stopping mechanisms ready. You can take a break by saying something like: "I appreciate your point of view. Give me a couple of minutes to take this information in before responding." Or "I think that I am getting a bit more emotional about this because it's been my project for so long. Let me step back and look at it from your point of view and I think

DISCflex™

that will help me get some balanced perspective." Or if you are dealing with friends or family members say: "I hear what you're saying and I know that you listened to me, too. How about if I don't make the decision right now. Give us both an hour to think about it. I think this will help us both come to the right decision."

2. Listen To Others.

While in a meeting or talking to someone, let them do most of the talking for a change. Sit back and listen attentively. When they're done talking, make sure you have at least one second - preferably three seconds, before you respond. At the same time, use verbal mirroring to rephrase the problem or solution in their own words. For instance, if they say that they are excited about the solution, you should use the word 'excited' instead of saying something similar like, "I am eager to see this implemented." Use the same words to describe emotions and the other person will feel that you care about them more and you'll find that you can empathize with them a lot better. Verbal mirroring is one of the most effective ways to accomplish comprehensive communication. This is an excellent way for you to practice dialing down your Dominance. Bottom line on listening: People like people who take a genuine interest in them. Listening involves not only hearing the other person, but comprehending them. People are usually annoyed or offended if you pretend to be listening without trying to understand what they actually mean.

3. Let Others Speak For Themselves.

Then, even if you have to prep them, let them shine. After they speak, don't explain to the rest of the audience what you think they meant. Let them do it. Failure to do this is considered rude and you take away the other person's personal power.

4. Understand Feedback & Coaching.

People with Elevated Dominance personalities often feel compelled to provide feedback and coaching whether appropriate to do so or not. Refrain from coaching them in front of others. Wait until after the meeting. Write down what you wanted to say and save for later.

If you remember from the feedback and coaching course, you should never provide feedback in front of an audience anyway. Plus, you should prepare your feedback words for maximum impact and this is best done with forethought. One final thought on feedback - determine if it is appropriate to deliver feedback. Unsolicited feedback is often not warranted. If you do feel that feedback could be a gift to the person, ask them if you can provide it. Have respect if they say "No!" This information is in the Feedback and Coaching course.

5. Follow The Rules.

You may feel tempted to break the rules or insist that they don't apply to you. Do not do this. Listen to the rules and follow them. When you are working in a rules-based environment, you must dial down your Dominance to comply with those rules. The Dominance Factor can cause you to ignore rules or create your own guidelines which can lead to lawsuits and possibly your firing. It can be frustrating for Elevated Dominance individuals to have to play by someone else's rules, but it is necessary if you work for a large organization.

There are reasons why organizations put policies and procedures into place. The Elevated Dominance individual may need to consider dialing back their Dominance Factor when they are in positions that require rules to be followed. Fortunately, this is a part of the Dominance Factor that you can dial back on the long term fairly easily, eventually depleting your stress from the situation.

6. Look Through The Perceptual Prism.

Remember that this is not your universe. We all have a tendency to see the world in our eyes and forget that there are other people in this universe as well. By looking through the Perceptual Prism, you are able to get a better view of the overall situation. This is incredibly important in the workplace. Get the second and third perceptual positions so that you are able to make a good decision. If you want more information about this, view the Perceptual Prism session in the Change Course.

7. Think Through Situations.

When faced with a decision, take the time to think about it and what it means. If you find that you make a decision and stick with it, and that there's no way your mind will be changed, take the time anyways. Look back at the facts and be thoughtful about the consequences that could occur.

"When we allow ourselves to adapt to different situations, like is easier."

~Catherine Pulsifer

The Dominance Factor can lead you to make decisions that are intuitive and quick. If you haven't had prior experience in a certain decision making situation, you should absolutely take a step back and go through the Rational Decision Making Process. Review these sessions in Indaba's Decision Making Course.

8. Get One Task Completed At A Time.

Elevated Dominance individuals have a tendency to shuffle between projects or tasks. This can delay these responsibilities from being accomplished and can hinder the job responsibilities of others. You may have found that you leave little, minute tasks to the last minute because you're focusing on bigger and better things. Or, you may have pawned those things off on lesser people to do. Make sure you do those things yourself. Leaving small tasks is a sign that you don't think you should do them, and that maybe you're too good to take care of it. You need to understand when it is appropriate to delegate and when others will think poorly of you for it. This can cause conflict in your life that you could otherwise avoid. You'll find that you will have better time management when you start focusing on and completing one task at a time.

9. Target More Energy Into Building Trust and Strong Open Relationships and Friendships.

Sometimes the Dominance Factor can make you focus too much on getting a result, instead of thinking about how relationships help you in the future. Whenever you feel yourself getting annoyed about little things that your coworkers, family members, or friends are doing, remember that you need to build your relationship with them by focusing on their perception of the situation.

This important relationship quality is an important part of life, even in animals. Think about the shark and the pilot fish. The sharks, which are the top predators in the ocean, will not eat a pilot fish because of the purpose they serve. The pilot fish eat all of the leftover food that gets lodged between the sharks' teeth. This is a collaborative relationship that satisfies both parties. This is the same logic that can be applied to relationship between people. You will occasionally have to take leaps of faith and assume that the shark won't eat you if you help it out. If you can learn to target energy into cooperating and helping to meet the needs of others, you can build trust, which

"The bamboo that bends is stronger than the oak that resists."

~Japanese Proverb

will inevitably build better relationships. "Trust is a calculated risk made with one's eyes open to the possibilities of failure," says Robert Levering, "but it is extended with the expectation of success."

After going through the immediate steps, here are some secondary steps that can help you dial down your Dominance Factor.

Secondary Steps:

1. Let An Argument Go.

In the immediate steps, you learned to take a time out and step back. In this secondary step, you need to actively decide to let things go unspoken - even if things are heated. This might be a lot harder to do than when things aren't so emotional or uncomfortable. If you begin to butt heads about something, just make the decision to let it go. Do not fight to the death over your opinion. State what you think and let it go. If the other person is as adamant about their idea to fight over it, chances are, you won't change their opinion. Say "I appreciate your idea/opinion, but I do disagree," and let it go. Do not let your anger or drive take you into an argument that is unnecessary or unproductive - especially one that could potentially do long term harm. It will cause unnecessary conflict in your life and push people away from you.

2. Periodically Review Your Biases.

Biases can affect your life in ways that you aren't even conscious of. Until you make a conscious effort to uncover your biases in decision making, you will continue to let them affect your life. Biases can come in the form of anchoring, where you base your decisions on only one key item; framing, where you continually frame a situation in a way that benefits you; or a plethora of other biases. It is recommended that you review all of the biases in Indaba's Decision Making course for a comprehensive understanding.

3. Let Someone Else Be The Leader.

In a group or team setting, let someone else be the leader and let them take control. This may be difficult for you, but let someone else use their talents and skills to take control of the situation. Although you may think that you can do it best and that you know exactly what to do, trust their judgment and let them do things the way they see will be best. There are times in your life when someone else will have more experience and be better suited to leading. You will gain credibility if you can spot those times and help that person lead, instead of leading yourself. This can build better teams and improve productivity across the board.

> *Bob Uecker is a former major league catcher for the St. Louis Cardinals. During one interview with Johnny Carson on the "Tonight Show" he told Carson, "You know, I made a major contribution to the St. Louis Cardinals' pennant drive in 1964." "What did you do?" asked Carson. "I came down with hepatitis and had to be taken out of the lineup." "How did you catch hepatitis?" asked Carson. "The Cardinals trainer injected me with it." There are times in our lives when we have to realize that we may not be the most skilled person to complete the job. Take a step back and assist in the best possible way you can when you believe it can lead to better project completion.*

4. Ask Someone Else What You Can Do Around The Office or Your House.

Rather than taking control and doling out responsibilities and tasks, ask someone else what you can do. This will show you what it's like to be on the other side and give you a chance to see how other leaders act. Ask the leader or someone else what you should do to contribute. They'll be surprised you're asking them rather than taking matters into your own hands. They will feel more status because of this and will return the favor by promoting your status as well.

"Everything is in a process of change, nothing endures; we do not seek permanence."

~Masatoshi Naito

7 How to Dial Up Influence

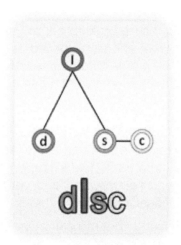

Influence is a necessary ingredient in today's world. The Influence Factor is the primary DISC Factor that deals with relationships, communication and interactions. Every day we put our influencing skills to the test, whether they are working for us the way we need them to or not. Situations may come during group settings or one-on-one contact where your current level of influencing ability is inadequate. Dialing up your influence powers will make you better able to make sure that others buy in to your ideas and put them into action. When you are able to dial up your influencing aptitude to an appropriate level for situations you face, you make your work, family, or social life change for the better. In this session, we'll concentrate on giving you tips and tactics to enhance your influencing skills.

There are several benefits of an Elevated Influence Factor. One important reality is that it might give you the ability to instigate change. We need to be able to deal with change in order to operate effectively. More than that, relationships with other people are constantly changing so being able to maneuver during changing times is important. Being able to influence the changes in your relationships; in your workplace, family life, and social life is important for your overall wellbeing. This ability to impact change is closely related to goal achievement and leadership, too. Moving forward and getting things accomplished means that you have to constantly change - moving from where you are right now to where you want to be in the future. Leading people toward a goal efficiently and without a good deal of stress demands a heightened level of influence. Even though you were not born with this natural ability, you can most certainly become proficient at communicating well and presenting ideas that people will buy into and follow.

Another important benefit is that by elevating your Influence Factor you can be particularly effective in building and maintaining rapport with others. Rapport building and trust go hand in hand. Especially if you have been working with the same people for a while you'll find that if you don't regularly reinforce the Influence Factor, team spirit or motivation may suffer. In your personal life, if you've been in a relationship over a long period of time, you can become complacent about how you interact with them. If you bolster your influencing talent on a regular basis and keep communication channels open by listening and paying attention to what's important to those you care about, you'll make certain that you won't lose interest in one another or become irritable toward them. In the DISC world, the Influencing Factor revolves around a desire to interact with and understand people. Being able to dial up this important function is critical.

Immediate Steps:

You can start to dial up your Influence by taking some immediate steps to practice using the Influence Factor in your everyday work and personal life. If you do not have a naturally Elevated Influence Factor, you may have to step outside of your comfort zone to realize the full potential of this Factor, but it will be worth it when you see what it can do for you and those you interact with.

1. **Control and Monitor Your Self-talk**

   Your subconscious mind is an extremely powerful and largely untapped resource that has the ability to think in the past and future as if it were happening in the present. The subconscious mind holds control over how you see yourself and your future. Unfortunately, most people don't understand that their subconscious mind is theirs to control!

   When we let our mind wander and dream or imagine the future that is our subconscious mind directing us. So, wouldn't you want to fill your subconscious mind with as many positive thoughts as possible? Positive self-talk is how you harness the power of your subconscious mind and direct it on the path that you want to go. By controlling the dialogue that goes on in your head, you are able to control how you act and feel. If you think you aren't a very good communicator it's going to be hard to have the confidence to talk to people. What if instead of saying to yourself "I'm a terrible public speaker", you said "I am amazing myself at how quickly I am becoming more comfortable speaking in front of people because I am willing to learn and try it." Quite a difference, isn't it! Whatever we tell our subconscious is what we will feel and how we will act, so be positive! It is shocking how many people talk themselves down in their own mind and therefore put a harness on their potential.

   Positive self-talk is extremely important in life and especially in areas where you might think you aren't quite as successful. Learn to recognize when you are using negative self-talk and change it. Our possibilities in life are endless, but unfortunately too many people hold themselves back by telling themselves they can't do something or they aren't good at that. Learn to control your self-talk and create a positive subconscious mind and as it becomes a habit you will notice that you are constantly energized and encouraging yourself to pursue your goals. Review Session 6 of the Life Skills Part 2 course to better understand how you can change your negative self-talk to positive, encouraging self-talk.

2. **Be Enthusiastic**

   Look on the bright side of things and ignore the negatives. Ask yourself a double-barreled question (and be realistic when you answer): What's the worst that could happen and what's the probability of that happening anyway? Most of the time you'll probably answer that even the worst thing isn't probably going to happen and even if it does, you can handle it. As soon as you put your fears into perspective with this line of self-questioning, you'll be surprised at what a positive impact this can have on your attitude. Happiness and excitement are magnetic and spread like wildfire. The happier you are, the happier everyone else around you will be. Just having a smile on at the office can improve the morale of people working around you. People will instinctively mirror your personality when they are talking with you. This is an excellent way of dialing up your Influence Factor.

You have more control of conversations if you realize that your body language speaks louder than words. Being able to have enthusiastic body language will cause others to mirror you, making them feel better when they are around you. These good feelings help to build relationships and ultimately build trust.

> *Theodore Roosevelt possessed the kind of enthusiasm the Influence Factor exhibits. According to Bernard Levin, Theodore Roosevelt went buffalo hunting in the Badlands of South Dakota with only one companion, Joe Ferris. During the trip, they almost died of thirst, and they slept on the hard ground. To make their matters worse, wolves caused their horses to flee away, which took them a good while to recapture. Then, they went to sleep another night to wake up lying in four inches of water due to the heavy rain. Ferris heard Teddy Roosevelt enthusiastically say, "By Godfrey, but this is fun!"*

When you need to dial up your influence, there is no better way than ramping up your enthusiasm. It will help you become more extroverted and it will cause you to talk to more people. As you continue to do this, you will learn to build on your confidence, just like Teddy Roosevelt.

3. Learn How to Mirror and Match

This will take practice and a conscious awareness of people you are conversing with. Mirroring and matching allows you to build rapport with another person through your body language and vocal qualities. As humans, we naturally feel comfortable with other people that have similar body language to our own and those who communicate like we do. If you can use that knowledge to gain rapport with others, you will find yourself with a masterful advantage in business relationships and you can effectively use it in your family and social relationships, too. If you can successfully mirror and match other people's body language, people will like you more and open up to you more. When done effectively, this skill will help so that you will in turn have a better understanding of people. Review Sessions 10 and 11 of the Life Skills – Part 3 Course or the Influence & Communication sessions of the same name in the Sales Course for a better understanding of these concepts.

4. Extend Invitations to Others

When you're going places such as lunch or grabbing coffee, invite your coworkers with you or ask if they'd like you to get something for them. They will be flattered that you thought of them and may come along for the company. Initiations have a profound effect on relationships. People are honored when you think of inviting them to join you. It doesn't have to be something fancy or formal, it's flattering to know that someone liked you enough to invite you to spend some time with them. Remember that simple gestures like this around the office, with your family, or with your friends is a great way to build relationships. You will learn more influencing skills this way because of the personal interactions you will have. This is the best way to learn about behaviors.

5. Share Your Knowledge

When you find out something new, share it with the people around you and your team. Make sure everyone is on the same page and has the up-to-date information and knowledge. The Influence Factor helps to build cohesive team units by making sure that everyone has the knowledge base required to make them successful. The better you are able to help other people understand all of the information involved in a project or undertaking, your team will run more efficiently and with better results.

"Attitude is a little thing that makes a big difference."

~Winston Churchill

Sharing knowledge can sometimes be against a person's first inclination because they might buy into the old saying that 'knowledge is power' but don't understand that it is not as powerful if you don't share it. They might want to feel in control of situations by controlling the information flow. Unfortunately some believe that if you give the information away, another person might be able to take over their superior knowledge-based position. If someone does believe this, they should change their thinking and realize that when you are working on a project, you must give a team member all the information they need to get the job completed. Otherwise there will be a lack of team unity and the project will end up worse off than it could have been. So holding onto knowledge in instances like these is detrimental to the whole.

Plus, on a personal level it is bad for you. You lose your influencing edge if you have the information but refuse to share it. People aren't stupid. They'll soon figure out what you are doing and they will work out ways to make sure that you don't get into that sort of powerful position again. They can go around you and get the information elsewhere. Or they can make decisions without your input, which is bad for many other reasons. For all these explanations, make sure that you don't make the influencing mistake of holding onto information. It might be a short-term gain but in the long run it hurts more than it helps.

6. Work in Teams

If the option comes up for you to work on a team, take it. Work with as many people as you can and connect with them. Get everyone together and start everyone working towards a common goal; you'll feel your influence increasing and it'll be easier to get to know and work with new people. As you become more experienced in working with teams, you will begin to realize how to find a common goal for everyone to work toward. Then you'll understand how to link that goal to each person's motivators in the team. As you practice this step and get better at teamwork, you might begin to see yourself becoming a true leader - someone dedicated to helping bring people closer to achieve their goals.

Secondary Steps:

After trying out the immediate steps, there are some secondary steps that you can take to dial up your Influence Factor.

1. Talk to People

This is a secondary step because it is more advanced than the immediate steps because we are going to use a technique that is designed to make you overcome a natural fear of approaching new people. If you don't naturally take the time to get to know people, look around your office or department. You'll soon find out that although you talk to people, if you're like almost everyone, it's probably the same people almost every day. To up your influencing abilities, make it a point to talk to people that you don't know very well. These may be new people or those you've worked with before but haven't taken the time to get to know beyond a surface level. Introduce yourself and strike up a conversation. The more social you are with them, the more social they'll be with you.

The goal is to systematically put yourself into conversations that might at first seem uncomfortable because getting to know people can be just that. However, the more practice you have at being uncomfortable, the less uncomfortable you'll feel. This process is called systematic desensitization - where you methodically, systematically desensitize - through repeated exposure - and build up your resistance to feeling awkward, stressed, embarrassed, or any other negative feelings when you talk to people. And remember, the first few times you do this, it might not go very well or it could go great. You never know, but the point is to get out there and just do it. Don't expect everyone to love you, but rather look at it as a game of numbers. The more people you talk to, the more you put yourself out there, the more you are building up your influencing abilities. The bottom line: You should be able to take a genuine interest in the people that you interact with everyday.

"You can make more friends in two months by becoming interested in other people than you can in two years by trying to get other people interested in you."

~Dale Carnegie

Everyone can teach you something that will give you better skills or knowledge to handle situations better the next time. You will learn influencing skills as you continue to learn from other people during conversations.

2. Get Others' Opinions

While you work, especially if you are working alone, get help from your peers or solicit input from others. Have them review your work or have an informal meeting for them to look at it. Just run ideas past people. You'll be pleasantly surprised at how much this can dial up your Influence Factor. They will be glad to give input into your situation and will often see something that you missed. Therefore, they will help you twofold, by first catching mistakes that you overlooked and second by helping to foster a better relationship between the two of you. It is not often thought about how helpful working together and get another person's opinions can help to produce stellar relationships between people.

3. Become More Convincing

When you're trying to get your point across, first remember the lessons from perceptual positioning. To gain an influencing advantage, you have to target their perceptual prism and only then move them into your way of thinking. If you forget to think about how they currently think before trying to influence them, you are fighting an uphill battle during the influencing process. After you have acknowledged what the perceptual positions are in the situation, use your verbal skills to put together a compelling argument. Don't forget to use mirroring and matching through verbal and body language cues. In this way you will be much better able to convince others around you. I suggest that you practice your speaking skills prior to launching them in front of a live audience if you are not yet competent in this area. This is wise even if you are delivering an influencing pitch to an audience of one. You can do this by talking in front of a mirror or by rehearsing what you plan to say while you're in the car. Keep replaying objections and counter-arguments in your mind until you have a persuasive answer for them. After you continue to practice this, you will become much better at influencing people.

"Teamwork is the fuel that allows common people to attain uncommon results."

~Unknown

Remember that sometimes people will persuade themselves if you know how to influence them to talk. If you influence people to talk, they will often convince themselves in unexpected ways. Let others talk and input key information and you will be surprised by the lengths they will go to persuade themselves for you.

4. Practice Public Speaking

This may be your worst nightmare, but if you don't practice it, you won't ever become good at it. You'll find that when you practice getting up in front of a group enough, it becomes easier and less frightening. This is another area where systematic desensitization has proved highly effective. Start with one or two people in an informal setting and methodically build to a point where you are competent at speaking in front of anyone, anywhere. And remember, you might never completely overcome your fear of speaking in front of people. That's okay. To those of you who know this is true for you I will give you this advice: Feel the fear but don't let it stop you. It's ok to feel the fear, just so long as you do it anyway. People are generally good-hearted and do not disparage a person for speaking in front of a group. Think about your attitude to people trying to speak. Don't you cut them a bit of slack? Sure you do, and people will do the same for you. As long as you try your best, have something to say that they find interesting or helpful, you'll do just fine. So just get out there and practice. Whenever you have a company fundraiser or a business gathering, try and get your name on a list of speakers or address smaller groups that you are comfortable with. Remember, in the human brain, four is a crowd. If you can practice in a small setting and gradually work your way up, you will find that speaking becomes easier and you'll get better at it.

DISCflex™

8 How to Dial Down Influence

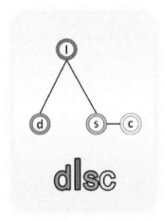

Since everyone has a bit of each of the four primary Factors, it is important to understand that the mix of levels or elevations determines how much governance these four Factors will have over your behavior. In this session we are going to talk in depth about the Influence Factor's potential negative impact and when it is appropriate to dial it down. A word of caution regarding ethics: By situationally adjusting your Influence Factor, you must make certain that you are using it to make the situation better. Never plan to use it in a scheming calculating way and always think of Noble Intent.

In general terms, an Elevated Influence Factor gives you an extroverted, relaxed style that can be useful when you need to persuade others to help you or when you want them to open up to you. Although this is highly desirable in most situations, in some cases, you must learn how to dial down your Influence Factor. This may come during a group meeting on a team project or when speaking to individuals one-on-one. You must learn how to dial down your influence when the situation calls for less friendliness or diplomacy. And think about this: Although it might seem counterintuitive, if someone views you as very good at influencing others - that you already have an elevated and highly skilled Influencing Factor, this can work to your detriment in an influencing situation. If people know that your skill level is far superior to theirs in the influencing arena, they become more guarded and in a strange way your heightened talent has worked against you. When you suspect this, it is critical to know how to dial down the perception of your Elevated Influence Factor. This doesn't mean that you forego influence and refrain from using influencing tactics; it just means that you dial down their impact significantly in order to make others feel more at ease.

Let's discuss specific instances when you might make the choice to dial down your Influence Factor. Imagine a project team just getting started. The team leader's goal is to make sure the team members get to know each other's strengths and weaknesses and to make sure that they bond to form a cohesive unit. Now jump forward. The team has been operating for a few months and deadlines are looming. But a couple of the team members are consistently late to meetings and critical deliverable dates slip. This is creating stress because the person next in line finds that they have to work overtime to catch up. It seems that the team leader has created such team camaraderie that the people think it's okay to let their team mates down as long as they apologize for doing so.

You might need to dial down influence to address this and hold people accountable for their behavior. This doesn't mean that you don't communicate effectively, it simply means that you deliver your message in a less easygoing manner. You are more forthright and pointed. The same is true whenever you need to hold people accountable. Examine precisely how you communicate your expectations and performance guidelines. For a team to be efficient and productive, the team members must all be held to a certain standard. The type of message a team leader must deliver sounds something like this: "Promises to other team members are important. Business is business and fostering team spirit is different than thinking it's ok to become a little lax in your responsibilities to your team mates. Letting team mates pick up the slack every once in a while when you get in a crunch is fine but when it becomes a habit, it is not effective teamwork." By delivering this type of message in a more efficient rather than friendly manner, you dial down your customary Influence Factor to make a point. This is usually enough to make sure people get the message.

Another example is when you are in a position where you need to get the facts right or when you need to be in a purely objective state of mind. Getting rid of emotional involvement is critical when you put yourself into the 3rd perceptual position.

In order to truly put yourself into this state, you need to dial down your Influence Factor and significantly dial up your Steadiness Factor. It doesn't take much to understand that if you are in an emotional state or in a mode where you are thinking about whether other people will like you rather than respect your rationale and judgment, that you might not be as impartial as possible. Finally, when you are in tactical mode, because the Influence Factor deals primarily with establishing the initial motivation and inspiration for a project, reliance on the Influence Factor at an elevated level when trying to accomplish the project's deliverables can lead to problems like missed deadlines, unfulfilled objectives, and inefficiencies.

When you have decision making authority to exercise; consider dialing down your Influence Factor and dialing up your Dominance and Steadiness Factors. The problem with an Elevated Influence Factor is that it skews the decision making process toward group consensus or putting together ad hoc teams. Rarely is authoritative decision making the first option when the Influence Factor governs. But authoritative decision making is the hallmark of a respected leader. When situations require it, the leader needs to be the final decision maker and set their vision into motion by making authoritative decisions. Be warned: The Influence Factor can hinder this ability.

"How do geese know when to fly to the sun? Who tells them the seasons? How do we, humans know when it is time to move on? As with the migrant birds, so surely with us, there is a voice within if only we would listen to it, that tells us certainly when to go forth into the unknown."

~Elisabeth Kubler-Ross

Immediate Steps:

As you think of situations in which your Elevated Influence Factor might hinder your performance, you can use these immediate steps to dial down your influence when it can help propel you forward.

1. Corral Your Instincts

An Elevated Influence trait is the reliance on gut feel and instinct. While having great instinctive judgment can be a particular strength, this tendency can prove disastrous if instincts and rationale don't match up. The key lies in understanding this and being able to keep the pony called 'Instinct' in the corral; letting it out only when prudent. The combination of instinct and reason – when honed and working synergistically – are powerful!

2. Close Yourself Off From Interactions During Certain Periods of The Day

When you need to get things done, or you need to become completely focused and objective, you can't afford to be social. Close your door and tell everyone that you'll be unavailable for a while. This will help you to focus on dialing down your Influence Factor and building up your other primary DISC Factors rather than talking to others. It's perfectly acceptable to tell everyone else to stay away for awhile while you get things done. This type of behavior - closing your door and not interacting with other people - can be a major issue for a naturally Elevated Influence individual. This is because they need frequent interaction to remain satisfied and happy. This is particularly true of extroverts. It is often painful for them to be alone for extended periods of time. It is hard for the influential person to say no when someone wants to talk to them. Make sure that you understand this might make you miserable at first but in the long run, having periods of uninterrupted alone time for planning, strategizing, or simply recharging your batteries will be highly beneficial.

I can't change the direction of the wind, but I can adjust my sails to always reach my destination."

~Jimmy Dean

3. Say What You Need To Say Once

If you're trying to convince someone to come around to your point of view, don't keep repeating yourself. Plan your message - ideally targeting precisely what your audience would love to hear, and say it just once. Because naturally Elevated Influence individuals are passionate in communicating, they often approach things by repeating and reiterating their strongest points. But this can also cause them to appear redundant or scattered. Plus, people with an Elevated Dominance Factor in particular will become annoyed and lose interest if you repeat yourself too often.

Dial down your influence by just saying it once and then move on. If you are trying to curb this tendency, just assume that the person listening will understand precisely what you are trying to say the first time you say it. Thinking like this goes a long way in changing your behavior and helps dial down a negative trait of an Elevated Influence Factor. If this worries you, remember that you can gauge whether they are willing to pursue the issue further if they bring it up again. Only then should you delve back into the topic.

4. Let Others Talk

While in a meeting or talking to someone in your personal life, let the other person do most of the talking. Curb your enthusiasm as a messenger. Concentrate on the other person's message instead. Sit back and really listen without interrupting their words. It is especially important to squash your self-talk when you are listening. You should not let it interrupt your thoughts either.

Concentrate on paying close attention to what they are saying. An Elevated Influence Factor can sometimes cause you to feel the need to interject. Perhaps you feel compelled to keep the conversation flowing during moments of silence. By doing this, you end up actually taking control of the dialogue and this is not always beneficial. When the other person finishes talking, it's okay to be silent. The other person might truly appreciate you giving them a few moments to think and reflect.

> *"The ideal condition would be, I admit, that men should be right by instinct; but since we are all likely to go astray, the reasonable thing is to learn from those who can teach."*
>
> **~Sophocles**

An excellent influencing tactic is to actually let someone convince themselves rather than you persuading them. When you let other people talk, you might find that you don't need to use your Influence Factor as much as you think. By letting the other person think and talk through a situation they'll often come to the conclusion you want them to. Just listen and make sure their logic is going along the track you want by proving cues like nodding and smiling. If they veer off track you can interject but don't jump in too fast. Often, if they talk aloud they'll counter argue against their own flawed logic.

There is a story about a man who stopped at a local flower shop to wire his mother, who was two-hundred miles away, some roses. Outside of the shop, the man noticed a little girl sobbing on the curb. He asked the little girl what was wrong, and she explained to him that she wanted to buy a single rose for her mother, but she only had seventy-five cents of the two dollar price tag. He bought the rose for the girl and offered to take her home. She agreed, but only if he would take her to her mother. The little girl directed him to the cemetery, where she placed the single rose on her mother's freshly dug grave.

The man, touched by the girl's actions, went back to the flower shop and cancelled his wire order. Instead, he took the roses himself and drove the two hundred miles to his mother's home to personally deliver the flowers.

You may find that they will keep talking and they will be the ones taking control of the situation and thinking of the idea that you wanted them to accept. This is an excellent way for you to practice dialing down your Influence Factor.

5. Do What You Can for Your Team (without asking!)

An Elevated Influence Factor puts too much emphasis on talking rather than action. It's easy to help if you are tuned into what other people's goals are. Figure out what you can do to help them by being aware. Don't ask them, be proactive, and just do it. Take the initiative to find an opportunity to help out, even if it is a small task. Your team members will appreciate your efforts and see you more of a go-getter than just being a social butterfly who talks to them and commiserates but doesn't pitch in.

We can all learn that taking just an extra step, without asking other people, can help create better relationships with the people in our lives because of the thoughtfulness that preceded the action.

6. Find The Root Cause Of Problems Rather Than Focusing On Superficial Problems.

Quite possibly one of the biggest weaknesses of an Elevated Influence Factor is its lack of focus and its willingness to go in different directions much as conversations lead from subject

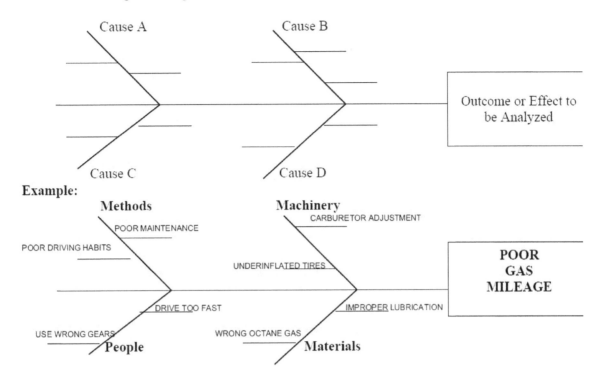

Example:

to subject depending on the interests of the current speaker. These traits cause behavior that focuses more on talking through the problem's fixes in circuitous ways - leading here and there without discipline or clear focus. An Elevated Influence Factor loves to debate possible solutions rather than spotlighting finding the actual reason why the problem exists in the first place. When this happens, you need to dial up your Dominance Factor to counterbalance the impact your Elevated Influence Factor has.

It is absolutely critical if you want to dial down your Influence Factor to review the session 2 of the Decision Making Course. In this session, you will learn how to identify the problem and how to use specific techniques such as the Fishbone Diagram and the 5 Why's model to the root cause of a problem. This is a great way to improve your ability to situationally flex your behavior so that your Influence Factor does not sidetrack you away from the actual problem that you need to solve.

Secondary Steps:

After completing the immediate steps to help you dial down your Influence Factor, there are some secondary steps that you can take to build upon your skills. Each step can be useful in helping you to foster a different set of abilities to manage situations and bring about better results.

1. Let Things Happen

Most often people associate the Dominance Factor with control but an Elevated Influence Factor desires control over relationships and communication. Don't try to manipulate every situation you are in. Sometimes the Influence Factor can lead you past influence and bring you into an area where you are manipulating outcomes and people. This can be disastrous in your long-term career or your long-term relationships with other people.

While working with a team, let others make connections and work together. Don't always be the orchestrator, peace maker, and networker. If there is an argument that ensues, stay back and let situations work themselves out. Although you are used to influencing or manipulating people to work together or solve the problem, let them bring out ideas to figure it out. If you are not an expert in the decision that needs to be made, sometimes your involvement can hinder the process. Look through the facts. Are you really the best person to influence the decision or action?

2. Concentrate on Following Through With Tasks in A Methodical and Systematic Way.

The Influence Factor causes almost erratic behavior at times that can jump around from place to place very easily. Focus is not one of the strengths of the Influence Factor. In fact, many people with a naturally Elevated Influence Factor love to multi-task and love a variety of activities buzzing around at once. But, persistency is required to commit and finish most tasks. A highly Elevated Influence Factor can interfere with and undermine this goal. This might make it hard to maintain concentration on following processes that need to be accomplished to reach the end goal. And following through with tasks might mean that you have to curb the Elevated Influence Factor's tendency to disrupt the single-mindedness required for complex assignments.

3. Translate Ideas Into An Implementable Action Plan.

Taking ideas and putting them into a plan that can actually be implemented is essential for the Elevated Influence individual to become skilled at. Sometimes the enthusiasm of new ideas can be motivating, and goodness knows that people with an Elevated Influence Factor love talking about and debating new ideas! But you have to remember to annex an implementable action plan to put the idea into practice. This requires dialing down Influence and gearing up thoughtfulness by amping up the Steadiness Factor.

Fleshing out action plans can help determine if your ideas will bear fruit. By going through an analysis process like a SWOT or a pros and cons exercise, which we'll discuss next, you may realize the strengths and weaknesses associated with actually carrying out your vision. Putting together a model for how your idea will work in practical terms is necessary to avoid obstacles and threats while simultaneously capturing the most profitable and beneficial opportunities. The Influence Factor can inhibit linear thinking because of the enthusiastic nature that it brings about in a person. When you get excited and inspired, ideas flow fast and furious. This is the

A 24-year-old, pregnant mother, sought a way to increase her family's income. She did not have much money, just the two-thousand dollars saved from her wedding gifts, but she nevertheless proceeded to use the money to submit an ad to Seventeen magazine. She was promoting personalized handbags and belts. At the time, putting initials on a person's products was a revolutionary idea. Lillian Katz decided to implement her idea with the slogan, "Be the first to sport that personalized look." Her business grew, eventually growing into the Lillian Vernon Corporation, with annual sales of one-hundred-forty million dollars.

influence of creativity in motion. While this is great, at some point you have to nip it in the bud. Often that point occurs when you move ahead toward action. Then you will need to learn to dial down the Influence Factor when you need to bring your idea to action.

Action-oriented people realize "those who want milk should not sit in the middle of a field and wait for a cow to back up to them". Lillian Katz did not wait for someone to offer her an opportunity or for some investor to agree with her about her idea. She took her ideas and translated them into an implementable action plan. As I mentioned, one of the models you can use to analyze your position is to Weigh The Pros And Cons before making a decision.

An Elevated Influence Factor can lead you to make decisions in an undisciplined manner. If you get caught up in discussions where people get excited and in the heat of the moment make decision that haven't been properly thought out yet you corrupt the Rational Decision Making Process. Snap decisions, spontaneous excitement and spur-of-the-moment choices are things to watch out for if your Influence Factor is in overdrive. In this regard, the Influence Factor is more associated with the Intuitive Decision Making Process, which can be skewed by individual perceptions and Groupthink.

Dialing down the effect of an Elevated Influence Factor will give you a distinct advantage when it comes to making decisions. If you take the sessions on the Rational Decision Making Process in the Decision Making Course, you will find yourself with an improved skill set that will help you in a plethora of different situations.

4. Watch Out For Groupthink (and other biases)

Groupthink affects every Factor, whether you are falling into it or causing it. Sometimes you may actually use your influence to cause Groupthink without even realizing it. Most people with an Elevated Influence Factor instinctively understand the Law of Societal Pressure and the affect that it can have on groups. Make sure that you are NOT using this to get your ideas put into action. From a logical standpoint, others can significantly improve your ideas and give you input into your strengths and weaknesses. You do not want to put into action a half-baked idea that will inevitably fail. Watch your influencing skills when you are putting forth an idea and make sure that one person is the Devil's Advocate that will stimulate debate. Review the Groupthink sessions of the Decision Making Course as well as the sessions on biases to learn how they could affect you and your Influence Factor.

9 How to Dial Up Steadiness

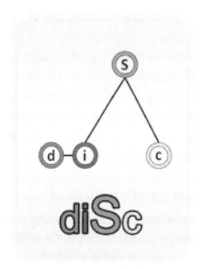

Since everyone has a bit of each of the four primary Factors, it is important to understand that the mix of levels or elevations determines how much governance each of these four Factors will have over your behavior. In this session, we are going to talk in depth about the Steadiness Factor's potential positive impact and how you can dial up its effects. As with all of the Factors you begin determining how to adjust them by first asking yourself: When is it appropriate to dial Dominance, Influence, Steadiness or Compliance up or dial it down? Remember our warning of caution regarding ethics: By situationally adjusting your Steadiness Factor, you must make certain that you are using it to make the situation better. Never plan to use any of your growing abilities to situationally adapt your behavior in a scheming, calculating way and always think of Noble Intent.

In some situations, you have to learn how to dial up your Steadiness when you are working alone. You may need to alter the depth of your thinking or the pace you are operating at; or you might need to dial it up in groups to make sure the decision making processes have adequate thoughtfulness or that people are considering all the options appropriately. The situation you find yourself in may call for increased patience and persistence, for which you must consciously make an effort to dial up your Steadiness Factor governing power. The Steadiness Factor is the Factor to turn to for thinking through situations, becoming committed to responsibilities, and becoming more empathetic to other people. This is a great Factor to learn to dial up if you are a manager, coaching at work or in social situations, or are a salesperson because you can better understand the needs of your employees or clients and effectively function in each situation.

Immediate Steps:

As you learn how to dial up your Steadiness, put extra consideration on how to pick up the positive qualities of this Factor while avoiding its weaknesses. Specifically, do not let the Steadiness Factor cause you to be resistant to change or to be passive aggressive. We want to ramp up the strengths of the Steadiness Factor to enhance our thoughtfulness, persistence, and patience.

1. The Perceptual Prism

Remember that there are three perceptual positions to any situation you encounter. The first perceptual position is your point of view. It is what you perceive and believe. The second perceptual position is the alliance position, where you see the situation from the point of view of the others involved. The final perceptual position is the observer or the fly-on-the wall position. This is from an objective viewpoint regarding the situation.

Learn more about the Perceptual Prism in Session 3 of the Change Course. This may seem difficult to do, but think about how others are feeling and about an objective view without emotional involvement. Think about how a new change or decision affects others. Our first instinct is to think about how this affects ourselves, but think about how this may change things for others. Think about the people involved and what this new change may mean for them. By putting yourself in someone else's shoes, you are now one-step closer to being able to look at a situation objectively. When a person is in the third position, they are able to make decisions for the good of the group, not just for the individual. For instance, a manager has two proposals to choose from and chooses proposal A because they like the way it looks and/or because their team is used to working with the company who submitted the proposal.

"I love people who do what's expected of them, and then go the extra mile. They are thoughtful, but not by some small measure. They are over achievers in this regard. They meet their obligations and responsibilities while being fair and considerate. It all comes back to the level of thoughtfulness they have. You can count on them to deliver. You can guarantee that they think long and hard about the consequences of letting people down. It's just not in their nature to disappoint."

~Hellen Davis

Proposal B happens to be significantly less expensive than proposal A and offers more features, but because the manager is making their decision from the first or second perceptual position, the correct decision is not made. If the manager took a step back and looked at both proposals from the third perceptual position, they would be able to make an unbiased, unemotional decision that would benefit the company and employees. The ability to look at situations through the different perceptual positions is a great strength of the Steadiness Factor.

2. RA² Interface Document

The best way to dial up your Steadiness Factor is to have a holistic approach to the responsibilities, accountability metrics, and the authority parameters that are involved with a task or assignment - whether this is at work or in any other areas of your life. A parent can use the RA² Document around the house to set up chores and make sure the family knows who is accomplishing what tasks. Alternatively, the coach can use the RA² document to set up responsibilities and accountability metrics for their coaches. Because the Steadiness Factor is acutely aware of the intricacies and consequences of decision-making, the RA² Interface Document can help carve out that picture for you so that you can properly manage your time and effectively produce the needed results according to your and other people's expectations.

"A small group of thoughtful people could change the world. Indeed, it's the only thing that ever has."

~Margaret Mead

Further than just defining the responsibility, accountability, and authority areas of a task in a work environment, the RA² Interface Document represents how to delegate authority with dotted and solid lines, who is in the communication loop, and what the legal, moral, and ethical constraints are. This is an invaluable tool for aligning your organization or team to become more cohesive and effective along horizontal and vertical lines. Whenever I work in a team setting, my first goal is to fill out the RA² Document and make sure we all understand our responsibilities. This makes us a more cohesive unit when we know to whom we can delegate to, who we can communicate with for more information, and what metrics we have to achieve. It makes sure no surprises come through at the end or people on the team say they did not fully understand what was being asked of them. Review the RA² Interface Alignment Course for a full description of how to receive the benefits from this method.

3. Stick to What You're Doing

Another component of the Steadiness Factor is the pace you operate at and your degree of persistence. Inconsistent pace is a sign of a low Steadiness Factor and happens when someone multitasks, procrastinates, and is easily distracted. This step can help you work and live at a more consistent pace by understanding the Law of Commitment and the Law of Consistency. The Law of Commitment states that people are more likely to listen and trust a person if they see that person taking action directed at achieving their goals.

Bottom line: Actions speak louder than words. The Law of Consistency states that people are more willing to trust someone who is stable and predictable in their behavior.

"Personality has the power to uplift, power to depress, power to curse, and power to bless."

~Paul Harris

When people jump from project to project and do not stick with what they are doing, they are working at an inconsistent pace which is detrimental to their performance and influence. Inconsistent pace is mainly due to having a lower Steadiness Factor. This Factor is responsible for persistence and the ability to keep on track with a project or activity. Use Steadiness to stay with your project and see it through.

If you need to, take a break, but get back on track quickly. Don't say you're done till you're really done with what you're working on.

Commit to the responsibilities that you accept in your life. Hold to your promises and achieve the results that you set your sights on. The more you are able to commit yourself to achieving success, inevitably the more success you will find. Review Session 5 entitled The Law of Commitment and the Law of Consistency in the 21 Laws of Influence for Sales Course - Part 1.

DISCflex™

On September 6th, 1995 in front of a sold-out, screaming crowd at Oriole Park at Camden Yards, Cal Ripken Jr. broke a record that had stood for 56 years in Major League Baseball. On that night, Cal played in his 2,131st consecutive game, breaking the record set by the great New York Yankees first baseman Lou Gehrig. He went on to play an additional 501 straight games after setting the record, and in 1998 he voluntarily took himself out of the lineup after playing in 2,632 consecutive games. Known as the "Iron Man", Cal's streak stretched from 1982 to 1998 and during that time, he made the All-Star team sixteen times, was a two time Gold Glove Award winner, and a two time Most Valuable Player Award winner. In 2007 he was inducted into the Major League Baseball Hall of Fame. His consistency and persistence is an example of how sticking to what you are doing and staying focused can lead to success.

4. Have A Purpose When Talking To Someone

People consider Steadiness individuals thoughtful and considerate, but just talking to someone does not make you thoughtful or considerate. Before you talk to someone, create an agenda. For example, a salesperson could make it a point to find out something new about an existing customer. By doing this, the salesperson shows that they care about their customer and are serious about continuing the relationship. Take the time to talk to someone and find out something you didn't already know about them. It is much easier for people to talk about themselves and their interests than other people. This small act of kindness could change someone's day and make them feel noticed and appreciated. The more you do this, the more considerate and thoughtful you'll become.

As you become more comfortable talking to others, you will find yourself beginning to understand what their motivators are and what their feelings are about topics and issues. You will begin to see the different behavior types associated with people and the way that they respond to various situations. Remember when talking with others that the MOST favorite word a person likes to hear….is their own name.

5. Plan

If you get a new project, plan exactly how you will complete it. Planning specifically will naturally dial up your thoughtfulness by causing you to think about the specifics involved in making your plan successful. More importantly, creating a plan enables you to make a roadmap for you to follow and allows you to set deadlines, which will keep you consistent. This will give your plans a greater chance of success. Make a list or a timeline of how you will get things accomplished.

Planning and organizing will make you feel like you have more control over things and you'll feel more relaxed knowing exactly how you'll accomplish your project's goals.

Strategic plans can greatly benefit your thoughtfulness and your ability to see how your decisions will affect the people around you. Be cautious, however, of creating plans without enough thought. As you continue to use plans over time, you will notice your Steadiness Factor growing, helping you to incorporate it into your life.

Secondary Steps:

After completing the immediate steps associated with dialing up the Steadiness Factor, some secondary steps can help you achieve situational behavioral flexibility of the Steadiness Factor. Practice these steps often so that they become second nature to you when you need these skills.

> "They were trying to send a message. I have to be more sensitive in the way I express myself, and I have to be more thoughtful in the positions I take."
>
> ~James P. Moran

1. Define What You're Doing

As we said in the immediate step, clear definitions of responsibilities, accountability, and authority parameters motivate individuals with the Steadiness Factor, which is the ultimate goal for someone who has a low Steadiness Factor. If you feel that you have become distracted from your original goals, remember your job description and what you're expected to do. You may want to ask your boss or superior what exactly they expect of you. If you feel unsure while completing a project, think about the benefits and consequences of why you are doing what you are doing.

Think about how to accomplish this better. When you think deeply, you will be more consistent about your pace, the planning process, and the efforts you put in will be more in alignment with the original goals. Take the time to look up those parameters you started with during your goal setting. Do this on a consistent basis to dial up your Steadiness Factor.

After you define what you are doing, you can then take the extra effort to exceed the expectations given to you. Don't get trapped into a mindset where you believe it is alright to simply meet expectations. Think about process improvement. Process improvement involves always checking your current position and seeing how you can improve it. Benchmarking and evaluating where you are can help you improve the process you are using to reach your goals. The persistence and determination from the Steadiness Factor helps you continually exceed the expectations set forth by your bosses, your family, or your friends. Remember, you control the amount of effort you put in to improving yourself and your responsibilities.

The difference between the status quo and a standing ovation can be found in a comment by Abraham Lincoln. "I do the very best I know how – the very best I can; and I mean to keep doing so until the end." This statement accurately describes how Peter Ueberroth ran his company, lives his life, and is an excellent example to follow.

2. Eliminate The Distractions From Your Life.

Distractions are the enemy of thinking because distractions kill thoughtfulness and pull you away from completing your goals. Having the ability to stay focused on task or a project can improve productivity and performance. The time and thought, which most people waste in aimless effort, would accomplish wonders if properly directed with some special object in view. Unless you can concentrate upon the object, which you have in view, you will have but a hazy, indifferent, vague, indistinct and blurred outline of your ideal and the results will be in accordance with your mental picture. Meditation, visualization, and deep breathing techniques can help you stay focused and consistent.

Take a few minutes each day to stop what you're doing and handle the small matters that might prove as distractions later. Close out of your browser, do not respond to text messages or emails, and turn off notifications. You cannot get things done and pay attention when you are giving your time and attention to everything that pops up on your screen. Set aside time during the day to complete any tasks that might later prove as distractions to your work responsibilities. Complete the Eliminate Distractions Activity from the How to Dial Down Friendliness session to help you eliminate distractions.

Peter Ueberroth was one man who was never satisfied with the status quo. The son of an itinerant aluminum-siding salesperson, Peter went on to become Time's man of the year in 1985. Ueberroth also built one of the finest travel companies in the United States.

His commitment to a personal lifestyle of excellence is reflected in his business practices as well. For example, Ueberroth's employees wore coats and ties at all times and when an employee looked a little shabby, they were admonished to purchase new threads. Oh yes, Ueberroth customarily provided a check to cover the cost, putting his money where his mouth is.

He later spearheaded a tremendously successful twenty-third Olympic games in Los Angeles, California. Unlike the twenty-two that preceded it, this event blasted the status quo of causing huge financial losses and generated a $215 million profit. To top off this effectively orchestrated event, eighty-four thousand people attending the closing ceremonies gave Peter Ueberroth a standing ovation.

10 How to Dial Down Steadiness

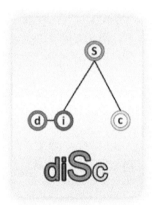

In this chapter we will go into how to dial down your Steadiness Factor. In certain situations, you must learn how to dial down your Steadiness. This may occur when you must make split second decisions or need to quickly recognize the best way to go about things. In these cases, it is necessary to dial down your Steadiness to act quickly.

"The challenge of leadership is to be strong, but not rude; be kind, but not weak; be bold, but not bully; be thoughtful, but not lazy; be humble, but not timid; be proud, but not arrogant; have humor, but without folly."

~Jim Rohn

In management positions or leadership roles within your team, you should dial down your Steadiness Factor in order to allow more extrovert-type behaviors to take effect. Although the Steadiness Factor can help you be thoughtful about situations, it can hinder you from adequately taking command and taking action. You need some degree of assertiveness in order to fulfill leadership duties; such as delegating tasks and dealing with conflict. It is imperative that you improve your ability to give and receive feedback, too. An example of this can be found when instructing young children. Young children have a short memory and when they do something wrong, you need to let them know right away or they will forget what they did and will not understand why you are instructing them. The Steadiness Factor can hinder this ability because it is an introverted Factor, meaning that it obstructs effective communication between others. Even though the Steadiness Factor is people-oriented, it is more introspective. Dial down this Factor and use it in tandem with the more extroverted Factors for effective management and leadership.

Conflict is the other major problem with the Steadiness Factor. There is an unwillingness to deal with problems or differences, which can cause someone with an Elevated Steadiness Factor to become passive aggressive. If you can't get your feelings or ideas out in the open, they might build up and cause resentment toward the people or person that you aren't able to express your true thoughts. This can cause serious problems in work and personal relationships and cause unwanted stress.

Take note of any situations in which your Steadiness Factor may be hampering your proficiency to accomplish your tasks and responsibilities.

Immediate Steps:

As you begin to mark areas of your life in which to dial down your Steadiness Factor, take note of these immediate steps that you can use to build your skills at situationally behavioral flexing or with long-term behavioral morphing.

1. Be Efficient

Focus on the actions you need to take. Occasionally, multi-tasking can be a waste of time and detrimental to performance; even causing stress and fatigue in the long run. Focusing on what you need to get completed can help your productivity and relationships. Although you may want to stop and talk to your coworkers and be thoughtful, to get things finished, you must put others on the backburner to complete your tasks. Close your door and focus on what's on your plate. Just get it done!

You may find it helpful to set a specific period of the day to focus on your work materials, and make that time known throughout the office. If others recognize that you are unavailable during certain points in the day, you will find yourself completing more work and achieving more of your goals each day. In this way, they will still think you are thoughtful, but you just need time to work without interruptions.

2. Forgive and Forget

Too many times individuals with an elevated Steadiness Factor will tend to hold in their thoughts and feelings, causing resentment and bitterness to build up. Being able to communicate your thoughts, forgiving a person that has wronged you, and moving on will help lower unwanted stress and allow you to focus on the many positive aspects of your life. Resentment and bitterness can also hold us back from achieving our goals because we are so focused on what another person said or did to us and how it hurt us, that we lose focus of our original goals and objectives. Learning to forgive and forget can help you regain that focus and press on to achieving success in your life.

How someone is able to forgive and forget is unique to each person's situation; however, communicating your hurt is a key step in that process. Communicating your hurt maturely allows you to let the other person know that you hurt them and gives them the chance to explain themselves. Allowing others to apologize and realizing that everyone is human and makes mistakes are other areas that are important in the process of forgiving and forgetting.

"If you don't like something, change it. If you can't change it, change your attitude."

~Maya Angelou

3. Try Something New

You may be getting comfortable in your routine and what you do; try something new! Change can be an extremely good thing! When a person sticks to the familiar they give up on the infinite possibilities and outcomes of any circumstance or opportunity. Trying new things will challenge you and can lead you to a level of success that you never thought possible. Try taking a class or simply go to a new restaurant. Take a break from your routine and get out of your normal habits.

You could even try to take on a new responsibility at work. This will show initiative and earn you respect from your bosses or peers. If you continually show this type of behavior, people will come to you with new tasks that will inevitably enhance your career.

The example that Liz Claiborne exhibited shows that coming out of your routine or comfort zone can push you to new heights, personally and professionally.

> *What do you do if you've invested sixteen years of your life with a company and your ideas for change are disregarded? Just ask Liz Claiborne. Claiborne was a clothing designer with the Jonathan Logan Company. She believed their limited variety of patterns and sizes were insufficient to meet the changing needs of their market. Efforts to convince management that body types and style preferences warranted innovation in design fell on deaf ears.*
>
> *Undiscouraged, Claiborne became a vehicle for stylish and affordable woman's apparel by starting her own company. Her versatile designs appealed to the growing number of women in the workforce and to store buyers. Liz Claiborne, Inc. experienced enviable growth throughout the 1960s, 1970s, and 1980s, ultimately attaining the number-one position in the woman's fashion industry.*

4. Take a Calculated Risk

People with Elevated Steadiness tend to get what is known as analysis paralysis. They become paralyzed by fear because they think so deeply and they conjure up all manner of negative consequences that they never even try to take a step forward. This can cause someone to miss an opportunity to reach their goal. If your boss offers you a project and you haven't done anything like that before, take the chance on it and try to achieve success. You may feel uncomfortable risking something and entering unfamiliar territory, but it will help you to learn how to dial down your Steadiness.

Calculated risks will lower your Steadiness Factor because of the initiative and assertiveness that risks require. For risks to occur, you need to make assumptions. An assumption is when a person thinks that a cause, a situation, facts or data are correct, but they cannot or have not yet uncovered irrefutable evidence to prove them true. We make assumptions every day. When we leave for work in the morning and see that it is sunny, we assume that it isn't going to rain and that we don't need our umbrella. Assumptions are a part of life, but making erroneous or false assumptions can be extremely detrimental in the decision making process. It is highly recommended that you visit and review the Decision Making Course and the Session entitled Analyze Options. Complete the Threat Mitigation of Fear Activity in Session #7 of Part 2 of the Life Skills Course.

> *"Change brings opportunity."*
>
> *~Nido Qubein*

DISCflex™

> *Charlie House took what many would consider the ultimate risk. As head of corporate engineering at Hewlett-Packard, he ignored an order from co-founder David Packard to stop working on a high-quality, large-screen video monitor. Charlie pressed on. The monitor has been used in heart transplant operations as well as space travel. Seventeen thousand of the units were sold instead of the projected thirty, and Hewlett-Packard gave House a medal in 1982 for 'extraordinary contempt and defiance beyond the normal call of 'engineering duty'. He took a calculated risk, made a decision, and took action.*

5. Open to Change

It's important to understand why people are wary of change in the first place to begin to dial down your Steadiness Factor. You have to go through the Transitional Time Line and determine what your behavior looks like in each of the ten phases. As you learn how to deal with denial, the depths of suffering, commitment, achievement, and the other phases, you will gain better insight into human behavior, both in yourself and in others. People tend to get stuck in phases and halt their forward movement through the Time Line. It is important for the elevated S to propel themselves into the decision making phase of the Transitional Time Line. It is too easy for an individual with an Elevated Steadiness Factor to become stuck in the Narrowing Options phase, which is right before the Making Decisions phase. Spending too much time in this phase will keep a person from accomplishing their goals and achieving success. Learning about the different phases in the Transitional Time Line may help you become more open to change and truly adapt to your environment.

Something that can hinder being open to change is what is known as hindsight bias. It is also called the 'I-knew-it-all-along' effect.

It is the inclination to see past events as being predictable. It sometimes occurs in reaction to a surprise and is used to try and cover up embarrassment of not being aware of anything that foreshadowed the occurrence. When a person exhibits this bias, they can refuse to learn from making a bad decision because "they saw it coming all along". When this happens, they are likely to carry on repeating the same mistakes. It is important to check your biases so that you don't continue making the same mistakes and become resistant to change.

You can review the Transitional Time Line in the Change Course in the Session entitled Understanding Human Behavior and the sessions on the Transitional Time Line. These courses provide invaluable material that will help you dial down your Steadiness Factor and become more open to change.

6. Be Flexible

The Steadiness Factor usually locks you into a certain belief pattern or a particular way of doing things. In order to adapt your behavior to different situations, you must become flexible. Flexibility allows you to utilize different Sub-factors in different situations which can help you achieve success in life and work. Dialing down the Steadiness Factor will open your mind to many more paths and approaches to accomplish your goals.

Flexibility entails practice, but your mind can accomplish it quickly if you become determined. Learn to focus on becoming more flexible and you will find plenty of success throughout your life.

Secondary Steps:

After practicing the immediate steps to dialing down your Steadiness Factor, there are several secondary steps recommended to help you improve your ability to dial down the Steadiness Factor.

1. **Think About the Most Important Aspects of Your Life, Both Professionally and Personally**

   If you have to make a decision quickly, think about the most important criteria required to make an acceptable decision. When you need to make that decision for yourself, you need to have a keen sense of where you want to go, not where other people want you to go. Trust your gut and make the decision on the best possible options. There are times in life and work where you have to make a quick decision. Having this skill set will benefit you as you work toward achieving your goals. This may seem hard to do but it'll get easier as you practice more.

2. **Take a Break from the Major Project,**

   When you've been working steadily on something for a long time, take a break and complete some of your smaller tasks. Occasionally, a break can help clear your mind and allow it to relax before starting on the major project again. You have to establish a balance between your determination to finish your most important tasks and your smaller responsibilities.

   Taking a break at work is extremely important for your physical and mental health and it can also have a positive impact on productivity and performance.

   Taking periodic breaks if you work at a computer helps circulation throughout the body, can lower heart risks, lowers stress and helps you from becoming burned out. Understand that breaks are needed to help you refocus and reenergize not only your brain, but your body as well. Breaks aren't just needed in the workplace, though. Taking time to refocus while around family or friends can help strengthen your relationships and keep you balanced.

3. **Find a Mentor that is the Opposite of You.**

   Observing and learning from someone showing different behaviors and diverse modes of thinking helps you develop your behavioral flexibility. Studying a mentor's actions and mindset gives you insight into developing new skills and can help you learn from their experience so that you don't have to make the same mistakes they did.

   More than just viewing your mentor's behaviors, the mentor will scrutinize your actions and give you a valuable perception of yourself. Then you can begin to improve and adapt your skills to fit the situations in your life.

4. **Become More Task-Oriented**

   Since the Steadiness Factor is people-oriented, you must dial down your Steadiness if your job or life requires you to be task-oriented. If you become more task-oriented then your productivity can increase and even stress levels can decrease because you aren't trying to rush to finish a project that you put off or analyzed too deeply. This may only be for a limited time or a few minutes, but you need to know how to situationally flex in order to progress.

   A task-oriented focus is the characteristic of the Dominance and Compliance Factors. Simply dialing up those Factors may be enough to dial down your Steadiness Factor. Review those two dialing up sessions in DISCflex™ Part 2 to learn more tactics to dial down your Steadiness Factor.

DISCflex™

11 How to Dial Up Compliance

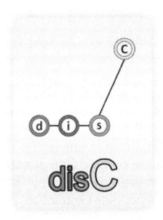

In some situations, it's necessary to know how to dial up your Compliance Factor. This may be the case while working on a team or working individually. Knowing how to dial up your Compliance Factor is a skill that is necessary to be successful.

The Compliance Factor is the behavioral link to accuracy, cooperativeness, and consistently meeting accountability metrics. Being able to follow guidelines, whether in your work tasks or in personal relationships, will help you learn the expectations of everyone involved and allow you to meet the appropriate standards. It is important to understand that the appropriate standards may not be high quality. For example, management may need a starting point for a project as soon as possible and they don't care about typos or inaccuracies, since they just want it as a starting point. This may seem counter intuitive to dialing up your Compliance Factor, but it is important to remember that your standards are not always the standards needed.

Observe team sports if you want to see the benefits of dialing up the Compliance Factor when the situation calls for it. Following the rules so the umpire or referee does not penalize the player is important but there are times in life, as in sports, where following the rules to the letter can keep a team or yourself from achieving success. Understanding the situation you are in is crucial to making the decision on whether or not it is appropriate to follow the rules to the letter. In some organizations there are unwritten rules that, even though they may not be completely aligned with the governing rules, are not considered wrong by others. For example, in 2005 during on NCAA college football game between the University of Southern California and Notre Dame, the USC running back helped his quarterback score a last second touchdown by pushing him into the end zone. The unusual play solidified USC's victory and preserved their number one national ranking. According to NCAA rules, helping or aiding a runner is prohibited, but it is rarely enforced and happens all the time.

A corporate example can be found in information sharing. Corporate policy calls for companies to be transparent and report all information to shareholders, though this doesn't always happen. Does this make it right? No, but that is how some situations in life are, and understanding that can help you be prepared and be more successful. The Compliance Factor also builds cooperative relationships between the different team members based on guidelines for dealing with situations and building team unity.

Even culturally, we complacently agree to customs and traditions, some of which we take part of unconsciously. We all obey social expectations, complying with the demands we put onto each other. Even through this, different countries and cultures agree to diverse sets of behaviors and mannerisms.

For instance, the American 'V' sign for victory is actually an insult when the palm faces in to a person in Britain. That sign in Britain means, well, suffice it to say, it is not a pleasant symbol. More than just gestures, culture influences our very conduct and thought patterns. This is due to our natural adaption to the Compliance Factor and its usefulness in our life.

Caveat on Compliance: It is important to understand that the Compliance Factor should not be used as a hammer. An individual with an Elevated Compliance Factor is typically exacting, precise, accurate, and a perfectionist. While these traits are very useful, when taken to the extreme they can become extremely damaging and counter-productive. A person with an elevated Dominance Factor should be very careful when dialing up their Compliance, because an elevation in both Factors can be extremely detrimental for them relationally and for an organization. An example of both Dominance and Compliance being elevated can be found in Herbert Hoover at the beginning of the Great Depression. Hoover's stance on the economy was that public-private cooperation was the way to achieve high long-term growth.

> *The Serenity Prayer by Reinhold Niebuhr puts the idea of accepting change and focusing on the things you can control into a well known prayer:*
>
> *Grant me the serenity*
> *to accept the things I cannot change;*
> *courage to change the things I can;*
> *and wisdom to know the difference.*
>
> *Living one day at a time;*
> *Enjoying one moment at a time;*
> *Accepting hardships as the pathway to peace.*

Hoover thought that too much intervention or coercion by the government would hurt individuality and self-reliance, which he considered important American values. He rejected Treasury Secretary Andrew Mellon's 'leave-it-alone' approach at the outset of the Depression because Hoover wanted business leaders to not lay off workers or cut wages. His pro-labor policy after the 1929 stock market crash is purported to account for close to two-thirds of the drop in the nation's gross domestic product over the two years that followed. His combination of Dominance and Compliance was one of the main reasons why what might have been a bad recession, turned into the Great Depression. Be cautious that you don't use Compliance as a hammer to drive home the rules and your own agenda.

As you learn how to dial up your Compliance Factor, you will enhance your ability to follow guidelines to keep you on track, organized, and form cooperative relationships.

Immediate Steps:

We have come up with several steps that will help you work towards dialing up your Compliance Factor. These steps come both at the immediate and secondary level. Both are equally important and require the same amount of attention and care.

1. Prioritize Your Tasks

Write down everything you need to get done; you might do this just for the day or for the entire month. After you write down what you need to do, prioritize it from the most important, to the least important. After organizing by priority, organize your list by how long it will take. If you group tasks together that are due around the same time and you put easy, short tasks first, you may not have enough time or stamina to get the longer tasks done. If you prioritize your task, you make it easier to stay organized and accurate. It also helps to add an incentive to finishing tasks on time. For example, a family could use the incentive of going to get ice cream if they finish the yard work on time. This helps motivate the each individual in the family to stick to the group's priority.

You need to find a method that works for you. You may want to speed through the quick tasks and take your time with the longer ones, or you may choose to get the long, cumbersome tasks done first and then breeze through the quicker ones. No matter how you choose, the most important tasks must be completed.

2. Structure Your Day

Plan your day out and schedule when you will be completing tasks. This will ensure that you do not forget anything and that you plan enough time for everything. This way, at any time during the day, you will know exactly what you should be doing and how long it will take. You'll find that there is no reason to get anxious or worried that you'll get things done or remember to do them when you have everything planned out and organized.

Our minds need structure to function more effectively. No structure is the same for everyone, however. You need to find an organization style that works for you and that is adaptable to your approach. An efficient way of structuring tasks during the day is called chunking. Chunking is when you organize tasks of the same nature together so that you can complete them more efficiently. For example, if a salesperson has to contact prospective clients and existing clients

> *A former president of the General Motors Corporation started out as a stock boy and had a career that was the epitome of the American dream. At the time of his retirement, a reporter asked him whether it was still possible for a young man nowadays to start at the bottom and get to the top – and if so, how?*
>
> *"Indeed, it is," was his answer. "The sad fact, however, is that so few young people realize it." Then he outlined a formula for success that will prove out not only in the auto industry but in any business.*
>
> *Keep thinking ahead of your job! Do it better than it needs to be done. Next time, doing it well will be child's play. Let no one, or anything, stand between you and a difficult task. Let nothing deny you the rich opportunity to gain strength in adversity, confidence in mastery. Do each task better each time. Do it better than anyone else can do it. Do these things and nothing can keep the job ahead from reaching out after you!"*

and make two sales calls during the day, it would be more efficient for the salesperson to do all of their communication at one time, then make their sales calls rather than space them out. In this way, the salesperson practices good time management.

3. Know The Guidelines and Regulations that Surround Your Work.

To be sure you are following the rules correctly when appropriate and do things the way they ought to be done, check and read up on the guidelines. You may be starting a new project and not move forward correctly or finish the project correctly because you did not read the rules and know exactly what you should be doing. Understanding what you need to do will give you a path to follow that can help you accomplish your work in an effective, competent manner.

4. Create Appropriate Quality Standards for the Situation.

Your potential of effectiveness is only as high or low as you set the standards appropriate for the return on the investment of your time, energy, and resources. Let's first look at the obvious - dealing with high standards. If you want to exceed expectations at work, set your personal expectations higher. If you work toward an elevated goal, you are much more likely to achieve more, even if you do not reach that goal.

The example of setting high standards for yourself and your work is important to remember when it is appropriate to have high quality standards. There are times when high quality standards aren't required, but they can be few and far between. Completing a project to the best of your ability is always a good rule to live and work by. It is especially important to set higher quality standards for yourself to assist with the way that your subconscious mind works. When you give your subconscious instructions, it will consider them and give you ideas to help you reach those expectations. If you combine the ability to talk to your subconscious with positive self-talk, you will continuously improve the results you get in your life.

High quality standards are not the only standards that are appropriate. Low quality is sometimes not only necessary, but wanted as well. An example of this can be found when a deadline is

DISCflex™

moved up and a starting point is needed for the project. The first drafts of a project don't always need to be high quality and when time is of the essence, high quality isn't efficient. I know that when I need a starting point quickly, I don't want my team wasting time trying to get it perfect when it will be changed anyway. Understanding when the appropriate quality standard is needed will help you dial up your Compliance to insure the best possibility for success.

5. Create an RA² Document for Yourself and Your Team.

The RA² Document is one of the most effective ways to dial up your Compliance Factor. Having the document in front of you and examining it often will likely bolster that Compliance Factor up in a matter of minutes. The reason is the design. From the table you can determine the responsibility, the accountability metrics, and the authority parameters you have been given in a simple glance. Knowing these, you will automatically dial up your Compliance to meet those standards.

The RA² Document can dial up the Compliance in your team as well. Because it is visible to everyone, especially the boss during performance reviews, there is more trust from both parties on what needs accomplishing. With more trust and visible standards, your work, along with other team members, is likely to improve dramatically. Visit the RA² Interface Alignment Course to learn the benefits and methodology for using RA² Documents.

Secondary Steps:

After you complete the immediate steps to help dial up your Compliance, some secondary steps can also be helpful. These steps require a significant amount of practice, but can be invaluable when you learn how to properly use them in your life situations.

1. Plan a Major Project

When your organization presents a new opportunity for a project, volunteer for it and take it on. To finish it on time, plan it out and organize it in a logical manner. Planning and organizing a project takes accuracy and organizational skill, which will automatically dial up your Compliance. Albert Einstein said, "If I am given sixty minutes to complete a task, I would take fifty-five minutes to figure out the problem and five minutes to come up with a solution."

> *"In order to succeed, your desire for success should be greater than your fear of failure."*
>
> *~Bill Cosby*

Identifying the problem is the first place that you need to start at when you handle a project. Learn more about it in the Decision Making Course in the session entitled Identify the Problem.

You may choose to prioritize the tasks and steps involved in the project and its structure. The more you plan, the more manageable the project will be for you. Try to follow the Rational Decision Making Process to ensure appropriate logic is in place before the actual implementation of the action plan.

2. Outline the Boundaries and Expectations When Working with a Team.

When you take on a project with a team, you may need to be the one to pay attention to the guidelines surrounding it. While others are brainstorming and thinking of ideas, you may have to be the person to point out that some ideas are not possible because of the guidelines or rules. If you do this when it is appropriate, then you will be tapping your accuracy and dialing up your Compliance. Just remember that you're not raining on their parade; you're keeping the team grounded and remembering the boundaries. Otherwise, the team could finish the project and then have to start all over because they overlooked major rules that made their finished project unusable.

3. **Ask A Manager, Subject-Matter Expert, or Leader to Check Your Work and to Give You Explicit Feedback.**

After completing a project or task, ask someone qualified to look over your work to give you feedback about what you could do better next time. You will want to follow the rules and make sure that you did your work correctly. This will give you the chance to get specific feedback about the work you've done. Doing this will improve your accuracy and improve your chances of improvement on future tasks.

4. **Refer Back to the Instructions or the Guidelines.**

This may seem rudimentary, but it is something to remember when you want to dial up your Compliance. Remembering the structure and guidelines of a project can help you dial up your Compliance by keeping you accountable to sticking to the plan and not deviating from it. When it is appropriate this may help your productivity as well as your Compliance. Keeping a copy of the guidelines of a project nearby can help remind you to stay on track if you find yourself trying to go outside the rules.

> *"Inaction breeds doubt and fear. Action breeds confidence and courage. If you want to conquer fear, do not sit home and think about it. Go out and get busy."*
>
> *~Dale Carnegie*

12 How to Dial Down Compliance

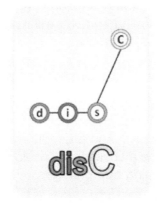

You must learn how to dial down your Compliance. This may occur when you're working in a group or in a meeting. It is important for you to speak up and take initiative.

A person with elevated Compliance is naturally task-oriented and process-oriented. Because of that, the Compliance Factor can morph into a hemorrhage on relationships. You need to dial down your Compliance Factor when you want to become more people-oriented and relationship-focused. Relationships require more than just informal guidelines and relationship standards. It is at those moments that the Influence or the Steadiness Factors will help you build better relationships, whereas the Compliance Factor might hinder them.

Another caution against the Compliance Factor is Groupthink. When you are leading a team, or if you are part of a team composed of Elevated Compliance individuals, you must watch out for Groupthink. Make yourself or someone else the Devil's Advocate in the group. You don't want creativity to be stunted or ideas prevented. Unfortunately, the Compliance Factor causes that to happen in stressful situations. During those times, you need to dial down your Compliance to allow your creativity and innovative nature to be unleashed.

Throughout history, compliance to rules without contemplating new ways of thinking has proven disastrous. For a long time, scientists believed the Earth was flat and that the Sun revolved around our planet. The Compliance Factor can force people into a state of agreement, even when the facts prove otherwise. That is why the Compliance Factor must be tempered when it can negatively affect your performance or the performance of your team or organization.

Immediate Steps:

First, let's examine some immediate steps that you can take to dial down your Compliance Factor. Try to incorporate these steps incrementally into your everyday life so you can build the skills for when you need to use them. You have to practice these steps to become comfortable with them and enhance your ability to situationally flex your behaviors.

1. Be Open-minded.

Question yourself when you are being close-minded. Ask yourself, do I need to hammer my point home by quoting the rules? Am I forcing people to fall in line without thinking about what is best? Sometimes the Compliance Factor can force us to strictly adhere to the rules, or our perceived guidelines of how things should be run.

Allow yourself to listen to other people's ideas, even when they go against the status quo. It is important to bring in new thoughts and solutions because the old way of doing things might be the wrong way. Keep an open mind and you will reap the benefits of your team members and help your organization, friends, or family.

2. Question Why People Create Rules and What Their Benefits and Consequences are for Your Organization, Family, or Social Life.

A great way to dial down the Compliance Factor is to question the authority parameters and rules. Questioning rules, policies, and procedures, helps create methods that are more effective when put into practice. As a society, we would not get anywhere without questioning the old ways of life and implementing new changes.

Alter your perceptions so that you can become more efficient and think of better ways to accomplish tasks and responsibilities in your life.

3. Speak Up And Engage in Respectful Debate.

"When we are no longer able to change a situation, we are challenged to change ourselves."

~Victor Frankl

When you have an idea, make sure you speak up and offer your opinion into the discussion. You may feel that the group won't listen to you anyway, so why bother speaking, but that may not be the case. No matter what, get your ideas out there. The more you speak up and assert yourself, the more people will notice and pay attention to what you have to say. A word of caution: You cannot simply hammer down the rules and only talk about the guidelines. People will shut you out if you barrage them with policies and procedures when they are trying to brainstorm. You need to help foster an environment where respectful debate is the norm. That means loosening up on the talk of rules and allowing for the brainstorming process to produce ideas. Save the rules for later in the Rational Decision Making Process when your organization absolutely cannot break certain policies.

Changing your behavior patterns and displaying it to other people will allow them to view you as more assertive and creative. If you want others to listen to you, dial down your Compliance Factor by speaking up and dialing up your Dominance and Steadiness Factors at the same time so that you speak with thoughtful courage. It is a surefire way to get the attention of others. If you can effectively combine the aspect of dialing up Dominance and Steadiness while at the same time dialing down Compliance Factors, you are building a surefire behavior pattern for enhancing your leadership currency.

4. Be Creative and Innovative in the Various Areas of Your Life.

Although you may like the analysis and planning parts of a project, volunteer for the creative

DISCflex™

part. If there is a PowerPoint or a poster that your company needs, volunteer to work on it. You may ask someone else to join in on your brainstorming efforts to help you along, but expand your horizons and try that new part of the project.

Even in your life, volunteering for more creative projects and tasks will give you new skills. You can learn a lot from helping to put together a fundraiser or assisting your children with a school project. Try to expand your horizons to enhance your creativity and build on your skills.

5. Take Calculated Risks and Make Decisions.

If you usually play it safe and stick to what you know, try taking a risk on something new. Although it may take longer or may not be the most straightforward way of going about something, try it and see what happens. Although it may not be logical, it will be a good experience for you to open up your opportunities to see what it's like to try something new.

It is wisest to start small with your risk-taking ventures. Do something new that may lead either to rejection or to something minor that could embarrass you. Once you realize that taking risks can actually help you achieve more in your life, you will understand the benefit of taking risks when it can help you improve.

6. Change Your Routine.

If you do the same thing every day in the same order, rearrange it and try things at different times of the day. The Compliance Factor is associated with structure and organization. If you have both an Elevated Compliance and an Elevated Steadiness Factor, this can lead to an unchanging environment where you have the same routine every day.

You can change that monotonous routine by changing up the structure of your everyday life. You may feel that you have much more energy trying this new procedure and doing things out of order. Changing your routine can help enhance your creativity.

7. Learn Rapport Building Techniques.

The Compliance Factor often reduces your ability to develop genuine rapport with others because the Compliance Factor is task-oriented and mainly more of an introverted behavior style. You have to develop a people-oriented approach when trying to build trust and rapport with your coworkers, clients, friends, and family.

The best rapport building techniques are mirroring and matching. Subconsciously, you trust others that move the way you do and have the same posture and stance as you. Use mirroring and matching to help become more empathetic to others by getting into their zone. I recommend viewing the sessions entitled Building Trust 1 and Building Trust 2 in the Life Skills Part 3 Course.

Secondary Steps:

After practicing the immediate steps in your life, try these secondary steps to build your ability to dial down the Compliance Factor. As you continue to practice these secondary steps, assemble a knowledge base of useful information about dialing down the Compliance Factor that can help you achieve your goals.

"Only the wisest and stupidest of men never change."

~Confucius

1. Confront Your Biases

There are four main biases that affect the Compliance Factor. The first is the framing bias. The compliance-based individual typically frames everything around rules and guidelines with a strict need for organization. The second bias is the confirmation bias. This is when the Compliance individual looks for proof that the rules work, rather than looking at how to improve them. The third bias is the anchoring bias. When in an argument, compliant people anchor on the rules, hammering down the point so that no debate can take place. The fourth and final bias typically associated with the Compliance Factor is called déformation professionnelle. This is the tendency to listen only to those in your profession or to a certain person about issues.

You must confront your biases and learn to question them when they affect your judgment of an issue. Unfortunately, déformation professionnelle affects many college students who are trying to abide by the perceived guidelines of their chosen professions.

One student that I know currently wants to attend a top 10 law school because he spoke with a lawyer who told him that if he could get into a top 10 school, he should take it.

Now, this student will not listen to anyone else about the matter because a lawyer told him what he should do. Even though going to a top 10 school will cost about $100,000 more than going to a top 50 school, this student's mind is set because of the déformation professionnelle bias. We all need to be aware of how we can get so easily influenced by people that we respect or even people in professions that we respect. I recommend you review the Cognitive Biases sessions in the Decision Making Course on the eLearning site.

> *"The mind has exactly the same power as the hands; not merely to grasp the world, but to change it."*
>
> *~Colin Wilson*

2. Take Initiative

When starting a new project, try your best to start it yourself and see where it goes rather than stopping and asking for help or reassurance that you're on track. You'll be very proud of your efforts after you're done if you do it all yourself and figure it out on your own. Initiative is one of the qualities that your bosses look for when assessing who they are going to promote or give a raise to. Show initiative and you will impress your bosses and your peers.

3. Focus on Behaviors

Instead of focusing on the rules, try to focus on people's behaviors. There are always times in our lives when we know that the rules are hindering people's ability to get their jobs done. Sometimes our own structure can affect the behaviors of other people in ways that we did not previously think. Take the time to examine the benefits and consequences of rules and their effect on behavior to influence positive change in your organization or life.

If you focus on rules instead of behaviors, you will inevitably kill the momentum of your organization, social structure, or family life. The only people that will be able to survive in your world are other Elevated Compliance individuals. This can be disastrous for organizations that need to focus on innovation.

Some of the defense companies have seen this happen over recent years. During the expanded growth in defense after 9/11, the defense companies grew so rapidly that they had to put new rules in place to prevent low quality results. Now that the economy is weaker, their rules are actually hindering their ability to become innovative and make money. Organizations have to focus on how the rules are affecting their people depending on the economic, social, and other situations in their business environment.

4. Look at the Big Picture

The Compliance Factor focuses on the smaller details and the working structure of projects or tasks. When you need to establish a vision, you have to look at the big picture. See how all the parts fit together before working on each specific part. In this way, you will have a better idea of how to accomplish your tasks and improve the project or task.

"The most useless are those who never change through the years."

~Sir James M. Barrie

I recommend you review the Bull's Eye Model in the supplementary activities section to understand how the motivation to keep a rule changes as you move out through each level on the model. You start with YOU and the motivation to keep the rule. You may think it helps you do your job easier or keep everything organized.

Then, you move to the team portion of the Bull's Eye Model and realize, in the team context, the rule is only benefiting you and is actually hindering the abilities of your team members. This alone can cause you to realize the rule should be improved to allow a more efficient performance. The further you get away from the Bull's Eye (YOU), the more you will see the different perceptions of how the rule affects people's effectiveness.

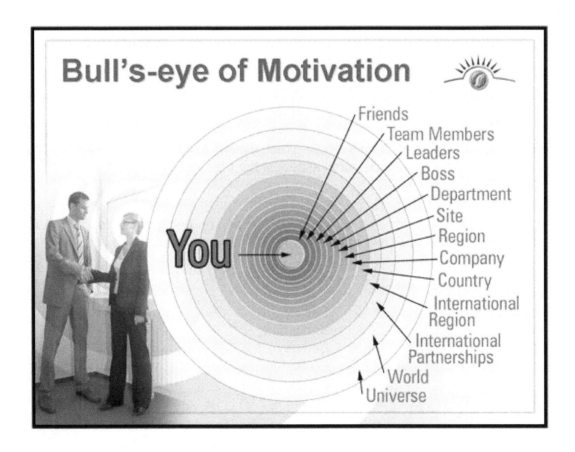

13 Efficiency Generic Profile

Definition

When your Dominance Factor has a greater impact than your Influence Factor, you will be driven toward being efficient. When D (Dominance) overrides i (influence) we call this the Efficiency Sub-factor. Depending on the degree of the elevation between the D and the i, the more the spread between Dominance and Influence, the more pronounced the level of efficiency will be. The Efficiency Sub-factor is sometimes described as robotic. A person exhibiting or being driven

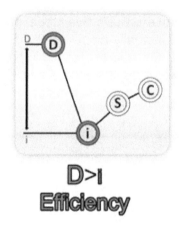

D>I
Efficiency

by the Efficiency Sub-factor is often seen as direct, assertive, and can be viewed as having little or no interest in dealing with the personal aspect of the situation.

Descriptors
Let me go over a list of words that might describe a person being motivated by the Efficiency Sub-factor. The characteristics and personality traits that might describe an efficient person are:

- Aptitude
- Capability
- Efficacy
- Faculty
- Performance
- Productivity

- Skill
- Competency
- Facility
- Know-how
- Potency
- Proficiency

Strengths

The inherent strengths of the Efficiency Sub-factor are objectivity and a drive towards achieving goals in the most effective, resourceful, and competent manner possible. People with this Sub-factor know how they want things done and will complete them as quickly as possible, with a minimum amount of fuss. They dislike excessive talking and deliberating about the best possible route, preferring to get on with it with a minimal amount of discussion. Efficient people tend to be more productive and have an easier time achieving goals.

I love having at least one or two co-workers with the Efficiency Sub-factor. They are able to keep me and my team on track when deadlines are approaching. When putting together coursework, I have my efficient team member keep track of deadlines and make sure that we don't spend an inordinate amount of time on research. This helps us stay focused, instead of going off on continual tangents, and makes our information more concise and to the point. Without having an efficient team member, our research and writing could go on for years with no actual script being produced.

Weaknesses

The inherent weaknesses of the person driven by the Efficiency Sub-factor are that even though they are results-oriented, they are sometimes too willing to compromise quality or detail just to see results. Also, without adequate debate in the planning process, efficiency can suffer. Sometimes this will manifest itself in a reluctance to change the way people currently do things. This can lead to rushed work and unfinished ideas. Usually there is little discussion about why things are being done, with more focus being put simply on getting it done.

If you have ever been frustrated by someone telling you, "We do it this way because that's the way it works best" or "We have to do it this way because that's how we've trained everyone and we want to be consistent". If you hear words like these, you might be dealing with someone that makes things happen by hustling forward with the Efficiency Sub-factor. Take note, however, that just because they want to be efficient, and this goal drives them, their actions might not be in line with what others think is efficient. They only do what they know works to get the job done the way they currently know how. In other words, they might not know the most efficient way to do something. But unfortunately, sometimes people like this think they do. The consequence is that they get locked into certain behaviors because they think it's a waste of time - more ineffective - to change.

It is interesting to note that just because they have an Efficiency Sub-factor it doesn't mean that they are the best at what they do either - they just happen to think that they are. In fact, sometimes efficient people can become so narrowly focused that they are unwilling to look at continuous improvement. In others, they are constantly driven to better their last best, consistently participating in continuous improvement initiatives like Total Quality Management or Six Sigma. Many successful process improvement initiatives use the Japanese Management approach known as Kaizen. This method became famous in the book by Masaaki Imai entitled "Kaizen: The Key to Japan's Competitive Success." Loosely translated Kaizen comes from the Japanese word 'kai' meaning "change" combined with the word 'zen' meaning "good" or "improvement". This philosophical bent has crept into almost every area of the business world.

In the spring of 2008, disaster loomed in the global food market. Triple digit increases in the price of staples like rice and maize resulted in food riots, and threatened the lives of countless millions across the globe. Forty years after the global efficiency initiative called the Green Revolution was enacted, and after waves of market reforms intended to transform agricultural production, the world's governments are still having a problematical time making sure that people aren't starving. In fact, the global food supply seems to be more vulnerable to supply shocks than ever. It wasn't supposed to be this way. In the eighties and nineties, the World Bank put efficiency protocols in place designed to maximize crop yields and minimize the problems associated with transporting food staples across the globe.

The logic behind the IMF's reforms was simple: The goal was producing food with little waste and therefore with little excess inventory. In the car manufacturing business, if the just-in-time system for producing automobiles runs into a hitch and the supply of cars contracts for a while, people adapt by delaying purchasing a new car. When the same happens with food, people go hungry and they can die. For example, bad weather in just a few countries can trigger havoc across the entire system. Then prices spike, so poor people cannot afford to buy the food they need to survive. The upshot of this drive to efficiency now is: Instead of a more efficient system, we should be trying to build a more reliable one as well.

As with anything too much of a good thing can be bad. So if you are prone to being rigidly efficient or if you don't consider the unintended consequences of too much efficiency, your best intentions can go bad. The bottom line: Make certain to guard against going over the top in striving for too much efficiency.

Situational Adaption - Dial Up or Dial Down

Looking at the strengths and weaknesses of being efficient, you have to determine where to set your efficiency level during certain situations. If you have a month to get a project done, it is much better to think it through first before delving right into it. Use your drive for efficiency to get through the thinking process and then the implementation stage will tend to go smoother. Remember what Albert Einstein said. If he had only one hour to solve a problem, he would spend 55 of those 60 minutes defining the problem, and only then would he would give 5 minutes of his time to actually finding the solution. We could all use that advice when striving to be efficient.

The key is to strike a balance between the opposite Sub-factors of efficiency and friendliness. If you want to include people and build relationships, efficiency will most often suffer. But if you want to be more efficient and less concerned about hurting people's feelings in your quest for robotic effectiveness, your relationships will suffer. Think of the short and long-term goals. You can indeed strike a balance between efficiency and friendliness. Sometimes the situation calls for dialing down your overall efficiency for the greater people-oriented good. Imagine a situation where you know exactly what to do for a client, but you know that being efficient and 'just telling it like it is' will cause the client to be uncomfortable.

> *"Change alone is eternal, perpetual, immortal."*
> *~Arthur Schopenhauer*

You have to step back, dial your motivation to get it done way back, perhaps realizing that it is frustrating to be patient. In dialing back under these types of situations, you have to pause, and listen to options that you clearly know won't work. Conceivably you even have to dial back your natural inclination to jump immediately in and tell the person precisely why their idea is not going to work. Although this might be efficient and save valuable time, in the long run a more friendly approach might be just the ticket to getting your organization's contract renewed down the line.

Clients rarely renew with vendors who don't listen, are blunt, or those they perceive as too businesslike, uncooperative, or unfriendly. In this regard, you might consider using the 'Moving Forward Goals' strategy, whereby you split your efficiency into individual segments - into segmented 'Moving Forward Goals'.

You must go into every meeting with a goal in mind. This is true whether it is a staff meeting or a meeting with a client. These 'Moving Forward Goals' can be as simple as increasing rapport with the client or generating thirty options with your decision team. At each client interaction, it is particularly important to plan and ideally be able to concisely state the reason you are communicating with the client. With your own staff and peers, have the same goals in mind. Are you trying to come up with new ideas? Are you trying to narrow down your options? Or how about implementing the decision?

> *"When you are through changing, you are through."*
>
> **~Bruce Barton**

'Moving Forward Goals' are a juggling act between the internal movements needed to keep the process alive and the external actions required to keep the team or the customer moving forward. You cannot drop the ball on either one of these or else the process will come to a stop. Mastering this skill will have a significant impact on your efficiency and the efficiency of your organization.

Keep in mind three important objectives as you create your 'Moving Forward Goals':

1. The first objective is the timing of the 'Moving Forward Goals'. When should you launch a new idea? When should the goal be accomplished? One hour? One week? You have to set a timeline for when you expect your 'Moving Forward Goals' to be accomplished.

2. The second objective is to procure an acceptable return on investment. Ask yourself, what will we gain by accomplishing this 'Moving Forward Goal?' There must be a positive return on the time that you spent into accomplishing the goal.

3. The third and final objective to consider as you create your 'Moving Forward Goals' is to preserve the business team's valuable resources. Keep an active log of how much time it took to get a commitment or achieve your goal. How can you make sure that the team has enough resources for the long haul and contingency planning?

I have dealt with many clients before where it is essential to get through the initial differences in philosophies to achieve the end goal. When creating programs for companies, I always make my first 'Moving Forward Goals' center around working with the philosophical differences and working it around back to my side. Sometimes, even when I am called in to give my expertise on a subject, others in the organization try to give their own expertise from a different field. Fortunately, this leads to some great ideas. When confronted with different philosophies, my first 'Moving Forward Goal' is to build trust and rapport. Once I have established trust, I can move to my next 'Moving Forward Goal' of setting my teachings into the program. As the decision makers realize the importance of the concepts I teach, they begin to incorporate more and more of them. Then, I can reach my final 'Moving Forward Goal' of proposing how all the pieces fit together in the program and how they align to the company's procedures. Once this final 'Moving Forward Goal' is met, I am able to reach my end goal.

The bottom line: Know your 'Moving Forward Goal' and focus on accomplishing it during your interaction.

The opposite is true as well. If you have a project due in a week that your team wasn't told about, you will have to dial up your efficiency to get the project done as fast as possible. I've experienced this numerous times in my life. My team will get hit with a contract that is due in a few days. We have to shift our personnel to keep operational efficiency in other areas, while perfecting the contract for the deadline. Efficiency helps us turn up our energy as a team and better delegate responsibilities to get more accomplished, even when we are faced with a new task. Efficiency, just like all the other Sub-factors, is a gift to be used in any situation; you just have to determine the right amount of efficiency to use.

Take another example of Efficiency. A boss has worked for a company for three years and has a set way of doing things. He considers himself to be an efficient boss and knows that his process is the best way to get tasks completed in a timely fashion. Imagine some new employees get hired, that have the Friendliness and Cooperativeness Sub-factors. These employees would be coming into a system where they could not use their strengths. The boss would force them to work his way. This can lead to problems between work relationships and also hinder quality work. The 'too efficient' boss needs to dial down their Efficiency Sub-factor to allow each individual employee's Sub-factors to flourish.

Next Steps

Next, you will explore the benefits and consequences of the Efficiency Sub-factor. If you think that this Sub-factor is important for your success, you can target your knowledge by investigating various ways to dial up or dial down your Efficiency Sub-factor in our 'How to' sessions.

DISCflex™

14 How to Dial Up Efficiency

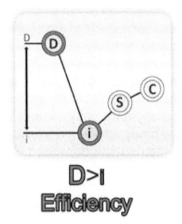

D>I
Efficiency

Now let's examine how to Dial Up your Efficiency. Today's session will explain the specific steps to take if you need to become more efficient. Every day at work you may ask yourself questions that pinpoint your desire to become more efficient. These might sound like:

- Where did my day go? I didn't get nearly as much done as I thought I would.

- Why do I get distracted with busy work when I need to be tackling the goals and projects that need my full focus?

- How can I feel more engaged, satisfied, and fulfilled when I'm at work knowing that I am doing the best job possible?

With the right commitment and desire to stay focused, resourceful, and proficient, while creating habits to make you more competent and efficient, you can accomplish more and feel better about your work.

It really doesn't matter who you are or what your current level of efficiency is in some of the areas of your life, we have found it is the rare individual who is efficient at everything they do. Especially when you are learning new things - before you become unconsciously competent at doing anything, there is a period where focusing and dialing up your efficiency quotient will pay a high dividend. So, let's talk about some steps to being more efficient. These suggestions can be tailored to fit your personal goals and needs as you see fit. The key to remember: Becoming more efficient - dialing up your efficiency - requires focus and dedication!

Immediate Steps:

When we tell ourselves to become more efficient, it inspires an immediate change. What we often don't know, however, is how to get there exactly. Some people believe that efficiency is a natural skill. They believe it's an inherent talent; and not something that can be learned. While we do concede that some people are talented and more naturally adept at being efficient, becoming efficient is a process. Then, once you know the process, by practicing and perfecting it, you can decide whether you want to just use it on a situational basis or you can turn efficiency into a lifelong habit. Just remember, it is a skill that you can learn. If you want to be more efficient, here are some immediate steps that you can take to begin your journey.

"Always bear in mind that your own resolution to succeed is more important than any other."

Abraham Lincoln

1. Focus

Staying focused on the task at hand can be one of the biggest roadblocks on the road to greater efficiency and productivity. Keep your schedule close throughout the day to review what you have accomplished and what still needs to be done. Give yourself permission to work on one task at a time. Most studies prove that multi-tasking is much less efficient than focusing with concentrated effort. Also, when you have a lot to do and perhaps feel overwhelmed, just take a deep breath and start at the top of your priority list and begin working methodically through each item on your to do list. Many times we feel so overwhelmed because we feel we are not getting enough done, which can distract you from the task at hand. Focusing on one project or task at a time frequently allows you to complete your goals in much less time and with a lot less effort than you would have ever thought possible. Also, set periods of concentration time. Then, make the decision to stay focused on your task for the time period you established.

After you finish each task, take a few minutes to refresh your mind and then get into a 'state of concentration' mindset to focus on your next goal.

2. Eliminate Distractions

Distractions can be extremely frustrating when you are focused on a project and, unfortunately, workplace distractions are always abundant. You can't get rid of them, but you can certainly manage them better. Distractions can come in various forms. Some that are especially prevalent are people popping in to gossip, ask questions, or say hello; email, phone interruptions, as well as internet messaging and updates, or online chat. To compound these distractions, your physiological needs can also distract you. If you are too hot or too cold, too thirsty or hungry, or if you are in pain or in discomfort; all these can dissolve your focus. Additionally, your environment can cause distractions from noise, smells, or other nuisances. It's the way you manage, plan for and ultimately handle distractions that will make you either more or less efficient. The first step is to become aware when distractions emerge. Once you realize you are being distracted, you have a choice. Integrity and determination in the moment of choice will help you steer yourself away from distractions and focus on what you're doing. Here are some strategies to help you.

Write down the things that typically distract you during the day and the times these distractions occur. Most often, you'll see patterns emerge. The goal here is to recognize how you get distracted and by what things. Next start grouping some together with the goal of handling distractions as a cluster. By grouping many of them all into set time periods, you allow yourself to do other work in a focused targeted manner, but still get in your distraction time without worrying about when you'll get to things that distract you but still need your attention. I call these 'distraction breaks'. I find it best to set a time later in the day to take care of distractions: say, from 3-4 p.m. rather than dealing with them first. However, some people cannot focus until certain distractions are eliminated first.

Another approach might be to do them for ten minutes at the end of each hour, making sure that you only spend ten minutes on them. Find a way that works comfortably for you that allows you to deal successfully with distractions that will inevitably occur. You know your personality so make the decision about which time frames and philosophy work for you. Make it a point however to set a finite period of time to deal with distractions, otherwise they will erode your time. That is precisely the flaw of distractions - they eat away at your time if you don't limit them in a closely controlled manner. The key here is that once your time limit is gone, to dial up your efficiency, you must force yourself to be completely disciplined: don't even look at the things that typically distract you during the day before your next distraction break.

On July 4, 1952, the California coast was blanketed in fog. Twenty-one miles to the west of Catalina Island, was Florence Chadwick, a 34-year-old, long distance swimmer. She began to wade into the water to swim toward California. Prior to this swim she had already conquered the English Channel, swimming in both directions. She had the experience, the determination and the fitness to make the swim a success. She was determined to be the first woman to swim the Catalina Channels. Millions of people were watching on national television.

As the minutes turned into hours Chadwick fought off bone chilling cold, dense fog, and sharks. The sharks would come so close to her that they had to be driven away with rifles. Fatigue never set in, but the icy waters numbed her to the point of desperation.
She constantly strained her eyes to make out the shore through her goggles. All she could see was dense fog. After a while she knew she couldn't go on. She wasn't a quitter, but she shouted to her trainer and her mother on the boat and asked to be taken out of the water. As they urged her not to give up, she turned around and looked toward the California coast again, but all she could see was the thick fog.

She couldn't see a thing and was totally discouraged. Florence swam that freezing cold Catalina channel for fifteen hours and fifty-five minutes before giving up. She fought the elements valiantly and was hauled out of the water, exhausted, into the boat. She was frozen and her spirits was broken because she didn't complete her dream.

More unfortunate news would sink her further into the depths of despair. She was absolutely devastated when she discovered that the California coast was only a short half-mile away. She felt the shock of failure. After the swim, she told a reporter, "Look, I'm not excusing myself, but if I could have seen land, I know I could have made it." The fog had done it. She couldn't see her goal. Florence had given up, when she was so close to reaching her goal, but fatigue and the cold weren't the reason she couldn't go on. The fog alone caused her downfall. The fog stopped her because it had obscured her goal. That fog blinded her reason. It forced her not to see her goals and when you don't see your goal you can't possibly have the motivation and the determination that your heart, your soul, and your mind needs to carry on.

There is a good ending to this story. Two months later, Florence Chadwick swam the same channel and the fog clouded her view, as it does on most mornings in the summer, in California. But this time she swam with her faith intact, and she knew, she just knew that somewhere behind that fog was land. She had envisioned it in her mind and that's how she kept her goal in sight. And this time she succeeded. Not only was she the first woman to swim the Catalina channel, but she beat the men's record by more than two hours.

The story of Florence Chadwick and the Catalina Channel is an excellent portrayal of how distractions can blind us and keep us from achieving our goals. Through her clear focus and faith, she was able to fight through the distractions during her second attempt and successfully swam the Catalina Channel.

Secondary Steps:

Now, let's move on to some secondary steps that you can take to dial up your efficiency. Many times, we go throughout our day without taking even five minutes to take a step back and evaluate what our goals are in the short, mid, and long term and how these tie into the decisions we make on an hour by hour basis. We also compound the problems associated with not planning out our hour by hour tasks by forgetting to align these with what we need to accomplish on big projects. Then, as a consequence of too little planning, we can become so overwhelmed that what started as a small project turns into an all day event. Each and every day you have to prioritize your activities so that your short, mid, and long range objectives are met on a consistent basis. Too many times we forget to simply sort and prioritize before beginning the day. This can be a huge determining Factor in whether or not we are being efficient.

Sounds easy, yes? But in reality, you have to be honest and think about how you usually operate. How many of us get sucked into many 'urgent' but really not important tasks for all sorts of reasons? It's planning and prioritizing that can help fix those issues. The solution to training yourself to dial up your efficiency is that we have to understand how important it is to make time to plan. It is critically important for achieving what you want from life.
If your life is full of incessant urgent demands, it may seem difficult or nearly impossible to do this. But you have to do it.

Authors Steven Covey and Roger and Rebecca Merrill, wrote about this type of concept in their best-selling book, First Things First. The book's basic concept is easy enough to understand. Divide your tasks up based on four criteria that will result in four categories. The authors propose that planning be done with the recognition that activities fall into one of the following quadrants:

Quadrant 1 - Important and Urgent
Quadrant 2 - Important but Not Urgent
Quadrant 3 - Not Important and Urgent
Quadrant 4 - Not Important and Not Urgent

I have spent years coaching people on how to become more effective and efficient. After all these years, I've concluded that most of us spend the majority of our time in Quadrants 1 - the Important and Urgent and Quadrant 3- the Not Important and Urgent. However, the quadrant of quality - the one that really has the potential to make us highly efficient - is Quadrant 2 - those things that are important but not necessarily urgent right now. Think about it, if you are planning properly and being highly effective, not much would be urgent because you handle things in a calm, proactive manner. You are so efficient that you are way ahead of your peers - you are an efficiency machine!

When you spend the majority of your time in the important but not urgent quadrant you are positive, upbeat, and most important you get down to business in a practical methodical way. You steer your efforts and your time rather than getting pulled hither and thither by whatever urgent, important things pop up. This highly inefficient behavior is often characterized as behaving in a firefighting mode. Examples of spending time in the important but not yet urgent arena include planning, preparation, relationship building, clarification of strategic direction, solidifying core values, making sure that your employees stay mission and purpose focused, fleshing out goals and implementation plans, and participating in any threat mitigation or prevention activities, and finally making the time to ferret out opportunities so that you can grow and prosper. The more time you spend on activities like these, the less time you'll be forced to spend fighting fires and the more effective and efficient you'll ultimately become. Think about it: It's just logical!

Use your common sense and be flexible when categorizing and planning out your days. Dealing with customers who are angry and need immediate help is important and urgent. But, calling a customer to set up a golf outing isn't urgent but it is important for the relationship. You have to have an appropriate mix in your quadrants, but always remember that getting out ahead of the urgent is highly efficient.

The authors, Steven Covey and Roger and Rebecca Merrill also discuss why the "integrity in the moment of choice" in implementing any plans is a critical point. Along these lines, we suggest that you consistently review your quadrant choices before making decisions about how you will expend your time. It is the process of planning and proactively determining what you want that is ultimately responsible for the quality of your life.

For more information on this topic, we suggest you go to the Ranking Goals session in our Life Skills course.

The bottom line is that you should take the time to sit down every day to map out your goals, prioritize your focus, set time limits for each task, and tackle tasks with focused intention and gusto. That is the key to better time management and efficiency. Here are some additional ways you can do that:

1. **Think About What Your Short-Term, Mid-Range and Long-Term Goals.**

   Perhaps short-term goals are the ones you need to accomplish for the day, or the week. Then do the same for your mid-range and long-term goals. Schedule a time to prioritize your to do list every morning. I suggest that you think about what is most important to accomplish before you turn on your computer. Just spend some time reflecting on your priorities for about your day for a few minutes before you jump into action. Ask yourself questions like: What goals are realistically attainable today or this week? What projects deserve my attention immediately? What deadlines are coming up? What things to I have to monitor to make sure everything is on track? Take a blank sheet of paper and write these down or use electronic means to keep track of what you need to do. Periodically review your priorities and what you have accomplished throughout the day. I suggest that you can do this every day, and at the beginning of every week make certain you are shuffling and reviewing where your mid and long range goals are, too. Doing it before the week starts, like on a Sunday evening or first thing on Monday morning, is a good way to prepare you mentally for the week ahead. It sets your frame of mind and provides great momentum for the upcoming week.

   The emphasis Lou Holtz put on goal setting at a young age gave him the direction he needed and allowed him to achieve more in his life then he ever thought possible.

> *How does a five-foot-ten, one hundred and fifty two pound man who wears glasses, speaks with a lisp, and has a weak physique become one of the most successful college football coaches of all time? Lou Holtz attributes his success to his wife and the emphasis he puts on goal setting. In 1966, Holtz was fired from an assistant coaching position at the University of South Carolina. After being fired, his wife gave him a book to read called The Magic of Thinking Big, by David Schwartz. Holtz devoured the book and in 1966 he sat down and wrote out a hundred and seven goals he wanted to achieve in his life. His goals ranged from winning a national championship to being on the Tonight Show. One of his goals was to become the head football coach at the University of Notre Dame. In 1986, twenty years after writing down his goals, he became the head football coach at Notre Dame and two years later he led the Fighting Irish to a national championship. To this day, Lou Holtz has achieved a hundred and two of the original hundred and seven goals that he wrote down.*

2. **Prioritize Tasks and Goals that Will Make Sure All of Your Short-Term, Mid-Range and Long-Term Goals Get Done.**

   Remember the concepts from First Things First. Determine out which tasks have an urgent deadline and are most important; and schedule them to be completed first. I always highlight these by marking them in bold, by underlining, calling them out with stars, or by putting an asterisk or two next to them. Sometimes those will be your least favorite and the hardest tasks, but by doing them first and marking them as important you save yourself from the stress of having it on your mind all day. This will also allow you to direct your full energy and attention to the task you have at hand. And most important -- make sure that you schedule some time into your day for planning. Also remember Murphy's Law: "Anything that can go wrong, will go wrong". Make sure that you allow for contingency plans and enough recovery time for unforeseen circumstances.

   An example of prioritizing is to look at your time during the day as a bucket and your tasks as big rocks or sand. The big rocks are all the major tasks that need to be done during your day. These could be things like writing a report, attending a strategy meeting, putting together a briefing or presentation, or setting up an agenda and preparing for a client meeting. Next come your smaller tasks - the pebbles. These are tasks that have to be finished but take less time. These might be things like getting paperwork filled out, reviewing documents, sitting in on a conference call, or attending short meetings. The sand is all the smaller items that you do during the day, such as quick phone calls or responding to email. If you fill your bucket up with sand first, this leaves no room for the big rocks. By taking the time to recognize what your major tasks are and scheduling them first, this allows you to get more done and become more efficient throughout your day.

   > *"A successful man is one who can lay a firm foundation with the bricks others have thrown at him."*
   >
   > **~David Brinkley**

3. **Give Yourself Deadlines for Each Part of the Task or Goal.**

   When writing down each goal or task, create a time frame to finish it. Don't rush yourself by allocating yourself less time than you think you might need, just be realistic. I think about time in terms of actual goals and stretch goals. If I think something might take me 90 minutes, I actually allocate the full 90 minutes; however, my stretch goal is to complete it in 75 minutes. By doing this I congratulate myself whenever I make my stretch goal but I don't sabotage my day if I was right on the money with how much time I thought it would take to accomplish that task. Be careful not to give yourself too much time either. Being realistic doesn't mean sandbagging your time and overcompensating by allocating too much time. This is actually highly inefficient. Analyze the goals and determine the correct amount of time that should be allotted to each and write your estimated timeframes down. For example, if it usually takes you two hours to research for a project, write it down and keep yourself to that time frame. Make a stretch goal to motivate you to complete it efficiently and in a timely manner.

Remember that you can make even the smallest task last as long as you want, so be careful when making deadlines. If you wanted to take 45 minutes to put together an agenda for tomorrow's meeting or review a contract, or to do something as simple as putting away the groceries, you will find a way to do that. You also need to realize that you will not always finish your tasks by the deadline you stipulated, but by at least having a set deadline, it keeps you focused and accountable. You will be surprised at how much time you really save if you get into the habit of setting deadlines to meet; and stick to meeting them.

4. Grouping.

Do you ever find yourself switching from one task to another and feeling a bit scattered or perhaps feeling disorganized? By grouping tasks, you can start to learn when multi-tasking is good and when it's not. Take your plan of goals for the day and group similar tasks together in the same time frame. Or group tasks that will work well together. For example, if I know that I will be on hold for several minutes, I will do mundane tasks like sort through receipts, put away filing or update my contacts. These types of tasks don't take a lot of focus or energy. To make this easy, I have a pile of some tiny taskers right next to my phone. By whittling away at these 'grain of sand' type duties, I find that I don't have to waste an afternoon or morning dealing with them when they pile up and have to be dealt with. By grouping like type tasks together, like email, writing, and putting together a presentation, you are already in the language type frame of mind so it's easy and efficient to stay there. This will allow you to minimize the time wasted from switching between tasks that have mental or physical ramp up time. This in turn will certainly minimize the energy, stress, and the time it takes to complete them. An example of grouping would be to do all of your mail, email, and instant messaging in the same time frame.

15 How to Dial Down Efficiency

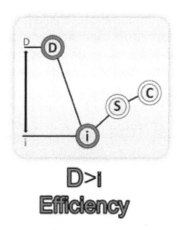

D>i
Efficiency

Remember that the opposing Sub-factor of Efficiency D>i is Friendliness I>d. So all that might be required is that you dial up the Influencing Factor in your Friendliness Sub-factor and this alone will have the immediate impact of dialing back your Efficiency. So as you learn the techniques in this session, immediately review the session on How to Dial Up your Friendliness to understand the polar opposite of Efficiency. We all know that Efficiency is an excellent trait to have. It allows people to accomplish goals faster and more often. Efficient people can be extremely successful because they usually know how they want things done and they use the quickest means possible to get there. Unfortunately, like all Factors that are not used properly, too much efficiency can cause problems as well.

The first thing that comes to everyone's mind whenever I ask them when it might be appropriate to dial down Efficiency is in the realm of relationships. While this is true, I want to start of this session by looking at Efficiency and effectiveness. In looking at deliverables, efficiency and effectiveness are not the same to many people. In our definition of efficiency - you also need to be effective. If you look at the RA² Interface documents, being efficient to many people is simply going systematically through your responsibilities and tasks assignments and getting them accomplished. But being effective is hitting all of your accountability metrics and adding value while being efficient. The efficient person might just meet expectations, but the efficient and effective person will exceed expectations because they add value.

So when would you have to dial down efficiency? Well, perhaps it's to become more effective - to add more value. For example, it might be highly efficient to shorten conversations with customers from an efficient time management point of view, but highly effective to keep them on the line and spend more time to find out more about the issues they are facing. In this way you can add value by coming up with solutions to address their needs. In analyzing this, your Dominance Factor - your desire to get on to your next task - will want to override your Influence Factor - the influencing

Factor's desire to talk and build rapport. In allowing Influence to govern, you create value for your organization and the customer. This is a clear cut example of when it is important to dial down efficiency.

Now that we understand Efficiency and effectiveness and adding value, let's move on to relationships. Imagine providing feedback to a project manager who initially had a month to complete an assignment, yet didn't take the time to analyze the best way to achieve success. Now, three weeks into the job, their team is floundering because they dove right into action - hell bent on handling this project exactly the way they handled the last. Unfortunately, the last project was entirely different and the same set of elements that made them successful just aren't present on this new assignment. The last team just followed instructions and got down to business. This team is dysfunctional and every team member wants to do things differently. They aren't a cohesive unit. To compound matters, the project manager decided to put the most experienced person in charge - the one with the most knowledge - but that person has the least effective leadership skills. By directing them start to tasks without first finding out how to best manage them, the project manager created a whole host of problems. Now he is dealing with the fallout of not building trust and rapport. Bottom line: In his quest to be efficient, he didn't bother to take the time to develop a fully functioning high performance team prior to giving out task assignments. The project manager has had to pull people into his office time and again to keep them on track. He feels that he is spending more time babysitting and smoothing ruffled feathers than getting anything accomplished. This is a fine example of how not dialing down the motivation to be Efficient resulted in lost time, broken trust, and schedules slipping.

Team leaders and managers who fail to recognize when to dial down their Efficiency in order to ultimately be more effective will create more problems than good through their desire to immediately have a high level of efficiency. The manager will be so focused on getting the job done that they will be willing to sacrifice the integrity of the project in several ways: in the relationship realm and communication, the innovation and brainstorming components, and knowledge acquisition.

First let's look at communication. If the manager was able to dial down their efficiency and dial up their friendliness, they could take advantage of the input that their team has to insure the greatest possibility for success. Too often people that are highly efficient overlook communication in their quest to get their job done, too. This failure to focus on communication can alienate their co-workers and peers. The same is true in groups outside of work. If you want to get things done but don't consider the impact that your Elevated Dominance Factor compared to a lower Influence Factor will have on family members and friends, you will annoy them because they'll feel that it's your way or the highway, your goals taking preference over what they want to do.

Learning to dial down your efficiency will help your relationships with the people around you. It will help you establish rapport, communicate better, and ultimately gain their respect because they'll think that although you have goals and objectives that you want to get done, that you'll listen to them, too. Building rapport and gaining their respect will help you influence them and achieve success in your life and at work. It will make your relationships much stronger and more fruitful for everyone. Like anything else though, it will take the right focus, practice, and dedication to learn to dial down your efficiency.

"One key to successful leadership is continuous personal change. Personal change is a reflection of our inner growth and empowerment."

~Robert E. Quinn

Now let's loop back to innovation and brainstorming. When you want to get something done in the most efficient way possible, you often don't have the time or patience for building a better mousetrap. You can become so focused on the end result that you think that taking the time to be innovative or getting the team together for a brainstorming session will just slow you down. And you know what? You'd be right. Innovation and brainstorming do take time. But what is the cost associated with not making time for these vitals aspects of business? Even worse, think of the effects of not doing this but your competitor does do it. Sooner or later your products and services are going to be out of date and stale. The end result: Your goal of efficiency cost the company dearly.

In this case, dialing up your Influence Factor is not the appropriate answer. For innovation to occur you need independent ideas and creativity as well as contemplation. Therefore you should employ the Independence and Self-motivation Sub-factors as well as ramping up your Steadiness Factor as in thoughtfulness. You needn't do this yourself. The best innovation and brainstorming occurs when team members have these traits. This is called cognitive diversity. For more information on cognitive diversity in teams, go to the Teambuilding course and look at the session entitled Selecting the Best Team Members to Ensure Cognitive Diversity.

Now let's take a moment to discuss Efficiency and knowledge acquisition. Imagine a final scenario. You are driving from Florida to New Jersey. You map out your route and see that 95 North is the quickest and most efficient way to go. But, will this expand your horizons and knowledge? If you take the most direct route you won't get to see the fabric or culture of America. You might miss out on the fun things you could see on the way.

Liken this to getting so locked into process - being super efficient - that you forget to raise your awareness or step up your knowledge base.

One of my colleagues brought up a great point about efficiency when he was discussing the work atmosphere in college. Many professors expect the students to get their work completed on time, maintaining the professor's pace. The problem is that students work at different paces and learn differently than their professors expect. This can cause college students to simply complete the work without building their knowledge base. Students come out of some classes without learning much. This is because some college classes are based around efficiency, which hinders the ability of students to learn at their pace.

Immediate Steps:

"Always do your best. What you plant now, you will harvest later."

~Og Mandino

If you feel like you need to learn to dial down your Efficiency Sub-factor it will take time and practice to succeed. Having the perseverance to achieve your goal of being able to dial down your efficiency will be important as you need to strengthen your relationships and build a higher level of trust. And please remember, that as with everything in life, it is perception that must be managed. If people think you are getting goals accomplished at the cost of their relationship with you, doing things like not asking their opinion, not stopping to find out how they are coping, or forgetting to ask about what is important to them, they will tend not to be as helpful or forthcoming with information that might help you. This is the softer side of efficiency - making sure that the relationships you must have with those involved in getting your goals accomplished are solid. If you can keep a high level of efficiency but give the perception that you are not forgetting about the softer side of managing how you work

DISCflex™

cooperatively and build your relationships with others, you'll satisfy everyone, including yourself. Here are some immediate steps you can take as you learn to be less efficient. Remember that these changes don't just happen overnight! Be persistent and stay focused!

1. First, Establish Your Standards

The first thing to look at is your criteria and standards for what you currently think efficiency is. Examine your thoughts on time and deadlines. Does efficiency mean that deadlines are sacred? Is it inconceivable for you to imagine missing a cut-off date? Does efficiency mean getting something off your plate as quickly as possible? Too often, highly efficient people sacrifice quality, standards, or accuracy for the need to get something done as soon as possible. They think that being efficient means getting something done on time and out the door no matter what. People like these just check the box without thinking too much of the next stage in the process or of the person who has to deal with their work output. If they just stepped back, they could have been a little less efficient but in taking more time and doing something that wasn't required but that would significantly help others be more efficient. This type of thinking has spawned many corporate initiatives like TQM (Total Quality Management) and Six Sigma and Supply Chain Management systems - where the goal is to take a system's approach in examining efficiency and effectiveness. In meeting deadlines, think about why the target date for your part of the initiative has been set. Who is the next person who will see or add to your work product? It is often wise to take a systems approach, but what if that is not possible? Well, most of the time even if you just talk to people you are getting the assignment from and those you are delivering to you can come up with better ways to become more efficient as well as effective.

Ask yourself and those before and after you: Is there a way we can work more effectively together? What can I do to make your task easier?

Are there improvements that will make the sum of our efforts better for us all and for the customer? Questions like these spawn a climate of efficiency. Next, look at the integrity and quality of your work product.

Problems can be created when an employee or boss compromises the integrity of their work merely to get their work done quickly. Understand what your standards are, as well as those you will be judged on, and the customer's opinion as they relate to what you have to accomplish. As we taught you in the Law of Satisfaction and Standards, different people have different standards and you have to determine what these are and try to satisfy them if you want others who judge your work product to think you are a stellar producer. Always try to do what is required of you with a view toward always producing a quality task.

Understanding what other people require can help you produce the best work you are capable of through their eyes. An example of not knowing your standards or requirements is when a manager asks an employee write a report. The employee writes the report quickly, yet doesn't use the best citation or sources available which would give the report more credibility. If the employee had communicated with their manager, they would have been able to understand the standard that was expected of the report and successfully accomplish it. Be careful to not assume that other people or organizations standards are the same as yours. Take the time to find out exactly what they need and then proceed with your work. This can save time in the long run and help you achieve greater success. I suggest that you review the lessons in the 21 Laws of Influence for Sales to learn more about this important topic.

2. Continuous Improvement

Where is the gap between where you are today and where you want to be as far as efficiency is concerned? In examining this you have to be willing to be vulnerable and look past your current ways of doing things. For example, you might have been taught to do something a certain way, but if you keep an open mind, you might find that someone else can do it better. Imagine looking at a different department's numbers and discovering that they are delivering 14% more product to customers with the same budget and staff that your department has. If you were in a protectionist frame of mind, you might not like to highlight the fact that you aren't as good as them. But by reaching out and letting them know that you want to learn from them and admitting to yourself and your team that you don't have all the answers, you are doing your organization a great service. You might find out that it took several months to retrain the workforce to be able to reach that improvement. So you have to be willing to dial down your efficiency in the short term to be better in the long term. Ask yourself: What you are willing to sacrifice to become better or more effective, even if you at first seem less efficient.

3. Engage in a Conversation

Take time today to have a conversation with someone. It is extremely easy for the highly efficient person to see communication as somewhat of a waste of time, because it may take time away from actually completing a task. While there are situations when this is true, communication is still vital to establishing rapport and increasing the success of a project. Whether it means that you converse with someone during lunch about something you usually wouldn't or you take some extra time to analyze possible scenarios related to a project, understand that this is vital to being effective.

Communicating with your fellow team members will help you gain their trust and respect, which can, in turn, allow you to accomplish more by utilizing their talents and traits. When a manager is so efficient that they overlook the need to share ideas and brainstorm, over time they lose the respect of their employees. Plus, they destroy motivation and morale because people work best for someone who communicates effectively and cares about them. Team motivation and drive is a valuable asset that could improve the manager's and the team's success. Learn to take time to engage in a conversation and if the situation allows for it, encourage others around you to do the same. A word of caution though: This doesn't mean standing around all day jawboning to the detriment of everyone's responsibilities. You can still have short conversations or see people during breaks and accomplish delivering on what you are tasked to do.

4. Understand Different Situations

There are situations where efficiency is not only encouraged but needed. For example, if you and your team are given a project suddenly that is due in a week, it would be wise to dial up

> *"Adaptability is not imitation.*
>
> *It means power of resistance and assimilation."*
>
> *~Mahatma Gandhi*

DISCflex™

your efficiency in order to get the project done on time. There are other times when efficiency is not the main priority and you have the time to analyze and discuss your work. Learning to understand when and where you should dial down your efficiency will help you achieve success. It is crucial to understand that different situations call for different actions, but understanding when to dial up or down your efficiency may not be easy. When given a project take a minute to understand what is needed and what you time frame you have to work with. This will give you a moment to think clearly and organize your thoughts to allow you to be efficient when needed, or to dial it down in order to communicate and brainstorm with your team members.

There are many instances where short-term efficiency can betray long-term motivation. This is important because a lot of companies hire on the basis of short-term tests and colleges look at SAT scores to admit our children.

Paul Sackett, a psychologist who in the 1980s measured short-term efficiency against long-term efficiency, found some interesting research on this matter. A test was performed in supermarkets where the speed of cashiers was measured in scanning a few dozen items. After taking in the results, Mr. Sackett decided to measure the cashiers over the long-term by tracking their speed through the new electronic scanners that could benchmark this data. Although it would seem logical that the cashiers who scored the fastest on the short-term test would be faster over the long-term, it actually did not turn out that way. Mr. Sackett was surprised to find a weak correlation between the short-term and long-term results.

The reason for this is based in behavior. Some people are able to situationally adapt better than others, while not being able to morph their long-term behaviors. Others are worse at situationally adapting when they are under stress, even though they may be good at it over the long term. We have to take into account how our behaviors can affect our perceived efficiency. Make sure that you don't make this mistake when hiring people in your organization or in performance evaluations. Take your perceptions into account and try to understand each person's overall behavior.

Secondary Steps:

When you recognize the need to dial down your efficiency it takes time and practice in order to successfully achieve this. The immediate steps mentioned before will help start you on your way to being able to dial down your efficiency. Here are some secondary steps you can take to build on what you have already learned and applied. Practicing these steps can help you dial down your efficiency.

1. **Be Humble**
   The highly efficient individual will sometimes be so wrapped up in what they think is the right way to do something, that they can become arrogant and closed off from ideas and suggestions that other might put forth. This attitude can be detrimental personally and professionally. Learn to be willing to accept advice and criticism from others. This can help you grow and which, incidentally, can help you efficiently do things the right way. Sometimes the overly efficient person will ignore advice or warning about a project because in order to address the issue, they will have to change or postpone the project. Be open to advice and welcome criticism from those who are experienced enough to give it constructively. This will help you establish rapport with your team members and gain their respect.

Now let's turn our attention to a story about being humble.

> *A well known speaker finally worked up the nerve to take his wife along with him on a speaking engagement. His wife's approval would be the ultimate compliment and encouragement as he endeavored to become a respected public speaker. He feverishly memorized the key points, practiced his illustrations, and worked on voice fluctuation.*
>
> *When he stepped on the podium on the night of the speech, he felt confident in his ability to deliver a flawless and inspiring speech. Forty-five minutes flew by and the crowd applauded his efforts. The pride swelled up inside of him as individual audience members shook hands and thanked him for a memorable address.*
>
> *In the car on the way home, the speaker turned to his wife and asked, "Sweetheart, how many great speakers do you think are in the world today?"*
>
> *She smiled, placed her hand on mind and softly said, "One fewer than you think, dear."*

The example given in the story is an excellent one to remember. A thin line exists between having pride in our abilities and being conceited. Sometimes others have a better view of our position than we do. If you can handle their honesty, an objective outsider might be able to help you keep yourself from crossing that line.

2. Respect Others

When you respect everyone's ideas, they are more comfortable talking and giving ideas to the group. When a manager is so set on getting a job done and snaps at the employee who brings up a question, they are breeding an atmosphere of negativity and groupthink. Learn to respect the ideas and opinions of others, even though you may not always use them.

It can be beneficial to hear others ideas and concerns about a project because the extra ten minutes spent discussing it might save you a big headache in the end. Being disrespectful is a negative habit and can ruin a team's effort. Be positive and encouraging when others speak. Welcome their comments and respect their ideas.

3. Accept Changes

> *"You have to be fast on your feet and adaptive or else a strategy is useless."*
>
> *~Charles de Gaulle*

One of the weaknesses of the efficiency Factor is a possible reluctance to change the way they do things because that would mean directing time away from the actual project and more toward the process. Changing the process may be necessary in certain situations, so being able to change will help the highly efficient individual be more successful. Learn to accept changes that will help the organization and aid in increasing productivity around your office. Not all changes are good, but when an opportunity arises to change something in order to increase productivity and encourage a positive atmosphere, learn to dial down your efficiency so that the changes can be effective.

16 Self-Motivation Generic Profile

Definition

When Dominance is greater than Steadiness, you have the Self-motivation Sub-factor. A person with the Self-motivation Sub-factor is able to take action without instruction. This type of person tends to be very active and on the move. This person is a thinker and looks to themselves to create new plans and ideas. There is hardly ever a dull moment in the mind of a person with this Sub-factor. The Self-motivation Sub-factor allows the individual to be creative and imaginative, but this doesn't necessarily show itself in the self-motivated person.

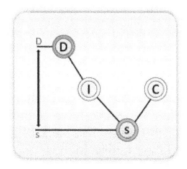

Descriptors

Some words that describe a person with the Self-motivation Sub-factor:

- Lively
- Energetic
- Forceful
- Full of life
- Creative

- Active
- Vibrant
- Vigorous
- Visionary

Strengths

The inherent strengths of the Self-motivation Sub-factor are quick thinking, integrity, and action. Self-motivated people typically have more energy and are more alert. This is useful in any profession. Self-motivated people are usually very honest with themselves and will stand corrected if they are proven wrong. Usually this person can only be proved wrong if they see something or learn something themselves. The self-motivated individual rarely takes another person at their word, therefore lacking a bit of trust.

Let's say you see five birds on a wire and one of them made the decision to fly away, with the rest following behind. Without self-motivation, how many birds would be left on the wire? You would have the same five birds sitting on that wire waiting for one to be the first to take flight. Self-motivation is the momentum that turns our decisions into actions. People with self-motivation are excellent co-workers because they take the initiative and act when they see something that needs to be accomplished. Self-motivated people have a sense of achievement and feel proud and pleased with their performance, without resting on their laurels. This allows them to be ready, willing, and able to succeed even more. When I have self-motivated team members, they take the initiative to get things done without having to be told, which allows the team to accomplish more and act more efficiently as a group.

> *"We continue to shape our personality all our life."*
>
> *~Albert Camus*

Weaknesses

The weaknesses of the Self-motivation Sub-factor are quick reactions (without thinking), impatience, and lack of empathy. Sometimes, people with the Self-motivation Sub-factor can't lower their pace to that of others and this causes conflict. They also have a hard time understanding why others aren't as motivated and go-getting as they are. This lack of empathy can also cause conflict between the self-motivated person and their family, friends, and co-workers.

When motivation causes conflict between you and the people around you, it can be a weakness. Have you ever worked with someone so motivated about a project that they left everyone in the dust and became annoyed when people couldn't keep up? They became angry and impatient with the other people on the project, putting a strain on the cohesiveness of the group. Though your co-worker may not think that they are hurting the efficiency of the group, the issues that arise from the lack of empathy can create an atmosphere of resentment. This can be the reason for poor production and the overall lack of success of the project.

Sometimes motivation causes people to stretch themselves too thin over numerous projects or tasks. When we take on too many tasks at once our success can be altered because we aren't able to give each assignment its needed focus. It's like when you are given a project with a deadline and as you are working on it, a co-worker seeks your assistance on another project. As you help your co-worker, another colleague comes over to ask you to create a spreadsheet for them by lunch. Being motivated to be successful, you take on the work and as your deadline approaches and you find that your original project hasn't been done yet, you rush to get it done and sacrifice the integrity of your work. Self-motivation is an excellent trait to have but examine yourself and how you use your motivation.

Too much of anything can be a bad thing. If you are prone to being impatient with others because of what you think is a lack of motivation or if you lack the empathy to understand circumstances, even your best intentions may go wrong. Bottom line: Understand that other people may not be as motivated as yourself, so be careful to not let your motivation blind you to others needs and issues.

Situational Adaptation - Dial Up or Dial Down

The degree of self-motivation is measured by your ability to get yourself to act, but not by your ability to get others to act. You can't focus on getting others to act, and, therefore, you can't let yourself get emotionally upset when they don't act. You have to dial down your self-motivation when trying to motivate others. What motivates you doesn't necessarily motivate them. The flip side is when you are determining your weekly routine. You have to dial up your self-motivation to actually accomplish that goal. Usually, whenever you set a goal, you need to dial up your self-motivation in order to see it through.

Being a self-motivated individual, your personal initiative is very strong. Just imagine a boss who is a self-starter, one who needs no one to propel him/her forward on thoughts, actions, and plans. This Sub-factor will be extremely beneficial as new ideas are being formulated, while other employees will be able to follow along with plans and goals generated by this individual. The self-motivated individual can show their forthright personality of knowing 'how to get the project done,' and they can be very decisive about the process. This type of behavior can be beneficial in many situations, especially when timeliness is crucial. A self-motivated boss can be seen as a great leader because they do their share of the workload. This type of boss doesn't delegate all of their work to their employees, therefore gaining leadership currency with the staff.

If you find yourself bored with your job and unmotivated, it becomes your responsibility to do something about it, even if the people around you seem apathetic to the causes of your boredom. You need to find what motivates you to succeed. An amusing example of this is a man who was hired by the circus to clean up after elephants. A friend observed him in his new position and couldn't help but share his perspective. "You have the worst job of anyone I know," the friend began, "The elephant poops and you scoop. What a demeaning job. Why don't you just quit?" His friend responded, "What, and give up show business?" It isn't the job we do, but how we perceive it that affects our inspiration in it. A sense of achievement and belonging is cultivated when we believe what we are doing is important. For the man at the circus, he found show business as his motivation to continue scooping. What motivates you?

Consider also, the same scenario - the boss has ideas and wants to move forward - at his pace. When sharing this 'great idea' with the staff, self-motivation may cause the boss to be so impatient that even gathering or considering input from staff will simply take too much time in his mind. The staff will usually work at a slower pace at first trying to understand the new idea, but the self-motivated boss may expect the staff to work at his or her pace, therefore creating conflict. If the D>s individual would demonstrate the opposing Sub-factor of patience, new and possibly even better ideas on how to implement the idea may prove extremely beneficial to the success of the idea or plans. By muscling and stretching his behavior and displaying more patience into the process, the boss may have the opportunity to make a good idea even better.

Self-motivation can sometimes lead us into making decisions without waiting because we are so focused on succeeding that we don't take the time to clearly think about what the right course may be. We can often overlook other people's input because we are in such a rush to accomplish our goal. Take for example the person who decides that they want to buy a house, against the counsel of his friends and family. He goes to the first realtor he finds, sees a few houses, then makes an offer on a house he's enthralled with, and after a little negotiation he buys it. The day comes to move in and with much excitement and enthusiasm, the man moves into his new house. He soon learns that the beautiful house that he bought is filled with termites, has electrical problems, a leaky roof, and is infested with rodents. If he had taken the time to listen to his friends and family, he would have seen that though his intentions were good, they became blinded by his motivation to take action. Situations like this arise in life and learning to dial down your motivation will help you to analyze what you need to do to successfully achieve your goals.

Next Steps

Next, you will explore the benefits and consequences of the Self-motivation Sub-factor. If you think that this Sub-factor is important for your success, you can target your knowledge by investigating various ways to dial up or dial down your Self-motivation Sub-factor in our 'How to' sessions.

"Remember happiness doesn't depend upon who you are or what you have; it depends solely on what you think."

~Dale Carnegie

17 How to Dial Up Self-Motivation

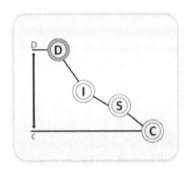

D>c
Independence

As children, we can learn to rely on our parents or other people to propel us into motion or we can self-propel - also known as self-motivation. One day we have to learn that we can't always depend on someone else to provide motivation for us otherwise we won't achieve much in life - especially what we want to achieve for ourselves. Have you ever created a plan and set goals, but you just didn't have that drive to start much less achieve them? Without self-motivation, it becomes hard to accept new challenges, opportunities, and directions in life. People get tired of pushing you to achieve. That is why self-motivation is important.

Dialing up self-motivation takes practice, especially when you need enthusiasm for a task that you have little interest in. Motivation and stimulus may come from external Factors, as well as internal Factors. For example, an encouraging or kind word from a friend might well be the trigger to get you started even if it had nothing to do with a particular goal. It simply made you feel confident which in turn prompted you to take action. Or it might be something inherent in your belief system that may motivate you positively to take action. This might be the case where your value system tells you be motivated to help co-workers who have too much on their plates, clean up the neighbor's lawn as a kind gesture when they are under the weather, or simply let a teacher know that they have been an inspiration in your life years after you graduate.

Negative Factors may also encourage you to self-start. Fear is the best self-motivator. Fear of loss, fear of embarrassment, being fearful of disappointing people of care about can make you egg yourself on. And this fear can bring about entirely positive results - even though the initial motivating Factor was negative - fear. For instance, if you get let go from your job, you might be afraid that you cannot provide for your family. Through this fearful state, you might be motivated to start your own business. Learning to be self-motivated may take time, but the key is to start now! Here are some steps that you can take to become more self-motivated.

Primary and Secondary Motivation Factors

General behavior and motivation have consistent patterns. Nowhere is this more important than in the area of our Primary Motivators in Life. I like to think of primary and secondary motivators as the ignition switches that I use to turn my motivation on. Without the ignition being on, I can't set myself in motion. Without these primary or secondary motivators, we wouldn't feel compelled to do anything. Understanding what they are and then leveraging them are critical components in achieving our goals.

Love & Fear

The primary motivators - the most compelling reasons that people are induced to do anything - are because they are in a state of either Love or Fear. Think about it. If you love someone you like to do things for them. If you love yourself, you will look after your body better, nurture your spirit, and continually develop your mind. Love and respect are similar and in terms of motivation are considered equal. If you like and respect your boss, you'll work harder to please them. On the flip side, if you are afraid of them, you'll also tend to work hard because you fear their wrath. If you are afraid of dying of cancer, you'll also look after your body - perhaps eating a healthy balanced diet and not smoking. The same results of accomplishing the goal but acquired through different motivational Factors - love or fear. Most people view love as a positive motivator and fear as a negative motivator. So, which one is most powerful? I like to think that love is more potent than fear.

And in looking at how people sacrifice for those they love, it's not hard to prove this. Think about parents diving into dangerous waters when their children are in peril. Or rushing into a burning room to save family members, without thought of personal distress. Imagine a world where people didn't love their fellow human beings. Would most humanitarian causes exist without people motivated by love of fellow man? If you study Maslow's Hierarchy of Needs - the Pyramid of Motivation, you can easily see that the top half of the pyramid - the levels closest to self-actualization - are externally focused - predominantly on love-based motivation.

The more you drop down through the levels of the pyramid to the base, the more focused people become on fear-based motivators like the fear of losing income, shelter, or the basic necessities of life. As you move up - ever closer to the goal of self-fulfillment - the motivation changes from fear to love and attainment. The basic criteria of motivation can be viewed in terms of what people move towards or what they move away from. This is akin to the old motivation analogy of moving people along with a carrot or a stick - a reward or a punishment.

Here's an example of how you could be motivated to accomplish the same goal but with the entirely different motivators of love and fear - moving toward attainment and abundance or compelled to do something out of fear - moving away from something that you fear might happen. I want to go get my degree so that I can learn leadership skills that will help my organization grow. I am afraid that my skills aren't up to the level where I can compete in the future for my job. I need to ramp them up by going back to college in the evenings.

Here's another goal coached in both a positive attainment manner versus in a fearful moving away from fashion. I have to conserve cash right now so that I can take advantage of opportunities that come my way as we move through tight economic times. And the fear-based equivalent: I want to minimize my overhead so I that I don't lose even more money during a down economy.

The key with self-motivation is to determine - for the particular goal that you are examining - what are your primary and secondary motivators. Doing something because you are afraid is not necessarily a bad thing if your fear propels you toward your ultimate goals. Remember that fear can be precisely the lift you need to motivate yourself. In looking at fear as a gift, you can effectively channel it and have it help you achieve success throughout your life.

Secondary Motivating Factors

Now let's move on from the primary motivating Factors of love and fear to the secondary motivational Factors. Secondary motivating Factors tend to be less powerful - less motivating than love or fear, but make no mistake about it - they are still very powerful when it comes to propelling you forward or stalling you.

There Are Four Secondary Motivating Factors:

1. Affiliation.

This is the motivation that centers on relationships and connectedness. The desire for social interaction is a strong motivator and many people will work to keep channels of communication with others open. They might feel stimulated and inspired to take action in order to fulfill an obligation to another person or when combined with the primary motivator of fear, they might be afraid that by not doing something they could negatively impact a relationship.

This impetus is a strong motivator because most people do not like to damage relationships with those they care about or with those they have a symbiotic or beneficial relationship - as in the customer/vendor relationships, any partnerships, or teaming associations.

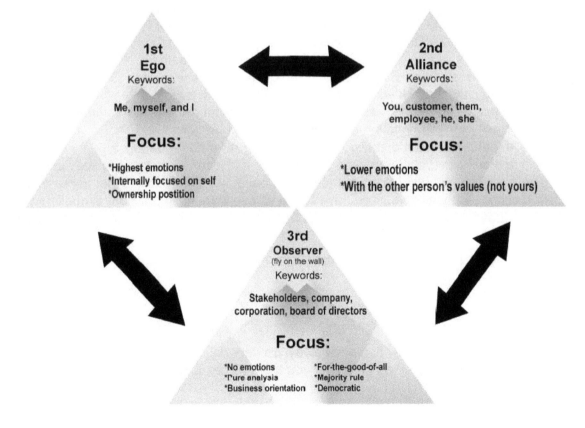

2. Dependency.

This is most often a fairly negative motivational Factor. Being dependent on things like alcohol or drugs does set up a situation where people will be aroused to satisfy their cravings. Many other dependencies exist that motivate people to indulge themselves. These can be physical cravings or mental dependencies.

3. Need for Certainty.

Perhaps this will motivate people to do things like seeking more knowledge about their areas of interest, uncovering information when they are forced to make decisions or seeking out advice from others so that they feel comfortable moving ahead. Living with too much uncertainty could mean that a person would feel obliged to wait until they are comfortable before taking action - thereby stalling them from taking action. The bottom line is that at some point in time, the degree of uncertainty will become so uncomfortable that the person will have to start moving forward. That is how this motivational Factor takes effect. Knowing that it exists can help you start gathering information and moving ahead sooner.

4. Desire to Meet (Or Exceed) Standards.

Fear of disappointing others or self (not living up to what is expected of you). People will take action to make sure that they do not disappoint or that they themselves are not disappointed. With regard to this motivational Factor, I suggest that you review the Law of Satisfaction and Standards in the 21 Laws of Influence and the 21 Laws of Influence for Sales.

Now that you know a bit about how primary and secondary motivational Factors work, use the perceptual position model and look at the things you think you need to be motivated to do in terms of the 1st perceptual position only - from the 'Me' mode. Ask yourself: "What's in it for me? And is it worth it?" If the answer to "Is it worth it to me?" is no, understand that it's going to be very difficult to motivate yourself! If the answer is yes, determine which of the motivational Factors are currently in play and ask yourself how you might enhance their efforts. Can you leverage them and make them more compelling or powerful? Next, can you combine another motivational Factor to add additional impetus? If you are striving towards saving for a home because you want to provide for your family, can you perhaps add leverage to this positive motivator by telling yourself that you need to make more sales because you are afraid that prices might go up if you continue to wait? Now you have fear and love working in harmony propelling you to your goals. Leveraging in this way works for any area of your life - work, family, or in a social setting.

> "Relentless self-talk is what changes our self-image."
>
> ~Denis Waitley

Now we're ready to move ahead to some Immediate Steps you can take to capitalize on dialing up your self-motivation.

Immediate Steps:

First, understand that when motivation goes away, it's very difficult to jump-start it again. So you have to take some immediate steps whenever you feel yourself losing motivation.

After laying out a plan and writing down your goals, sometimes you may be at a loss on how to start down the road to achieving success and accomplishing your goals. Self-motivation needs a primary or secondary motivational Factor to turn itself on. You need to keep the ignition turned on and continually fuel the fire of motivation from within - by yourself - to sustain self-motivation. With the desire and will to do it, self-motivation can be learned and practiced. If you feel that you need to become more self-motivated, here are some immediate steps that you can start with right away:

1. Stay Positive.

Learn to see the good in every situation. Negativity limits our drive and creativity, and stops any hope of positive outcome by convincing ourselves that the negative view is appropriate. Be rational. I understand that negative consequences are possible but dwelling on them tends to make them occur more often. Understanding this fact, it just not in your best interests to dwell on the bad rather than making the choice to concentrate on the good. Look realistically at the probability of the good outcome versus the bad. The bottom line: If there is truly a greater chance that you will fail, you might want to step back and consider your options. But if after consideration, you decide to go for it - that the potential benefits far outweigh the risks, try to stack the deck in your favor as much as possible and go for the gold! Remember, no guts, no glory! As for being realistic, when a potentially negative situation arises, defer leaping to conclusions. Examine your motivation and temper your judgment and examine your response. For example, if you don't have the funds to afford that new car you want, thinking that you can't afford it isn't going to help you eventually buy it. Instead, think about how you CAN afford it. What steps would you have to take to afford that car? That simple difference in thinking how you CAN activates your mind and begins the motivation process. If you have been recently passed over for that promotion you thought you deserved, think about why you were passed over and make a new game plan so that it won't happen again. Be objective and stay self-motivated to get the results you want.

> *"You were not born a winner, and you were not born a loser. You are what you make yourself be."*
>
> *~Lou Holtz*

2. Create a Task List.

To be self-motivated, you need to have something to be motivated for. Start by creating a list of goals and tasks that you need or want to do. The list should include goals and tasks that benefit you, and also those that benefit others you care about. Set yourself a deadline to complete them, leaving room for unexpected interruptions or changes to your plans. Stick to one task at a time, staying focused and inspired on the project at hand. We have so many things going on in our everyday life that we sometimes tend to set aside our goals or try to take on more goals than we can handle at a time. With that frustration, we can lose focus. Your goals should be realistic and attainable, but you should make sure that you have stretched yourself. A huge component of sustaining self-motivation is in continually surprising yourself by achieving more than you thought you could. Follow the SMART goal format and challenge yourself so that you are continually striving to better your last best and achieve your full potential.

Far too often we are tempted to dream so big that we create goals that will be difficult to accomplish or realize in the present. That's just part of human nature. Think about what children want to be when they grow up. They almost always have high aspirations, but over time, most people temper their dreams and squish their self-motivation down. Why does this need to happen?

It doesn't make a lot of sense but by squishing your goals you kill your drive and self-motivation. Resist the urge to do this with your whole being. Question why you allow yourself to do this to yourself? In questioning, you'll probably find all the right reasons to dreams big hairy dreams for every area of your business and personal life. If you have a big goal, start with the small goals you need to accomplish along the way to get to that big dream. For example, if you want to buy a house, but don't have the down payment money or you can't currently qualify for the mortgage you need, set up a three to five year goal. Pay off your debt in the first 18 months, then save for two years and the result will be that you'll get to that dream of owning your own home sooner than later.

> *John Goddard always had a great determination. He learned this early when his grandmother said to him, "If only I had done this when I was young." John Goddard never wanted to play the 'if only' game. He sat down and wrote out exactly what he wanted to do with his life. 127 goals were on the list when he finished. His goals were a combination of travel, adventure, learning skills, reading, and other activities. These goals included climbing mountains, learning to fly an airplane, retracing the travels of Marco Polo, and committing himself to reading the entire works of several classic authors. At 47 years old, John Goddard had accomplished 103 of the 127 goals he set for himself. John Goddard is a man determined to create his own task lists and make use of them.*
>
> *Through his determination and motivation, John Goddard was able to accomplish things in his life that most people can only dream about. Learn from his story and take the time to write down your goals. This will help you dial up your self-motivation.*

John Goddard is an incredible man and an amazing example of how you can accomplish more than you ever thought possible if you write down your goals. Let's take a look at his story.

3. Surround Yourself with Positive People or People That Encourage You To Grow.

Bad character or negative people can corrupt good morals, and the same goes for motivation. If you surround yourself with unmotivated people or people that try to put your goals down, you are making it that much harder on yourself to become self-motivated in your endeavors. Start meeting and making friends with people who will encourage you on your path to your goals, and find ways to spend time with them. Learn to share your goals with the people that support you, not those who will respond with cynicism and indifference.

If your goal is to get more work completed during the week, would you be motivated by the guy on the computer next to you playing solitaire? Though he most likely gets his work completed on time, is he keeping you motivated towards reaching your goal of getting more work completed? Plus, if you are hanging around people like that and your boss thinks you condone this type of behavior, this might curtail your opportunities for mentoring or advancement. People always assume that like-minded people hang out together. So, instead why not find someone who has improved their work motivation, spend time with them, and learn what helped them achieve their goal. This will make your goal personal and help you stay focused on reaching it.

Secondary Steps:

The desire and focus to become self-motivated does not always come naturally. There can be times in your life that you just don't want to take the next step forward toward achieving your tasks. This process will take practice and dedication. These next steps can help you on your journey to becoming more self-motivated when you feel yourself losing energy and focus.

1. **Know Yourself, So You Can Grow Yourself.**

   Knowing how you performed during your corporate meetings helps you understand what your strengths and weaknesses are. The same thing applies to becoming more self-motivated. Keep notes on when you're lacking motivation and also when you feel like you could move mountains. Begin to understand what your patterns are and how you can work around and develop them. Recognize what makes you bored and avoid it. Boredom can be the water that douses your motivated fire. Learn how to make your boredom a trigger for making the task interesting and creative. As you progress with your goals, keep track of your accomplishments. This will help keep you focused and motivated when you see yourself succeeding.

2. **Help Others.**

   Learn to share your ideas with friends and help them get motivated themselves. Seeing others succeed will help motivate you to do the same. Even the smallest thing can be a huge help to someone. The great thing about helping others is the boost you receive to achieve your own goals. Remember that if you struggle from being unmotivated, there will be other people who struggle from the same thing. As you learn how to teach and help other people realize their dreams, you'll find that your dreams are that much easier to achieve. This will not only give you the satisfaction that comes from helping another human being, but also the motivation to realize success in your own life.

3. **Continue to Learn as You Make Decisions and Take Action.**

   Sometimes the biggest roadblock in accomplishing our goals is a lack of experience. Don't let this deter you from reaching your goal. If your goal is to write a resume, read as many books as you can on resume writing, take a class online, or ask a friend who has experience to help you build it. By learning what it takes and how to achieve your goals, the goals become more attainable and personal. If you want to learn more about being motivated, listen to motivational speakers or read a motivational book. Don't stop learning!

4. **Commit Whole-Heartedly to Your Goal.**

   If your goals are really important to you, learn to minimize the opportunities you give yourself to escape completing that goal. "In for a penny, in for a pound!" Once you decide on your path, go for it with gusto. Having an easy escape route can cause doubt to creep into your mind and undermine your self-motivation to see your task to the end. Leaving an easy 'out' sends a message to your subconscious mind that it's ok to quit. Understand that on your way to reaching your goals you will encounter roadblocks and trials. Sometimes, having an easy escape decreases your chances of succeeding. Commit whole-heartedly to your goals from the beginning to the end and determine to see them finished.

A great example of acting on a goal or need and committing whole-heartedly to it is Henry Ford. Let's look at how he did that.

> *Ford was a pioneer of 'welfare capitalism', designed to improve the lot of his workers and especially to reduce the heavy turnover that had many departments hiring 300 men per year to fill 100 slots. Efficiency meant hiring and keeping the best workers.*
>
> *Ford astonished the world in 1914 by offering a $5 per day wage ($110 in current dollar terms), which more than doubled the rate of most of his workers. A Cleveland Ohio newspaper editorialized that the announcement, "shot like a blinding rocket through the dark clouds of the present industrial depression". The move proved extremely profitable; instead of constant turnover of employees, the best mechanics in Detroit flocked to Ford, bringing their human capital and expertise, raising productivity, and lowering training costs. It also set a new, reduced workweek, although the details vary in different accounts. Ford and Crowther in 1922 described it as six 8-hour days, giving a 48-hour week, while in 1926 they described it as five 8-hour days, giving a 40-hour week.*
>
> *Detroit was already a high-wage city, but competitors were forced to raise wages or lose their best workers. Ford's policy proved, however, that paying people more would enable Ford workers to afford the cars they were producing and be good for the economy. Ford explained the policy as profit-sharing rather than wages.*
>
> *Henry Ford saw a need and took action to fill it. His five dollar workday helped improve the life of his workers and increase efficiency through lower employee turnover.*

5. 'Moving Forward Goals'.

Once you set a goal for yourself, act immediately. Procrastination is one of the worst self-motivation killers. As you begin working on a fresh new goal, focus on separating that goal into smaller 'Moving Forward Goals'. For every meeting or task, know exactly what you want to accomplish during the day or during a meeting. By achieving these smaller goals, you will reach your end goal before you know it. Plus, you'll be able to sustain your self-motivation because you can congratulate yourself along the way as you reach your moving forward goals.

Too often people get stuck in the state of analysis paralysis and never reach the action stage. Identify your plan of action and just do it! For example, if you decided you need to lose weight, go straight to your refrigerator, and throw out all the junk food. Don't analyze whether you should throw them out alphabetically or by size or expiration date, just do it now! One of the secrets of success is recognizing that motivation follows action. The momentum of continuous action fuels motivation. So act boldly, as if it's impossible to fail. Continue to add fuel to your desire and you can reach the point of knowing that you can't quit, and that success is only a matter of time.

18 How to Dial Down Self-Motivation

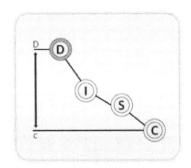

D>c
Independence

Learning to successfully do something new takes practice and learning to dial down your self-motivation is no different. Thankfully, if you recognize your need to dial it down, you already have the Self-motivation to get things done - so in a strange way, this Sub-factor™ is perfect for what you want to accomplish!

Let's begin this session with some general information about self-motivated people. An individual who is highly self-motivated is usually quick thinking, alert, and full of energy. They generally have lots of opinions and are solid in their convictions. This sense of self-assurance is often portrayed through a high level of integrity and make no mistake about it, these people will stick to their guns when they believe they are in the right. However, if their Steadiness Factor isn't too low they will stand corrected if proven wrong.

The confident characteristics of this Sub-factor are useful in any line of work and should be admired. Unfortunately, like every other Sub-factor, Self-motivation has its weaknesses, too. An overly self-motivated person will tend to make quick decisions without thinking, become impatient, and lack empathy for those around them that may not be as motivated. These weaknesses can cause problems with family and social relationships and in dealings at work. Having strong rapport and trust is crucial to success in the work place and in social relationships. Self-motivated individuals are often described as have tunnel vision in their quest to achieve or they're seen as steamrolling over people to get their goals accomplished. The bottom line: The important elements of trust and rapport can be damaging if self-motivation is forceful.

Even if you manage to maintain trust, if your self-motivation is too amped up, you may come across as appearing too impulsive, eager, or driving. You might look like you are overly stimulated, zealous, or too inspirational to some people. They might perceive that you appear excessively animated or inappropriately hyped up relative to the situation in your quest to get results quickly.

Teammates or friends may feel overwhelmed if you come at them with an abundance of agitation, pent up tension to get things done and your over-the-top motivation when you talk about projects. This is especially true when you are dealing with more reserved types or introverts.

The first thing to remember when determining that you want to learn how to dial down your Self-motivation is that Self-motivation's D>s opposing Sub-factor™ is Patience S>d. So, all that might be required is that you dial up your Patience and this alone will have the immediate impact of dialing back your elevated level of Self- motivation. Dialing down your Self-motivation doesn't mean that you nix the elevated level of Self-motivation you have at your core. I don't think that anyone would say that a person should eliminate their drive to succeed. However, perception is the key and using the other Sub-factors™ to balance out how you come across will help you achieve your goals without others perceiving the negative aspects of Self-motivation. So, remain Self-motivated at your core and show your outward-facing behaviors through your balancing behaviors. This will allow you to empathize with others and strengthen your relationships with those around you.

Understanding the importance of learning how to control other's perception of your self-motivation will be critical to your success if one of your governing Sub-factors™ is Self-motivation.

Appropriately channeling your internal drive and then determining what works to get others perception and buy-in to line up with your goals is the primary objective. Learning how to do this effectively will take time, practice, and persistence. Fortunately, in time you will be able to dial down your external self-motivation while still retaining your internal impetus without stress.

Again, before we go into some immediate steps you can take to help you dial down your self-motivation, I will reiterate that being self-motivated is definitely not a negative attribute. In fact it can be extremely beneficial. It only becomes a weakness when it is taken to the extreme and compromises the success of a project or negatively impacts a relationship. If you feel that you need to learn to dial down your self-motivation please understand that it will take time and diligence is vital.

Immediate Steps:

1. Empathize

Self-motivated people tend to find it hard to empathize with other people's situations when they are driving to get things done. This can put a strain on their relationships and create conflict - especially in the work place. The self-motivated individual is so ready to accomplish a goal that they will sometimes fail to acknowledge how another person may feel about the goal or how it may affect them. By learning to empathize, you can help increase your rapport with your co-workers or subordinates and influence them. Learn to understand that some people may not be motivated the same way you are or by the same things in life. This will help you understand and gain the trust and respect of the people you work with. And don't forget that the same is true in your friendships and family life. Being understanding of the people around you will help you build solid relationships and quickly establish rapport. Now let's look at understanding through the story of Patricia Moore. Patricia Moore took the time to understand how her grandfather truly felt and it helped create awareness for the needs of the elderly. She empathized with her grandfather's position in life and set out to more fully understand it so she could make a difference.

Patricia Moore, the only female industrial designer at Raymond Leowy's internationally renowned design office in New York, was moved by her arthritic grandfather's challenges to take on an unusual experiment. In 1976 at the age of twenty six, Patricia Moore reconstructed herself into an elderly woman with bound joints. She padded her back into a hump and wore contact lenses smeared with Vaseline. To complete her make-over, she wore support panty hose and a fuzzy wool coat.

Her results were extremely thought provoking. Moore found herself being ignored in stores, struggling to complete simple tasks, too slow to cross the street before the light changed and encountering people apathetic to her circumstances. As a result of her reporting her experiences, several companies became more sensitive to the needs of the elderly.

Moore challenged people to try their own experiment. "Play tennis until your muscles ache; put on gloves with a couple of fingers sewn together; wear sunglasses with scratched lenses; then go and make yourself a bowl of soup. It won't be easy but you'll learn what life often is like for people with arthritis and cataracts."

2. Distract Yourself

Impatience is one of the main weaknesses of the elevated Self-motivated individual and can cause stress in the individual as well as in their relationships. Being patient can be difficult for an individual where the Dominance Factor is much, much greater than their Steadiness Factor. When this degree of separation occurs the results could be dire. They can compromise work relationships, destroy family relationships, annihilate friendships, or devastate the joint efforts of a project team. Some of the things you have to do to avoid this are to learn to channel your frustration to something else instead of focusing on the person or thing that is causing you to become impatience or frustrated. Looking at pictures that make you laugh or reminding yourself of a happy, relaxing event can help relieve stress. Create an album of pictures that you can look at when you are feeling frustrated and impatient. The album could include anything from funny pictures you found on Google to snapshots from your favorite vacation. Make this album accessible and turn to it when you become stressed.

3. Focused Breathing

Another way of relieving stress and channeling your frustration at not getting enough accomplished in the timeframe you want is to focus on your breathing. This will take your focus away from the external Factors that are causing your frustration and allow you to concentrate on your internal state. It is a simple exercise but can be extremely effective. With practice you can find yourself becoming more patient and less stressed at work and in life.

4. Take a Minute

The self-motivated individual is usually full of energy and ready to jump right in and take on a task. This can backfire when they don't analyze the situation properly and allow their motivation to blind them from issues that may compromise the success of the project. Learning to take some time and step back from a project or to step back from a heated debate to discern what is needed for success is crucial to accomplishing your goals. Take a minute before you take on a new project and think about what is needed in order to insure the highest possibility of success. Think about what others might find stressful about what you are trying to accomplish and try to discuss things before they become flashpoints. Analyze what situations might arise and how you would respond to them in a proactive and calm manner. It is hard to find a project that doesn't meet obstacles and road blocks at one time or another so being prepared can give you the edge needed to achieve success.

5. What Irritates You

A highly self-motivated person can easily become irritated at those around them when they perceive them as not being as motivated. This can cause the self-motivated individual to become frustrated and impatient with their co-workers or subordinates. Impatience can lead to loss of rapport as well as trust between the individual and their team members, which can affect the success of the team and individual. The same is true in families. If the motivated person wants to get something done and the other family members are not on the same page, this can cause conflict.

Think about what irritates you in your work, family and social relationships as it relates to your motivation versus that of others. Write down the top five things that come to mind. Remember these five things and learn to recognize when you become frustrated so you can learn to control it and shape your behavior to better suit the situation. Being able to dial down your self-motivation and dial up your friendliness in this type of situation will help you maintain good rapport with your colleagues.

Secondary Steps:

If you feel like you need to dial down your self-motivation to help you accomplish what you want in work and life, the immediate steps that we just went over will definitely help you. Now, here are some secondary steps that can help you become aware of different situations and how to dial down your self-motivation. Remember that these steps take practice!

> "You cannot expect to achieve new goals or move beyond your present circumstances unless you change."
>
> ~Les Brown

1. Preparation and Foresight

When you're creating a plan for a project, plan for delays, complications, and setbacks. Although your motivation to jump right in and tackle the project may want to keep you from planning for unforeseen events or problems, you must prepare for encountering them. If they happen, you are already prepared and not caught off guard which will allow you to stay motivated and confident to finish the project. Where you may have been stressed and angry, you're now confident because you had planned for those situations. Should these events not occur, you're delighted and happy that your foresight to prepare served you in the end. Learn to think about each situation and create a successful plan that you can stick to - especially with adequate and realistic timelines. Then track your time estimates. Many self-motivated people become agitated and stressed when they believe that timelines are slipping. When this happens many of the negative behaviors associated with stressed out more dominant individuals occurs. To avoid this train try to be realistic about how much time it actually takes to get things accomplished. It's ok to have to stretch your goals when you do this, but you have to be reasonable otherwise people around you will not like it. This process will help you be more accurate with your work, too. Now let's enjoy the story of Scottie Pippen.

DISCflex™

How do you get yourself into the position to become a member of a world-championship basketball team? The answer may be different than you think. At least it was for Scottie Pippen. As a six foot two inch, one hundred and forty five pound point guard playing on his high school basketball team, Scottie's prospects for college ball were dim, and that's being kind. The state campus at Monticello failed to come through with an opportunity as Pippen had hoped for, so he ended up at the University of Central Arkansas, under head coach Donald Dyer, as a work-study 'manager'. His job allowed him to prepare himself by working out with the team and continuing his own skill-building practices. Later on, at Central Arkansas, his body changed, dramatically! Pippen grew to six feet eight inches and enjoyed an average of 23 points per game, earning him a full scholarship. He later went on to win six world-championships with the Chicago Bulls and become known as one of the best small forwards of all time. Through his many years of preparation, he was able to play a major role in the success of the Chicago Bulls. Even though his chances were slim, Scottie Pippen didn't quit practicing and educating himself about the tactics and strategies of the game of basketball. His constant preparation meant being ready and adequately prepared when opportunity presented itself.

2. Listen

As mentioned before, one of the weaknesses of self-motivation is lack of empathy and understanding. Learning to listen at a deeper level will help you in situations where you need to dial-down your self-motivation. This is a secondary step only because training yourself to listen well takes time, energy and practice. In learning how to listen there are a few tried and true techniques that are easy to implement. This might mean being quiet so another person may say their side of an argument without interrupting them. It might mean taking the time to listen to someone who just needs to talk. Taking the time to learn to listen will help you empathize with other people and understand them better, which will help you keep a strong rapport with them and gain their trust. Avoid the bad habit of simply thinking about what you plan to say next in the conversation instead of truly listening to the other person.

3. Rome Wasn't Built in a Day

Sometimes a D>s individual will be so full of energy and ready to take on a project that they can become impatient if the project takes longer than they expected. For example, a manager might be given an assignment for their team to accomplish and after jumping right in and tackling the project, they become frustrated when they meet the inevitable road blocks that appear in almost all projects. Becoming impatient when things aren't going as expected is not a sign of a mature business person. Often, a self-motivated person will simply turn their focus to something else that can be accomplished quicker. In this regard they might annoy workers when they change their mind and do things like moving resources and switching out team members midstream. These types of managers might perhaps even lose the motivation needed to complete the project and they may abandon it entirely. Learning to understand that some things take time will help you stay focused and motivated when a project hits an obstacle.

> *"Man's main task in life is to give birth to himself, to become what his potential is. The most important product of his effort is his own personality."*
>
> *~Erich Fromm*

19 Independence Generic Profile

Definition

When Dominance is greater than Compliance, you have the Independence Sub-factor. This is the type of person that creates their own rules and doesn't submit to authority. They form their own ideas, prefer to work alone, and take pride in what they can accomplish by themselves. The Independence Sub-factor is most common in the entrepreneurial field. People with the Independence Sub-factor feel the need to create things themselves. Independence can also mean that this type of person is more objective to other people's affairs. This isn't necessarily true when this person has a stake in the affairs, but from afar they are typically more neutral and impartial.

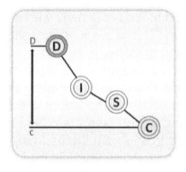

D>c
Independence

Descriptors

Here is a list of words that describe someone with the Independence Sub-factor:

- Autonomy
- Self-determination
- Self-reliance
- Self-rule
- Self-sufficiency

Strengths

The strengths of the Independence Sub-factor are self-reliance, the ability to self-regulate, and a strong sense of freedom to be innovative. The independent person doesn't rely on other people to get their work done. They continually find their own resources without the assistance or guidance of others.

They also regulate themselves well, usually sharing a part of the efficient Sub-factor. The best features of the independent person are the creativity and innovativeness displayed. They are the visionaries that create new ways of thinking.

Having the independence to be self-reliant and the freedom to utilize creativity has been the reason for success for many people. A salesman during the Great Depression squeezed out his living walking dogs, washing cars, and doing anything he could to make ends meet. At night, he worked on developing a board game that he envisioned would be in every home in America. Today, twenty thousand of those board games are sold every week. This type of independence and innovation helps major companies today stay successful in an ever changing world.

When working with a team, I always try to have at least one person with the Independence Sub-factor. They are able to accomplish tasks efficiently and creatively, without my constant supervision. Their independence helps keep everyone motivated and working efficiently towards the goals that need to be accomplished. When independence is lacking, creativity suffers and work becomes stagnant.

Weaknesses

The weaknesses of the Independence Sub-factor are a tendency to be too egotistical, belligerent, and a poor team player. Their ego can sometimes prevent them from learning anything from someone other than themselves. They can also be very hostile to other people when they are told what to do or how to act. People with an independent Sub-factor can also be weak team players, usually trying to win for themselves rather than for the team.

Arrogance is the killer of growth. When independence turns to arrogance, growth becomes stagnant in not only the work place, but in life.

If you have ever tried to instruct someone on how to do a task but they don't listen and continue to do what they want, you are most likely dealing with someone who is highly independent. This can be an enormous hindrance in the business world.

A successful, yet arrogant, professional athlete was brought to a team to help them on their journey to winning a championship. It soon became evident that the particular athlete was more interested in personal glory than the overall team's accomplishments. Resentment set in among the other players who were all working as a team toward one goal and the team began to fall apart. The team ended the season well short of their overall goal. Bottom line: Don't let arrogance kill your personal or professional growth.

Imagine a boss who is an independent, creative, efficient, and motivated person. Unfortunately, this boss is hostile to other ideas or opinions and thinks his or her way is the only way. This creates a 'my way or the highway' atmosphere in the office which suppresses growth and communication. When new ideas are brought up, they are shot down because they don't go along with the boss's agenda. Production is hurt because communication becomes strained throughout the office and the overall moral is at an all time low. Unfortunately, this happens all too often in the business world today.

Independence can be a very good Sub-factor to have, but having too much of it can be a recipe for a bad team player. Be careful not to let your independence cause you to become arrogant and forget that there are other people who have ideas that might help you and your team become successful.

Situational Adaptation - Dial Up or Dial Down

It is critical to a person with the Independence Sub-factor to know how to dial up and dial down their independence. When working with a team, or anything that requires someone else to be a part of the process, you have to dial down your independence. You have to dial it down enough to be open to other people's thoughts and ideas and objectively judge them. You still want to keep it high enough so that you can provide your own insight and vision to the team. It's important to achieve balance between your ideas and other's ideas when working in a team environment. When working alone or creating new ideas, you want to dial up your independence. Independence can be the best Factor in innovation because you are doing it for yourself and your own creativity.

"The intellectual is different from the ordinary man, but only in certain sections of his personality, and even then not all the time."

~George Orwell

Working as an independent individual, you will be the person who displays their independence in the various working environments. This can be very positive for the boss, the team, and for individual employees. An independent person will most likely not be a 'yes man' for every idea and project that gets discussed and reviewed. Most bosses like to have an employee who is willing to stand out from their peers and be independent enough to share their ideas and opinions. One of the reasons for this is that the independent person can single-handedly stop Groupthink from occurring in team meetings.

It is easy to let other people tell you what you can and can't do in life and in the workplace. You might find yourself involved in a group project that you believe isn't going to be successful unless change is implemented. You may have a goal that people around you say is impossible to accomplish. Dialing up your independence will help you find creative and innovative ways to accomplish your goal. A man who worked for a company that manufactured sandpaper, asked himself what do you do with rejected sandpaper materials?

He spent so much time trying to find a solution that his company fired him because they thought he was wasting too much time. However, he continued to come to work. He went on to become the vice-president of one of the divisions in the company. He found the answer to his question and it is found on the roof of millions of homes across the world in the form of asphalt shingles.

The boss needs employees who are independent enough to speak up when the time is right, and to not speak out when stepping on the toes of other employees. If they speak out too much, displaying too much independence, they may push others away and display a lack of caring about other employees and their ideas along the way. That is when the cooperative Sub-factor would be helpful. By dialing up their cooperative Sub-factor, they can still show their independence while cooperating and working well with others.

An example of cooperation is a football team. Often making less pay, with little publicity, the offensive lineman's job is to make sure the quarterback does not get sacked by an onrushing defensive player.

Although the quarterback often makes a much higher salary and appears in TV commercials and magazine ads, the offensive lineman knows that their cooperation is what enables the team's success.

If a new assignment has been given to a team, being a leader with a dialed up cooperative Sub-factor will be productive. Initial meetings and discussions will be great when everyone has the chance to feel important and be a valued member of the team. Being too cooperative can also be a detriment. What if the independent individual becomes too cooperative and the meetings become more of a social gathering instead of coming up with true working plans? It is always very helpful for a team to work together to accomplish the final goal, but when there is too much cooperation and not enough independent leadership, the meetings may accomplish very little.

Next Steps

Next, you will explore the benefits and consequences of the Independence Sub-factor. If you think that this Sub-factor is important for your success, you can target your knowledge by investigating various ways to dial up or dial down your Independence Sub-factor in our 'How to' sessions.

20 How to Dial Up Independence

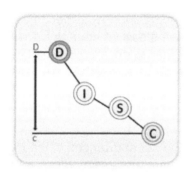

D>c
Independence

Sometimes life puts us in positions where we are dependent on the generosity or helpfulness of others. Growing up, for the most part, we had to rely on people to take care of us and provide us with our needs and wants. It is difficult to be completely independent when we have health or financial issues. This is also true when we are at college or have the misfortune to lose a job. However, there is a typical pattern of children being dependent and then maturing to become independent. Even when times get tough most adults prefer being self-reliant. Responsible adults prefer to maintain their personal freedom, self respect and confidence, and once they have established their independence and let go of external aid, they are loathe to return to a dependency status.

This session deals with independence. I want you to consider that there are degrees of independence. Independence comes in various forms and there are pros and cons to the extent that you are completely independent from others. Examining financial independence, it is desirable to be self-reliant, but if you want to purchase a home, you have to depend on the bank to provide a mortgage, otherwise, without this dependence, you would rent for years; perhaps never being in the position to purchase the home of your dreams. In most situations, there is indeed a period of dependence before independence - just as in purchasing a home, then after the mortgage is paid off, you will independently own it.

Mental independence is similar. To be an independent thinker is good to a certain extent, but at times this can hurt you. Imagine being so independent that you refuse to ask for assistance in getting critical information because you want to keep everything secret -- only to find out that in doing so you've missed a vital piece of data. Or picture a situation where you don't think about soliciting other people's input, with the result that you waste valuable resources when you find that another team has been working on the same problem set and are well ahead of your efforts. Or just consider the potential negative consequences of declining to seek out other people's ideas because your team wants to remain completely autonomous.

DISCflex™

Do you recognize how too much independence might be a detriment? The key is in knowing how much independence to have - in other words, how much should you dial up your independence? Think about this question: Have you ever wanted to accomplish a goal, but never did because you did not think you could achieve it on your own? Becoming more independent can give you the confidence to tackle your goals and successfully complete them.

Just like most things in life, to become more independent you need to set your mind to it and continually be motivated to be more self reliant. Independence is a frame of mind that you must commit to. Learning independence can take time, but if you feel that you need to become more independent, it is imperative that you start now! Here are some steps you can take to dial up your Independence Sub-factor.

Immediate Steps:

Whether you are a young person beginning to spread your wings and leave the family nest or a mature adult who has had to rely on someone else due to possible health or financial issues, you will probably find that your dependence or cooperativeness has spread to other areas of your life. Dependence has its time and place, such as relying on others to get their portion of a project completed, but the degree of independence you choose to exhibit in a situation focuses on your internal motivations and behaviors.

"To exist is to change, to change is to mature, to mature is to go on creating oneself endlessly."

~Henri L. Bergson

Dialing up your independence will help you tackle problems yourself, achieve goals that you have to labor on that you deem important, and possibly allow your self-reliance to increase. Taking the first steps toward becoming more independent and self-sufficient will be difficult. Fortunately, once you start down the road toward independent status you'll find it gets easier. So, with that in mind: Here are some immediate steps to help you become more independent.

1. **Make the Decision to Become More Independent.**

    An independent mind set begins and ends with you. Learn to understand that you are responsible for your life. If you get sick, get laid off, or are just having a bad day, recognizing that there is nothing holding you back except yourself is the key to becoming more independent. Be confident in your decision, knowing that with time and dedication, you can rely less on the people around you and achieve success on your own.

Christopher Reeve made the decision to overcome the incredible adversity in his life and is an amazing example of how to use mental independence to push yourself toward a goal.

On May 27, 1995, life for Christopher Reeve, the man who the world knew as Superman, changed in one devastating second. Reeve, an avid horseback rider, was competing in an equestrian event in Culpepper, Virginia. During the event, Reeve's horse started to jump over the third fence but suddenly stopped, throwing Reeve to the ground. His helmet saved him from brain damage, but the force of his two hundred and fifteen pound frame hitting the ground shattered his first and second vertebrae. The damage to the vertebrae was so substantial that his head was detached from his spine. The man, who will be forever remembered as Superman, in an instant, became a quadriplegic.

Many people would have given up on life, but Christopher Reeve made the decision to press on and live his life to the fullest. He was confined to a wheelchair and required a breathing apparatus for the rest of his life, but he didn't let it keep him from lobbying on the behalf of people with spinal cord injuries and founding the Christopher Reeve Foundation. He made the decision in the days following his accident to not allow his injury to keep him from leading a useful and productive life. His life has been an inspiration for thousands of people throughout the world. He co-founded the Reeve-Irvine Research Center, which is now one of the leading spinal cord research centers in the world. In 2002, the Christopher and Dana Reeve Paralysis Resource Center was opened in New Jersey with the mission to teach paralyzed people to live more independently. His decision to not let his injury affect his life and his independence gave him the self-determination to live a life that inspired and helped thousands.

2. **Set Goals.**

Setting goals for yourself is the epitome of independent thinking. Focus solely on yourself with questions like: What do I want to achieve? What type of work/life balance do I want to have?

What is important for me to accomplish so that I reach my full potential? What do I need to do to be the person I want to be? While answering questions like these, start to make a list of short term goals that you want to accomplish. You can sit down every day or once a week and write down what you want to get done that day or week that are 'Me' focused. Create deadlines and keep yourself accountable to them. Even if your personal goals for the day are to go to the grocery store and buy food for a new recipe you wanted to try, write them down! Be specific!

For example, if you want to get a promotion, don't just write "I want to get a promotion". When you are broad and vague when making your goals, you make your goals less personal and attainable. Be detailed and check your goals regularly to see if you are staying on track. For the example of getting a promotion, you could write, "I want to get a promotion to be the Associate Director of Sales by next April". Giving the title of the position and the date when you want it to happen makes it more solid and embeds it into your subconscious mind. By creating a list of independent lifestyle goals, your subconscious immediately begins making decisions that affect how you want to live your life. Try not to judge your goals by what others might think. Write the goals down that you want to achieve; even if they might not seem remotely important to anyone else. Sticking to your deadlines and successfully completing your self-governing goals in the time frames you established will instill confidence in your ability to get things done on your own; based on your own wants, dreams and desires. As your confidence grows, begin setting individual mid-range and long-term goals, too. Take the time to decide what you want to accomplish in your life during the next five years and write them down. Start a bucket list of things you would like to do before you die.

3. Be Positive.

Sometimes when we become accustomed to being dependent, we lose confidence in our ability to accomplish goals autonomously - without other people's assistance. Without having someone to guide or support us, we can become doubtful or negative about our chances of success. Negativity or insecurity can keep you dependent on other people because it can cause a fearful state of mind -- which in turn might limit your drive and desire to take on that goal and achieve success. When a situation arises where you feel like you can't do something, stop and ask yourself instead how you actually could do it. By using this type of question to propel your mind forward, toward finding a solution, you leave fear behind in your quest to find an answer to how to get your goal accomplished. This questioning and answering creative process will motivate you toward success and a more positive outlook.

Secondary Steps:

After following the immediate steps to help yourself dial up your independence, there are also some secondary steps that will help you achieve this goal. You can learn to appreciate independence and how it can positively affect you and your road to success. The will to be more independent doesn't always come naturally though. Accomplishment takes time, desire, and dedication to be successful and this is no different. Here are some more steps you can take to leading a more independent life:

1. Take Initiative.

Becoming independent and successful takes a willingness to be proactive and to take initiative in the situations where you want to dial up your independence. Don't wait for someone to tell you what to do at your work or around your house. If you see something that needs to get done, do it yourself! You have the freedom to become more independent! When you're at work, seek out work in your own area or department and also look for opportunities outside your comfort zone. Ask to join a team to offer support or volunteer on extra projects around the office. By demonstrating you are willing to go the extra mile with your job and accomplishing things on your own, you create a confidence in not only yourself, but from your coworkers and peers. This will aid you in becoming more independent.

"No problem can be solved by the same consciousness that created it. We need to see the world anew."

~Albert Einstein

Let's look at the story of Mother Teresa and how she took initiative.

2. Surround Yourself with Independent People or Take on an Independent Person as a Mentor.

Spend time with a person that exemplifies the Independence Sub-factor. Learn from them and begin to implement what you see into your own life. By spending time with dependent

Mother Teresa was born on August 26th, 1910 in what is now known as the Republic of Macedonia. From a young age, Mother Teresa was fascinated by the stories of the lives of missionaries and their service in India. When she was twelve years old, she was convinced that she should commit herself to a religious life. She left home at the age of eighteen to become a missionary, never seeing her family again. In 1946, Mother Teresa experienced what she later described as 'the call within the call'. She felt that she needed to leave the convent she was at and help the poor while living among them. Four years later, she founded the Missionaries of Charity in Calcutta, India. For over forty five years, Mother Teresa ministered to the poor, sick, orphaned, and dying, while guiding the Missionaries of Charity's expansion, first throughout India and then in other countries. She won a Nobel Peace Prize in 1979 for her humanitarian work and at the time of her death, Missionaries of Charity was operating six hundred and ten missions in one hundred and twenty three countries. The missions included hospices and homes for people with HIV/AIDS, leprosy and tuberculosis, soup kitchens, children and family counseling programs, orphanages, and schools. This and more came from her willingness to take initiative and make a difference. She saw a need in the world and dedicated her life to it, impacting thousands, if not millions, along the way.

The example that Mother Teresa sets is an excellent one. Through her independence and initiative she was able to make a difference in the lives of thousands of people that actually brought people closer together. Sometimes independence can lead to better connections between people.

people you surround yourself with the same attribute you are trying to stop using. Being around independent minded people will push you to rely on yourself because people that are independent and successful expect things to get done and don't usually let things go undone. They will push you to expect more from yourself, and not from the people around you.

3. Self-Evaluate Yourself.

Start by evaluating what your strengths and weaknesses are and determine what additional training or education is needed. Be candid about what you are good at and what you need to improve upon and write them down. Learning to be independent requires knowledge of who you are, what you're good at, and what you may not be good at. Knowing your areas of strengths and weaknesses gives you the ability to make positive changes in your life to create a path to success.

4. Keep Learning.

One reason you may be dependent is because you might currently lack the knowledge or training needed to accomplish your goals. Once you've created your list of strengths and weaknesses, start searching for ways to increase your knowledge and skills. Begin reading books that can help turn your weaknesses to strengths, participate in training seminars or conferences, or learn from a friend or coworker. If you have a dream or a goal you wish to accomplish, but don't have the skill set or knowledge to complete it yet, don't hesitate to learn! Take fifteen minutes a day and devote it to bettering yourself through education. The knowledge you gain can allow you to confidently go after any goal you might set for yourself.

21 How to Dial Down Independence

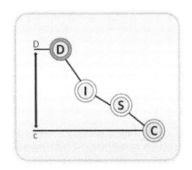

**D>c
Independence**

Remember that Independence D>c has the opposing Sub-factor of Cooperation C>d. All that might be required is that you dial up your cooperativeness and this alone will have the immediate impact of dialing back your Independence. As you learn the techniques in this session, immediately review the session on How to Dial Up your Cooperativeness, to fully understand the polar opposite of Independence.

Imagine a situation that you must work together in a group but you truly dislike group projects. You are fairly independent by nature anyway, and you believe that getting work done in a timely manner means just working on it alone. Besides, you're much more effective without all the hassles and time wasting that teams typically do - especially in your organization! Do you think teamwork on a project that is forcing people to work collaboratively together will go well and yield good results with people who have this belief? Have you ever been on a team and one person absolutely refuses to participate? Even if they were right about independent work sometimes being quicker and more efficient, were you excited to work with them? Would you avoid working with them again on another project? Probably so!

We all find ourselves in situations where we must be cooperative and collaborative in team or groups settings. In this type of environment, where teamwork is necessary -- even if we are naturally self-sufficient and autonomous -- we must dial down our independence for the benefit of the organization and those that we are working with on the team. Although it may be difficult, we must find ways to dial down our strong dominant Factors and dial up our teamwork parameters and regulations. In this case, we have to dial down our independent nature, and dial up our cooperativeness to be more efficient at work. If we don't we could miss out on people saying things like this about us: "She is an excellent team player - very cooperative." Or "He is willing to do whatever it takes to make the team successful and understands that teamwork is critical to our customer service program." Or "Susan led one of our most successful cooperative efforts. By working with other departments, she achieved something that many thought was impossible to accomplish." As you can hear from these comments, a lot of leaders value a commitment to teamwork. That doesn't mean that all instances require teamwork, being independent is also highly valued in employees. However, it does mean that you need to know how to dial down your independence when the situation requires it.

Immediate Steps:

Here are a few Immediate and Secondary steps that you can take to learn how to dial down your Independence at work.

1. **Be Helpful**

    When you learn that you are working with a team or will be collaborating, rather than instantly thinking the worst, perhaps immediately jumping to getting annoyed and frustrated, put yourself in a collaborative, helpful mindset. By helping others, you can guide them towards moving at your pace - which in the long run - will frustrate you less. Bringing your talent at getting things done - with your Elevated Dominance tendency - can really help the team and will satisfy your need to control some aspects of teamwork - even if you are not in charge. By collaborating it means that the project will be finished twice as fast. By channeling your elevated assertive behavior towards a team environment, everyone wins. An added benefit, by steering and guiding, you probably won't require having as much work to perform yourself.

    You'll be teaching others how to get more accomplished quicker if they don't have as much of an Elevated Dominance Factor.

    A word of warning here though, you have to make certain that you are not driving too hard and too fast; otherwise, your good intentions here can be misconstrued. For example: People may think that you are overstepping your boundaries, telling them what to do when you have no right to do so, or are being pushy.

2. **Context**

    As we said in many other sessions, understanding why you're working together in a group will make cooperating less intimidating. If team members feel like they don't know why they're working with a team, everyone may get frustrated and start questioning what purpose it holds to work together. When you recognize why you're collaborating, when you understand the mission and the purpose of why the team has been pulled together, and when you fully comprehend the benefits that are expected as a specific result of teamwork, it will be easier for you all to work together towards the common goal. In order to make sure that the team functions properly, you must first address the question of context. If you don't you are sure to have negative consequences as a result.

3. **Collaborate With Others.**

    When working on a project, if you have extra time, ask a coworker to look over your work product, mull over ideas, and get their slant on the issues your team is facing. When you are sharing ideas and getting insight this will open up dialogue with a view toward better communication.

Lilly Tartikoff understood that working with others was beneficial and used that belief to help thousands of people. Tartikoff was a member of the New York City Ballet Company from 1971 to 1980, and in 1982 she married Brandon Tartikoff, the newly named president of entertainment for NBC. During that same year, Brandon Tartikoff was diagnosed with Hodgkin's disease for the second time. On the advice of a physician friend, Brandon went to see a young oncological researcher at UCLA named Dennis Slamon. Dr. Slamon started treatment on Brandon in 1982 and one year later, amazingly, Brandon was free of the disease.

Once Hodgkin's disease was driven from her husband's body, Lilly Tartikoff didn't just move on. She started looking for ways to help other cancer patients. In 1989 she teamed up with Dr. Slamon to help him find funding for his research into breast cancer. She created a partnership with Ronald Perelman, the CEO of Revlon, together with Dr. Slamon. Perelman donated 2.4 million dollars to the scientist's work, with no restrictions. In 1990 they created the Revlon/UCLA Woman's Cancer Research Program as well as a successful new treatment for cancer that was soon saving numerous lives.

Lilly went on to establish the annual Fire and Ice Ball in Hollywood to raise money and a few years later she put together, with the help of the Entertainment Industry Foundation, the Revlon Run/Walk. These events have raised more than 18 million dollars for cancer research. In 1996 she helped create the National Woman's Cancer Research Alliance.

The incredible, significant task that Lilly Tartikoff took on could not be done by an individual. Her willingness to work with others and partner with people who could help her, made her and Dr. Slamon's dream possible.

Lilly Tartikoff's ability to utilize other people and be a part of a team has helped hundreds, if not thousands of cancer patients. She understood that she couldn't make a difference on her own and she took the necessary steps to seek help, which in turn helped thousands of people.

4. Make a Valuable Contribution.

It's important in group settings to remember that everyone provides a valuable contribution. Although you may keep thinking about all the ways you would do it better by yourself, it's important to keep in mind that everyone contributes something - even if it's not precisely what you would have done or how you would have done it. When a team is able to best use the skills of all team members efficiently and productively, teamwork magic happens. This is where a tendency for recognizing individual contributions to the team goals can provide a boost to the team. Giving an 'Atta boy!' or 'Atta girl!' can truly reap tremendous benefits. Recognizing contributions, skills, and talents makes people proud of themselves and solidifies their commitment to the team. It enhances their motivation to be more effective. So, understanding

> *The Law of the Bench states that "Great teams have great depth". John C. Maxwell in his book, The 17 Indisputable Laws of Teamwork, gives an example of how this is true.*
>
> *In 2000, Maxwell and a few of his friends and family went to a football game between the Georgia Tech Yellow Jackets and the Florida State Seminoles. The games between the two were usually close and extremely competitive. Even though FSU was the favorite that year, the game promised to be an exciting one and on that day, they weren't disappointed. The two teams battled for three quarters and at the end of the third quarter with Georgia Tech leading fifteen to twelve, Maxwell told his friends, "Come on, guys. This one is over."*
>
> *His friends were astonished that he wanted to leave the game early and they asked why. On the way to their car, Maxwell explained why the game was already over. Yes, the Yellow Jackets were hanging in there against FSU, especially when it came to the way Georgia Tech was playing defense, which was impressive considering the vaunted offense that FSU had. Maxwell noticed something throughout the game though.*
>
> *While Georgia Tech had kept their starters in for the majority of the game, FSU had substituted freely without a noticeable drop in performance. Because of that, Maxwell knew it would only be a matter of time before the Georgia Tech players became worn down. Sure enough, the game ended with FSU on top, 26 - 21.*

this, be the one who makes the concentrated effort to recognize people's contributions.

That is the impact of the Law of the Bench. Great teams have great depth. The Law of the Bench is an excellent illustration of how by being able to trust and use your teammates, you and your team can accomplish more.

5. Volunteer for Group Projects.

Although you may loathe group projects and avoid them at all costs, you must practice being on teams in case you find yourself on a very important group project in the future. You have to make sure that you are already well versed in dialing down your independence and dialing up your cooperativeness, collaborativeness, and teamwork skills well prior to being in a situation where you really need those skills. The more you practice and get comfortable in a group setting, the better you will react when forced to work on a group project. I suggest that you review the course on Teambuilding in the online suite if this is a skill that you need to enhance.

6. Let Others Speak And Refrain From Interrupting.

Although you may be used to taking control of meetings or in situations where people might be reluctant to speak, refrain from doing so immediately. Silence has a way of bringing people out because it is uncomfortable -- unless someone breaks that silence. Usually, the quieter people don't have long to wait before a more dominant person chimes in. I caution you to wait though. Just sit back and let someone else say something for a change. You may realize that someone else in the room is a valuable player, but has been waiting for a more opportune moment to speak out.

You'll never know what you might hear from the more silent folks until you sit back and listen. Remember to avoid interrupting people when they are talking. Many people do not even realize that they have a habit of doing this! And if they knew, would be embarrassed because they consider it rude behavior. People interrupt for any number of reasons, but mostly it is because they are excited to add to the conversation. Rarely do people do it to be rude. Another reason people interrupt is to move the conversation along. They are frustrated with the speaker's pace and in an effort to remove their frustration, they interrupt and finish the speaker's thought.

Although this indeed might make the conversation go quicker, it might make the project go slower if that person is not allowed to finish what may have been a very important point. The bottom line: Don't interrupt. There are many other more effective tactics for moving people along if they are moving too slowly during meetings or in conversations. Many of these are detailed in the Facilitation course. I suggest that you review them if you do uncover a habit of interrupting people.

Secondary Steps:

After completing the immediate steps, you can turn your attention to a few secondary steps to help dial down independence.

1. Build Trust.

Remember from the session on dialing up cooperativeness that you always have to build trust, so make sure you put an emphasis on trust and rapport building.

2. Participate in a Team Sport.

If you belong to a gym, see what team sports are available. The more you work with a team, the more comfortable you will be relying on others and understanding that a few people coming together to work on a goal is often better than one person working by themselves.

22 Friendliness Generic Profile

Definition

When Influence is greater than Dominance, you have the Sub-factor of friendliness. People with this Sub-factor are naturally friendly and love communicating with other people. The friendly person is an extrovert and is usually not afraid to make small talk with anyone. They are very outgoing and get along well with others. Many see people with this Sub-factor as fun, entertaining, and a pleasure to be around.

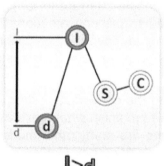

I>d
Friendliness

Descriptors

Here is a list of words that relate to the Sub-factor of friendliness:

- Openness
- Easiness
- Responsiveness
- Kindliness
- Camaraderie

- Sociability
- Outgoingness
- Affability
- Amiability
- Congeniality

Strengths

The inherent strengths of the Friendliness Sub-factor are the ability to communicate effectively with other people, gaining rapport with others, and building trust. Communicating effectively means that this type of person inherently understands the laws of influence and is able to command them to their needs. Gaining rapport with others is a particularly good strength because it allows this type of person to make friends easier, use effective body language, and gain a connection with other people.

This is my preferred Sub-factor at networking events. When I am networking, I remember to use the strengths of this trait, such as gaining rapport and building trust, to meet new people and get more business. This Sub-factor can even help you when you don't realize it.

One of the luckiest moments I've had in my sales career happened when the restrooms were out of order in my client's building. My client had made an arrangement with the business owner next door to use their restrooms until repairs were made. I had never seen such nice restrooms. I was in a really friendly mood, so I took the time to thank the receptionist for letting me use the restrooms. I mentioned that I admired the modern look of the whole office. I made some conversation and asked if the owner was a man or a woman and commented on how young looking and hip the décor was. The receptionist responded by telling me that the female entrepreneur always said that she was 70 years young. It was evident by my facial expression that I was expecting someone much younger to have such a modern taste. Then luck entered the picture. As I was about to leave, the receptionist gestured and asked if I would like to compliment the owner myself since she was entering the building. The receptionist was in total rapport with me because of our great conversation. By sheer luck, I was introduced to the owner and she gave me a tour of the office. We began to talk about business, and through our dialogue I was able to pique her interest in what we had to offer. Within two weeks, I made a huge sale by taking advantage of an opportunity that had presented itself thanks to my unintended use of the Friendliness Sub-factor.

Weaknesses

The weaknesses related to the Friendliness Sub-factor are a lack of concentration on mundane tasks, a resistance to doing task-oriented work, and getting easily distracted from daily work for social interaction. Ordinary tasks don't interest a person with the Friendliness Sub-factor because they don't provide the sort of entertainment and communication they crave. The same is true of task-oriented work. People with the Friendliness Sub-factor prefer people-oriented work. This type of person is a great salesperson and spokesperson. Other weaknesses relate around dominating the social environment and controlling conversations.

I remember being at a company dinner where I encountered an employee who overused his friendliness to the point that he dominated every conversation he was in. Although this employee was very good-natured and wanted to build a friendship with the guest speaker that night, he ended up pushing the speaker away from him. It all started when this person was put at the same table as myself and the guest speaker. During dinner, the entire conversation was dominated by this employee and everyone else was looking around at each other, wondering what was going on. My personal rule is that for every ten minutes of conversation, you should divide that time by the number of people in the conversation.

Since there were five people at our table, each person at the table should have had two minutes to talk. But ideally, the guest speaker would have had more time to talk since we were there to hear from him, a decorated colonel. Later that night, after dinner, the colonel was talking to me and a few other people. The same man from dinner barged into the conversation and again dominated the conversation. I knew what he was going to do, so I looked at my watch to time how long he would speak for. During this time I noticed the colonel trying to politely get out of the conversation. By the time I found someone to step in and take the colonel out of the conversation, it had been seventeen minutes! The colonel went so far as to call the man a 'blowhard' and thanked me for saving him. It wasn't until I was giving feedback to this employee that I realized he thought he was doing something good. It turns out this employee thought that the conversation was getting dull between the colonel and some of the people he was talking to, so he wanted to step in to make sure that the colonel had a good time. I explained to him that I understood his intentions, but it actually produced the exact opposite result.

It is important to understand there are three perceptual positions to each Sub-factor in each situation you are in. The man from the example only looked at the situation from his perceptual position, which caused the colonel to become annoyed with him.

> *"I pretended to be somebody I wanted to be until finally I became that person. Or he became me."*
>
> **~Cary Grant**

Situational Adaptation - Dial Up or Dial Down

Friendliness has to be dialed up and dialed down according to the occasion. If you are a manager, you need to dial down your friendliness in order to show your employees that you are serious about getting work done and won't accept mediocre work. Sometimes friendliness can harm you in managerial situations because employees think that they can get away with not doing things or failing to make deadlines. You need to dial up your friendliness, however, when at a networking event or when you are with a client. You need to be able to build rapport quickly because you don't have much time to talk to each person at a networking event. When with a client, you need to be able to build rapport and trust during each conversation. Friendliness can be one of the best Sub-factors to have if you know how to use it effectively.

Just imagine your best employee's ability to talk to customers. He is able to dial up his Friendliness Sub-factor and build rapport with them. I look for employees that are able to dial up this Sub-factor. When I am in the hiring process, I make note of how each person does in terms of rapport building with me. If I feel they do really well, I am much more likely to hire them, because I know they will treat customers right. If they seem oblivious to building rapport and building good relationships, I know that I shouldn't hire that person because of the adverse effects it will have on customer service.

> *I always remember the story of Jackie Robinson and Pee Wee Reese when I think of how powerful the Friendliness Sub-factor can be when it is dialed up by just a simple gesture. When Jackie Robinson went to the Brooklyn Dodgers, he knew that he was going to face extreme discrimination, from both the fans and other players. In one of the games that season, he was playing poorly and having a bad day. The crowd was particularly loud and mean with their slurs and boos that day as well. Imagine being in Jackie Robinson's situation and facing nothing but rejection from everyone around you. Something happened that day that brought Jackie Robinson through those horrible ordeals. The shortstop for the Brooklyn Dodgers, Pee Wee Reese, come over to Jackie Robinson when the crowd was getting very rowdy and put his arm around him. That simple gesture was enough to keep his determination to play the game he loved. He is even quoted as saying, "That gesture saved my career. Pee Wee made me feel as if I belonged."*

DISCflex™

On the opposite side, you have a very efficient boss who is encouraging the team to move along with the project. He is aware of the best way to handle the details due to great organizational skills. Add to that his ability to get the team motivated and excited with his friendly approach and the boss could get great results. If he shows too much efficiency, the team will wait for his ideas on how to move forward. He will have to dial up his friendliness and rapport to coach the team to get pumped up, work hard, and come up with their suggestions of how to approach the situation. Friendliness can be a great Sub-factor to get your employees or team motivated and input their ideas into the process. It can also help team members with lower self-esteem to stand up and feel supported in the workplace.

I want you to remember that story whenever you have the urge to exclude someone or make fun of someone. Jackie Robinson will go down in history as one of the best baseball players and also one of the most courageous people to ever walk this planet. A friendly gesture can go a long way to making your organization a better place to work. Take the time to dial up your friendliness to get to know your co-workers and you will find your career will skyrocket with promotions.

Next Steps

Next, you will explore the benefits and consequences of the Friendliness Sub-factor. If you think that this Sub-factor is important for your success, you can target your knowledge by investigating various ways to dial up or dial down your Friendliness Sub-factor in our 'How to' sessions.

23 How to Dial Up Friendliness

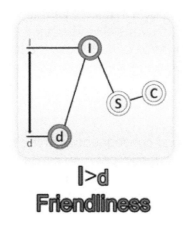

I>d
Friendliness

The brief definition of friendliness would consist of being nice to, and interested in, other people. It isn't always easy to be nice and considerate to the people around you. It's easy to point out when other people aren't being friendly, but we tend to ignore it when we ourselves are unfriendly. Being friendly and having a pleasing personality increases the rapport we have with people and helps to build and maintain relationships with not only our coworkers but our friends too. It can take a dedicated and desired effort to become friendlier because sometimes it takes us out of our comfort zones. With the right commitment and understanding, you can increase your friendliness to successfully build your relationships, not only at work, but in life.

Here are some ways for you to increase your friendliness. By dedicating your time and efforts, you can become friendlier. Remember that it might take work, but with enough practice and perseverance you can dial up your friendliness to build more rapport with those around you!

Immediate Steps:

First, you can take some immediate steps to help become friendlier. How many times have you walked down the road and gotten a friendly smile and a wave from a neighbor? Or had a coworker ask you about your day? We all enjoy it when people show interest in us and our lives, but how many times have we passed up the same opportunity to do the same for someone else? Here are some steps you can take to immediately begin your journey to becoming friendlier.

1. Find out What Irritates You or What Your Pet Peeves Are.

We all have things that other people do that irritate us, but have you ever thought that you might do some things that subconsciously annoy others? No one likes to be around people with annoying habits or mannerisms. Recognize that all your efforts in trying to be friendly will be wasted if you don't examine this area and correct anything that people won't like. Take a piece of paper and write down the top five things that irritate you that other people do. This could be things like being late for a meeting, tapping a foot, chewing gum, or other things like this. Do you do the same thing? Put yourself in their shoes and examine where you can be friendlier. Be honest with yourself and make it a goal to not do the things on your list to the people around you that you have marked pet peeves for. Finally, ask some trusted friends or coworkers to be brutally honest with you. Ask them point blank if there is anything that you do that is annoying. Make sure that you tell them that you are trying to be less annoying and need their honest feedback. Make sure you thank them when they tell you the truth - even if it stings! Remember you can't fix something if you don't know it exists.

2. Make a Concentrated Effort to Engage in a Conversation with People in Your Life and Ask Questions About Them.

Have you ever tried making pleasant conversation with someone you've run into, and they blew you off by giving one word responses and obviously looking disinterested? You most likely left that conversation thinking they were pretty unfriendly. When someone is trying to chat with you, make an effort to give them something back in return and to take an interest in them. Ask open-ended questions that stimulate discussions. There may be times when you don't have the time to stop and talk, but by being considerate and asking questions to find out about what is happening in other people's lives, you can help your relationship with that person.

If you see someone you know, go over and see what's going on with them. There doesn't have to be a reason, just show an interest in their lives. Maintaining friendships and relationships is tantamount to being successful in business and life.

3. Be Positive

Not many people, if any, enjoy the company of someone who continually takes a negative view of life. "Smile and the world smiles with you, weep and you weep alone." Everyone has down days, but the world doesn't beat down the door of someone who looks on the negative side of things. Learn to be positive and cheerful. There is usually a positive side to every situation and learning to see that will help you become friendlier. Every day wake up knowing that great things will happen. This will make you happier by simple cause and effect and will allow you to significantly dial up your Friendliness Sub-factor. Be positive before any meeting and you will find that people will like you more and in turn more will get done.

4. Listen to Other People Much More Than You Talk.

You were born with two ears and one mouth for a reason. The friendliest people I know use the ratio of ears to mouth and do a lot more listening than talking. This is great advice for a number of reasons -- but the most important is that when you truly listen to people, they open up more and tend to be friendlier in return. Attentive listening is the key to long lasting friendships.

> *"Personality is an unbroken series of successful gestures."*
>
> *~F. Scott Fitzgerald*

Secondary Steps:

Now that you know some immediate steps to take to dial up your Friendliness Sub-factor, here are some secondary steps. Being friendlier isn't just so you can have more companions and friends, though you probably will with the use of this Sub-factor in your life. Becoming friendlier will help you be more successful at your job and create more opportunities for you to accomplish your goals. Here are some additional steps you can take to help you become friendlier:

1. Invite People to Spend Time With You.

Ask if they would like to go out to dinner, participate in tennis or golf, or other activities like scrapbooking or going for a walk or to a museum. Make sure that the activity you pick is one where you have plenty of discussion time. Activities like plays or movies most often run counterproductive to the goal of becoming friendlier.

Have you ever transferred to a new job or town and felt out of place until someone invited you to hang out? It most likely felt nice to have someone extend an invitation to spend time with you. Learn to do the same thing. Start being the one to invite people to do something, rather than the other way around. You don't have to know the person especially well, because spending time with them will give you the opportunity to take a genuine interest in their lives and who they are. Be open and generous in your invitations. Obviously, your invitations won't always be accepted, but by doing so, you show people that you are willing to spend time with them and get to know who they really are.

2. Go to Places Where People are Having Conversations.

It can be hard to practice becoming friendlier if you spend all your time alone. It may seem simple, but go where other people are. If you're at work and everyone is going to lunch together, join them. If you are at a networking event and everyone is talking in one area of the room, go be with them. This doesn't mean you have to do everything the crowd does, but when you have a chance to interact and engage other people, take advantage of it. Make it a habit to be a part of whatever the group might be discussing or doing. This will show that you want to spend time with people and that you make the effort to. Eventually, you will be seen as a fun, outgoing person who gets along well with others. This type of perception can work wonders in the workplace.

3. Remember the Golden Rule.

"Do to others as you would have done to you." This is the key to becoming friendlier and achieving success in not only your professional life, but your personal life as well. Learn to put yourself in other people's shoes and try to see the world through their eyes. Do you enjoy it when someone you are talking to seems disinterested? Remembering that there are other people involved besides yourself will help you to be more approachable, less arrogant, and friendlier.

4. Practice Humility.

Many people think that humility is a negative virtue in today's society. Nothing could be farther from the truth. The book Good to Great by Jim Collins shows that the best leaders have a great

DISCflex™

sense of humility. There are certainly times when humility isn't appropriate, but arrogance can be the killer of growth and it can be extremely hard to make friends when you aren't humble. Humility is essential for the type of personality you need to achieve personal success, no matter what your goal is.

It is a positive force that shows no limitations and even though it may seem like a small thing, don't over look it. Humility is a vital ingredient of greatness and anything you might look to accomplish in life.

5. Be Genuinely Interested in Learning From and About Other People.

This can be very difficult to do genuinely, but it can help you tremendously if you strive to be friendlier. People can tell when the person they are talking to is disinterested or bored, even if it they only recognize it subconsciously. This can give them a negative perception of the person they're talking to, which can be hard to change. When you are engaged in a conversation with someone, try to learn something new about them. Ask people open ended questions that let them know you are genuinely interested in them. Remember, people love to talk, and giving them a forum to do this will make you appear very friendly. This will help you gain their trust and be perceived as friendly and approachable.

> *Dale Carnegie is a master at helping us understand how to communicate with other people. The best way to do that: Take a genuine interest in the person you are talking to.*
>
> *Dale Carnegie outlined this principle in his bestseller How to Win Friends and Influence People. Carnegie believed that to be good at communication and improve your friendliness, you had to take a genuine interest in the people that you are trying to befriend. Dale Carnegie outlines six ways to make people like you. They are:*
>
> *1. First, become genuinely interested in other people.*
> *2. Second, smile.*
> *3. Third, remember that a person's name is to that person the sweetest and most important sound in any language.*
> *4. Next, be a good listener. Encourage others to talk about themselves.*
> *5. Fifth, talk in terms of the other person's interests.*
> *6. Finally, make the other person feel important- and do it sincerely*
>
> *Dale Carnegie's work helps us understand how genuinely showing interest in someone else can help you establish rapport and gain their trust.*

24 How to Dial Down Friendliness

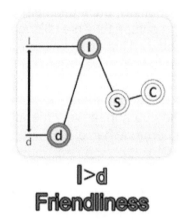

I>d
Friendliness

Can you imagine trying to get your work done while your coworker talks your ear off and hangs around having a conversation? Or, knowing that a deadline is fast approaching and your coworker wants you to go to lunch with them? If you are constantly talking and socializing at work, you won't get much done, at least not as much as you could do if you were more focused on your task at hand.

In times like these, we must dial down our friendliness to get things accomplished and stay on track. You have to ascertain how to become more efficient while not destroying or damaging your relationships.

In these cases, you must learn to dial down your friendliness in order to get things done. Remember that the opposing Sub-factor of friendliness I>d is efficiency D>i. Fortunately, all that might be required is that you dial up your efficiency and this alone will have the immediate impact of dialing back your friendliness.

Immediate Steps:

Here are a few steps that you can take to learn how to dial down your friendliness.

1. **Stay Focused and Don't Get Distracted.**

    Usually, we start talking and looking for a distraction when we're unfocused and bored. If you've been typing away at a project for hours and you want a break, generally you'll look for a diversion. Although this may be a nice break for you, you may get carried away and talk too long or your coworker won't get the work they need to get done finished. Don't go looking for distractions to take you away from your work, especially talking to others during crunch times.

The story of the Ant and the Grasshopper provides us with a good example of how being too friendly can keep you from doing your job efficiently. Be careful to not let your friendliness distract you from your job. Are you an ant or are you the grasshopper? Don't wait until winter arrives to find out!

Now let's look at Aesop's fable of the Ant and the Grasshopper.
Once there lived an ant and a grasshopper in a grassy meadow.

All day long the ant would work hard, collecting grains of wheat from the farmer's field far away. She would hurry to the field every morning, as soon as it was light enough to see by, and toil back with a heavy grain of wheat balanced on her head. She would put the grain of wheat carefully away in her larder, and then hurry back to the field for another one. All day long she would work, without stop or rest, scurrying back and forth from the field, collecting the grains of wheat and storing them carefully.

The grasshopper would look at her and laugh. 'Why do you work so hard, dear ant?' he would say. 'Come, rest awhile, and listen to my song. Summer is here, the days are long and bright. Why waste the sunshine in labor and toil?'

The ant would ignore him, and with head bent, would simply hurry to the field a little faster. This would make the grasshopper laugh even louder. 'What a silly little ant you are!' he would call after her. "Come, come and dance with me! Forget about work! Enjoy the summer! Live a little!" And the grasshopper would hop away across the meadow, singing and dancing merrily.

Summer faded into autumn, and autumn turned into winter. The sun was hardly seen, and the days were short and grey, the nights long and dark. It became freezing cold, and snow began to fall.

The grasshopper didn't feel like singing any more. He was cold and hungry. He had nowhere to shelter from the snow, and nothing to eat. The meadow and the farmer's field were covered in snow, and there was no food to be had. "Oh what shall I do? Where shall I go?" wailed the grasshopper. Suddenly he remembered the ant. "Ah - I shall go to the ant and ask her for food and shelter!" declared the grasshopper, perking up. So off he went to the ant's house and knocked at her door. "Hello ant!" he cried cheerfully. "Here I am, to sing for you, as I warm myself by your fire, while you get me some food from that larder of yours!"

The ant looked at the grasshopper and said, "All summer long I worked hard while you made fun of me, and sang and danced. You should have thought of winter then! Find somewhere else to sing, grasshopper! There is no warmth or food for you here!" And the ant shut the door in the grasshopper's face.

Don't let yourself be distracted from your job by your surroundings and let your friendliness take you away from your work. You must stay focused on the task at hand and complete it efficiently.

2. Find an Appropriate Break.

If you must take a break, resolve not to talk to anyone just to pass the time. This might be great for you as a distraction but could really hurt the other person if you put them behind on their task list. Instead, stand up, stretch, or close your eyes for a few seconds and take a few deep breaths. When you start talking to someone, you may find it hard to stop and then you'll lose important time needed to get things done.

3. Make a Priority List.

Make a list of things that MUST be accomplished and the order they must be done in. Pay attention to deadlines. If you think you have too much time and can slack off a bit to socialize or do something else, you may end up shooting yourself in the foot and not being able to finish in time. This will cause you undue stress. When things must be done, there is no time for socialization and friendliness must come only in reason. Work first, fun later!

Let's consider this situation. You just won a million dollars and you decide to buy two building lots to erect a couple of homes. You hire an architect to design two identical houses and he gives you the blue prints. All the materials are delivered to the sites and you hire a couple of carpenters. You tell them all about the house and even show them a picture of what it's going to look like.

You give one carpenter a blueprint and you give the other carpenter the picture of the house and say 'go to it, boys'. The carpenter with the blue print builds the home efficiently, step by step. Unfortunately, the carpenter without the blue print ends up spending much more time on the house which costs you more money and causes everyone on the project greater stress and anxiety. The blue print is a plan that is used to help the carpenters utilize the time, money, and materials that they have to construct the house. Its instructions help cut down on wasted time and effort, bringing the project successfully to completion, on time, on budget.

Having a plan can help you stay focused and on task at work and in life. It can help you work efficiently and successfully, thereby reducing unnecessary stress.

Without a clear, defined plan, it can be hard to accomplish your goals in life and at work. Creating a list of goals and items that need to be done will help you stay focused and work efficiently.

"Self-improvement is the name of the game, and your primary objective is to strengthen yourself, not to destroy an opponent."

~Maxwell Maltz

Secondary Steps:

1. **Recognize That Others Will Understand**

   You may feel bad turning down an invitation to lunch or feel uncomfortable by telling a coworker that you'll have to cancel on them, but they will understand if you explain the situation. Whenever you have to dial down your friendliness, just take a moment or two to tell others why you have to do so. This is important for maintaining relationships. You are there to work and you have work to do. However, you are still dedicated to being their friend. If you have to turn someone down or tell them you'll get together another time, they may be disappointed at first, but they will understand. That's what true friendships are all about after all. Please remember that you have to have balance. All work and no play makes Jack a very dull boy! Strike a fair balance between friendliness and work responsibilities. Communication is the key. The hardest thing for thoughtful people to say is 'no'. If you say yes to everyone, however, you'll lose track of your work priorities and end up becoming less efficient and getting less done. This may result in having more friends and less chance of promotion! Remember that efficiency and friendliness are on opposite ends of the behavior spectrum. You must say no occasionally for efficiency's sake, and believe that your friends will understand and know where you're coming from.

2. **Roles and Responsibilities Dictate the Level of Friendliness**

   Imagine a situation where you worked hard for promotion of an extremely friendly team. You proved your worth and were recognized as a leader. Now you have gone from team mate to team leader. Whenever events like these occur, the level of friendliness must change. Again, the best thing to do is communicate with all team members and let them know why your level of friendliness is changing and precisely how you intend to dial down your friendliness. It might be that at work you will no longer go out to lunch as much. However, you plan to keep work and social friendliness completely separate. Talk through how things might change and how your situation requires you to have to dial down your friendliness and you'll find that you and those you care about will make the transition easier. If you fail to communicate, you fail in your responsibility as team leader. Explain your new responsibilities and how these will affect your relationship parameters.

25 Enthusiasm Generic Profile

Definition

When Influence is greater than Steadiness, you have the Enthusiasm Sub-factor. This is an extrovert Sub-factor and has the signs of an outgoing person. People with the Enthusiasm Sub-factor offer a great deal of positive energy into any activity they participate in. They also have a very energetic pace and are able to keep up with others. People with this Sub-factor do not hide their interest in a topic; rather they show it very strongly.

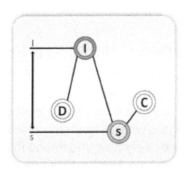

I>s
Enthusiasm

Descriptors

Words pertaining to the Enthusiasm Sub-factor are:

- Eagerness
- Keenness
- Passion
- Zest
- Earnestness

- Interest
- Fervor
- Zeal
- Conviction
- Vivacity

Strengths

The strengths of the Enthusiasm Sub-factor are positive energy, openness of self, and an ability to motivate others to have enthusiasm as well. Positive energy is important to your way of life. Thinking positively and acting positively allow good things to happen to you which motivate this

Sub-factor further. People with this Sub-factor are more open about their feelings and thoughts due to the mixture of being an extrovert and having positive energy. Motivating others is another great strength of the Enthusiasm Sub-factor. Positive energy flows through the enthusiastic person to others and makes the people around them enhance their Enthusiasm Sub-factor. If others around them have the Enthusiasm Sub-factor as well, then you will be able to dial up their enthusiasm too.

People who make great use of the Enthusiasm Sub-factor typically have a certain frame of life. Everyone knows the person that is constantly exuberant and energetic, whether they are facing problems or getting rewards.

A good story to understand the frame that a person with the Enthusiasm Sub-factor puts themselves in is the story of an old woman. This old woman quite poor, seemed to face an unusual amount of trouble, and was often said to have back luck. Yet all the while she had the most consistent cheerfulness of anyone in the town. Eventually the townsfolk started to wonder how she was able to keep such an enthusiastic outlook on life. She replied openly, "Well, you see, it's like this. The Bible says often, 'And it came to pass,' never, 'It came to stay.'" That frame of mind is what defines enthusiastic people. They are always looking at the brighter side of life, finding pleasure in daily events.

Weaknesses

The weaknesses of the Enthusiasm Sub-factor are an inability to effectively understand and help people in negative moods and a tendency to delve into things too fast without thinking it through. People with a lot of enthusiasm have a hard time understanding how some people can get so down about things. This leads to an inability to help those people get through their negative mood. The Enthusiasm Sub-factor also gives off the tendency to delve into things too fast and without thinking. Although there is usually positive energy flowing into the project or activity, it sometimes falls through when there is little forethought and only emotions going into making the event happen.

I notice the Enthusiasm Sub-factor as a weakness when new ideas are brought up. Even though I believe we should defer judgment until we do research on an idea, sometimes team members dismiss it rapidly. I've seen some of my team members have genuine excitement in an idea, only to be shut down by the first peer they tell it to. This causes their mood to swing from enthusiasm to anger, frustration, or a similar negative emotion. I've taught my co-workers to understand that the other party isn't trying to ruin your day, but rather give advice from their perspective. Too much enthusiasm can lead us to negative emotions if we or our ideas are rejected.

"The best contribution one can make to humanity is to improve oneself."

~Author Unknown

Situational Adaptation - Dial Up or Dial Down

Enthusiasm is a great Sub-factor to have in business. You can dial up your enthusiasm throughout the Sales Process in order to get your client excited about your product or service. In management you can dial up your enthusiasm to your employees in order to get them genuinely excited about completing a project.

Even though you will have to learn which employees or which clients have the behavioral tendencies of an enthusiastic person, the positive energy that you create is sure to help the mood of the workplace.

Sam Walton was one of the best at dialing up his enthusiasm. He prided his business on friendly service and low prices. The one thing that he learned throughout his career was celebrating achievements. He would give goals to his company and promise to celebrate them one way or another when they were achieved. For one goal in particular, achieving a net pretax profit of more than 8 percent, he vowed that when the goal was met he would do the hula on Wall Street. Sure enough, Wal-Mart met the numbers for that year and Sam Walton, at age 71, was off to Wall Street to do the hula with some Hawaiian dancers. Sam Walton knew how to use the Enthusiasm Sub-factor to encourage growth in his organization.

There are also times when you will need to dial down your enthusiasm. Most of these instances revolve around whether or not the moment needs to have a serious tone. This can be when you are helping out a friend in a rough spot, where you will need to dial down your enthusiasm while they are in the negative phases of the Transitional Time Line and dial up your enthusiasm during the positive phases of the Transitional Time Line. Enthusiasm can help make every day of your life better, but you still need to understand when to dial down your enthusiasm. Use the degrees of attitude to specifically list when your enthusiasm works well and when it doesn't quite fit the situation.

The positive side to working with an enthusiastic person is usually their overall enthusiasm. It is easy to get caught up in the excitement of the plans because enthusiasm can be contagious. Just imagine if you were working on a team project and the members of the team all present a down and negative view of the work to be done. They would all reluctantly trudge forward – unless you toss in an enthusiastic individual into the mix. Their enthusiasm may just be the needed impetuous to motivate the team to get moving. On the negative side, this committee member may not exercise control over their actions, words, and emotions because they are excited. They need to focus on facts and take the time to plan in a rational logical manner rather than relying too much on emotional involvement.

Next Steps

Next, you will explore the benefits and consequences of the Enthusiasm Sub-factor. If you think that this Sub-factor is important for your success, you can target your knowledge by investigating various ways to dial up or dial down your Enthusiasm Sub-factor in our 'How to' sessions.

"Many people who excel are self-taught."

~Herb Ritts

26 How to Dial Up Enthusiasm

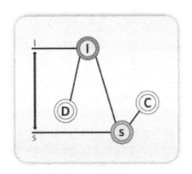

I>s
Enthusiasm

A famous football coach once said to his team, "If you aren't fired with enthusiasm, you will be fired, with enthusiasm!" He went on to tell his team, which had won just one game the year before, "You are to have confidence in me and enthusiasm for my system….let enthusiasm take hold of you – beginning now!" The next season his team won seven games, the following year they brought home a division title and a world championship in the third year. Through his enthusiastic leadership he was able to influence and motivate his team to the ultimate success in football, a world championship. With renewed passion and enthusiasm for the game, hall of famer Vince Lombardi's Green Bay Packers players produced astounding results.

Enthusiasm and passion are important in anyone's life and through practice and determination, they can be implemented. Think about those times in life when you or other team members lost enthusiasm for a project. I'll bet that the burning desire and perhaps even the motivation to keep working on the project went with it. That doesn't mean that you didn't finish; it just means that the party went out of the project. It might just be that when your enthusiasm left, it went from fun and exciting to mundane. In some instances, when enthusiasm leaves, a project can get pushed to the side and forgotten about. Learning to be enthusiastic about life and work can help you be more successful. Helping team members sustain their enthusiasm is a valuable talent. So knowing that enthusiasm is a valuable skill, let's learn how to Dial Up your enthusiasm. Taking the time to practice the steps we're going to over today will help you become more enthusiastic.

"Never neglect an opportunity for improvement."

~Sir William Jones

Immediate Steps:

When you are working on a project, who would you rather be around? Someone who exudes vitality, enthusiasm, and passion about life or a pessimistic, down trodden bore? When given the choice, the majority of people from all walks of life would rather befriend the optimistic, enthusiastic, upbeat person. Enthusiastic individuals are able to establish rapport quickly with others which helps to influence them. Remember that enthusiasm, just like any other trait, takes time and dedication to master. Here are some immediate steps that you can take to dial up your enthusiasm right away.

1. Be Positive

A positive mental attitude is a critical component for having enthusiasm. It is the foundation and without being positive you cannot become excited. Since excitement and enthusiasm are sister emotions, it stands to reason that you have to put yourself in a positive, upbeat state of mind before becoming enthusiastic. Our mental state can determine how we think and react to different situations and when we are negative our actions will follow our mindset. Practice seeing the good in things and learn to use positive self-talk. All religions and philosophies understand the power of being positive and looking on the brighter side of life. Learn to recognize when you are using negative self-talk and change it to positive self-talk. Be especially aware of your thoughts and the phrases you use to influence yourself and those around you. Words have impact on your psyche - so choose them well.

When you are dialing up your enthusiasm it doesn't matter if you say things aloud or silently - they have the same effect. Write down some words or phrases that remind you to be enthusiastic and excited. It's not hard to conjure them up if you already have thought about precisely what they are. Preparation and repeating your enthusiasm mantras are the key. Being positive and having the right words on the tip of your tongue can help change a possibly boring situation into a fun and exciting occasion.

2. Take Action.

Too many times we can become bogged down by thinking and formulating too many ideas and not enough action. If you stay in the 'ideas world' without seeing results, enthusiasm will wane. Most people will quickly lose enthusiasm over even the most exciting plans when nothing ever moves forward or actually gets done. Make an effort to take action, even if it is something small. Attack your tasks with energy and jump right in. Even if a task may at first seem mundane and boring, stay positive and keep moving. Telling yourself that "It's so boring!" doesn't make anything better and will only slow you down. Use positive self-talk. Remember Mary Poppins' advice that a 'spoonful of sugar helps the medicine go down'. Mary Poppins knew that positive self-talk and positive beliefs would lead to a more enthusiastic outlook toward completing tasks. In the movie, even the task of cleaning up the children's room became fun and soon the children were enthusiastically helping complete what they had thought was an initially boring project. Continually bring a higher level of energy into your projects when you need to dial up your Enthusiasm Sub-factor. This can help you in every aspect of your life and lead to more success and motivation -- both professionally and personally.

Martin Luther King Jr. blended enthusiasm with his non-violent method of protesting. He had taken from Gandhi the process, but added on the influencing Factor of enthusiasm. Examining his speaking style, he was able to motivate people to follow him. His "I Have a Dream" speech is considered one of the most motivating and life-changing experiences of all time. The reason it was so influencing was King's ability to take action on his beliefs. The March on Washington itself showed his ability to take action. The result was growing enthusiasm on the part of Martin Luther King Jr. as well as all of those supporting the Civil Rights movement.

Martin Luther King Jr.'s life was filled with enthusiasm and action. He saw something that needed to be changed and he spent his life making a difference.

Secondary Steps:

After taking immediate steps to help dial up your enthusiasm, there are some secondary steps that will assist you as well. The word enthusiasm comes from the Greek roots 'en' and 'theos' and means "God or spirit within". It is a fire, a passion within. Real enthusiasm is not something you 'put on' or 'take off' to fit the occasion. It is a mindset and it can be cultivated through practice and determination. Here are some secondary steps you can take to become more enthusiastic.

1. Focus.

To be enthusiastic about a goal, learn to keep your mind on your goal day after day. The more worthy and desirable your objective, the more dedicated and enthusiastic you will become. Keeping track of your progress will help you stay motivated too, because as you get closer and closer to your goal, it becomes more realistic and attainable. Do this by having a table showing your progress. When the possibility of achieving a goal becomes real, being enthusiastic about it comes naturally as you press on toward successfully completing each goal. Practice keeping track of your progress and stay focused on your goals each day.

2. Be Interested in People.

Enthusiastic people are interested in everything that is going on around them and how they can affect the other people in their lives. Curiosity and enthusiasm are linked. Finding out about what is happening in other people's lives is exciting. Asking them questions that bring out their enthusiasm is not difficult to do. Just make a short statement and ask a simple question that keys in on their excitement or enthusiasm like this: "Wow, you must be excited to be starting that new project. What are you really eager about accomplishing?" Or, make it team centered: "Your team looks so enthusiastic! What's driving their passion?" Or, ask people questions like: "What's happening? What's exciting in your life?" And don't forget that people get excited about their friends and family, too. Ask them about the people they love -- but make sure you center it around positive enthusiasm "Anything exciting happening with your family?" Or "Do you have anything interesting or energizing planned for this week?"

Find ways to take interest in things at work and in other people's lives. If there are problems at work, communicate with your co-workers to find out how you can improve things in your office. For example, a telephone operator working on the switchboard at a very large organization was dismayed at the amount of calls to a department that were being transferred around the office. She knew it was really frustrating the customers and staff as well. After some investigation she found that the department had moved people and telephones around without letting the operators know which people were at which numbers. She then went on to collect and consolidate the new information for the switchboard database. This greatly improved the customer service throughout the organization. By showing interest in things around her and doing something about it, she was able to enthusiastically change her surroundings for the better. Taking an interest in people and things around you and getting things changed for the better is a quick way to dial up your enthusiasm.

3. Surround Yourself With Enthusiastic People.

If you want to become more enthusiastic, spending your time with pessimistic, negative people will not help you. These types of people will squish your enthusiasm. Diligently seek out enthusiastic people who live their lives with vigor and passion and spend time with them. Enthusiasm is contagious. Learn from them and find out what makes them so enthusiastic. Spending time with passionate people can make it easier for you to cultivate and express your own enthusiasm.

4. Keep Your Energy Levels High.

It is extremely difficult to be enthusiastic about life and work if you find yourself exhausted and tired most of the time. Enthusiasm and excitement about your life requires that you are alert and awake. You can't conjure up passion if you're tired. It's tough to be energized if you are exhausted, stressful, overwrought, or drained. Your mind is the engine and your body is the frame and the wheels. Without a healthy car, it's hard to get anywhere. If a positive, healthy lifestyle is not already a priority, take the time to learn how to make it one when you need to dial up your enthusiasm. Exercise is a great way to keep your mind and body active and it is recommended that you work out regularly. You will find yourself with increased energy. This will help you become more enthusiastic about life and work.

You also have to be careful about what you put into your body and when you do it. Energy flags when you get hungry. When blood sugar levels go up or down with big swings this affects your drive and in turn your drive affects your ability to be enthusiastic. By taking care of your body, you free your mind to focus on taking on new tasks and goals and not be bogged down by your lack of health. Your stress levels will decrease and you will not only find it easier to be passionate about life but you will be happier as well. It doesn't take a lot to maintain a healthy, vibrant lifestyle; however, it does take work and dedication. With this in mind, sit down and plan out time to participate in some form of exercise. By making this a priority, you can find yourself with more energy than you have ever had and will be ready to enthusiastically accomplish your goals.

5. Make a List.

Sit down and create a list of all the things in your work life that you love and are grateful for. When someone focuses too much on what they want and believe they can't attain it, the mind can create reasons why they can't have it. This can lead to that person dwelling on their weaknesses and things they haven't accomplished, which can quickly drain anyone's enthusiasm. Consciously become aware of things in your life that you are thankful for and that inspire you. Enthusiasm and inspiration are closely linked. Look at the word inspire as being 'in spirit'. If you are in the spirit of things, you are very close to being enthused. Be fully associated and 'in spirit' as you compile your list. Imagine yourself reliving some of the things that motivated and excited you - ones that you are thankful that you had the opportunity to do. Set aside time daily to mentally list everything you have to be grateful for. Recall your past successes, unique skills, good relationships, and positive moments. Studies show that remembering just one positive moment in your life can be the kick start you need to get you back on track and dial up your enthusiasm. Can you imagine the benefits you would have if you did this on a regular basis? What wonderful enthusiasm you would have!

> If you have ever wondered what a high energy level looks like, look no further than Richard Simmons. He has an eccentric, outgoing personality that many people seek as inspiration for weight loss and fitness. Simmons energy level allowed him to seek out ways to lose weight which eventually helped him lose 123 pounds. Not only did he lose the weight, but he kept it off for over 42 years now! Through his high energy level and method of teaching, he has helped humanity lose approximately 12,000,000 pounds.
>
> The enthusiasm that Richard Simmons continues to show for physical fitness continues to inspire thousands of people today.

"Change yourself and fortune will change with you."

~Portuguese Proverb

27 How to Dial Down Enthusiasm

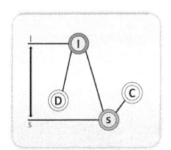

I>s
Enthusiasm

In the workplace, there may be situations in which you must dial down your Enthusiasm. You may come across as too overbearing, eager, passionate, zealous, or too excited for some people. They may feel overwhelmed if you come at them with an abundance of excitement and motivation. This is especially true when you are dealing with more reserved types or introverts.

When you think about when you might have to dial down Enthusiasm, think about being in a meeting looking at two people interacting. Tom is calm, while the Debra is passionately making her point. Debra alertly notices that they are not getting anywhere as they try up their influencing efforts. Instead of being calmer, they make an influencing mistake and become more heated and passionate as they thrash out ideas with each other. They simply let their enthusiasm override logical communication. If someone isn't responding to your enthusiasm, perhaps your coworkers might even be a little overwhelmed by it, you must dial down your Enthusiasm.

Looking back, have you ever made a mistake where you might have been a bit too excited or too enthusiastic for the situation? Have you ever been irritated when someone on your team seemed a little too enthusiastic or eager during negotiations and let the other side know that, potentially giving away a negotiation advantage? Do you know someone who gets enthusiastic about too many suggestions? Don't they seem like just like a bounding puppy chasing three ideas at once? Being too gung-ho about too many things isn't a great strategy if you want to appear thoughtful and contemplative -- especially when taking risks with corporate resources. Whenever you want to be perceived as someone who is dependable and considerate, dialing down your enthusiasm to an appropriate level is one of the best strategies in looking conservative and trustworthy. Another way that being too enthusiastic might hurt your reputation is when people may think you're a little too enthusiastic about your bosses' ideas or when others notice that you consistently become more animated whenever higher ups are in the room.

Although most people will tell you to show passion and to be enthusiastic, as you are already gathering, you have to have an appropriate level of enthusiasm and excitement. Balance is the key!

DISCflex™

Immediate Steps:

Here are a few steps, both Immediate and Secondary, to help you learn how to dial down your Enthusiasm.

1. Use the Opposing Sub-factor.

The first thing to remember is that Enthusiasm's I>s opposing Sub-factor is Thoughtfulness S>i. Recognize all that might be required is that you dial up your thoughtfulness and this alone will have the immediate impact of dialing back your Enthusiasm.

2. Check the Enthusiasm Levels of Everyone Around You.

If you notice that everyone around you is a little sluggish or not very excited, it's okay to be a level or two above them in enthusiasm; you must remember what you learned about mirroring and matching. If you not yet developed enough rapport with these people, you should always ramp your enthusiasm down – and do the same for any other potentially overt Sub-factors. Get them close to the other people's level of enthusiasm.

Then once you've established an appropriate level of rapport or trust, slowly lead by ramping up to a level both you and they are comfortable with. This might be significantly lower than the enthusiasm level you personally started with. If the entire office is in a serious mood and you are bursting with enthusiasm, they will feel overwhelmed and may think of you as obnoxious if you don't dial it down a bit. It's okay to be a level or two above everyone else's enthusiasm levels, but having too much enthusiasm - too much excitement or passion - can sometimes cause others to see you as annoying. Your goal is to have an appropriate degree of enthusiasm for the specific situation - as well as a proper balance of enthusiasm that the people you are interacting with feel comfortable around.

If you are able to be subtle about adjusting your degree of enthusiasm, they will feed off your energy and you can excite everyone around you. This requires you to be observant of other people's energy levels and stay in their range. Then, by using the techniques of mirroring and matching and pacing – which is doing the same thing they are doing at the pace the other person is doing it at, and then leading them to an increased level of enthusiasm by dialing up your personal enthusiasm bit by bit, you can gradually ramp up the other person's enthusiasm along with yours. Pacing and leading is explained in detail in the Rapport Building sessions of the same name. If you would like to master these skills, I suggest that you study this material. The key in pacing and leading is to stay within their range before they get annoyed at your high energy.

3. Know When the Situation Requires a More Settled and Reserved Mood

There are times in all of our lives when a serious, dispassionate, or calm demeanor is required. This can be hard for the naturally enthusiastic person because they genuinely and seemingly effortlessly put a high amount of energy into their work. They are naturally passionate and dialing this characteristic down for any prolonged period of time is stressful on these individuals. An example of specific times where a naturally enthusiastic person must dial down their enthusiasm is when they are attempting to help someone get through in the negative phases of the Transitional Time Line™: Denial, Resistance, Sabotage, and the Depths of

Suffering. Often, when someone is in any of these negative phases, they will not respond well to enthusiasm. In fact, enthusiasm can propel them further into a pessimistic state of mind. This could potentially extend how long they will take to accept the change and make it harder to break through to the positive phases. It is imperative for the enthusiastic person to take a genuine interest in the Transitional Time Line™ in Indaba Global's Change Course. The enthusiastic person needs to understand that their optimistic or high energy simply won't bring another person out of a negative mood. Adopting a more serious or a more caring tone is necessary at these times to deal with negative situations. Leading people through to a more positive state by dialing down enthusiasm is a much better tactic.

4. Remember to Listen Instead of Talking.

This seems simple, but the enthusiastic person is usually the one talking the most in a conversation. They are passionate and this means getting excited and conveying that fervor through their words and passion. More than that, even when they are not talking, they are typically thinking about what to say next rather than listening. They're already planning and celebrating and figuring out how to tell everyone how excited they are about everything! This makes it tough to communicate with an overly enthusiastic person.

If you've ever felt that the person you're talking to is talking over you because they just can't wait to blurt out what they're thinking, that's precisely what it feels like to be 'not listened to' by an enthusiastic individual. It's not pleasant! This reminds me of an old quote I was read: "People don't care how much you know until they know how much you care." The good news is that enthusiastic people usually really care about communication effectively with people because they do have an Elevated Influence Factor. Imagine if this weren't the case! By taking a step back and developing a genuine interest in listening attentively to others, the enthusiastic person can dial up their Thoughtfulness so that it balances their overpowering Influence Factor.

This is particularly true when you are trying to relate to someone. Michael Faraday knew that successful selling was a product of understanding what was important to other people. Faraday wanted the backing of Prime Minister William Gladstone for his invention of the first electric motor. Gladstone was clearly not impressed with Faraday's crudely made invention. "Of what possible good is it?" Gladstone asked. "Of great benefit to our country," Faraday responded, "For some day you will be able to tax it!" They both got on the same page and agreed to cooperate. Faraday did not go on to boast about his creativity, describe his product, or convince the world it needed an electric motor. Rather, he was thoughtful about what Gladstone wanted and would be convinced by instead of trying to win him over with his own enthusiasm.

> *"You will never change your life until you change something you do daily."*
>
> *~Mike Murdock*

Secondary Steps:

1. Take a Step Back and Take The Time to Think Through Your Actions.

Dialing down enthusiasm requires that you make sure that you don't jump right into things without thinking it through. The enthusiastic person is usually the most spontaneous of the Influence Sub-factors. Sometimes this can lead to rash decisions or ill-thought actions. Instead of letting spontaneity harm your career, family, or social life, the enthusiastic person can learn to dial down their Influence Factor when it is necessary. Stepping back before making a decision will invariably help you to keep away from rash decision making. Alternatively, you should consider going through the Rational Decision Making Process in the Decision Making Course. The six steps of the Rational Decision Making Process are essential for good and well thought out decisions. But for implementation to be fun and to create a thriving, growth filled environment, an enthusiastic approach could be just the magical ingredient it takes to motivate everyone around you.

2. Make a Mental Effort to Observe Your Surroundings and Thought Processes.

Being acutely aware of the environment around you can lead to greater success in your work and personal life. Typically, the Influence and the Steadiness Factors are on different ends of the spectrum in behavioral tendencies. They are polar opposites in temperament and disposition. An extraordinarily enthusiastic person is likely to have a highly Elevated Influence Factor and a much lower Steadiness Factor. The Steadiness Factor is the driver of situational awareness, however. It's just logical – to be aware of what's happening, you have to think at a deeper – more thoughtful level. To dial down enthusiasm, you have to make a conscious effort to dial up thoughtfulness.

3. Set Triggers Become Less Enthusiastic.

Triggers are defined as events or cues that when sensed by a person, they set in motion automatic responses. The concept of triggers was studied through a series of experiments by physiology and neurology scientist Ivan Pavlov. Most of his work involved research in temperament, conditioning and involuntary reflex actions. In his most famous experiment, known in pop culture through the widely used phrase 'Pavlov's Dog', he studied what triggers would make dogs salivate. He successfully trained dogs to have involuntary reflex reactions to the sound of a bell signaling that food would be delivered. This occurred whether or not the food was actually given to the dog. It was a trigger.

Triggers can contribute reactions to a wide range of reflexes – physiological and psychological. Often, there will be a trigger to dial up your thoughtfulness that will work to dial down your enthusiasm. It is actually quite easy to set a trigger for yourself; you just have to be consistent about it. A trigger to be more thoughtful might be a picture in your mind of Rodin's statue of The Thinker. It might be a phrase as simple as, "Take a step back and look at this." Setting triggers will help you to reel in your enthusiasm and make sure that it doesn't blind your Thoughtfulness Sub-factor.

> Henry Ford was often asked, "How can I make my life a success?" He would reply with the same line every time, "If you start something, finish it." Henry Ford learned this advice when he was building his first car. He was so motivated to get it completed, but then he figured out another design that might be superior to it. After almost forgetting about the first car and focusing on the new design he was enthusiastic about, he stopped himself. He realized that he had to get one thing done at a time and not make any excuses about it. He pressed on and finished his first model of the car. After finishing, he realized that he learned much more about the details and was able to use that information to create an even better design than he would have without the experience.

28 Self-Confidence Generic Profile

Definition

When Influence is greater than Compliance, you have the Self-confidence Sub-factor. People with this Sub-factor are social extroverts that don't doubt themselves often. This type of person will typically doubt others before they begin to doubt themselves. Self-confident people feel at ease with themselves when they are in social situations and initiate conversation easily and effectively. This type of person makes conversation and social situations seem easy. For a movie reference of this type of person look at James Bond and how he acts in a variety of situations.

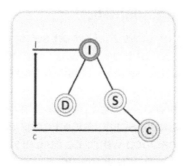

I>c
Self-confidence

Descriptors

Here is a list of words that relate to the Self-confidence Sub-factor:

- Poise
- Potency
- Power
- Self-assurance
- Dominance
- Sureness

Strengths

The strengths of the Self-confidence Sub-factor are an ease of interacting with others, the ability to continually assure themselves of their strengths, and a sort of power of presence around others. This type of person instinctively understands the Law of Status and makes their presence known in any situation.

DISCflex™

They easily interact with others by striking up interesting conversation. People with the Self-confidence Sub-factor have above-average positive self-talk and continually assure themselves of what they do right.

Self-confidence exhibits a certain 'can-do' attitude. Even when faced with adversity, negativity, and criticism of ideas, the Self-confidence Sub-factor pushes a person to explore their visions and ideas. Think about all of the major innovators and revolutionaries in the world. Michelangelo, at a time when even one of the premier Italian sculptors Agostino d'Antonio said marble was impossible to work with, saw a vision in his mind and worked at it. He ended up with one of the greatest masterpieces in the world, the statue of David. The Wright Brothers were ridiculed for wasting their money on a supposed flying contraption. Yet they had the self-confidence to push forward with their idea and created the launch of the plane. Even Henry Ford encountered criticism for his idea of the motorcar from none other than Thomas Edison. Edison told Ford to come work with him instead of spending money on a worthless idea. But Ford held steady to his vision and produced the car. History shows us that visionaries had confidence in themselves. They were the ones that were likely to say, "I can solve that problem", or "I can make that happen".

Weaknesses

The weaknesses of the Self-confidence Sub-factor are when it is taken to an extreme and you are perceived as over-confident or egotistical, acting impulsively, and perceived as not caring or having empathy. This can sometimes lead to negative self-talk instead of the positive self-talk that is common with the Self-confidence Sub-factor. Although this type of person will still act confidently, inside they are suffering. People with this Sub-factor will act impulsively because they believe that they can do no wrong. This can sometimes lead to trouble and ill thought out plans. Sometimes people with this Sub-factor become so wrapped up in themselves that they forget other people have different feelings and thoughts than they do. This can lead to problems with relationships if not handled properly.

There have been many times in my life when I have experienced the Self-confidence Sub-factor gone wrong. When I used to be a sales manager, I would notice all too often that my salespeople would go into a sale with too much self-confidence. Because they knew they were going to get the sale, they forgot to build rapport and perfect the initial steps of the process. As a manager, I had to show my team the proper dosage of self-confidence to have, and when to have it. Sometimes we can become so self-confident that we start acting impulsively, instead of thinking about the situation logically.

Situational Adaptation - Dial Up or Dial Down

You must be able to dial up and dial down your self-confidence in order to succeed in life personally and professionally. Self-confidence must be dialed down when you are talking to others about how they feel and when you are trying to help them get through something. If your self-confidence is too high, the person will have a hard time believing you care about them and are really just thinking about yourself. Dial down your self-confidence so they see that you care and know that you mean it.

When you are trying to connect with a co-worker to push them through a tough assignment, there are times when you need to dial down your self-confidence. Whenever I see my team members struggling with a project or an idea, I take a step back and look through their perception. This allows me to be more empathetic and find out what will really help them through the situation. If I went into the situation with a self-confident attitude, explaining how I could do that assignment, it would just cause resentment toward me. You have to try and understand how the other person in the situation is thinking. Use the Perceptual Prism Model to dial down your Self-confidence Sub-factor when appropriate.

> *I remember the story of a young man who wanted to be a journalist. While combing through the newspaper ads one day, he found an opportunity to write for the newspaper. He decided to go to the interview session the following morning. As he walked to the office in the morning, he was delighted by the possibility of getting the job. Unfortunately, when he got there, he found out that he was tenth in line. Instead of letting this bother him, he calmly went up to the receptionist and told her to give a note he had just written to her boss, saying it was very important that he looked at it right away. When the boss read the note, it said, "Hello sir, I'm the young man that is tenth in line. Don't make any decisions until you see me." The boss smiled and was excited to meet that young man.*

Self-confidence can be your biggest asset as well. You need to dial up your self-confidence when going into an interview or when managing a team. For the interview, you need to show the person interviewing you that you are confident in your abilities. For managing a team, you need to be able to show leadership and you have to show confidence in every decision that you make. Self-confidence will help you achieve your goals, you just need to understand how far to dial it up or dial it down in any given situation.

Sometimes self-confidence can be what separates you from the rest of the pack. You should know what you are capable of. Everyone has unique characteristics that make them special or the best at something. Figure out what your characteristics are and learn how to use your unique characteristics to be successful in any situation. An example of an I>c, highly confident individual, is the one in the meeting who is always the out spoken one. This is really a gift sometimes in a meeting, when other committee members may be too shy to speak up and share their opinions. Not the I>c individual though. They will be helpful and will be able to be confident when speaking on behalf of others. This is good…most of the time.

Next Steps

Next, you will explore the benefits and consequences of the Self-confidence Sub-factor. If you think that this Sub-factor is important for your success, you can target your knowledge by investigating various ways to dial up or dial down your Self-confidence Sub-factor in our 'How to' sessions.

DISCflex™

29 How to Dial Up Self-Confidence

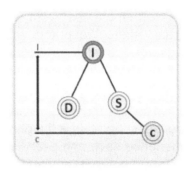

I>c
Self-confidence

Self-confidence can open doors and create new opportunities for success at your job and in your personal life. You can learn to interact with others more easily and utilize positive self-talk to be successful at anything you focus on. With practice and commitment you can become more self-confident, poised, and self-assured.

Immediate Steps:

First, we will outline some immediate steps that will help dial up your Self-confidence Sub-factor. People aren't born with self-confidence. They learn it and practice it throughout their lives. Most often when we see others who have this trait, we admire it, and model our behavior from theirs. Psychologists call a central point or an internal locus of control the reason for self-confidence. This means that individuals who are self-directing, and who believe they control their destiny through their actions and behavior, accept responsibility for their own results. Ultimately, individuals like these have greater self-confidence. By dedicating your time and effort to modeling effective ways to self-direct and have a higher locus of control, you can become more self-confident. Here are some immediate steps that you can take that will help you become more self-confident.

1. **Start by Dressing the Part.**

    You may be thinking, how is dressing sharp going to make me more self-confident? Clothes don't make a man, but they certainly affect the way he feels about himself. When you don't look your best, you usually know it and you may consciously or unconsciously portray that. Think about that time you bought a new suit or dress that you knew looked great on you and think of how you felt looking in the mirror and leaving your home that day. That is the feeling of self-confidence, a positive energy that flows through you and affects everything you do during the day. The good news is that you don't need to go and buy a whole new wardrobe or spend a lot on clothes to feel self-confident. In most cases, significant improvements can be made by bathing and shaving frequently, wearing clean clothes, keeping your hair neat and being aware of the latest styles. Taking care of your personal appearance by being cognizant of how you look will help you as you learn to become more self-confident. For more information on image and status, review the Law of Image session in the 21 Laws of Influence for Sales Part 2 and the Law of Status session in the 21 Laws of Influence for Sales Part 3.

2. Self-Talk is the Next Step in Becoming More Self-Confident.

Self-confidence means confidence that comes from yourself. This requires you to take the time and energy to pump yourself up. The best way to do this is to align your self-talk for building your confidence.

"Employ your time in improving yourself by other men's writings so that you shall come easily by what others have labored hard for."

~Socrates

Self-talk is the dialogue that takes place inside your head and controls how you act and feel. It even controls how you remember events and think about your perceptions. Self-talk is the constant internal discourse that we all experience each and every minute of our waking hours. Most important, your self-talk is the driver of your actions. Self-talk can be the expression of fear that holds you back or the pronouncement of a 'can do' attitude. In other words, self-talk will propel you forward or tell you to hesitate. Learn to recognize when you are using negative self-talk and change it to positive self talk.

For example: if you find yourself saying that "I wish I was self-confident", you could change it to something positive: "I am truly amazing with my new cooking abilities because my family really enjoys the new recipes that I learned in my cooking class."

This is one of the most important actions you can take in life that will not only make you more self-confident but successful as well. You can review the Self-Talk session in our Life Skills Course to get more information on this topic.

3. Adjust Your Posture

Another helpful, yet simple step in become more self-confident is to adopt self-confident postures, even when you don't particularly feel confident. Smiling makes you appear relaxed and confident and positively effects how you feel as well. Being aware of your posture will help you be more confident and self-assured. It has been proven that when people are told to display confident gestures

"Repeat anything often enough and it will start to become you."

~Tom Hopkins

and postures in meetings or social functions, they are much more likely to take control of situations and be able to command your ideas well. A person that has slumped shoulders and is lethargic in their movements almost always displays a lack of confidence and enthusiasm for what they might be doing. Practicing good posture will automatically make you feel more confident. Stand up straight, keep your head up, and make solid eye contact when you interact with other people. When you do this you will make a positive impression on the people you are communicating with which in turn will make you instantly feel empowered and sure of yourself. Plus, understand that people judge you by what your body language displays. If you look confident, they'll think you are. People respect confident people more and this will be reflected in how they talk to you and how they behave with you. When people address you as if you have confidence, you in turn will live up to their expectations. It's a self-fulfilling aspect of communication.

Former Minnesota Vikings hall of fame head football coach Bud Grant took great pride in posture and what it conveyed. He ingrained his team with the philosophy that winners prepare to win, think like winners, act like winners, and look like winners. New additions to his team were likely very surprised with Grant's first drill at the first session of training camp. Grant would line up the entire team and show them how he wanted them to properly stand for the national anthem. "You're winners," he would say, "so look and act like winners every second you're part of this team." Winners believe they are winners because they've learned to act like winners, right down to their posture. Mr. Grant led his team to four Super Bowls.

Secondary Steps:

Self-confidence also requires secondary steps in order to become part of your life. An example of building self-confidence was a man who had a dream of creating an affordable motorcar. It seemed so farfetched at the time that even one of his closest friends discouraged him from trying and invited him to come and work for him. But this man was so confident in his idea that he continued trying and in 1908, Henry Ford unveiled the Model T car. His self-confidence was one of the traits that kept him committed to his dream and allowed him to succeed. Here are some secondary steps that you can take to become more self-confident.

1. Find a Role Model to Learn Self-Confidence From.

"The art of life is a constant readjustment to our surroundings."

~K. Okakaura

Earlier, I mentioned that we learn to be confident through looking at people who already have this trait and by modeling them. Sometimes it can be hard for us to start being self-confident because we may not know what it looks like. Look for someone who is already successful in your field or interests and learn from them. What is it they do that makes them confident?

Identify yourself with behaviors that they portray that convey self-confidence and apply these behaviors to your own life. An example of self-confidence can be found in the character James Bond, the fictional MI6 super agent. The character in the movies exudes confidence in every situation that he comes across and interacts easily with all those around him. Henry Ford's role model was Thomas Edison. Ford even hung a picture of him near his work area to remind himself of his hero.

2. Take Calculated Risks.

It may seem strange, but taking calculated risks will actually raise your self-confidence as long as you adopt the right attitude at the beginning. Assume responsibility for the risk you are contemplating and have a clear idea of what you need to accomplish and where you are heading. In this way you turn a risk into a calculated risk - one with a better chance of succeeding. With a positive attitude toward calculated risk-taking you can increase your self-confidence. When you take calculated risks and successfully achieve them you gain the confidence that you can accomplish more than you thought possible. Utilizing calculated risk-taking, combined with positive self-talk, can help you become more self-confident and successful at your job and life. Let's look at the story of King Camp Gillette.

> *Safety razors had been around for a while before Gillette introduced the disposable razor. King Camp Gillette took the risk that he could create a type of disposable razor that could add convenience to the user. The biggest calculated risk he made was the cost of the razor itself. Gillette decided to retail his razor at $5 (about $140 in 2011 dollars). This was about half of the average worker's weekly pay. And yet the razors sold in the millions in America. King Camp Gillette made a career out of taking calculated risks based on the marketplace and people's behaviors. Now Gillette is one of the best known razor companies in the world and is still expanding its business.*
>
> *Gillette took a calculated risk in trying to develop disposable razors, but his confidence in his idea helped him create the first disposable razors.*

3. Don't Fear Criticism.

Often when people are criticized, they get caught up in their emotions, become sensitive, and their confidence is shaken. Learn to not fear criticism and to not go into immediate denial and counter-attack mode. Think of criticism as feedback. Think of feedback as a gift. Analyze the source of the criticism and determine if they have expertise and knowledge to back up their criticism. If you decide that there is truth in the criticism, tell yourself it is information that you prefer to know, view it as great feedback and take the opportunity to improve yourself based on your newfound knowledge. You can't fix what you don't know about. So, remember that feedback is truly the gift of knowledge.

By taking the opportunity to develop your self-awareness and adjusting it according to the feedback you receive throughout your life, you will gain confidence in knowing that you are better prepared for any situations that arise. Understand that you can only control your thoughts and actions, not the thoughts and actions of others. Some feedback is incorrect and should in fact be ignored. As you gain more self-confidence you will know how to judge best what feedback to incorporate into your development plan for yourself and what feedback to ignore.

For more information on how to successfully do so, please review the Feedback and Coaching sessions in the eLearning Suite. This will help you have self-confidence in a variety of situations and circumstances. Even Henry Ford's mentor Thomas Edison told him as previously mentioned, that he was wasting time and energy trying to make a more affordable motorcar. Fortunately, Henry Ford had already developed enough self-confidence to withstand Edison's criticism and went on to make a household name for the famous automobile company.

4. Compliment Other People.

When we think negatively about ourselves, we can often project that same feeling of negativity on to others in the form of insults or gossip. Break the negative cycle by getting in the habit of praising and complimenting other people. Abstain from engaging in negative gossip about others and make an effort to compliment people throughout the day. It may just be a small thing, but people respond more to praise than criticism and by complimenting others you will in turn be more liked which will help your own self-confidence. Learning to look out for others and not merely yourself will help you keep a positive focus on life.

30 How to Dial Down Self-Confidence

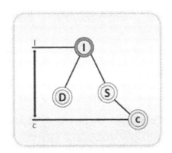

**I>c
Self-confidence**

It is important to remember that Self-Confidence I>c has an opposing Sub-factor™ of Accuracy C>i. As with the other Sub-factors™, all that might be required is that you dial up your Accuracy and this alone will have the immediate impact of dialing back your Self-Confidence. As you learn the techniques in this session, immediately review the session on How to Dial Up your Accuracy to understand the polar opposite of Self-Confidence.

In some situations your elevated Self-Confidence may come across as arrogance and turn people away from you. We've all seen people who are overconfident, some are borderline smug or cocky because they know they can hit it out of the ballpark when asked to do something. They are in no doubt of their ability to accomplish the goal; unfortunately, they may offer much too much for the situation they are facing. More often than not, this 'too-sure-of-themselves' attitude is seen as immature and swaggering. This is seen more often in the younger set because as folks mature, they realize it doesn't play well with others. Even if you don't mean it, some may begin to think of you as egotistical, or arrogant if you show too much Self-Confidence. In extreme cases they might think you are condescending or patronizing. In these situations, you need to learn how to dial-down your Self-Confidence. Here's a friendly word of warning: Self-confidence is valuable! Understand, you shouldn't get rid of it; you just need to know how to dial it back to an appropriate level so that people don't misjudge you. There is a fine line between Self-Confidence and arrogance. This is one of the Sub-factors™ where it might be best to know how to mask it rather than dialing it down. Bear this in mind as you look at the suggestions for dialing down your Self-Confidence. Other people's perception might be what you have to adjust here as you seek the appropriate level of Self-Confidence to exhibit. Some of the tips are designed to do just that while others are specifically to give you ways to truly dial down your Self-Confidence.

Immediate Steps:

Here are a few immediate steps that you can take to dial down your Self-Confidence.

1. Use Maslow's Pyramid of Motivation and Self-actualization.

If you use Maslow's Pyramid of Motivation and turn Self-confidence into Self-respect as you move toward Self-actualization, you will automatically appear to be less arrogant. If you receive a promotion or praise, say thank you. Never gloat or have boastful thoughts. In particular never brag about your accomplishments around the office. If you do I will bet that some of your coworkers will think of you as egotistical, arrogant, or perhaps conceited. Downplay your accomplishments and celebrate them inside, don't make a big deal about it. Act as if you have done it before! If you look at Maslow's Pyramid of Motivation, external gratification from others is lower on the quest for self-actualization than self-respect is. Knowing this, isn't it better for your soul to be content with knowing that you did a great job? Do you really need recognition from others to know that you did well? Probably not if you are solid within yourself. This is just another reason to always be humble.

2. Praise Others.

Focus on others' achievements and give them praise. When your coworkers see that you notice their achievements, and are vocal about giving them praise, they will start to think of you as more thoughtful and not simply focused on your own achievements. As you notice their efforts, you will also raise their self-confidence. This is especially important if you have a naturally high level of Self-confidence. Bringing up the level of Self-confidence of those around you will make your high level seem more normal. The spread between their new level and your natural level is diminished. You are making them more comfortable with Self-confidence in general. Therefore they will be more comfortable with you as a result. Now let's look at the story of the Wranglers and Stranglers.

Years ago there were two writers clubs at the University of Wisconsin. The first group, known as the Stranglers, was filled with men of extraordinary ability and creative literary talent. The men of the club had an incredible ability of being able to put the English language to its best use. The young men would meet regularly to read and critique each other's work. And critique it they did! The club members would mercilessly dissect the most minute literary expression into a hundred pieces and heartlessly criticize the author. This pattern of behavior led to the origination for their club name, the Stranglers.

The other literary club on campus was made up of women who had equal ability and talent; they called themselves the Wranglers. They too read their works to each other. However, unlike the Stranglers, their criticism was softer and more encouraging. Sometimes, there was almost no criticism at all and every effort, even the most feeble one, was encouraged.

Years later an alumnus of the university was doing a study of his classmates' careers when he noticed a vast difference in the literary accomplishments of the Stranglers as opposed to the Wranglers. Of all the bright men who were part of the Stranglers, not one had made a significant literary accomplishment of any kind. In contrast, the Wranglers had six or more successful writers, some of national renown.

The talent between the two clubs was on most accounts the same as was their level of education. The difference between the two was that the Stranglers strangled, while the Wranglers were determined to give each other a lift. The Stranglers promoted an atmosphere of contention and self-doubt, while the Wranglers highlighted the best, not the worst.

The example set by the group of woman known as the Wranglers is one that can help you establish rapport and gain the trust and respect of your co-workers or employees.

3. Be Open to Other Ideas.

Although this might seem obvious, often people block out other people's input when they have an elevated level of Self-confidence. How exactly does this happen? Well, perhaps your current level of Self-confidence makes you overly convinced your ideas are best. Even if you don't consciously think that they are, you might be too narrowly focused because of your experiences in life. Just because you are certain that your way will work, doesn't necessarily mean it's the best way. Someone else might have a more efficient, cost effective, or simply a better way. It doesn't mean that you are wrong or unwise to be secure in your knowledge.

It just might be that you haven't ever seen or heard of the different way another person may handle the situation. We urge you to leave room for new ways and new information to seep in. Remember, if you are overly convinced your way is best, you automatically might block out other suggestions. When this happens you might write off other people's ideas as not important, relevant, or worthy.

4. Stay Confident inside, But Adjust Your Outward Facing Voice.

Keep your self-talk intact so that you don't change who you are inside as far as Self-confidence goes. Knowing how to adjust and temper your outward facing voice will reflect a 'non-cockiness' appearance. Thankfully, you will not be perceived as overly confident. This is especially important to regulate if you are talking to people who do not have much faith in what you are trying to accomplish. If you state irrevocably that your goal will happen, and show your extremely confident nature, it may backfire when they resist your best efforts to bring the project home. To people like these, talking up your game is false bravado. Some people are even superstitious about being too confident. They think that you are tempting fate by being too confident with your words. They truly think that if you state your goals too confidently, that something will happen to stop you, that the universe will put you humbly back in your place because of your overly confident words. An excellent tactic might be to use a Statement of Expectations rather than direct statements. Start your sentences with phrases like: "I hope..." "I believe...", "I anticipate..." rather than direct confident statements like: "I am certain..." "I am sure..." or "I am positive..." By simply changing your outward facing voice, you will appear to others as one who is more reality-based in contrast to a person appearing full of themselves.

Secondary Steps:

After you have tried the primary steps, which are for the most part outward facing, it is prudent to do some introspection when thinking about Self-confidence. Now, let's look at some secondary steps you can take to adjust your Self-confidence to the appropriate levels.

1. Strengths and Weaknesses.

Performing a SWOT analysis on your strengths and weaknesses, as well as analyzing your opportunities and threats can be illuminating. Individuals who are overly confident usually don't have a solid grasp on the extent of their limitations. By performing a SWOT analysis, you force yourself to be realistic in analyzing your limits. Then, once you have this knowledge you can move forward and adjust your skills - bringing your strengths out and capitalizing on them. At the same time, by analyzing your weaknesses, you can come up with a plan to mitigate them so they will do the least amount of damage to you. Play to your strengths - build skill and enhance your strengths without nervousness and timidity. Nervousness leads to needing reinforcement from others - it's a vicious cycle that can systematically erode your Self-confidence. It is imperative to understand that dialing back your Self-confidence is not about eroding your sense of self-worth or your Self-confidence at all. When you dial back your Self-confidence you are simply exhibiting less of the outward, obnoxious traits of over-confidence. You should not erode your inner strength in this area. Strong, realistic, well balanced Self-confidence is the goal.

2. Know Your Limits.

While Self-confidence is a valuable asset, you must make certain that it is tempered with realism. You must take a look at your limitations - whether they are self-made or imposed on you - these will determine to a large extent whether or not you are being real in your level of confidence. Once you understand precisely what your strengths and weaknesses are, and you look at your opportunities and threats, assessing and addressing your current set of limitations becomes easy.

Then, once you have accomplished this task, you can make decisions about your confidence that you will indeed be able to carry out what you said you were capable of achieving. This ties directly into the probability of success you might have when undertaking goals. For more information on the process that this ties into, review the Analyze Options session in the Decision Making course.

"It is impossible for a man to learn what he thinks he already knows."

~Epictetus

3. Competitive Analysis of Yourself.

There's always going to be someone better, bigger, faster, richer, taller, more capable, more talented. Understand this and don't get wrapped up in having to be the best. Seriously, who exactly determines what the 'best' is anyhow? Look to your competition as a benchmark and figure out how they have reached their level and model the attributes, actions and behaviors that you want to emulate. By understanding that there will always be people higher up the talent ladder, this will make certain that you realize that others are in a higher position than you are - that even if you are very, very good, there are others with a more advanced skill set than you. This should serve as a regulator on your Self-confidence. That said, make sure that you continually improve and foster your sense of self-worth through your achievements. Always benchmark your progress against yourself and others as a gauge to how far you have come in your efforts to be the best you can be. Most important, always attempt to better your last best.

4. Make a Decision Not to Be the Big Fish in the Little Pond.

Never tie your self-worth to having to be the best in your world. Going out and finding people who are better than you are in your area of expertise can be a drain on your level of confidence; because where you once were seen as the best, you now are not. However, understanding that this is a natural part of life and always seeking out ways to become better at what you do requires you to find people that can coach you and help you become increasingly more skilled. My husband's college commencement speech gave a perfect and memorable illustration of this. When we start school we are in first grade and are the smallest kids in the school. We then pass through each grade until we reach fifth grade. We are now the biggest kids in the school and the leaders. We then depart to middle school in 6th grade and are now the

"They key to success is often the ability to adapt."

~Unknown

smallest and youngest kids in the school. After two fast years we are now 8th graders and again, we are the leaders. After summer vacation, we enter high school in 9th grade and quickly recognize how small we are compared to our older schoolmates. We then work our way up to our senior year and we are the 'big man on campus' once again. Just as quickly we graduate and enter college as a freshman…again, the youngest and least experienced person on campus. We then successfully make it all the way to senior year in college, feeling like we are on top of the world…we then attend a ceremony where they hand us a graduation certificate and a funny looking hat that you will never wear again and say 'good luck'. Guess what happens next?

We start our first job….you guessed it, as the newest and greenest member of the organization. Always remember, when you believe you are on the top of a hill, it may simply be the base of the next mountain. Each new challenge will test your Self-confidence. By anticipating life's many challenges, you will not be in for a rude awaking if your Self-confidence was a bit too pumped up for your own good.

You have two choices, stay in the environment where you are the best - never seeking promotion or things that will make you look inexperienced - or forge ahead into a world where you know that you will constantly be challenged by others more talented in any number of ways. The first choice, limiting your environment, and deciding to always be the big fish in the little pond, has severe consequences, but has a few benefits, too. If you decide to be the big fish in the little pond, never seeking those people who can teach you to grow, you limit yourself in profound ways. However, on some level you know that there are others more talented but you choose not to deal with them. In your circle, people look up to you.

This benefits you because it does stroke your ego. Yes, you might preserve your Self-confidence but at what cost? The next decision is to go out and widen your environment. You decide to be a smaller fish in a bigger pond. The benefit is that you can learn from others in that bigger pond and you have room to grow. If you've ever owned a fish tank, you know that the general rule is that the fish will only grow as big as their environment allows. This is a universal phenomenon. So, by deciding to expand your environment, you expand your horizons and your opportunities. Although your Self-confidence might take an initial bruising, by learning, expanding and being ever more accomplished, you'll find your Self-confidence will adjust to an appropriate level again. The most important benefit of deciding to be a little fish in a bigger pond on an ongoing basis is that you self-regulate your Self-confidence in the process. Every time you jump into a bigger pond and become the little fish again, your Self-confidence adjusts accordingly.

> *"Reasonable people adapt themselves to the world. Unreasonable people attempt to adapt the world to themselves. All progress, therefore, depends on unreasonable people."*
>
> *~George Bernard Shaw*

31 Patience Generic Profile

Definition

When Steadiness is greater than Dominance, you have the Patience Sub-factor. This is an introverted Sub-factor and is typical of a person that has a low sense of urgency. People with the Patience Sub-factor are naturally submissive and are able to handle mundane and ordinary tasks exceptionally well. Patient people are more realistic and typically more positive. This type of person works really well with repetition.

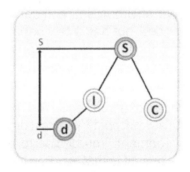

S>d
Patience

Descriptors

Words that can be associated with patience are:

- Endurance
- Tolerance
- Serenity
- Constancy
- Restraint

- Staying power
- Fortitude
- Composure
- Diligence

Strengths

The strengths of the Patience Sub-factor are the ability to think things through, to anticipate and welcome change, and handle others exceptionally well. Patient people think things through because they believe there is not a sense of urgency when something needs to be done right. Patient people are usually more open to change because they view change as a slow and steady progression, which is something that they are comfortable with. Patient people also handle others exceptionally well. They understand that the person is not going to just get over something, but rather they need to go through a slow step-by-step process.

James Gordon Gilkey had a great strength in patience and knew exactly how to explain it to someone:

> *"Most of us think of ourselves as standing wearily and helplessly at the center of a circle bristling with tasks, burdens, problems, annoyances, and responsibilities which are rushing in upon us. At every moment we have a dozen different things to do, a dozen problems to solve, a dozen strains to endure. We see ourselves as overdriven, overburdened, overtired."*
>
> *James Gordon Gilkey*

This is a common mental picture—and it is totally false. No one of us, however crowded his life, has such an existence.

What is the true picture of your life? Imagine that there is an hourglass on your desk. Connecting the bowl at the top with the bowl at the bottom is a tube so thin that only one grain of sand can pass through it at a time. That is the true picture of your life, even on a super-busy day. The crowded hours come to you always one moment at a time. That is the only way they can come. The day may bring many tasks, many problems, strains, but invariably they come in a single file. You want to gain emotional poise? Remember the hourglass, the grains of sand dropping one by one. We could all use this advice to understand what the strengths of the Patience Sub-factor are.

Weaknesses

The weaknesses of the Patience Sub-factor are that they can't change fast and can't make quick decisions. Usually the adapted style of a patient person is relatively the same as their natural style. They aren't able to change on the spot in any given situation. This can sometimes make them seem stubborn. Although it is necessary to make gut decisions at times, patient people still prefer to be diligent. People with this Sub-factor also have a hard time in management or leadership positions. This is mainly because they let their employees get away with too much and are too lenient with them.

Any decision maker needs to understand the weaknesses of patience. Although it could be good to step back and wait, it could also cost the company great opportunities. I remember when I had to make a decision about whether or not to cancel production of a certain course we were working on for a client. I decided to be patient and continue creating the program, waiting to hear from the company about whether they still wanted to do it. My decision to be patient ended up costing me time and money.

The company continued to delay the project and ended up not having the budget for the course. I learned my lesson and knew that my patience had become a weakness at that point.

Situational Adaptation - Dial Up or Dial Down

When managing others, patience is a beneficial Sub-factor to display in various scenarios. What if one of your employees was dealing with a serious situation, which may temporarily affect their work; some deadlines may be missed and some of the details required may not be totally up to your original standards. Patience may be necessary for their success. It may not be the employee's fault – they have always been a good and steady employee. By showing patience, the employee will feel less stress and they may be able to handle the situation more quickly and with a clear mind. When the time comes for them to dive back into their routine, they will most likely be very loyal and eager to please. If you use patience effectively in a situation like this, then you are much more likely to build respect and leadership currency. The employee will be grateful of any feedback you give them henceforth and will view you as understanding and even trustworthy.

"We can't solve problems by using the same kind of thinking we used when we created them."

~Albert Einstein

Whenever you are in a management type position and have to delegate tasks, you must be able to dial up your Patience Sub-factor to some degree. Although you have to meet deadlines, you must also allow your team members appropriate time to get their work completed. Whenever I delegate activities to other team members, I try and multiply the time that I believe it should be completed in by two or three. This is because of the Actor-Observer Bias. If I were to do the project from start to finish, it would probably take me longer than the initial time I gave when delegating it. That is a natural occurrence that managers need to realize. Therefore, we must dial up our patience when delegating to make sure that the projects are being completed effectively.

On the flip side, sometimes it is necessary to dial down your patience in order to get work done. If your employees see you as too patient, they won't be motivated to get the work done right away or to get it correct the first time. You have to be strict at times. What if when managing others, you continue to wait for them to get back to you on details and progress of the project. By dialing up your Self-motivation opposing Sub-factor, the employee will have the opportunity to see and learn from a boss who is self-motivated, and they may follow your lead and step up their pace too. Patience sometimes doesn't allow you to be an effective leader and gain enough leadership currency. You have to be able to balance patience with self-motivation in order to earn respect and build your leadership currency.

The same manager that has to dial up their patience when delegating, has to dial down their patience when meeting critical deadlines or dealing with unmotivated employees. At times I can be too patient with my other team members, which can cause our projects to fall behind deadlines. Usually this will transition what was patience into frustration. When managing projects, we all have to know when to complete projects and how to motivate our team members to get their parts of the project done. There is a fine line when we need to dial down our patience and get something done.

"We can change our lives. We can do, have, and be exactly what we wish."

~Anthony Robbins

Next Steps

Next, you will explore the benefits and consequences of the Patience Sub-factor. If you think that this Sub-factor is important for your success, you can target your knowledge by investigating various ways to dial up or dial down your Patience Sub-factor in our 'How to' sessions.

32 How to Dial Up Patience

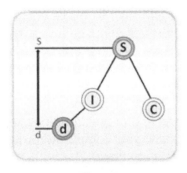

S>d
Patience

When we are impatient, we usually become stressed and frustrated when things don't go our way. Impatience can occur when we're sitting in traffic on the way to work, when we're waiting for an important email, or when we're anticipating feedback from a boss. Most of us - in particular high D's - have some degree of impatience. Many of us are used to, and expect, instant gratification. We like our messages and phone calls to be returned immediately. We become impatient waiting for things to happen in the timeframe we expect - especially when we want a critical response. Unfortunately, when we are already impatient, and things still are not happening in the time frame we expect, we become even more impatient. This spiraling effect of becoming more and more impatient is usually not productive or beneficial to ourselves or those around us.

Impatience can cause people to become more stressed, more frustrated, and can cause us to become angry at others around us. People on the peripheral sometimes bear the brunt of the emotions associated with impatience escalating or spiraling out of control - even when they don't deserve it. And this can damage relationships and make the impatient person be perceived as immature, angry, and unduly emotional. Truth be told, most of us wish that we were more patient, but we never really know how.

As a child, I am sure that you remember an incident where someone was unnecessarily impatient and they were told to calm down, count to ten, or leave the room. Can you think of some other tactics that you use when you're upset and impatient? Some people, when they are really impatient don't take advice well because they are in such an angry, emotional state. They feel chastised and perhaps are angry at themselves and a bit embarrassed. This might cause them to get even angrier. This technique obviously doesn't work for us and we throw the goal of 'learning to be patient' away for another day.

Let's look at different techniques that genuinely work. You must remember, however, that simply knowing these skills will not result in you being able to become patient. If you find yourself becoming impatient, you must practice the tactics that will make you more patient. Most important, if you practice, you will tend to remember these strategies in times of stress and anger. Over time, as you use your new patience-building skills, you will become more patient during those situations where it is vital for your success. Every day you should concentrate on being patient whenever you think it appropriate for the circumstance you find yourself in; until you build a habit out of it.

Immediate Steps:

There are two immediate steps you can take to make yourself consciously competent with the Patience Sub-factor. Usually, we do not think about being patient until we are thrust into the situation where our patience is being tested. If we have not prepared for it, we could potentially exhibit the signs of impatience. These include a wide range of emotions from showing displeasure all the way through to potentially exploding under the stress of intense rage. Let's imagine a scenario where you could become impatient. Think about the minute you find out through the rumor mill your project might be cancelled or lose resources. You don't know what exactly happened but you want answers now! Almost immediately, your temperature rises. You get angry and want to find out right away why you weren't the first to know.

You know that there is a team meeting scheduled but it's three hours away. You also know that other rumors have proven false and that logically you shouldn't panic. But you feel yourself becoming increasingly impatient as you think about getting answers. You should rather wait for the meeting to find out the reasons why someone is spreading rumors to uncover the source. Unfortunately, you feel compelled to take action. You just can't wait. You are increasingly impatient. There are a few simple steps to remember when you immediately find your patience being tested.

1. **Disassociate With the Root Cause of What is Making You Impatient.**

   There is a huge difference in thinking that happens when you are in a disassociated versus an associated state of mind. Associated means that you are in the 1st perceptual position - fully in your 'me' mode - in a state where you are fully engaged at your core level. Disassociated is when you step outside your 1st perceptual position - into another viewpoint or as if you are outside of your body. So let's look at how this works as it relates to dialing up your patience. Step back and imagine yourself looking at you - as if you are another person. This will quickly begin to grant you another perspective of the situation. You will automatically put yourself in the 2nd (Alliance) or 3rd (Observer) perceptual position where your emotional involvement will immediately lessen. This makes sense because you are stepping outside of yourself. After you are able to disassociate and step back and lessen your emotional state, you will go back and re-associate with yourself. Now, think about going into your body in a more focused way. Channel your immediate anger or frustration to something else. For example, rather than yelling or raising your voice at someone, consider counting to ten and thinking about ways to remain calm before talking. Take a time out to think of something else. As an example, browse through your email or look at an album of pictures from a vacation you recently enjoyed. Create a folder of images that relax you. This will work as an immediate de-stressor and is perfectly tailored to your personality. Your file, perhaps on your computer or phone, may consist of pictures of your wedding or of friends, your children, a family vacation, a tropical paradise, or a collage of places you wish to visit. Taking the time to stop and focus on something else will relinquish your immediate emotions and let you revisit the topic or situation more calmly.

At this point, there may be a new result to the problem that solves everything, making your patience help your work life be more successful.

2. Focus on Success and Achievements.

In difficult situations where you find yourself about to explode in frustration, anger, or any other negative emotion, remember your success and your achievements. Even in the most stressful situations, remember what you want to show the world about your behavior and maturity. You have proved that you can be patient before - and can do so now. Remember the challenges you have overcome in the past by being patient. Consistently remind yourself that you have done that before and can handle this new hurdle. Reminding yourself that you are competent and successful will relax you and make you more confident about tackling the problem. This is certainly more attractive than exploding and becoming impatient; both for your own personal self worth, as well as the image you desire to convey to your peers who may be present.

Even in a team environment, reflect on the achievements your team has previously accomplished. Understanding that the others on your team want success as much as you do is critical to becoming more patient.

Secondary Steps:

After you recognize that you want to become even more able to display patience, you can start practicing some secondary steps so that you have mastered this skill well before you find yourself in frustrating situations.

"To change your reality you have to change your inner thoughts."

~David Bohm

1. Anticipate When You Might Become Impatient

If you know you'll be waiting somewhere, bring something fun to do or something that will distract you from focusing on the cause of your impatience. It will decrease your stress level and keep you calm. Rather than spending your time waiting in the lobby being nervous and impatient about an interview, relax and make your grocery list, plan a vacation, or think about what you will do that evening. Personally, I love to carry a book with me everywhere. Then, when the receptionist calls you, you are calmer and more relaxed, rather than nervous and agitated that you had to wait. The same is true when you are waiting on important numbers for the month. Focus on other job responsibilities or cross some to-dos off your task list while you wait for the numbers to come in. This will allow you to de-stress and be more productive. A simple SWOT Analysis can be very helpful in anticipating what will happen. Refer to the SWOT Analysis in our Life Skills Course to become acquainted with how this will help you.

2. Rationalize the Situation

Rather than thinking about how waiting makes you feel, think about the reasons why you may be waiting. It is possible that while waiting for an important email, the sender may be writing it with very significant information and that the more time they take, the more relevant the information they send to you will be. The same goes when waiting for an important meeting with your boss. He hasn't been getting back to you and you're getting impatient that he hasn't responded. On your end, you're annoyed and getting agitated. If you take a step back and rationalize it, he may be collecting more information about you to give you a good, thorough performance review and accurate feedback, which is to your benefit. In these cases, stopping to think about the other side will help you relax and realize why you're waiting. Just being willing to do this simple process is often just the ticket you need to dial up your patience quotient.

3. Empathize With People Around You.

While driving to work, you're stuck in a traffic jam due to a car accident. Immediately, you get frustrated and think about how it affects you. Again, you launched straight into your 'me, me, me' mode. This is the mode where impatience and frustration thrive. You ramp up your negative self-talk by saying things like: "Now I'll be late to work, for sure." Or "I'm really going to be late for that meeting!" Rather than getting angry at the driver and honking your horn, empathize with them. Think about how you would feel if that was you. Realize that it would be a horrible situation, you would be late to work, you would have to endure costly repairs, and now you have an entire highway honking their horns and glaring at you. Empathize with that person's situation and relax. You might be late to work, but things could be a lot worse.

Actually, you should take a moment to thank your lucky stars that your car is moving and that you are not in the pickle the other driver finds themselves in!

4. Prepare a Contingency Plan for When Patience May Be Needed.

When you're creating a plan for a project, plan for delays, complications, and setbacks. Although you don't want to think about them, you must prepare for encountering them. If they happen, you are already prepared and not caught off guard. Where you would've been stressed and angry, you're confident because you had pre-planned for those situations and created contingency plans. When they don't occur, you're delighted and happy that your patience to prepare served you well in the end. Remember that impatience happens when timelines become strained. If you have contingency plans that adjust timelines with very little stress, you will be able to remain patient.

The example that Romana Banuelos set through her life is an excellent one of patience, preparation, and persistence. Let's enjoy her story.

The patience you need to succeed might be similar to that of Romana Banuelos. Romana Banuelos was handpicked by the President of the United States to become the thirty-seventh United States Treasurer. How could that happen to somebody who was just sixteen years old and living in Mexico when her husband deserted her and her two children? At sixteen Romana was poverty stricken; she was untrained, unschooled and unable to speak English.

She was determined however, to improve her life. She wanted to seek out the American dream. She thought it was the only chance for her and her children. Romana boarded a bus with her two children and headed for Los Angeles. She arrived in one of the biggest cities in the world with only seven dollars in her purse. Throughout this time in her life, she held on to an unrelenting vision of a better life. Of course she was beaten down, disappointed and rejected, often more than once a day. However, her willingness to work hard and a commitment to success never wavered. Romana started at the lonely, tiring job of washing dishes. Then, from midnight to six in the morning she started another job making tacos. From these mundane jobs she was able to save $500. She invested the $500 in a taco machine. One thing led to another until Romana became the manager of the largest Mexican wholesale food business in the world. She never doubted her American Dream would come true. She committed herself to accomplishing more than anyone expected of her. She exemplified everything that is good about overcoming adversity. Dwight Eisenhower said of her, "We succeed only if we identify in life or in war or in anything else in a single overriding objective by making all other considerations blend into that one objective that powered Romana Banuelos to achieve her goals."

Through adversity Romana was able to reach her goals and achieve success. Her patience helped her through each obstacle that came her way and gave her the persistence needed for success.

5. Remember That Good Things Take Time

Sometimes, we're offered two positions: One is available immediately, comes with a raise, but is far beyond where you're willing to travel. The second position will not be available for six months, but it also comes with a raise, though slightly smaller, and is right in town. The catch is, however, that the second job may not be available when it comes down to it. The less patient person will choose the first option and want the immediate job opportunity. The patient person may realize that the second job is a much better proposition and, although it may end up not being available, they are willing to take the chance to provide them with a more attractive work-life balance. Good things take time and you must realize that you may have to wait for a good opportunity and resist lunging at the first option. The same is true when hiring. It isn't enough to get someone to fill a position, you need to be patient and make sure that the right person is filling that position. The best way to accomplish this type of thinking is to list the pros and cons of the situation and think logically through the decision making process.

Let's look at the story of Johnny Unitas and how his patience helped him become one of the greatest quarterbacks in the history of the National Football League.

> *Johnny Unitas had an obsession with becoming a professional football player. After graduating from Louisville University, he went undrafted in the pros. Instead of letting this get him down and perhaps thinking that he may not have enough talent, he remained patient. Unitas remembered that good things take time, nothing worth having comes easy. He wrote letters to a bunch of football teams and eventually was offered a try out for the Pittsburgh Steelers. Unfortunately, he did not make the team. Not one to give in, and after sending out more letters, he still had not made a team. His friends told him that he "got a raw deal" and "I guess it's time to hang it up". Unitas understood that good things take time, so he remained patient. He continued to train and work out on his own. In his heart he knew he was good enough to play in the NFL. Eventually, he was given an opportunity to try out for the Baltimore Colts. For all of his training and long hours of patient waiting, he was offered a contract. His patience did not stop there, though. He ended up working his way up from the third string to one of the greatest quarterbacks in NFL history.*
>
> *The patience and persistence that Johnny Unitas had was the reason that he is now in the NFL Hall of Fame. This is a great example to learn from.*

6. Look at the Big Picture

What if you were rear-ended on your way to work and the car dealership said they won't be able to look at the car until tomorrow? Would it be so horrible to drive a dented car for an extra day? No, it won't be. The car will be taken care of and there is no use in being impatient and angry over one extra day. In the grand scheme of things, this little setback doesn't really matter. Realize that sometimes there is NOTHING that you can do. Understanding this simple fact is crucial to being less stressed and being more patient.

7. Find Your Patterns of Impatience.

Write down every time that you become impatient and lose your cool. First, this will result in a helpful distraction from your frustration, as we discussed earlier. Later, you can look back at your list and examine the patterns and connections as to why you've become upset and impatient. While writing down the reasons associated with your impatience behaviors, you may realize that you've become upset for no real reason. Sometimes, it takes a visual representation of our stress and anger to make us realize why we are even upset at all. You may feel like you didn't get upset during the day, but on your list, you recorded ten times that you felt impatient. After recognizing those situations, you can discover new ways to act and plan when encountering those situations again in life.

> *Bobby Jones was a master at golf, but he eventually learned to master himself as well. He was beating everyone at the local golf club by the age of twelve, but he had earned a nickname during that period. He was called the "Club Thrower" because of his hot temper on the golf course.*
>
> *Even though Bobby had a natural skill, his friend, Grandpa Bart, told him, "You'll never win until you can control that temper of yours. You miss a shot – you get upset – and then you lose." Bobby was a golf prodigy at the age of twelve, but he did not win his first tournament until he learned to have self-discipline and have patience with himself at the age of twenty-one.*

DISCflex™

8. Recognize Your Triggers

Rather than specific incidents, some people respond impatiently to triggers. There may be certain phrases, recurring incidents, or situations that always seem to set you off. Recognize your triggers and learn to realize when you're about to become impatient before it even happens. If your trigger is someone saying "You don't know what you're talking about," recognize it and learn to prepare your response. You may have been saying "I DO know what I'm talking about! How dare you..." and been unsuccessful in that encounter. If you know this statement will 'set you off', pre-plan a calm response or, even easier, do not say anything at all. Once you have developed a good, calm response, you can use it, such as "I understand that you're frustrated, I would be as well. Let's look back at the big picture..." You will have the upper hand in that situation and not let the other person get to you. Use your own key words to remember to be patient when you recognize triggers that will make you impatient. Rather than ruining that relationship, you steered your impatience and frustration away and brought the topic back to the surface rather than letting it get to you and exhibiting frustration.

9. Visualize Yourself as a Patient Person

If you have extra time to sit and think, think about stressful situations you've encountered. When are times that you've acted impatient or have been frustrated? How could you have reacted differently? What would you have said? Once you think about these situations and prepare a calm response, you will be prepared when dealing with that situation again. Visualize yourself responding to the situation. It's harder to react on the spot, but if you have thought it through and mentally practiced, you are more apt to use your patience and relax when it could be useful to your situation. Learn more about visualization by visiting the Creative Visualization session in the Life Skills Course.

33 How to Dial Down Patience

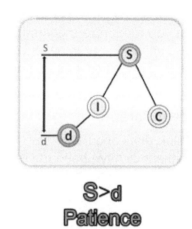

S>d
Patience

Patience S>d is not always a virtue and to accomplish many of your goals, you must learn to dial down your patience if the situation calls for it. Although self-motivation D>s is the opposing trait, 'Learning How To Become More Self Motivated' is not the same as 'How To Dial Down Your Patience'. Although they can be related, they are not exact opposites. Dialing down your patience includes different steps and different approaches than simply increasing your self-motivation, which we will discuss in this session.

Most of the time throughout our lives we've been told to be patient - not impatient. But, there are just as many circumstances where you might need to dial down your patience. The more you understand why and when you might need to become less patient, the more you'll realize that nothing gets accomplished if we have too much patience. Imagine a deadline is fast approaching and you don't have the materials you need from your coworker - even though they promised that it would be in your email bin yesterday. You have the choice to remain patient or take action. If you choose the latter, you can ask them where it is and when you'll receive it. You can tell them that you've assigned it to someone else. You can do it yourself. Or you can take the task completely off your to-do list and decide never to complete it. In this situation, choosing to dial down your patience, rather than waiting in limbo afforded you lots of options. Most importantly, you are moving forward.

Or think about this scenario... What if you're trying to sell an upgrade to a client and are about to close the deal, and you sense hesitation. You can be patient and book another appointment when the client says they need time to think about it, or you may need to drive the point home that the price you are quoting expires tomorrow and you know this will save the client money because they need the upgrade before

> *"Some people would rather die than think."*
>
> *~Bertrand Russell*

the end of the year anyway. By dialing down your patience and being assertive you can really provide a benefit to your client. If you don't dial down your patience, and instead wait for the client to make their decision, you haven't closed the sale and when the price rises, your client loses the benefit you could have provided. As you can see, both of these situations required immediate actions. So you have to be ready to launch into action whenever you make the decision to dial down your patience. You will need to practice the steps necessary to do so, in order to execute them confidently when needed.

Immediate Steps:

Here are a few immediate and secondary steps that you can take in order to learn how to dial down your Patience. These are a few steps that you can take immediately towards learning how to dial down your patience.

1. Prioritize Your Patience

Create a task list and write down everything you need to do on a piece of paper. Then, assign each task to a category of 'Important' and 'Not as Important'. Being patient, you may think that all tasks require the same amount of patience and waiting. This is not true. Once you have your list and you have prioritized what needs to be done, you must dial your patience down and act to get the 'Important' tasks done; while knowing you can wait on the 'Not as Important' tasks.

In the best-selling book, First Things First, authors Steven Covey and Roger and Rebecca Merrill wrote about this type of concept. The book's basic concept is easy enough to understand. Divide your tasks up based on what category they fall into:

Quadrant I - urgent, important

Quadrant II - not urgent, important

Quadrant III - urgent, not important

Quadrant IV - not urgent, not important

Then simply prioritize your time accordingly. This will go a long way in determining which tasks require you to become more proactive by dialing down your patience and getting down to action. For more information about this you can review the information in the Ranking Goals session of Indaba's Life Skills program, or peruse the best-selling book, First Things First.

2. Stop Making Excuses

Rather than making excuses and saying that you must wait for one reason or another, act! Rather than asking "Why?" ask "Why not?" When you are unsure, you usually wait around and let things work themselves out. In dialing down your Patience, you must ask and not hesitate. Make a plan to step up and start acting, rather than deciding to sit and wait. Then train yourself to ask the most important questions of all: "Why not me? Why not now?"

"Action is the foundational key to all success."

~Pablo Picasso

3. Surround Yourself With 'Go-Getters'

Make friends and spend more time with motivated and driven people who have balance in their lives. These types of people tend to know when to dial up and when to dial down their patience. You will see how they drive themselves to get what they want and sometimes may not wait to do so. You will be able to recognize situations in context and see what action they took to get to their goal. Talking to these people and asking them what situations they look for when deciding not to be patient will also help you.

4. Set Goals and Write Down an Action Plan.

Set an overall goal for yourself that is conceivable to reach. Then break it down into action steps. Do this for the goals that are most important to you. If you keep working towards those goals with a view to stepping up your timelines for achieving them, you will find yourself making more decisions that require you to dial down your patience.

Soon you'll be in the habit of assessing whether you need to start acting quicker rather than being less proactive about reaching your goals. Create specific steps that you WILL take you towards reaching your goal as you set down finite timelines. Then look at your goals again to see if you can accomplish them sooner. This type of thinking is what you do for stretch goals. Stretch your thinking a bit and challenge yourself by dialing down your patience appropriately.

Secondary Step:

The secondary step for dialing down patience may take more time to master than the Immediate Steps. However, it is just as important and is not harder necessarily, but will happen over a more extended period.

1. Practice Writing Down the Situations You Regularly Face.

As situations occur and you react, journal the situation, how you acted, and what occurred. As time goes on, you may start to fall back into your habits of being patient and waiting around, convincing yourself that it's for the best. Bear in mind that this is normal. When at first you dial down your patience, you'll be operating at a different speed than people around you are used to. Whenever you change pace, people become uncomfortable because it's not like the 'you' that they've come to know. So, make sure that you make an effort to maintain trust and adjust your tempo by using mirroring and matching as well as other rapport building techniques.

As you log events in your journal, you will have history to look back on. As you dial down your patience and increase your tempo you'll see patterns emerge and see your successes as a result of consciously making the effort to dial down your patience as situations warrant. Writing in your journal and reflecting on specifically what worked well for you and what didn't will also help you if you face a new situation and are unsure how to act. You can look at your past experiences and compare the new situation to something you've been through before and make an accurate decision of how to act.

34 Thoughtfulness Generic Profile

Definition

When Steadiness is greater than Influence, you have the Sub-factor of thoughtfulness. Thoughtful people think diligently about problems, relationships, or anything else that comes their way. They work hard at planning their words and even their actions. Thoughtful people never act on impulse; they always trust their conscious mind over their instincts.

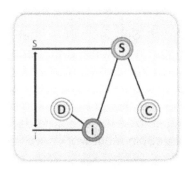

S>I
Thoughtfulness

Descriptors

Here is a list of words synonymous with the thoughtfulness Sub-factor:

- Caring
- Thinking
- Contemplative
- Sympathetic
- Deliberate

- Attention to detail
- Considerate
- Kindheartedness
- Diligent

Strengths

The strengths of the thoughtfulness Sub-factor are deep and logical thinking, great steadiness and reliability, and the ability to understand others well. Deep and logical thinking is important to the thoughtful person. They pride themselves on going through the rational decision making process and never acting on impulse.

Thoughtful people are very reliable and will always follow through on their work. They will also provide it in a manner that is well thought out and needs little editing or revision. People with this Sub-factor understand others well. They are very thoughtful in terms of relationships and how others are thinking or feeling. They show a great deal of empathy and are able to solve the personal problems of others. Therapists are a great example of a profession that has this Sub-factor.

I love working on teams with thoughtful people. They oftentimes consider every option to make the best possible decision. When they make a decision, I am confident that they looked at every detail and have made a good decision. I also never have to worry that they don't do their work. Thoughtful people are usually very reliable since they think things through and realize how important their contribution is. Also, they like to do things for others and see doing their work as something they're doing for me.

> *"Expect problems and eat them for breakfast."*
>
> *~Alfred A. Montapert*

Weaknesses

The weaknesses of the thoughtfulness Sub-factor are that they have a hard time making quick and on-the-spot decisions when necessary and they don't deal well with deadlines and time constraints because they like to get their thought process right before finalizing anything. This can sometimes be a crux for them because they can't complete projects on time and continually fall behind. Because the thoughtful person never acts on impulse, they fail to understand the importance of making quick and deliberate decisions at times. This is an essential quality of leadership, and thoughtful people must work hard at making these types of decisions.

Oftentimes, when people start new jobs, they fall into a rut of being too thoughtful. If they are unsure of what they are doing, they may be taking a long time to complete a project. They may be working so diligently in trying to make the project and process perfectly right before turning it in, perhaps making them miss the deadline. Usually, they need an extra push to be reminded that the deadline is coming and that they need to speed up their process.

Situational Adaptation - Dial Up or Dial Down

Thoughtfulness is an essential tool if you learn how to harness its power. You need to dial down your thoughtfulness when working on a project and try to dial up your efficiency when deadlines are nearing. This will combine the best of your logical thinking process with meeting deadlines. You should also learn how to dial up your thoughtfulness before having to make quick decisions in order to know what to decide beforehand. This will allow you to dial down your thoughtfulness when you have to make those on-the-spot decisions and will turn you into a great leader. You almost always want to dial up your thoughtfulness when making decisions; you just want to make sure that you limit how much time you think for. You don't want to be caught in a static position where you are only thinking and not ever acting. Thoughtfulness is a great tool to have if you know how to use it effectively.

Being an elevated S>i means you will tend to think long and hard before making any decisions.

This is an excellent trait when it's important to have a thorough understanding of all details in a project or goal before moving forward. This will generally translate into fewer mistakes since all of the details will have been researched and possible negative scenarios will have been considered before any real actions take place.

Unfortunately this can also mean taking too long to move forward with the project or goal. Imagine working with someone who had their feet firmly planted and is unable to move forward with a yes or no decision, at least not until all research has been thoroughly reviewed. This could mean the window of opportunity could close and it may mean that the opportunity to launch a new product may be delayed. The competition may beat you to the punch.

Being thoughtful while dialing up the opposing Sub-factor of enthusiasm may be helpful when dealing with a tentative customer. This customer may be unsure if the product is right for their needs. If you are able to answer all of their objections quickly and thoroughly while being enthusiastic, it may close the deal. On the other hand, having too much enthusiasm may make the customer more nervous than confident in the product or sale. You may come across as too pushy and assertive.

There have been times that I've had to dial up my Thoughtfulness when creating a new coaching session. I've wanted to get it done as soon as possible and launch it, but I had to dial up my thoughtfulness to develop it and create it in the best way possible. It is oftentimes difficult for me to slow down, dial up my thoughtfulness, and develop a project slowly rather than rush through it to get it done and to be a success.

When being the decision maker, I've had to ignore my thoughtfulness to make a decision and act fast. When it comes to the critical point where I must act, I have to ignore my feelings and emotions and make a decision. If I rested on my thoughtfulness too much, I would never make fast decisions and probably would not be where I am today. Dialing down and ignoring my thoughtfulness is oftentimes necessary in my line of work.

Next Steps

Next, you will explore the benefits and consequences of the Thoughtfulness Sub-factor. If you think that this Sub-factor is important for your success, you can target your knowledge by investigating various ways to dial up or dial down your Thoughtfulness Sub-factor in our 'How to' sessions.

"You must constantly change and adapt to a new environment."

~Jong-yong Yun

35 How to Dial Up Thoughtfulness

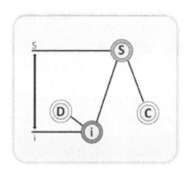

S>I
Thoughtfulness

Sometimes, by way of feedback, we're told by a co-worker or partner that we weren't very thoughtful in a specific situation. Fortunately, even if you've never been told something akin to this, I know that you might - after self-examination - have thought that you could have been more thoughtful at some time in your life. This session focuses on how to become more thoughtful; with an emphasis on how to dial up your thoughtfulness.

Thoughtfulness has many aspects. You can be thoughtful in an emotional and logical manner; in planning and strategy; in relationships. You may be a deep thinker and thoughtfully put together incredible technical solutions. You may be a thoughtful decision maker. You may be thoughtful about time - always thinking about the best use of this valuable commodity. You may focus on the past, present or future. Today we'll discuss how you can dial up thoughtfulness in any of these areas - in any of these contexts. For the purpose of best explaining how to dial up thoughtfulness, we'll assume that you can translate our examples and steps into any arena where you need to dial up your thoughtfulness quotient. In this session, we'll concentrate primarily on being thoughtful in the relationship realm.

Too often, we fall into the habit of going to work focused primarily on getting our responsibilities accomplished and we don't think to put in extra thoughtfulness or effort into forging relationships with those we work with. There are benefits and consequences to not being thoughtful as you interact with others. We've found that forging deep relationships is one of the best ways to become more successful. However, without consideration and thoughtfulness, it is almost impossible to develop the types of relationships that will ultimately help you stand out above the pack. You'll find that when you are more thoughtful, you will take the time to consider the consequences your actions have on your future. You will be considerate of the impact on those you care about. By being more

> *"It's what you learn after you know it all that counts."*
>
> *~Attributed to Harry S. Truman*

thoughtful, you'll also tend to have a better quality of work product.

Now, let's look at some specific ways and different skills to master in order to become more thoughtful in your relationships. Usually, after we realize that we're not as thoughtful as we want to be, we genuinely want to change our behavior. Often, however, we just don't know how to dial up thoughtfulness. Some people believe that thoughtfulness is not something that can be learned. We politely disagree. Although it takes time and practice to put thoughtfulness into recurring actions, there are a few simple steps that anyone can do to become more thoughtful. First, understand that thoughtfulness has many faces. It is the face of kindness and consideration for others. It is the face of contemplation and attention to detail; the face of caring and meditation. In thinking of the past and planning for the future, it is the face of reflection and introspection.

Immediate Steps:

Here are some immediate steps that you can employ to become more thoughtful in your dealings with others.

1. Attain Proper Nonverbal Behaviors.

Make eye contact with another person and keep an open stance with your arms unfolded and your shoulders relaxed. Studies have shown that when you talk to someone in a relaxed way, with your arms unfolded and make good eye contact, you are much more likely to be comfortable and stress free.

> *"A good listener is not only popular everywhere, but after a while he gets to know something."*
>
> *~Wilson Mizner*

In a less stressed state of mind the studies say that you will retain the information the person is telling you much more. Also, in retaining the information it will allow your mind to begin thinking of ways to use that information productively. When we're busy, we tend not to look people in the eye. We are absorbed with other things and are unfocused on the present moment or on the person at a deep level. Sometimes, we actively seek not to connect at a deep level with others. Perhaps we might think that if we stop to make eye contact and engage at a deep level, we'll waste a lot of time. And if we waste time talking all day, we'll get off track from our day's responsibilities and tasks at work and won't be able to focus on accomplishing everything we need to get done.

Recognize you simply must make time for thoughtful relationships. Yes, they do take time. Occasionally you will be stuck (trapped!) in a long conversation when you really do have pressing things that need your attention. However, they will feel important that you stopped what you were doing to really take notice of what they are saying and to look them in the eye. Making eye contact with them also makes them more comfortable and less intimidated. Eyes, after all, are the windows to your soul. Making eye contact enhances trust because you are more open in your communication. You are able to read people the best when you make eye contact. Whether someone is presenting to a conference room full of people or to a small group, everyone sitting down generally behaves in a similar manner. Most audience members look at their notes, jot a few things down, occasionally look up, and look around and many times stretch to stay alert. When was the last time you gave visual feedback - through great eye contact - to the presenter while they were speaking? Have you ever given a presentation and someone in the room was watching, smiling, and nodding as you delivered your presentation? Didn't that person appear more engaged - more thoughtful?

Receiving thoughtful signals from an audience member gives a presenter a surge of confidence that what we're saying is right on target and the members of the audience are listening and understanding the intent of the message. Do this the next time you are in an audience. Watch intently, smile, and nod as you're following along with the presentation. The speaker will appreciate it and may even say something to you afterwards about how thoughtful you looked.

2. Listen.

This may seem obvious, but to be more thoughtful, you must learn how to listen properly. There is a major difference between hearing and listening. People often hear what someone is saying, but they are not really listening to the message. This may mean making a conscious effort to remain silent - while focusing on the topic - during a conversation so the other person can complete their side of the discussion without interruption. When you're listening without interrupting, you may hear things you never thought you'd hear. Whenever you give people the opportunity to speak for an extended period of time without interruption they tend to talk more and provide more information than had you interrupted their entire train of thought. You may find out that a coworker has the same hobby as you do and you have a novel connection with them. Or, you may find that someone in your office is also from your hometown or region. Listening doesn't only apply to conversations you're already having. Sometimes, you may see that a coworker has been efficient lately and would make a great member for a team or a new initiative. Not only will they be grateful you asked them to join your group, the overall project will quite possibly have a better chance of success.

Simply by improving your listening skills may sometimes be the most thoughtful thing that someone can do, and it has a good chance of leading to positive consequences. Also, chances are that person will remember your kindness and tell someone else how much they enjoy talking to you.

3. Defer Judgment at First and Just Focus on the Positives

Small, positive thoughtful comments can be made at any time. You can compliment a coworker's outfit, their presenting skills, or even their attitude. It doesn't take much time to be attentive and just say something like: "Wow, Sheila, I loved that presentation! Your enthusiasm really spoke to me and I can't wait to hear you present again!" Not only will Sheila think of you as very thoughtful and kind, you have now given her a boost of confidence for when she has to present again. You can make small heart-felt compliments at almost any circumstance - if you take the time to consider what other people are doing.

> *"Talent is God given. Be humble. Fame is man-given. Be grateful. Conceit is self-given. Be careful."*
>
> *~John Wooden*

Genuine comments delivered in a considerate and thoughtful manner touch people. Like good deeds, compliments inspire people to give them to others. It takes just a little time and effort to make this practice a habit in your life. If you do so, you'll find that the benefits in brightening someone's day and being thoughtful are much greater than the effort you expended Positive reinforcement is a fabulous motivational tool. As you compliment your people, you will begin to see your staff flourish. More of their strengths will become apparent as they thrive under your praise. This positive energy will help your team realize new opportunities. This blossoming environment will help the company and its employees grow. An excellent way to focus on generating solutions to problems and creating a positive

DISCflex™

environment - instead of focusing on the negatives of the problem - is in the Generating Options session of the Decision Making Course.

Secondary Steps:

After you recognize that you want to be more thoughtful, it may take a while to naturally ingrain that habit. After you perfect the Immediate Steps, you can step back and look at the next things you can do. These Secondary Steps, like the immediate steps, come more naturally with practice.

1. Be Humble.

When you receive feedback, either privately or publicly, don't make a big deal out of it. Say thank you and be grateful, but don't boast. Keep your feelings of self-satisfaction inside. Sometimes, when we are thrilled, or taking pride in our accomplishments, or are in a state of self-satisfaction, it can come across as bragging or gloating, even if this was absolutely not our intention. When this misperception occurs, it can hurt our relationships with others. This is especially true if we were singled out for praise and someone equally deserving did not receive the wonderful feedback we did. To be more thoughtful of others' feelings, don't talk about your accomplishments openly, unless asked, and when you do so -- always be very modest. You can learn more about feedback from the How to Give Feedback session of the Feedback and Coaching Course as well as the Receiving Feedback, Noble Intent, and Coaching session from the same course.

Now let's see an example of humility and thoughtfulness displayed by George Washington when he was commander-in-chief of the American army.

> *George Washington was an exceptional general because of his humility. At one point during his tenure, soldiers from the Continental Army were fed up with the Continental Congress because they had fought for years without any pay. They gave an ultimatum to Congress: If we don't get paid, we will march on Congress and seize control of the Government. George Washington tried to calm the situation by addressing some of the leaders of this rebellion in New York. He urged the soldiers to "not take any measures which, viewed in the calm light of reason, will sully the glory you have hitherto maintained". At first, the men glared angrily at the general, believing that he was nothing more than a lackey for the Congress. Then Washington began reading a letter from one of the congressmen. He kept stumbling over the words and eventually stopped and reached in his pocket. He pulled out something that his men had never seen him with before: a pair of spectacles. Humbly, he addressed the soldiers by saying, "Gentleman, you must pardon me. I have grown gray in your service and now find myself going blind." The soldiers wept for Washington and agreed to give the Continental Congress more time to pay them. Thomas Jefferson recounted the incident by saying that "the moderation and virtue of a single man probably prevented this Revolution from being closed, as most others have been, by a subversion of that liberty it was intended to establish".*
>
> *George Washington's humility helped him take advantage of an opportunity to help his soldiers. His thoughtfulness helped him gain the respect and trust of his men. His example is an excellent one to follow and apply in our lives today.*

2. Do Good Deeds.

It is admirable to do a geed deed for others for no particular reason. When you're out getting your morning coffee, grab another for one of your co-workers or for your spouse. They will feel noticed and cared about that you did that for them. Change up who you do nice things for. Help one coworker load the copier one day, help another edit a project the next, and buy lunch for another coworker another day. You'll soon see that one good deed sparks another and you will be more apt to keep doing it. Also, your coworkers will be touched by your thoughtfulness and will, in turn, help someone else or help you in the future. This also builds your relationship with them, ensuring that one day you may need their help and they will be much more likely to offer you their support.

If you really want to understand how powerful this concept can truly be, read the book or watch the movie called 'Pay It Forward'. The concept of 'Pay It Forward' is a real life consequence of one child's thoughtfulness. The 'Pay It Forward' movement was the brainchild of a young boy, 11 1/2-year-old Trevor McKinney. He was inspired when his seventh grade social studies teacher gave the class an assignment to devise and put into action a plan that will change the world for the better. The idea Trevor came up with was simple, but ingenious. Trevor's plan is a charitable pyramid scheme, based on good deeds rather than greed and profit. He said that if a person just concentrated on doing three thoughtful things and told others to do the same and 'Pay It Forward' instead of paying it back, all these good deeds could really change the world. He had three simple tenets as the foundation for his idea:

'Pay It Forward' is a form of people pleasing and so is being thoughtful, kind, and considerate. A great session to learn how to do this is the Law of People Pleasing session in the 21 Laws of Influence for Sales Course Part 2.

3. Do Not Set Too Many Expectations of Others.

All too often, people go out of their way for others and then get hurt and annoyed when others don't go out of their way for them immediately in return. Thoughtful people do good deeds and do not expect anything in return. Although this may seem like a challenge and make you feel like your good deeds are going unnoticed and forgotten, they're not. You never know when someone may pay you back or pay it forward to someone else. Good deeds are like a domino rally - you never know when or where the rally will lead - you just have to know that if you put energy in motion that good deeds will happen. The best thing is to keep giving and keep helping others. The true reward is you will be the one making yourself happy by helping others. Again, review the Law of People Pleasing and also look at the Law of Reciprocity to know when you are subconsciously expecting people to do favors for you in return for your good deed. That can ruin relationships if not handled appropriately.

Pay It orward

#1 It has to be something that really helps people.

#2 It has to be something they can't do by themselves.

#3 I do it for them, then they do it for three other people.

4. Make a Mental Effort to Observe Everything Around You.

Watch how other people act. This is the best way to find out how to help people with good deeds. If you see that a coworker is always misplacing their papers, buy them a small organizer to help them out. If you notice that another coworker never eats meat at company meals, you may think to ask them if they're vegetarian before you order food for the company Christmas Party. Noticing little details like this will make people feel like you care. This will foster good relationships in your organization and lead to more effective outcomes. There is a reason why companies like Google and other companies that take great care of their workers often produce the best results. Being observant of everything around you can also help you make the right decision on a business deal or transaction. I'll admit that I've made a couple of mistakes in not observing my world to help discern what the future might hold.

5. Continually Remind Yourself to Be Thoughtful.

You may think it will take forever to make thoughtfulness second nature to you. The good news is that you don't need constant focus on thoughtfulness for it to become a major driving Factor in your life. All you need is to remember to use thoughtfulness often. Even though it doesn't take a lot of effort, you still have to remember to do it. At first, before it becomes a habit, you may need a little help to remind yourself to be thoughtful. You may choose to leave sticky notes and reminders to yourself to "Give someone a compliment. Smile. Be encouraging." Or use electronic reminders that pop up every once in a while to prompt you into thoughtfulness. After a while, you won't need those reminders and thoughtfulness and consideration will come naturally.

In the early 1980's a client of mine was very excited about a new machine that he had seen at a trade show in Chicago. At the time I was living in South Africa. Victor walked into my office with a gigantic machine that looked like a copier but it had something like a telephone attached to it. He explained to me that it was called a facsimile machine. I, of course, asked him what this facsimile machine did. He told me that it could send documents over a telephone wire out to anybody else. I said, "How would they get the documents, will they have to have two fax machines? One at each end?" He answered yes exactly, two machines were needed - one sending and one receiving. Then I asked him how much the fax machines cost and he told me that it was about 6,000 Rands. Now 6,000 Rands was an enormous amount of money to spend in any business in Africa at the time and was equivalent to approximately twelve thousand US dollars.

I asked him how many fax machines were already in operation in South Africa because I hadn't seen any. Victor told me there were only a couple because the machines were brand new. However, he said that would quickly change because he had managed to acquire the rights for Sharp, Sony, and Canon fax machines in South Africa. He was in my office because he needed some financial backing. I looked at the idea and came to the conclusion that fax machines were not viable. Too expensive and none too practical because of the sending and receiving requirements, which I believed was a huge problem. I told him that I would not financially back the product nor would I recommend that any of my clients put money into the deal that he was about to set up. Unfortunately for me and fortunately for him, this company went from $1M in the first year to $3M in the second to nearly $55M less than five years later. This was an expensive lesson for me to learn about being thoughtful and observing what the future might hold.

36 How to Dial Down Thoughtfulness

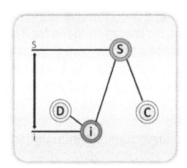

S>I
Thoughtfulness

Remember that the opposing Sub-factor of Thoughtfulness S>i is Enthusiasm I>s, so all that may be required is that you dial up your Sensitivity and this alone will have the immediate impact of dialing back your persistency.

In some situations, you must dial down your thoughtfulness. This may be when a deadline is approaching and your team is stuck in a mode of 'Analysis Paralysis' and can't seem to decide on the strategy to implement. Although you empathize with the team's need to create a perfect plan, you know you need to step up and bring the plan to action. You must meet the approaching deadline.

In times like these, you may need to dial down your thoughtfulness to be more efficient and motivated to get things done. Sometimes, we need to move to action. The Enthusiasm DISC Sub-factor™ can help you do this. Thoughtfulness often takes us into a deep thinking mode that is hard to break out of to complete our goal. You need to learn to set appropriate time limits to thoughtfulness and give yourself the okay to take your ideas to action.

With the Thoughtfulness Sub-factor, you may need to dial it down to decline a previously accepted lunch invitation to work on a project. Hard to believe, but your coworkers will understand. Dialing down your Thoughtfulness is the key to getting things done. If you were always thoughtful, you would be more focused on everyone else than your own work, possibly missing things or not getting things done.

DISCflex™

A couple of years ago, I worked with a colleague who spent an inordinate amount of time on PowerPoint presentations. We were presenting to a few executives and creating the slide deck for them. My colleague initially put over forty-five slides into the presentation for a thirty-minute meeting. Worse than that, the slides were filled with text and data that could not be adequately addressed in the meeting. I told my colleague that we would be lucky to get through fifteen slides with the executives because they will want to ask questions. My colleague was too thoughtful about the PowerPoint presentation and, when presented, turned out to be too much for the executives to comprehend in one meeting. Read the whitepaper on the Magic 7+2 Rule in the supplementary materials section to get a better grasp of how being too thoughtful can overload people's memory capacity.

Immediate Steps:

There are some immediate steps that you can implement to start dialing down your Thoughtfulness DISC Sub-factor™ when you need to during your daily interactions. Remember to practice these steps and complete the activities in the activities section.

1. **Understand Your Return on Investment.**

   What is the task you are undertaking and how long should it take you to complete? If you are trying to buy car insurance, you should not spend fifty hours to save a measly two hundred dollars a year. You need to think of appropriate timelines for the task. Your effort should be in correspondence with the result you need to produce. You can exceed expectations, but only to a reasonable amount.

2. **Know the Consequences of the Thoughtfulness DISC Sub-factor™.**

   There are many consequences to being too thoughtful or being thoughtful in the wrong way. Have you ever been in a situation where someone tried to console you after something bad happened and you just wanted them to leave you alone? Thoughtfulness can kill rapport when it comes across as persistent and unswerving. Show your thoughtfulness in one sentence rather than giving a whole story about it.

   Another problem with thoughtfulness is that it can come across as disturbing if you don't have a great deal of rapport with the other person. You have to moderate your thoughtfulness when interacting with people that you don't have a strong relationship with. It is important when building relationships that you understand the consequences of being too thoughtful with people. The best advice is to show more thoughtfulness the longer you know someone and the stronger the relationship is. If the other person doesn't meet those two criteria, edge on the side of caution when displaying thoughtfulness so you don't overdo it. If you don't dial down your thoughtfulness, you may find yourself missing opportunities.

> *There once was a man who desired a part-time job to help afford his tuition to Stanford University. He was told there was only a stenographer position available and he quickly responded, "I'd love it!" Then the young man added, "However, I can't start until next Wednesday."*
>
> *The young man reported for work on Wednesday and his boss said to him, "I like your promptness and enthusiasm. I do have one question. Why couldn't you start until Wednesday?" "Well, you see, sir," the young man replied, "I had to find a typewriter and learn how to use it."*
>
> *That young man was Herbert Hoover, the 31st President of the United States of America. President Hoover shows us that sometimes you have to dial down thoughtfulness to learn new things. A thoughtful person might have waited to find a job they could do. Know the consequences of the Thoughtfulness Sub-factor and its effect on opportunities in your life.*

3. Understand That They Will Understand.

You may feel bad turning down an invitation to lunch or when telling a coworker that you'll have to cancel on them, but they will understand. You are there to work and you have work to do. If you have to turn someone down or tell them you'll get together another time, they may be disappointed at first, but not for long. The hardest part for thoughtful people to do is say no. If you say yes to everyone, however, you'll lose track of your work and end up becoming less efficient and getting less done. You must say no occasionally and understand that those people do understand and know where you're coming from.

Even with your family and friends, you have to dial down your thoughtfulness when you have an important project at work. Try and keep a work-life balance, but understand that efficiency and achieving business goals requires you to sacrifice your thoughtfulness at times to achieve what you want.

The thoughtful person may get sidetracked into doing what other people want and helping to achieve other people's goals, which can negatively affect your life in the long run if there is no balance.

4. Create A 'Must Say No' List.

Have you even been in a situation where you know you should say no but decide that you can handle it and say yes? Then afterwards, you may regret it.

In an effort to be thoughtful and helpful, you may rationalize and think that you can handle whatever it is that they're asking from you. Before you run into any situations, make a 'Must Say No' list. This list may include things such as "Do not volunteer for another project when I already have three going" or "Do not accept a dinner invitation when I have a major project due the next day". If you will sacrifice your work for something and can't afford it, add that situation to the list. That way, if that situation comes up, you can refer to your list instead of being tempted to rationalize and accept the offer.

After completing the immediate steps to help dial down your Thoughtfulness DISC Sub-factor™, some secondary steps will help you further your ability to dial down thoughtfulness. These skills may take practice to incorporate into your life. Set aside time to practice the steps so that you can use them whenever a situation calls for dialing down your thoughtfulness.

Secondary Steps:

1. Avoid the Brain Dump.

If you have an elevated Thoughtfulness Sub-factor, you probably spend a lot of time giving information to others in your team or personal life. You may think that giving the detailed information is being thoughtful because you are making sure the other person is not missing any critical data. Unfortunately, too much tidings of knowledge at once is called the 'Brain Dump'. When this happens, the other person is rarely going to remember much of what you told them.

Instead of telling them everything you know at once, take steps to intersperse it throughout conversations. When working with a team, the first meeting should cover the overall objectives and goals. After you acknowledge those, you can move on to setting responsibilities and accountability metrics. Remember to always sequence information so that you are not overloading someone's brain in one conversation.

2. Reflect on Your Life.

If you said no to someone recently, what were the consequences? Did you have more time to get your work done? When you reflect on what happened, you give yourself a point to analyze your actions and make a plan to correct things if something went wrong or could be better. This also serves as a good reminder. If you feel like you want to return to your thoughtful ways and aren't sure that dialing down your thoughtfulness is a good thing, you can look back on situations that proved that they worked well.

3. It Takes Time.

You aren't going to dial down your thoughtfulness over night. You need continuous practice so that you can flex your behavior when you need to.

Although it may feel uncomfortable to say no to a few people and you may feel cold-hearted and uncaring, dialing down your thoughtfulness must be done. This feeling will go away as you start to realize just how much you're doing and what you're getting accomplished.

"I look back on the old Masters highlights and I watched some things that I've done, and I've learned from those experiences. It's taken me time and years of seeing what's worked well and what hasn't."

~Phil Mickelson

37 Persistence Generic Profile

Definition

When Steadiness is greater than Compliance, you have the Persistence Sub-factor. Persistent people are great at continuing to do their work despite having problems or difficulties along the way. They are a great asset to any organization because they stick to the current state of affairs and are predictable. People with this Sub-factor are determined and can usually get something done that others can't simply because they keep at it.

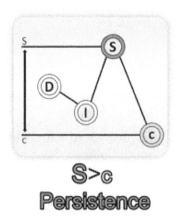

S>c
Persistence

Descriptors

Some words that describe the Persistence Sub-factor are:

- Perseverance
- Doggedness
- Resolution
- Endurance
- Tenacity

- Determination
- Diligence
- Constancy
- Stamina

Strengths

The strengths of the Persistence Sub-factor are that persistent people have a great determination, they can get past obstacles that would stop others, and they can typically work at something for a longer period of time than others. Persistent people are very determined in almost anything that they do.

"Success is almost totally dependent upon drive and persistence. The extra energy required to make another effort or try another approach is the secret of winning."

~Dennis Waitley

This is one of the best qualities to have for salespeople, because salespeople that are persistent do a much better job at getting sales than those that aren't persistent. Persistent people can work past obstacles because the only thing on their mind is the objective. Long projects that take a lot of time are best given to persistent people because they will be able to focus throughout the project and do the best job on it.

"Nothing in the world can take the place of Persistence. Talent will not; nothing is more common than unsuccessful men with talent. Genius will not; unrewarded genius is almost a proverb. Education will not; the world is full of educated derelicts. Persistence and determination alone are omnipotent. The slogan 'Press On' has solved and always will solve the problems of the human race."

~Calvin Coolidge

Using the Persistence Sub-factor allows us to continue working on things we believe in, our visions, our dreams, and other Factors. Whenever you look at successful people, you will find that they used this Sub-factor to achieve their goals. Take for instance Dr. Seuss. It is almost impossible to imagine not reading our children a Dr. Seuss book, but at one time Dr. Seuss himself was not finding any success. The first twenty-three publishers that he approached all rejected his first children's book. Could you imagine if he would have given up after the third rejection or the twentieth rejection? Fortunately, Dr. Seuss used the Persistence Sub-factor to make it to the twenty-fourth publisher who ended up selling six million copies of the book. This is a lesson of how persistence can be used in our lives to achieve our goals. We just have to push for the goals and dreams that mean the most to us.

Weaknesses

The weaknesses of the Persistence Sub-factor are that persistent people deal badly with change, can be stubborn, and aren't good at multi-tasking or changing directions. Persistent people become established in the status quo and have a very hard time at breaking out of their regular patterns in order to move into a new set of patterns. This can make persistent people stubborn as well, because people with this Sub-factor typically won't change their minds on any issue for a long period of time. Persistent people aren't good at multi-tasking or changing directions because their mind gets set on a goal and doesn't take its focus off of that goal until it is completed.

Persistence can sometimes be a weakness if you continue to work on a project that is bad for the company or for yourself. I've noticed this with myself and with my team members at times. Sometimes we will get so focused on a project that we think is a great idea and end up spending countless hours working with the wrong research or eventually find out that our idea was only half-right. Because of my team's persistence, we push until we get our projects completed, but that is sometimes a weakness if we realize later it needs to be redone. You must know when persistence can hurt your productivity.

Situational Adaptation - Dial Up or Dial Down

Now, let's talk about situational adaptation of the Persistence Sub-factor. You have to dial down your persistence when dealing with change. Use your persistence to get through projects and new obstacles, not to keep you in the same routine pattern. You should also dial down your persistence when handling multiple projects and even when balancing your work-life relationship. You can't constantly be thinking about a project at work when trying to have a nice night out with your family. Persistence needs to be dialed up when you are dealing with a complex project that needs a great deal of time. Your persistence will help you get through the routine work and the obstacles you will face in order to meet the final goal. Using your persistence wisely will help you become excellent at whatever you do.

In your professional life, you need to have a work-life balance. Sometimes work is your life, and that's alright. But for others who are trying to balance work with family and friends, knowing when to dial down your Persistence Sub-factor at work is important. Although you could stay a few hours overtime to finish a project that isn't due until next week, you may want to consider dialing down your persistence to spend some personal time with your family. The Persistence Sub-factor also makes the person responsible and dependable. I always look for team members that can display this Sub-factor because I know they will be dependable when I need them to be. I make it a rule in my office, however, to dial down the persistency of our office so that my team members spend time with their families and loved ones.

An example of an S>c boss is one who is very persistent and focused on the particular job or goal HE is most interested in. Obviously that should be the one that his employees are the most focused on too! This can be a very positive experience when the employee knows where their priorities should be at that time. The saying 'What gets measured, gets done' is very true and evident here. When the boss is persistently asking "How are you doing with…? Have you formulated the plans? Do you have the numbers for me," that is the project that will be first and foremost in his employee's mind. This is a positive situation when that particular project is the one most beneficial to the company. On the negative side, what if an S>c employee is too persistent during a sales call with a potential customer? Their persistence may be a turn-off to the customer and the sale may fall through. If they had been more sensitive to the customer's needs and not their own, the sale may have had a positive close.

> *"As human beings we do change, grow, adapt, perhaps even learn and become wiser."*
>
> *~Wendy Carlos*

Let's look at some famous people that had to dial up their Persistence Sub-factor to achieve their goals. Every successful person has met set-backs at one point or the other and that can help us realize how to be successful as well. Apple microcomputers were rejected by both Hewlett-Packard and Atari when they were first being created. Imagine a world today without the Apple line of products. Apple knew that they had a good product and pushed to see it to completion. Even when Apple ran into difficulties with its computers, it reinvented them and produced the iPod along with it. They continued to persist achieving tremendous success.

If the persistent boss wants to get 'his' project accomplished in the most efficient way possible, he may find that dialing up the 'sensitive' Sub-factor may also be beneficial to achieving the goal.

Sometimes persistence can mean quick and curt questions followed by the same style answers. This can oftentimes be very cold and non-motivating. His employees may avoid him, so that they won't have to feel 'badgered' by his abrupt discussions. This may backfire and the project will be reviewed quickly and without much thought. Being more sensitive to your employees and showing more empathy can be positive. Being persistent doesn't mean being rude; even if you are kind and more sensitive to others, your employees will probably still be motivated to work hard on their projects when you have more empathy and sensitivity. On the flip side, the too sensitive salesman does need to forge a customer friendly relationship, but within professional boundaries.

What would happen if all 'sensitive' salesmen had clients who could not make their payments on a product recently purchased? Being too sensitive may cause the salesman to feel too guilty about asking for the payments required. This could eventually cause the relationship to sour since it is too personal and the salesman would be unable to actively pursue the product payments.

Charles Goodyear is another example of persistence in the face of adversity. It was his idea to create a rubber that was unaffected by extreme temperatures. For years, he faced family difficulties, ridicule from the community, and even was imprisoned at one point for debt. His vision paid off in the end because he discovered how sulfur could be added to rubber to achieve his goal. Every successful idea is met with a person with the Persistence Sub-factor. These are the people that know how to dial up their persistence when they need to get to their goals.

Next Steps

Next, you will explore the benefits and consequences of the Persistence Sub-factor. If you think that this Sub-factor is important for your success, you can target your knowledge by investigating various ways to dial up or dial down your Persistence Sub-factor in our 'How to' sessions.

38 How to Dial Up Persistence

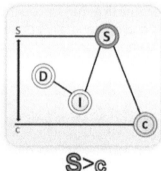

S>c
Persistence

"Persistence is the foundation of excellence. One is a matter of worth and value; the other, a matter of time."

~Hellen Davis

Here are some strategies for dialing up your persistence. Sometimes, we can become too comfortable and relaxed with where we are and what we've accomplished. We are happy and satisfied at home, with our friendships, and in our workplace. But looking at our situation, although we are satisfied and happy, and that is great; we just do not have the drive we used to have. That is the conundrum of life: We strive to be satisfied and happy with where we are but when this happens, it has the potential to severely impact our drive determination, initiative, and get-up-and-go; not to mention our persistence!

What happens if we stand still or step back when we should have acted and stepped forward? What happens if we don't go the extra mile? What will we miss out on if we aren't persistent? What could we go on to accomplish if we were just a little bit more determined or unshakable in pursuing our goals? What could we learn if we were unrelenting in our quest for knowledge?

Sometimes, it is necessary for us to be persistent, but there is a fine line between persistence and being pushy, unrelenting, and annoying or too dogged.

"Today, and every day, deliver more than you are getting paid to do. The victory of success will be half won when you learn the secret of putting out more than is expected in all that you do. Make yourself so valuable in your work that eventually you will become indispensable. Exercise your privilege to go the extra mile, and enjoy all the rewards you receive. You deserve them!"

~Og Mandino

In life we have to make a decision about what the appropriate level of persistence is for what we want to accomplish. Most people never think about this but it is critically important because the right level of persistence may make the difference between being successful or pushing through - by being just a bit more determined and persistent - and achieving things other will never achieve because they didn't persevere. Often the only difference between those who succeed and those who don't is that they keep at it. So appropriate persistence is an important skill to learn. If you determine that it is worth it to keep trying, and you've thought through the consequences of stopping, push for what you believe in or push to have your ideas heard. Some people may say their thoughts and give up after, while others voice their opinions and are persistent about having them heard.

What makes a persistent person? Some believe that it is a natural trait that can't be learned. They believe some people are just born to be doggedly persistent, while others struggle to summon up the initiative to go the extra mile. We do agree, as with all the Sub-factors, while some people have a natural tendency, anyone can indeed learn the skills necessary to acquire an adequate and appropriate level of any characteristic or quality. Now let's discuss precisely how you would do so for persistence.

The best way to become good at being persistent is to think of persistence in terms of the level of effort it takes to get something accomplished at the level you deem suitable for your particular goal. You have to do a cost benefit analysis for persistence. How much effort versus how much reward? As an example, imagine the difference in persistent effort it would take to learn how to play the piano at an amateur versus professional level. Now think about how much more effort and persistence it would require for someone to become one of the top concert pianists in the world. Each goal requires a difference degree of effort - a distinctive level of persistency and perseverance.

There is a process for determining how much persistence is warranted. Think of times in your life where it was necessary to become more persistent. What made you determine that you had to be more persistent? Did you look at the goal and then think: How much effort and time is this going to take? You probably do this a lot more than you think you do. Put pen to paper and start mapping out the time, energy, resources it will take to complete your goal according to the level of excellence or completeness you want to achieve. Be brutally honest with yourself. Is the effort relative to the expected outcome?

If want your lawn groomed, and you all you have are lawn shears, all the persistence in the world - taking all day and all night to finish - isn't the best path. Get the right tool and you'll have better results and expend less time, energy and effort. A final word on persistency as it relates to cost benefit - return on the investment of your persistent efforts is important. So you have to have an ending point when you decide that your persistency isn't going to work out as planned. The definition of insanity is doing the same thing over and over and expecting a different result. This is where persistency is folly. Smart persistent people understand that stuff happens and all the persistency in the world isn't going to help all the time. Even the most persistent people don't win all the time. Have an end in sight before you start. That's just smart and an appropriate way to keep your persistency in the right perspective.

> *"The majority of men meet with failure because of their lack of persistence in creating new plans to take the place of those which fail."*
>
> *~Napoleon Hill*

If your dream is to play in the NBA and you have already grown as much as you ever will and reached your full height at 5'4", all the practice in the world - all of your persistent efforts - will statistically not help you achieve that goal. Yes, it can be done, but what are the odds of it happening and is it worth the effort and disappointment? Perhaps a more realistic endeavor where your persistency would pay higher dividends would be more prudent.

> *"Success is the result of perfection, hard work, learning from failure, loyalty, and persistence."*
>
> **~Colin Powell**

It's the same with many things in life, from wishing you could sing and be the next American Idol, to hoping to become the CEO of a Fortune 100 corporation. You have to assess whether you have the capability - do you have the vocal cords, height, IQ, or other attributes to make your goal achievable? Then determine the odds and allocate the appropriate amount of persistence. Next, just because you want to do something right now doesn't mean you can. Do you currently have the qualifications, capacity, or talent? No one is going to let you do brain surgery if you haven't qualified as a surgeon yet. The bottom line: You have to assess whether persistence is the right attribute to use right now. And if it isn't, when should you use persistency in achieving your goals. So the next question you should ask is: When is the appropriate time?

Perhaps you really want to play the piano at a professional level but once you right down specifically what it will take to achieve that level of excellence, you are realistic with yourself and say: "There is no way I can do that right now. Not with my family, school, and work responsibilities." But once I finished my degree, I can put aside the energy it will take. This example shows the two aspects - time and timing - that are important considerations in determining how persistent you will decide to be with any of your goals and desires. With time, you have to consider whether you have the time available to go after your objective. If the answer is 'No' all the persistence in the world isn't going to help you achieve it. So, the next thing you determine is if you don't have the time right now, and you still want to accomplish your goal, will you have enough time in the foreseeable future? If the answer is 'No' then you need to rethink your time constraints and priorities. But until you do, dialing up your persistence for this goal is probably not a smart thing to do. All that will happen is that you will frustrate yourself and those around you. Although this seems logical, people frustrate themselves like this all the time. Dialing down your persistence would be more appropriate in situations like this until you come up with a plan to adjust your time constraints. On the other hand, if you do see your time constraints changing, it might just be that your timing is off. A crucial aspect of persistence is timing. This is where goal setting and planning rally together with persistence to create magic. If you can be persistent at the most opportune moments in your life, you can truly succeed beyond your wildest dreams.

Another tactic in learning how to dial up your persistency is to use modeling. Seek out information about how much effort it took someone else who already achieved a goal similar to yours. Then examine how they did it relative to persistent efforts. How much time, money, resources, energy, and mental fortitude did it take these people? Was their persistency something that most people would have considered normal or were their persistent efforts above the norm? This is important. If you know that persistency is not a strong Sub-factor for you, having to dial it up to an above average level might indeed prove problematic. The good news is that forewarned is forearmed. If you know that you do indeed have to dial it up at an inordinate level to achieve a goal, you can prepare yourself better and give yourself that much better odds of being successful. Modeling how others behave who are persistent is one of the most effective ways to become persistent yourself.

> *"Never let your persistence and passion turn into stubbornness and ignorance."*
>
> **~Anthony J. D'Angelo**

Although it may seem difficult to become more persistent, it is possible and through practicing these skills and by modeling others who consistently display how persistent they are, you can achieve your goals. Let's look at some ways that you can easily accomplish this in your personal and professional life.

Immediate Steps:

After you recognize that you need to become more persistent, it may seem impossible to step up and become appropriately persistent. There are a few steps that you can take right now towards becoming more persistent.

1. Keep the End in Sight

Focus on reaching your goals. SMART goals and smart persistency are the winning ticket. Remind yourself what you're working towards. Sometimes, we get distracted by what we're working for and give up when it becomes too complicated or the perceived benefit passes. You may be working overtime for weeks and exhausting yourself, deciding to quit. You may have forgotten that you decided to pay off your student loans once and for all and were almost there. Remind yourself often what your goals are. It may help to post them in places you see all the time, such as on your bathroom mirror, on your computer, or a note in your car. Keep reminding yourself what all your hard work is for. It will make it twice as hard to give up. And remember to always look at persistency in terms of appropriateness for the situation.

The story of John Roebling, Washington Roebling and the Brooklyn Bridge is an incredible story of focus and persistence.

> *John Roebling convinced his son, Washington, an engineer, to build the bridge that others said was impossible to build. The two of them developed the concepts and how they would overcome the obstacles. The project was only a few months under construction when John Roebling was killed during a tragic accident on site. Even worse, Washington was severely injured and left with permanent brain damage. He was unable to talk or walk. Because these two were the masterminds behind the entire plan, everyone felt that the bridge would be scrapped. Washington Roebling had a different idea. Even though he couldn't talk, he was able to develop a code of communication with his wife. He would tap out a message with his fingers and his wife would communicate it to the engineers who were building the bridge. For thirteen years, Washington tapped out his instructions with his finger until the spectacular Brooklyn Bridge was finally completed.*
>
> *John Roebling, Washington Roebling, and the Brooklyn Bridge story gives us an example of how staying focused on your goals and fighting through adversity can help us achieve success.*

2. Overcome Hesitation and Do Something

Sometimes, we let important things go simply because fail to act on them. Think about the last time that you let something important slide through the cracks. What if your boss offers you a raise, but it does not appear on your next paycheck? Rather than asking, you decide to let it go, thinking that he forgot and will do it next time. After a while, you feel strange bringing it up since time has passed. In reality, if you walked into his office right then and reminded him, gently asking about it, he would jump right on it and fix the mistake, apologizing for his forgetfulness. What would have happened if you never even asked? Your boss may have remembered later and wondered why you never brought it up. He may assume that you didn't care or weren't motivated. This is a situation that being more persistent can benefit you. You can read more about this in the Overcome Hesitation and Do Something session of the Life Skills course.

Secondary Steps:

1. Be Confident

When you have confidence in yourself and in your work, you have more energy. When you know you can achieve, you are more motivated and excited about what you can accomplish. Telling yourself "I know I can do this!" will pump you up and keep you inspired to keep working and accomplish your goals. What if you had a large task list and started it thinking that you may not be able to finish it and you might end up having to quit. You wouldn't put much effort into it, already preparing yourself for a negative ending. Be confident and certain that you can and will succeed.

2. Be Passionate

When you're involved with your work, you have a deep connection to its goals. If you have an idea you're crazy about, you'll go to far lengths to have it heard and listened to. Have you ever been handed a project you're not crazy about? When you're uninterested and bored, you're not as likely to be as passionate about that project. When you find something exciting or interesting, you're more inspired and want to work on it. Think about it. Would you try harder writing a report or playing your favorite sport? If we tried as hard on everything as we do our favorite things, we would be persistent, successful people in many spheres of our life. Although not everything in life is fun, there are ways we can make more things positive and interesting. Although that report may seem dull, finding the interesting part will make us want to finish it and be persistent about doing it.

> Michael Jordan did not have an easy path into the National Basketball Association. He was actually cut from his high school basketball team before making it. Then he wanted to realize his dreams of being a baseball player, but was held back in the minor leagues. Finally, he achieved his dreams in basketball and became arguably the best player in NBA history. If you ask Michael Jordan how he attainted success, he would say, "I've missed more than 9,000 shots in my career. I've lost almost 300 games. Twenty six times I've been trusted to take the winning shot and missed. I've failed over and over and over in my life. And that's why I succeed!"
>
> Through all of his failures, Michael Jordan maintained the confidence to succeed. He knew that his failures were the reason he was able to succeed and become one of the greatest basketball players of all time.

39 How to Dial Down Persistence

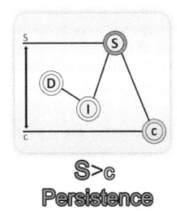

S>c
Persistence

There may be situations that you will run into that require you to dial down your Persistence. These situations may include dealing with clients, working with a group, or spending more time on a project. In these cases, it may be necessary to relax a little and become less set on having your own way. You might have to wait for things to work out before you jump on it again with renewed persistence. You might sense that people are tired and need a break from the sustained effort you have been putting in. You might decide to dial down your persistency for a little while and ramp it up later when people have recovered from their fatigue. Remember that the opposing Sub-factor of Persistence S>c is sensitivity C>s - so all that might be required is that you dial up your sensitivity and this alone will have the immediate impact of dialing back your persistency. Make sure that you review the session on how to dial up your sensitivity if dialing down your persistency is important to you.

> *"What you ardently desire, sincerely believe in, vividly imagine, enthusiastically act on, must inevitably come to pass."*
>
> *~Paul Meyer*

Immediate Steps:

Here are a few steps that you can take immediately towards becoming less persistent and perhaps more of one of the other Sub-factors - perhaps rather choosing to be more sensitive, friendly, cooperative, or patient while pursuing your goals. These steps must be practiced.

1. Make a List

When you have a large list of things to accomplish, make a list of your tasks and prioritize. Make doing this a habit! Figure out what needs to be done immediately and what can wait. If you MUST be persistent, decide what tasks are of the upmost importance and act on those only. Don't overload yourself and try to complete everything at the same time. Dial down the efforts on those tasks that don't require your persistent efforts. Sometimes you'll find that things will get done whether you are persistent or not. Or you might find that some of the things will fall by the wayside and weren't that important anyway. This would have been a waste of your finite, persistent energy.

2. Set Goals for Yourself

If you decide that you want to be more patient and dial down your persistence, you may decide that you should wait a certain amount of time before acting. When itching to act, however, you may end up shortening that time line. If you say that you'll wait 'a while', you may end up getting anxious and acting in five minutes. Set specific goals and hold yourself to them. If you say you're going to wait two days, wait two days and don't shorten that time. If you remember from the dialing up session, timing of when to be persistent is important to your success. In dialing down your urge to be persistent, you are actually becoming more effective! You should enjoy the adventure of pursuing what you ardently desire in life. The trick is in knowing how to dial down your persistence enough to allow more urgent needs and tasks to come first. Act on what is important and know when to dial down your persistence on long-term goals at times. It is good to keep persistence for these goals, but you have to remember what is important to accomplish right now.

3. Set Your Limits

If you're trying to relax and let things go as they will, you may find yourself becoming stressed as deadlines approach. The thing to do here is to set your limits. If you decide beforehand that three days before the project is due, if nothing has happened, that you will act then. If you have thought this deadline for stepping in and taking action through properly, you will feel comfortable dialing down your urge to be stubbornly persistent - giving patience a chance. In these situations, to keep your stress levels low make a plan that controls your persistency urge is of the essence. Having a finite point where you can turn your persistency back on once things reach a certain point will make you feel more confident about dialing down your persistency and will stop you from acting in an overly persistent, aggressive, impatient or pushy manner.

There is a story about Nick Sitzman, a strong man who worked on a train crew. It seemed that Nick had everything: a strong healthy body, ambition, a wife and two children, and many friends. However, he was a notorious worrier and often feared the worst in every situation. One day on the train yard, the crew was informed that they could quit an hour early. Nick was accidently locked in a refrigerator boxcar while the rest of the workmen left the site. Nick panicked and banged against the door until his fists were bloody. He thought, "If I can't get out, I'll freeze to death in here." He took a knife and wrote in the wooden floor, "It's so cold, my body is getting numb. If I could just go to sleep. These may be my last words." The next morning the crew found Nick dead in the boxcar.

The autopsy revealed that every physical sign of his body indicated he had frozen to death. The problem was that the refrigeration unit in the car was inoperative and the temperature inside was fifty-five degrees. Because Nick worried so much and didn't just relax, he literally worried himself to death.'

Secondary Steps:

"The quality of a leader is reflected in the standards they set for themselves."

~Ray Kroc

1. Take a Step Back and Reflect

Taking the time to reflect on what worked for you as you dialed down your persistence and congratulating yourself is motivating and will keep you on track as you adjust your behavior to the situation. This is especially important if you decide that long-term behavioral morphing is acceptable for this Sub-factor. After there has been a situation where you purposefully dialed down your persistence and have been a bit more sensitive, friendly, cooperative, or patient, write it down. What worked and what didn't work? Sometime in the future, you may find yourself questioning your efforts to slow down that persistent nature of yours and wondering if it is really worth it. If you have actual proof of instances where using other Sub-factors has worked effectively in certain situations, you will find yourself more motivated to keep doing what you've been doing and changing up how you get things accomplished.

2. Relax!

Participate in hobbies that you may have neglected lately. If you have nothing else to do than work, you will find yourself very driven and very focused. This often results in being too obsessed with completing goals and therefore appearing too single-mindedly persistent. If you have other interests you'll have to make sufficient time for them. By balancing them with work, you will find yourself less focused on dogged determination for work related issues. The expression 'worried to death' might have more truth to it than we think.

"By setting binding limits, we clarify what we can and cannot, will and will not do. In this way we solidify our resolve; we make our targets real.

If more people set reasonable limits, they would accomplish more; and with a lot less stress."

~Hellen Davis

40 Cooperativeness Generic Profile

Definition

When Compliance is greater than Dominance, you have the Cooperativeness Sub-factor. Cooperative people are very easy to work with and will do almost anything to help out another person or the team in general. Cooperative people use the established policies and procedures in order to make decisions. People with this Sub-factor need practical support from their friends and their colleagues, which is exactly why they work at building positive relationships with the people in their life.

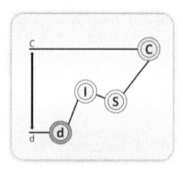

C>d
Cooperativeness

Descriptors

Some words that describe the Cooperativeness Sub-factor are:

- Agreeableness
- Amenableness
- Deference
- Obedience
- Accommodativeness

- Compliance
- Amiability
- Good-natured
- Submissiveness

Strengths

The strengths of the Cooperativeness Sub-factor are an easy-going personality, a rule-oriented philosophy, and a willingness to do what is required for the team.

Being submissive is not necessarily a bad thing if you know how to use it effectively, and the cooperative person can even maintain control of the group by knowing how to act around others. If you aren't the head of the organization you are working for, then you have to practice some degree of submissiveness.

Cooperative people are very rule-oriented, sticking to the guidelines and regulations of the company they work for. This is a great quality to have in order to make sure that everything you are doing is in compliance with company procedures and won't have to be overturned or reworked. Cooperative people are also ready and willing to do what is required of them. This is a great mindset to have in any area of life because it takes away excuses and gets you to your goals.

I love having cooperative people in the office. It's good to know that when they are handed a project, they will complete it according to the directions given, they build on each other's ideas, and they can work successfully with other people. I don't like worrying if someone is going to stray from the directions and spend a lot of time working on something that isn't correct or isn't done the way it was directed by whoever happens to have the responsibility for getting that project done. Having cooperative people in the office, I don't have to worry about that. Everybody works for the good of the project and for our clients. And, usually, when people give directions, they repeat it back to the person what they think they have to do. It's reassuring when people show they do understand what is being asked of them. Cooperating is ultimately about understanding what someone wants and knowing that we are all on the same page about what we have to do. It really doesn't matter who's in charge, as long as people cooperate with the team leader and their team mates. This helps us to stay focused and on track.

Cooperative people also work better in groups. Canadian Geese fly in V's, usually, with one side longer than the other. Geese instinctively know that by making this formation, they are able to fly faster and farther together. The geese regularly change leadership, another mark of their cooperation. The leader fights the toughest winds to create a partial vacuum for the rest of the flock to fly. As he becomes exhausted, another goose takes over. Studies have shown that the geese can fly 72 percent farther and faster by cooperating in this manner. The same works for people. When you work successfully together, you can accomplish many more things, faster and easier than you would by yourself.

> *"If you want to be incrementally better, it's all about self improvement. The solution: Be competitive. If you want to be exponentially better and make your organization better, you have to leverage others. The solution: Be cooperative."*
>
> *~Hellen Davis*

Weaknesses

The weaknesses of the Cooperativeness Sub-factor are an inability to make decisive and individual decisions in the workplace, allowing others to sometimes walk over them, and not willing to break the rules even if it means doing a better job. Cooperative people have a hard time making decisive and individual decisions. They like to get advice from others before making decisions. This is not a mark of leadership and needs to be worked on by people with this Sub-factor. Cooperative people sometimes allow others to walk all over them. They can be pressured into doing their colleagues' or managers' work. This can sometimes be a weakness. Corporations have to put rules in place for their own protection against lawsuits, but sometimes in order to be the most effective you can be at your job, you have to be willing to bend some of those rules to help the customer.

Have you ever been about to go out to lunch with a few coworkers and you ask where they would like to go, they respond with "I don't know, where would you like to go?" After pressuring them, their response stays the same. Cooperative people have a hard time making decisions, even small ones. In this case, they may fear having their decision judged by others or voicing their opinion and someone else saying that they're going to do it a different way instead.

Cooperative people like to satisfy the whole group, which may mean that decisions don't get made.

Situational Adaptation - Dial Up or Dial Down

Cooperativeness needs to be dialed up in any team meeting. You have to work with people in order to make your organization better. Coming to agreements and setting plans is essential to improvement. Dial up your cooperativeness to ensure effectiveness in your organization during team meetings.

You need to dial down your cooperativeness when you are in a leadership position or when you need to break a rule in order to get something done. You have to take the part of cooperativeness that allows you to listen to the ideas of others and be agreeable, but make sure that you can make independent decisions. You will have to make tough decisions in which you can't always get input from others on. Using your cooperativeness effectively will help you become a great leader in your organization.

Just imagine working for a boss who has the Cooperativeness Sub-factor. On the positive side, this individual will be very easy to work with, especially if all the members of the team want to feel included and have a say in the project. The cooperative leader will often be the one who will allow everyone the opportunity to 'add their two cents' and be able to share their ideas and suggestions. They will tend to listen to all of the facts before making the decisions needed to propel the project forward. The negative aspect of the elevated Cooperativeness Sub-factor IS their need for everyone to have a say. This behavior is not a plus if the project has a fast-approaching deadline. If you have ever been involved in a project or meeting where there is way too much discussion and not as much action, you know that this can be frustrating. The need to hear everyone's opinion and to listen to all the minute details before a decision is made can cause the project to get off track and move forward very slowly.

If this cooperative manager would simply tap into the Sub-factor of 'Independence,' then the project may move and progress faster.

Sometimes, the boss doesn't need to hear all of the ideas in order to make a decision. Sometimes the manager just needs to take that risk and say what they feel needs to get done, when it needs to be done, and who will be responsible for each detail. This may feel very foreign and not very cooperative, but it may be necessary. Many new inventions have been discovered by the leader who thinks independently. Entrepreneurs are often the individuals who step outside of the box and think differently or 'independently'. They demonstrate their leadership by showing an independent spirit, and they are more willing to take a risk, even though they may have some apprehension.

On the negative side, this boss displaying their independence may miss out on some great ideas that may have been shared by the team, had they been offered the chance to speak up. The other members of the team may feel like they are not being fully used for their knowledge and ideas, and this may cause them to shutdown and not offer important suggestions.

I have been in many meetings that have dragged on while everyone states their point of view and how they think a project should go. While listening to them, I knew that there was no way we could accommodate every point of view. With the deadline quickly approaching, I had to stop the dialogue to get the project moving and distribute responsibilities. While listening to every single opinion could have been nice, the reality is that things had to be done and actions needed to be taken immediately.

When working with other companies, with whom I do not have the final say, I've had to dial up my cooperativeness. Although I thought I knew best on how a project should go, I sat back and contributed to the group. It was not my place to take control and I had to learn how to sit back and work together with everyone else.

Next Steps

Next, you will explore the benefits and consequences of the Cooperativeness Sub-factor. If you think that this Sub-factor is important for your success, you can target your knowledge by investigating various ways to dial up or dial down your Cooperativeness Sub-factor in our 'How to' sessions.

"The more generous we are, the more joyous we become. The more cooperative we are, the more valuable we become. The more enthusiastic we are, the more productive we become. The more serving we are, the more prosperous we become."

~William Arthur Ward

41 How to Dial Up Cooperativeness

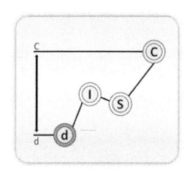

C>d
Cooperativeness

When we're focused on getting done what we want and not being as cooperative as we should be, it can make it difficult for everyone - including ourselves. Have you ever been summoned to a group meeting and you see one person not listening attentively, looking preoccupied or bored, giving the impression of wanting to leave well before it is appropriate, dragging their feet on signing up to help the team, having a sour attitude whenever anyone makes a suggestion that doesn't agree with them, and generally not participating to the extent you know they could? Were you excited and happy working with that person? It's an easy answer - probably not! Getting things done in a self-reliant and self-motivated manner is important; however being cooperative is a skill that we frequently need in the workplace as well as in our family and social groups.

> *"Teamwork is so important that it is virtually impossible for you to reach the heights of your capabilities or make the money that you want without becoming very good at it."*
>
> *~Brian Tracy*

As a child, we remember being told "Be nice and play with the other kids! Share!" We were constantly reminded that we needed help from others and to help people ourselves with sayings like 'two heads are better than one.' In this way we were taught to be cooperative and work collaboratively with others. It may have seemed, however, that as you worked on your own goals, career, and interests, you may have drifted away from collaborating a bit. This is normal. As you matured and moved out of your family home you became more self-directed. In your career, as you work toward promotions, you have to vie against your peers somewhat. It's logical to show how self-motivated and self-reliant you are because this is a trait of a leader.

As far as cooperating with your peers, well, only one person will be promoted on most teams so there is a fine line between working for the team's benefit and making sure that people know that your efforts deserve to be recognized on an individual basis, too. The ultimate goal is to strike a

DISCflex™

balance between being both self-determined and independent as well as cooperative. To reach goals effectively - especially when you work on goals on teams, in your family circle, or in your professional life - it must be so. Nonetheless, getting along with others and being cooperative is an essential skill in the workplace.

Imagine a scenario where you have been told during a performance review that you're not very cooperative. After possibly being defensive, you may think about how to alter your behaviors in order to get a better evaluation next time. Although cooperativeness seems like a natural trait, it's just like anything else, to get really good at being cooperative, it is something that can be learned and practiced.

> *"The best teamwork comes from men who are working independently toward one goal in unison."*
>
> *~James Cash Penney*

Immediate Steps:

Cooperativeness is sometimes seen as being absolute: either we are or we aren't cooperative and there doesn't appear to be much middle ground. There is middle ground, however, when you move from being uncooperative to cooperative. Being cooperative can actually be viewed as a combination of mental attitudes and behaviors. Here are some that you can implement immediately to focus on cooperativeness:

1. Be Positive.

When you hear that you are working with a team or will be collaborating, rather than instantly getting annoyed and frustrated because you think this will slow the goal down, be positive. You might be completely wrong about the negative impact you think it will have. In fact, it might reap great results. Collaborating may mean that the project will be finished twice as fast, won't require as much work from you in the long run, and that the project will be even better with five heads working on it than one.

If others see that you want nothing to do with group work and don't want to be involved, they will be instantly turned off and annoyed that they have to work with you.

You probably wouldn't want to work with a grumpy team member, so don't be that person for someone else. Be positive that it can be a good experience and you'll get things accomplished. Expectations set any team in motion. If you go in with the expectation of a fun, exciting collaborative, cooperative environment - that attitude will rub off on the team. If you expect the worst to occur, it will damage the level of cooperation you will receive from everyone.

2. Understand and Set Context.

> *"Somebody has to take responsibility for being a leader."*
>
> *~Toni Morrison*

The second step is to understand the context of why cooperation is called for and if it isn't defined, make sure that context is set for everyone involved. Understanding why you're working together in a group will make cooperating and collaborating a lot less intimidating. If you feel like you don't know why you're working with a team, you may be frustrated and questioning what purpose it holds. When you recognize why you're collaborating, and what everyone's roles and responsibilities are, and precisely what is expected from all, it will be easier for you and everyone else to work together towards the common goals.

3. Have Enthusiasm About Working With Others.

If you are able to dial up your enthusiasm to a level where the group is motivated by it and comfortable with it, and at the same time dial up your cooperativeness, this is a winning combination. After getting the first two steps in line where you understand the context and you are in a positive frame of mind, you may walk into the room to start the project and realize that your worst nightmares are in front of you. You can clearly see that no one else wants to cooperate. So if they don't want to, why should you even bother? Although it can be easy to be uncooperative or have negative expectations, be enthusiastic anyway. Make a concentrated effort and understand that when you do this, it might be the way to bring everyone to a better, more cooperative state of mind.

> *"A hundred times every day I remind myself that my inner and outer life depend on the labors of other men, living and dead, and that I must exert myself in order to give in the same measure as I have received and am still receiving."*
>
> *~Albert Einstein*

The more you are excited about a project, the more everyone else in the room will be excited. As we described earlier, would you want to work with the grumpy team member and be excited for collaborating with them? Even if others aren't excited and enthusiastic, your attitude can indeed change the attitude of everyone in the room. Through your enthusiastic attitude, you'll hopefully inspire everyone else to be excited and get the ball moving. The bottom line is that enthusiastic people who understand the benefits of cooperativeness realize that working together can yield great results.

4. Be Sure of the Goals.

Make sure you and everyone else knows precisely what your team's goals are. If you don't know what you're working towards, it makes it difficult to produce accurate, focused collaborative work, especially as a team. If you discover that a team member is working towards a different goal, everyone involved may feel frustrated and hold back, not giving it their best coordinated effort.

As an example, imagine if you're working towards getting a project done by the deadline and another team member is working towards getting it done at the best cost, but not worrying too much about timeliness or making the deadline. In their quest to make sure their goal gets accomplished, they take a long time scoping out vendors and trying to negotiate.

You on the other hand just want to get it done, thinking that saving a couple of thousand dollars on a big project isn't worth missing the deadline - especially when you have to explain why this happened to a customer. The result is that you get frustrated and annoyed at the other person's efforts which run contrary to working cooperatively together. The root cause of your frustration is that you and your teammates are not on the same page with your goals. It's best to be totally clear of your goals as a group and map them out according to each person's responsibilities. When you do this, it will make it easier to work together.

5. Know Who is Responsible for Each Section in the Project.

If you jump in and don't assign roles and responsibility, you may find that at the end of a project that things have been overlooked and forgotten, causing stress and panic. When you assign roles, you always know what is happening. Failing to assign responsibility can make you frustrated and make you shut down from being cooperative with your group. Always be sure to assign responsibility and know who is accountable for each task. Also, go one step further and make sure that the appropriate levels of authority are determined so that you know who is in charge of resources, decision making, deploying people and other important Factors as they relate to authority. I suggest that you review the RA² Interface sessions to become familiar with how to best accomplish this.

6. Mutual Respect is Important.

When you respect everyone's ideas, they are more comfortable talking and giving ideas to the group. Have you ever had an idea and someone ignored you or even worse, snapped at

The story of Charles Plumb is inspiring and emphasizes the value of each individual of a team. Captain Charles Plumb, a graduate of the Naval Academy, whose plane, after 74 successful combat missions over North Vietnam, was shot down. He parachuted to safety, but was captured, tortured and spent 2,103 days in a small box-like cell.

After surviving the ordeal, Captain Plumb received the Silver Star, Bronze Star, the Legion of Merit and two Purple Hearts, and returned to America and spoke to many groups about his experience and how it compared to the challenges of everyday life.

Shortly after coming home, Charlie and his wife were sitting in a restaurant. A man rose from a nearby table, walked over and said, "You're Plumb! You flew jet fighters in Vietnam from the aircraft carrier Kitty Hawk. You were shot down!"

Surprised that he was recognized, Charlie responded, "How in the world did you know that?" The man replied, "I packed your parachute." Charlie looked up with surprise. The man pumped his hand, gave a thumbs-up, and said, "I guess it worked!"

Charlie stood to shake the man's hand, and assured him, "It most certainly did work. If it had not worked, I would not be here today."

Charlie could not sleep that night, thinking about the man. He wondered if he might have seen him and not even said, "Good morning, how are you?"

He thought of the many hours the sailor had spent bending over a long wooden table in the bottom of the ship, carefully folding the silks and weaving the shrouds of each chute, each time holding in his hands the fate of someone he didn't know.

Plumb then began to realize that along with the physical parachute, he needed mental, emotional and spiritual parachutes. He had called on all these supports during his long and painful ordeal.

The parachute packer in the story is an example of how everyone has a responsibility and even if it is the smallest job, it can affect everything profoundly. Understanding that clear definition of people's different responsibilities is necessary and everyone should ideally dovetail their responsibility with others in a cooperative and collaborative fashion. This understanding of responsibilities will help you know what it takes to succeed and dial up your cooperation.

you, saying that it wasn't valuable? Did it make you want to propose ideas after that type of treatment? Being disrespectful is a negative habit and can ruin a team's efforts. Be positive and encouraging when others speak. Welcome their comments and respect their ideas. And if another team member is not respectful of ideas, take them aside and have a quiet conversation about the ramifications of appearing disrespectful or of discounting other people's opinions. For more information on how to do this, take a look at our sessions on Noble Intent and pick up the book for pointers.

"Trust men and they will be true to you; treat them greatly and they will show themselves great."

~Ralph Waldo Emerson

7. Make Sure You Have Open Lines of Communication.

Sometimes, we can feel like if we speak up about a problem, no one will listen and it will be drowned out. This can stew feelings of resentment or frustration in a group setting. In order to be cooperative, be open to communicating your ideas. While you will be respectful of others' ideas, you need to open your comfort zone to speaking out as well. Be comfortable with your team and voice your opinions. This will be especially helpful if there is a problem and you see it first. Helping your team will show your cooperation.

After you finish this session, I suggest that you watch the Life Lifter entitled Cooperation about how Alexander Norris's communication and the cooperation shown by Proctor and Gamble brought about the creation of a multi-billion dollar company. After you hear the story, you'll never underestimate how much communication and cooperation can help you achieve success.

"The greatest gifts you can give your children are the roots of responsibility and the wings of independence."

~Denis Waitley

8. Be Accepting of Changes

If a change emerges, be open to it and remain positive. As hard as working with a group may be, you may lose patience and refuse to be cooperative if another unexpected or impactful change comes up. You need to stay positive and be willing to try out new things. Although this may be difficult, it is necessary to do so when being cooperative. Here's the thing: You have to deal with the change anyway, so why not deal with it in the most positive way possible?

Secondary Steps:

After those initial steps, there are two additional steps that may take you longer to master. Learning to become cooperative requires patience and practice. These next steps will be harder to form into second nature, but will help you on your journey to cooperativeness.

1. Share

When working with others and being cooperative, you must share information and your expertise. Surely you've known someone who keeps all the information to themselves and because they don't cooperate willingly, asking them for help takes a while to yield results. If you are working towards a common goal, all information should be available to everyone on the team. Although you may feel like your work is YOURS, you should be open to sharing it and helping others whenever you can. Remember that the big wheel turns and by providing information and assistance to someone today, they might be more inclined to do the same for you or your teammates tomorrow. Be sure to help your team members and others in your organization and be willing to give them a hand with an open heart and mind.

2. Build Trust

You may not know your team members very well and may feel uncomfortable working with people you haven't worked with before. It's important to participate in team building activities, social events, and break bread together in order to get to know the people around you. The more you get to know the people around you, the easier cooperating with them will be. Plus, they will trust you more because you've taken the time and effort to get to know them. In turn they will be more excited about working with you.

"Adapt or perish, now as ever, is nature's inexorable imperative."

~H.G. Wells

42 How to Dial Down Cooperativeness

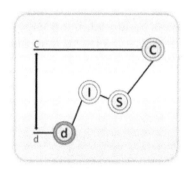

C>d
Cooperativeness

Remember that Cooperativeness C>d has the opposing Sub-factor of Independence D>c; so, all that might be required is that you dial up your Independence Sub-factor and this alone will have the immediate impact of dialing back your Cooperativeness. As you learn the techniques in this session, immediately review the session on How to Dial Up your Independence to understand the polar opposite of Cooperativeness.

Although working and collaborating with others is admirable, there may be situations where you must dial down your Cooperativeness. Remember that although Independence is the opposing trait, dialing down your Cooperativeness does not automatically mean that you must become more Independent. You might well choose to employ one of the other Sub-factors to override how prevailing your Cooperativeness Sub-factor is over your behavior. For example, you might dial up Self-motivation and use that Sub-factor to become the team leader, driving the team to a quicker pace in accomplishing goals. Or you may choose to dial up your Accuracy Sub-factor and hold yourself and your teammates to the highest standards possible.

"Think for yourself!

Resist GroupThink!

Do you know how many people tell me: 'It can't be done!'? I find that if you set your goals, and virtually ignore what everyone else in your industry is saying (except the ones everyone agrees is crazy), you're probably going to be a frontrunner. GroupThinkers aren't the lead dogs.

Seek answers with an open mind.

Do research, draw your own conclusions, set your own goals. Most of all, be determined - stick to your guns. When you're doing something new or just starting out, people will tell you you're wrong. As you fly past them, they'll tell their friends that you're going to fail. A few years after that, they'll ask you to coach them."

~Hellen Davis

By being accurate and holding people accountable, Cooperativeness and friendliness have to automatically take a back seat. Accuracy is precise and is a black and white area. Whereas Cooperativeness is based on team dynamics and has infinitely more shades of grey. As you already know, there are specific steps for dialing up and dialing down each Sub-factor and there are differences in how you approach the situation as to which course of action you will take when deciding which Sub-factors will govern your behavior. Here are a few steps that you can take to learn how to dial down your Cooperativeness when you need to.

> *"First, have a definite, clear practical ideal; a goal, an objective. Second, have the necessary means to achieve your ends; wisdom, money, materials, and methods. Third, adjust all your means to that end."*
>
> *~Aristotle*

Avoid GroupThink

If you think of the effect that Groupthink has in social circles and professional organizations, you can better understand why there are many situations where you might need to dial down your Cooperativeness Sub-factor. Imagine being on a team and things aren't moving along as they should. You, however, are the person responsible for delivering results. Because of this, you need to take action and lead everyone towards a resolution. Or, you may be fast approaching a deadline and even though you'd like to ask someone else's opinion, you just don't have time. Or think about this: You have promised the team that you would debate the points of your new program and try to come up with a solution that everyone buys off on, but after days and days of talking, you just can't reach consensus. You know the next step is to make a decision that is going to be unpopular with some people. To do so, you have to be less cooperative.

Although many of these situations demand immediate action, you must practice the steps in how to dial down your Cooperativeness so that you are prepared to take action before the situation arises. You have to be well equipped to recognize the effects of peer pressure and Groupthink. You also have to make certain that your skills in handling this Sub-factor's ramifications are solid. If you are prepared, you will not over-stress yourself by acting out of your comfort zone. For how to handle Groupthink, review the sessions in the Decision Making course by the same name. This course contains a large body of work on Groupthink and how to best overcome it. In addition, for choosing the best decision making methods, and to avoid always making consensus-based decisions, review the Decision Making Matrix materials.

Immediate Steps:

Here are a few immediate and secondary steps to practice in order to dial down your Cooperativeness.

> *"You are unique, and if that is not fulfilled, then something wonderful has been lost."*
>
> *~ Martha Graham*

1. **Prepare, Prepare, Prepare and Mentally Rehearse.**

   Try to think about future situations that you might find yourself in that will require you to dial down your Cooperative ways. When you do this, do it to prepare yourself to go against the group's current ways of doing things or of their thinking. In your preparation, you will mentally rehearse precisely what you will say to the individuals to make sure they understand why you are not being as Cooperative as they might like and precisely why - in clear and logical terms - you are not agreeing with them or going along with them right now. Remember to tell them that while you might not currently be seen as cooperating, it doesn't mean that you won't always be like that.

2. State the Parameters of Your Cooperativeness.

If you are dialing down your Cooperativeness on just a few points, let them know the parameters and limitations on your Cooperativeness. If you spell out the parameters and let them know precisely how you are thinking, you give them the opportunity to understand you. Also, when they understand where you are coming from, they can try to Influence you to Cooperate with them. You never know, they might bring you around, It might be the case that you were unwilling to Cooperate simply because you didn't understand or weren't fully on board with the benefits of the scenario. If you think about these situations you will be more prepared to deal with them before they arise.

"A mature person is one who is does not think only in absolutes, who is able to be objective even when deeply stirred emotionally, who has learned that there is both good and bad in all people and all things, and who walks humbly and deals charitably."

~Eleanor Roosevelt

If you analyze the earlier situation, working with a group but getting nowhere, you need to know your limits. If you decide beforehand that three days before the project is due, if nothing has happened, you will step up and get everyone moving. Once you're in the situation, and if you haven't set your limits, you may end up relying on your Cooperativeness and letting things go as the group directs. If you have your limits, however, and you're prepared to discuss your limits on your Cooperativeness, you will know when you need to act.

Even when you are cooperating, make sure that you have parameters around the relationship. You should make sure that appropriate accountability metrics are given for the responsibilities that you accept. In this way, you will know what you have to do yourself and what part is important for you to complete. Sometimes, if you are too cooperative, you will focus on helping with other people's responsibilities and will end up delaying your own responsibilities.

3. Avoid Peer Pressure.

Independent thinking and peer pressure do not go hand in hand. Peer pressure is a powerful force in compelling individuals to conform to the ideas, ideals, and goals of the group. Learn to say NO! This is the easiest step to take against peer pressure. It doesn't matter how much you respect your peers. They also should learn to understand your boundaries. Your own will comes before anything else. If there is something you think is inappropriate or might harm you or others in any way, then simply be firm about it and tell your friends that you cannot do it. Here are some tips and tactics to make sure that you are not being swayed by peer pressure.

- Be True to Yourself and Your Goals. When thinking about whether it is best to cooperate or go against the group, do some introspection. Honestly ask yourself if that's something you really wish to do or whether it would be the right thing for other constituents or stakeholders.

- Re-check your motivation and make sure that you are not making decisions based on whether the people in the group will approve or not. Do not manipulate your thoughts by thinking that you are making decisions because that's what the others want you to do. Think about the consequences both in the short and long term prior to making the decision to cooperate or go against the group. This type of thinking will make sure that you are not being unduly influenced by peer pressure.

DISCflex™

- Discuss the Issue With Objective Parties. Make sure that you have people outside of the group that you can talk to. Their objective advice and counsel can have a counterbalancing effect on peer pressure. So, always make sure that you have an avenue whereby you are able to discuss the issue with objective parties. Bouncing ideas off impartial or detached outsiders brings diversity of thought into the mix. This is a sure-fire way of combating peer pressure. Doing this can provide a voice of reason, or provide clarity.

4. Do What You Can.

On a group project, if you are given a part, try to do it by yourself first. Before you ask for advice or ask someone what they would do, do as much as you can by yourself before asking someone else. This is the first step in feeling comfortable working by yourself and not relying on anyone else.

> *Victoria Principal is a great example of taking on an individual project by dialing down her cooperativeness. When Victoria Principal signed a contract for her acting career, she omitted a clause that would have given the network the right to consent and profit from her outside endeavors.*
>
> *Unfortunately for the network, Victoria Principal was an independent woman who knew when to cooperate and when to hold her ground. She explained her philosophy, "As a result that's why, you can only notice in hindsight, I was the only person in the cast who did commercials, who was doing movies of the week, who wrote books and these all belong to me. I retained the control and ownership of my image. No one owns me."*
>
> *She ended up starting her own production company as well as a line of skin care products. Victoria Principal is a great example of someone who knows the benefit of dialing down the Cooperativeness Sub-factor when the situation calls for it.*

5. Take on an Individual Project.

To practice not relying on your group, take on an individual project. Make it a goal to get as much done by yourself as possible to prove that you are a valuable member of the office and that your work can stand on its own two feet. Although this situation may not come up immediately, you may not be thrown into a project by yourself, it will be good to practice this so that you can react in immediate situations comfortably.

6. Surround Yourself with Motivated People.

If you know people in the office who are always working independently and acting first, take the time to get to know them. Being around them and noticing how they act on their own and don't wait to talk to others will influence you. If you are around them, you may start to hold yourself to their standards and try to act more like them.

Although it may be uncomfortable at first, you will feel more comfortable as time goes on. Being a self-starter often means that you have to be less cooperative because you are pulling out ahead of the group.

Secondary Steps:

Now that you understand the primary steps, here are a few Secondary Steps that will further help you dial down your Cooperativeness Sub-factor.

1. **Take Responsibility for Your Actions.**

   If something goes wrong, don't blame it on your group members or say it was somewhere else in the process. If you constantly depend on your group, you will start to place the blame on them and not yourself. Realize where you may have gone wrong. Even if it was someone else's mistake, it was your responsibility as a team member to look across the team efforts, to notice where things are slipping, and bring it up, rather than just doing your part independently of the others. Although this might logically be the height of Cooperativeness because you are putting the team's efforts high on your priority list, you must understand that by doing so, other team members might view you as uncooperative - with them. Open lines of communication and talking about issues far in advance of them causing harm or stress to teammates is the key here.

2. **Learn and Grow.**

   Sometimes people mask their lack of self-confidence by constantly being in a team environment. So, while it looks like they are operating at the height of Cooperativeness they are really hiding in the herd. Cooperativeness can therefore inhibit your personal and professional growth. You may feel uncomfortable working by yourself because you don't have the proper training or expertise in that area. You might feel entirely uncomfortable bringing up fresh ideas that don't go along with the way the group has always done things. Recognize that you might be doing this and snap out of it! Boost your confidence and attend extra trainings and meetings so that you feel more comfortable when you're doing things on your own. Confidence is the key and if you believe that you can do it, simply try!

"Let's face it. In most of life we really are interdependent. We need each other.

Staunch independence is an illusion, but heavy dependence isn't healthy, either. The only position of long-term strength is interdependence: win/win."

~Greg Anderson

43 Accuracy Generic Profile

Definition

When Compliance is greater than Influence, you have the Accuracy Sub-factor. Accurate people take their time and rarely make errors. They check and re-check their work in order to make sure that it is of the finest quality. Accurate people don't take risks unless absolutely necessary. They want to be precise and understand the situation completely before making a decision. The Accurate person wants to be right the first time instead of finding out their mistakes after doing something.

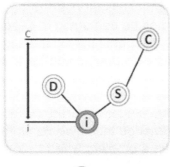

C>I
Accuracy

Descriptors

Words that describe the accuracy Sub-factor are:

- Correctness
- Precision
- Carefulness
- Definitiveness
- Faultlessness

- Exactness
- Truthfulness
- Certainty
- Meticulousness

Strengths

The strengths of the Accuracy Sub-factor are that the person with this Sub-factor will get their work right the first time, they will edit their work themselves, there is little worry about checking over their work, and they are great at finding the truth in things. Accurate people spend a lot of time finding the right way to get their work done. They work at a slower and more diligent pace in order to make sure they are being logical and factual. Accurate people continually check and re-check their work and barely ever make spelling or grammatical errors, which is why the quality of their work is always superior. Accurate people are also great at finding the truth in things. They find the factual statements and stick to them and rarely give their opinion outside of those facts.

> *"Fast is fine, but accuracy is everything."*
>
> *~Wyatt Earp*

Accurate people always surprise me. When I work with someone new, I expect to have to fix their work, edit it, or go in a different direction. It surprises me when work is done almost flawlessly in exactly the way I wanted it. Although it sometimes takes longer for accurate people to finish a project, I know that ultimately it will save time in the long run. I usually like to get work in early, before the deadline, so that I can check it and double-check it. It's sometimes hard for me to not receive something right away, but I know that if someone accurate is doing it, it will be done right.

Weaknesses

The weaknesses of the Accuracy Sub-factor are that these individuals spend too much time trying to be correct instead of getting projects done; they are prone to correcting the errors in other people excessively. Accurate people have an incessant need to be completely correct before they can get anything done. This can sometimes be damaging to deadlines and time constraints because the accurate person won't finish anything until they know it is completely accurate. Whether it is grammar, word choice, or ideas, accurate people can be blunt and expressive when correcting others. Accurate people also won't take risks easily.

In life, risks are necessary if you want bigger rewards, but accurate people usually aren't willing to sacrifice anything without the knowledge that it will be worth it, so they instead try to obtain all the information they can. This can be a problem when dealing with a situation that they need to take a risk on. Since accurate people dislike errors in their own work, they will notice it in others'. While typing out a quick email to my team, I may not notice a few spelling errors or a missing comma. I do know, however, that one of the accurate people in my team will notice it. I also know that person may take longer to complete tasks since they take the time to make it as perfect as possible. Although I understand this is their preference, it can be very frustrating to me when things need to be done promptly and I need to see results.

Situational Adaptation - Dial Up or Dial Down

You have to dial down your accuracy when determining whether to take a risk or not. Take a quick look at the benefits and consequences of the risk and then decide right there if it is worth it depending on the window of opportunity that is available. You also have to dial down your accuracy when conversing with others; don't correct everything that they do. This will cause them to resent you if they feel you will just correct them if you ever talk. You want to dial up your accuracy when working on an important project for your company or for a client. Especially with a client, you want to be as accurate as possible so that they won't think you are pulling a fast one on them. Use your accuracy wisely to help you, but not to hurt you. Accuracy can help you become more efficient and better at analyzing data if you understand how to use it.

Imagine that you are working on a team project with a fast approaching deadline. When you have an accurate team member on task, their constant fact checking may slow down progress. If this individual would simply dial up their opposing Sub-factor of self-confidence, they would trust their own judgment and the judgment of the team. Since they are often very accurate in the first place, checking, then re-checking will not change the overall outcome. However, their attention to detail may be extremely beneficial when dealing with high-risk situations. Possible mistakes may be avoided because of their elevated accuracy, which in the long run, may save the company from a great financial loss.

Imagine the accurate individual who has dialed up their self-confidence in discussing the company's rules and suggested operative procedures. A highly accurate individual would rarely think of questioning 'how things are done,' yet a self-confident individual would. They would have the confidence to do what is right and have the strength to speak up and feel good while saying it. However, being the individual having too much self-confidence while being too thoughtful may have negative effects. A high Compliant and detailed individual may come across as very smug when being too self-confident. Displaying the Self-confidence Sub-factor while correcting others' mistakes may make you seem too much of a 'know-it-all'. Your co-workers will not want to be corrected by someone they think acts 'too perfect' themselves.

There have been many times that I've had to dial down my own accuracy. When deadlines quickly approach, in my line of work, I have to act fast. Although there may be a few things that aren't fully explained, I must make the decision to move forward and take the risk that the errors will not hinder progress. Although, ultimately, there should be no errors, sometimes the deadline must be met and sacrifices, such as accuracy, must be made.

I've also had to dial up my accuracy many times. When making progress with a client and presenting a contract, it must be accurate. I will oftentimes take extra time to go over the contract over and over again to check it for errors. If a client noticed the errors in it, they may lose their confidence in me and the deal may be changed.

You should decide what the situation calls for in order to accurately dial up or dial down your accuracy.

Next Steps

Next, you will explore the benefits and consequences of the accuracy Sub-factor. If you think that this Sub-factor is important for your success, you can target your knowledge by investigating various ways to dial up or dial down your accuracy Sub-factor in our 'How to' sessions

"Success produces confidence; confidence relaxes industry, and negligence ruins the reputation which accuracy had raised."

~Ben Jonson

44 How to Dial Up Accuracy

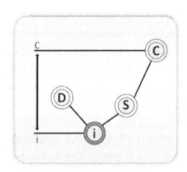

C>I
Accuracy

The general rule of thumb of 'Big Picture versus Detail Focus' as it relates to accuracy is this: If we're focusing too hard on an end product or on the big picture, we concentrate less on the details. They are inversely proportional. If you are too detail focused, your 30,000 foot view is diminished. If you do not monitor this tendency, it is logical that we can become inaccurate or less strategically focused - depending on your viewpoint. This may come about as an accident through lack of awareness or it can be that we just aren't naturally either a detail oriented or big picture-focus type person. It could also be that we just haven't thought about it before and therefore not focusing has become a habit forged over the period of our lives. If you want to dial up your Accuracy, so as not to forget the fine points or details of what you are working on, but as part of your responsibilities, you have to have a strategic or big picture focus. This means that you have to take care not to lose focus on either one - Big Picture or details. To add complexity, in your strategic planning, you may not know specific information, so you speculate or assume, lowering your accuracy further.

Accuracy, especially at work, can sometimes be a very big deal. As an extreme example, if you're a neuro-surgeon, being accurate while performing brain surgery is a life saving requirement. Simply being able to say that the person lived, even though they sustained permanent brain damage, is not a good thing. If you were told the twenty-story building you work in wasn't built accurately, but was built fast, you wouldn't feel very comfortable riding the elevator to the 31st floor every day. Sometimes, we expect others' work to be very accurate but in other instances where accuracy is not as important, we don't care as much. If an employee at a fast food restaurant puts too little mustard on our sandwich it's really not a big deal. In fact, often times we lower our standards based on how accurate we expect people to be. As for our own work product, many of us have varying standards depending on what we're trying to accomplish.

It is a human trait that we prefer to set our own standards for our work. Unfortunately, this is not always possible. It's all about expectations then - ours and those who judge us. Understanding the accountability parameters associated with accuracy, as well as being able to influence those, is an important skill to have. If you are not able to understand or influence the accuracy expectations, you leave yourself open to negative judgment from others. You can also beat yourself up pretty badly if you fail to be as accurate as you know you have to be. Making mistakes and lambasting yourself for doing so is the number one reason people whip themselves into a negative mental state. Think about it. If you mess up and make a simple mistake, don't you mentally beat yourself up? If someone else had made a simple error, would you have been so hard on them? Probably not! Unless it was something that really mattered to you. Remember, most events rarely rise to that level.

That said, accuracy for many situations in both your professional and personal life, is very important. When you are vying for promotion, you don't want to be seen as someone who can't look after the big picture as well as making sure that details are handled properly. Accuracy and being seen as someone who can be counted on - being someone people view as reliable and conscientious - is something to be proud of. No one likes people who seem like they don't care, who seems sloppy with details or numbers, or appears as if they consistently leave out bits of important information. Of course no one wants to be viewed like this! But what if being accurate is something that you are naturally good at? The good news: Accuracy is something that can be learned and must be practiced. There are specific steps that can get you there and all they require is practice, practice, and more practice. Out of all the Sub-factors, accuracy is the one that takes the most focus to get good at and to overcome a bent for inaccuracy.

Immediate Steps:

There are a few steps that can be undertaken immediately to dial up your accuracy fairly quickly. If you take them to heart and practice them they can get you started in the right direction as you begin to become more accurate and focused in your work. But remember this, just knowing how to do these steps isn't enough, you must put thoughts and 'how to's' into action where accuracy is concerned. The bottom line: You just have to put them into practice and be consistent.

1. Define Your Standards.

If your boss tells you to write a report, you may try to write it solely using your own information and opinions without first asking about how your work product will be judged. Imagine that you turn it in to him, and he is disappointed. He expected you to research other people's ideas and summarize how the top business leaders thought about the topic. He expected that you cite other proven materials and use resources other than your opinion. Your boss expected this because he really doesn't think that you have much expertise or knowledge of the subject. At the very least, he anticipated that you would use professional, educated opinions and refer to statistics that supported your theories in your paper.

If you had known the standards that your boss expected, you would have produced more accurate and precise work, the way he wanted it. If someone gives you a project or asks you to finish something, find out the basics about what they expect - especially with regard to how accurate they expect you to be about your research. Here are some guidelines for doing this: Usually you should ask why they asked for it and what question are they trying to address, how they want it done, when you should get it back to them, and finally enquire as to the amount of time they think you should spend on completing the assignment.

> *"Watch every detail that affects the accuracy of your work."*
>
> *~Arthur C. Nielsen*

This last question will give you a general idea - more than the other questions - of how thorough they are expecting you to be. Then if given the chance drill down a little bit more and ask any other related questions that spring to mind. If you don't ask these questions, you probably won't complete the work to their standards. You'll end up disappointing them and you might end up having to do the whole project over again after they tell you what they initially expected from you in the first place.

'Practice makes perfect' is a wonderful motto for learning accuracy. The more you practice being accurate, the more accurate you will get. Once you start reminding yourself to take care in all that you do and begin checking yourself to make sure that you are working to high standards, you will soon become an expert at working to those. You wouldn't expect someone to be perfect at writing reports and do it right the first time, would you? It takes time, focused attention, a willingness to correct any errors and learn from them, a vow not to repeat those same types of errors again, an action plan to ensure continuous improvement, and lots and lots of practice. Even if you start out far from your goals of being precise and accurate, you will become more and more accurate as time goes on. Just stick with the program - as you practice holding yourself to ever higher standards of preciseness, meticulousness, and accuracy.

A word of warning though: In your quest to become more accurate, make sure that you don't tip the scale too much. You don't want to spend time dialing up your accuracy in areas where it won't provide an adequate return on the investment of your time, energy, and care. Remember our examples about brain surgery and putting mustard on fast food.

There are absolutely different levels when it comes to being precise and accurate. Choose wisely where you will practice being more accurate and precise and you will make sure you target your efforts to dial up accuracy in the appropriate manner. Now let's look at a story about Ozzie Smith.

Ozzie Smith was known "The Wizard" for his defensive brilliance in the major leagues. For thirteen straight years, Ozzie Smith won the Gold Glove Award at shortstop, acknowledging that he was the best defensive player at his position. The reason he was able to accomplish this wasn't purely natural skill as most would think. Ozzie Smith spent hours and hours each day honing his skills, making sure that he was making accurate calls on how a ground ball would come at him before the game even began. He wanted to make sure that he didn't make an error on the field, rather preferring to make those during practice. All of his hard work and practice paid off for an excellent career. He even had his number retired by the St. Louis Cardinals.

Ozzie Smith was a model of how repetition and attention to detail can help you become successful. His accuracy and work ethic helped him become one of the greatest shortstops to play the game of baseball.

Secondary Steps:

After identifying your standards and practicing holding yourself to them, there are a few more steps to take in order to become more accurate. These steps will also require practice and dedicated time and effort to really solidify them into your work performance. Make no mistake though: If you follow these steps like the Immediate Steps, you will be well on your way to becoming much more accurate in the areas you give attention to.

1. Ask for Reviews.

After turning in a project or a piece of work, ask your boss to review it and to please get back to you with critical feedback. If you've been going in a certain direction and aren't sure about whether this is the right direction, just ask your boss. He or she will most likely be impressed that you're asking for them to give you feedback and showing initiative about the standards for your work product. This will also give you the chance to ask questions and be sure that you're headed in the right direction before you burn through much more of the organization's most valuable resources - your time and energy. The clearer you are about the expectations and standards for the tasks and assignments on your plate, the more accurate you will be. The goal is to effectively dovetail your work product with the expectations of the individuals who are ultimately going to be judging that product or holding you accountable.

"The game of life is a game of boomerangs. Our thoughts, deeds and words return to us sooner or later with astounding accuracy."

~Florence Scovel Shinn

2. Influence the Standard by Which You Will Be Judged.

Waiting until after you have turned in a project or a piece of work to negotiate the judgment criteria is way too late. You have to influence the standards by which you will be judged. You would be surprised how much influence you have in adjusting and defining standards. But you only have this power when you discuss the expectations prior to completing the assignment.

So, knowing this, start shaping the criteria by which people judge your work product sooner rather than later. If you think people's standards are too high for one reason or the other, speak up and discuss the reasons why this might be true. For example, imagine that the team leader wants you to find out how many competitors are going to bring out a similar version of a software release this year.

If they are expecting you to get back to them in two hours and you only have the internet at your disposal, you are going to be hard pressed to come up with a terribly accurate report. Bring up your concerns and negotiate your terms. Say things like: "If you give me a couple of days, I can probably speak to our competitive intelligence folks and have them research this for us. At the same time, I can do some internet research and also search the latest patent applications." Or "Bob, I think it's impossible to come up with anything remotely accurate in the timeframe you have allowed. However, if you just want preliminary and very rudimentary information prior to this afternoon's meeting, I can most certainly get something like that to you. It will at least give us a starting point." In this way you are negotiating and letting the other person know what the standard should be according to what you think is possible.

If they counter, you have opened up discussion. Imagine if you don't do this? You are going to be at a distinct disadvantage because you are not going to live up to their standards. So the bottom line: If you want to dial up your accuracy, you also have to be willing to negotiate and talk about the standards.

3. Be Humble.

Humility in asking for feedback is a vital key in becoming more precise and accurate. So be humble. Let go of your preconceived notions about letting your mistakes define who you think you are. Get over the fact that you aren't nearly as accurate as you would

"You were born to win, but to be a winner, you must plan to win, prepare to win, and expect to win."

~Zig Ziglar

like to be and that you are working to get better. Then, don't take everything personally when people point out your mistakes. Be willing to accept advice and criticism from others about your current level of skill as it relates to accurateness. In fact, demand that they be brutally honest with you and tell them that you are trying to up your game in this area and that you can't do it without their critical eye and feedback. From our other sessions, you'll remember that we said you should think of feedback as a gift of knowledge - that you can't change what you don't know about. Although you will also ask your boss, you may find times where you will ask colleagues to review your projects to look at them from a different point of view. If they give advice, be gracious and take it. Accept constructive criticism and learn from it.

Sometimes people will get criticism and ignore it, thinking they know what's best. It's typically wise to listen to what other people have to say, especially since they're looking at the project from a different point of view and with a fresh mind. You may miss your little mistake or overlook missing information because you're so used to re-reading your report. A new mind or a fresh set of eyes might not miss it and can help your work become more accurate. An important point to remember is that we tend to make the same types of mistakes over and over again. If you have a new set of eyes looking over your work, providing you with accurate feedback, see if you can discern any patterns. In behavior, it's always easier to change if you can uncover a pattern and then adjust for it. Be critical in looking to see if there are certain times of the day where you are less accurate - perhaps you are tired and shouldn't do paperwork at those times.

> *"It takes as much energy to wish as it does to plan."*
>
> *~Eleanor Roosevelt*

If you see that you have a pattern whereby your work tends to be less accurate first thing in the morning - because you tend to multitask at that time of the day - or because you are just getting in and haven't settled into work mode yet, you can easily adjust this. Perhaps you forget to write down times and numerical data accurately. If this is the case, make sure that when you do put numbers on paper that you always check them twice for correctness.

4. Stay Focused.

Accuracy and focus go hand in hand. If you find that your main issue is forgetting to fix small details, include other sources, or get your work double-checked, remember that. Perhaps leave a sticky note near your computer to remind you to look at minor details. The more you remind yourself and stay focused to areas where you've previously been inaccurate, you will fix those issues and become more accurate as time goes on. This will also help you to repeat your actions and keep focused.

5. Make the Effort.

> *"Continuous effort - not strength or intelligence - is the key to unlocking our potential."*
>
> *~Winston Churchill*

As you continue in your work, remember to always give additional effort in your projects to become more accurate. It may be that as you get busy, you start to spread yourself thin and don't put in as much effort to your projects that you used to, missing small details. Be sure to keep up the effort to be accurate and precise - especially when it really counts a lot - and try your hardest to work to at least the standards you and others have defined on every project. When you don't put enough effort into something, a part of the project will suffer - and one of the areas where this is most noticed is in accuracy.

45 How to Dial Down Accuracy

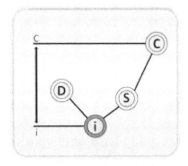

C>I
Accuracy

Occasionally, you may run into situations where you must dial down your accuracy. Because of the Accuracy DISC Sub-factor™, you focus on tiny details and make sure your project is absolutely 100% perfect before turning it in; sometimes missing deadlines because you took the time to hunt for mistakes. You may become less efficient as you take extra time to look through your work - often spending too much time on the details.

In some cases, for instance presentations and major deadlines, you may need to dial down your accuracy in order to complete the tasks on time. Another important aspect of dialing down your accuracy is when you need to be more innovative and creative. Accuracy is great once you have a project underway, but it stunts new and original ideas at the beginning of the process. Some of the greatest scientific achievements in history were the cause of innovation and not Compliance Factors, contrary to popular belief.

"A good plan violently executed now is better than a perfect plan executed next week."

~George S. Patton

There always has to be a crazy idea that breaks the social norms to first breakthrough a new way of thinking. Think of the Defense Advanced Research Projects Agency (known as DARPA). They were established to "prevent strategic surprise from negatively impacting U.S. national security and create strategic surprise for U.S. adversaries by maintaining the technological superiority of the U.S. military." DARPA's scientific advancements were accomplished through their dialing down of the Accuracy DISC Sub-factor™ because they have to think of new and innovative ways of preventing threats and ensuring a technological advantage. DARPA is immensely huge now because of that initial focus on innovation and allowing accuracy to fall into its rightful place later in the production process.

There is a caveat when dialing down the Accuracy DISC Sub-factor™. You must make sure that someone on the team is still complying to the accuracy Sub-factor. If everyone is dialing down their accuracy, this can be disastrous as accuracy may never come back into the equation. You can delegate this role to someone to maintain accuracy in the organization while the team is brainstorming. There has to be someone on the team that is able to be the devil's advocate, especially once you start to narrow down your options and select the best idea.

Immediate Steps:

To begin dialing down your accuracy, you can take these immediate steps to flex your behavior. As you continue to practice these steps, they will become natural and allow you to flex your behavior in any situation, so you can be more successful in your professional and personal life.

1. Plan Ahead.

If you find yourself double checking your work far in advance, set your deadline a week before it is due. Make sure the full project is done a week in advance to give yourself extra time to look over the details. If push comes to shove, it's done and ready to go. This way you won't be missing deadlines because you're going back over your work.

You also need to plan ahead during the brainstorming stage. That is why it is critical to have an accuracy person on the team.

Dialing down your accuracy may help you think of an innovative new solution, but forgetting to dial it back up will cause it to be ill thought out and you will have to spend more on fixing the problems caused by the lack of accuracy.

Let's look at the example of the Hubble Space Telescope.

The team that designed it was incredibly innovative and thought outside of the box to put together the impressive system. The only problem was that the main mirror had been ground incorrectly, which severely compromised the capabilities of the telescope. Because the Hubble scientists and engineers failed to have an adequate check and balance with accuracy, they made a huge error. It isn't enough to believe that someone else is checking the accuracy of the work. Someone needs to be delegated to that task so that others can focus on improving the system.

2. Deliver a Statement of Expectations For Any Changes.

One of the most effective ways to begin communicating changes is to start with a statement of expectations. A statement of expectations is a simple, concise, straightforward proclamation of why a company is making any change in the first place. A statement of expectations encourages the management team and employees to keep an eye on the results so that employees and managers do not become overwhelmed or distracted from the original purpose for the change. You can use the statement of expectations to dial down the accuracy of colleagues and give them enough information so that they do not need to constantly search or ask for what they are supposed to measure with their accuracy. This will put you into a leadership position with your peers.

To compose a statement of expectations, the management team needs to answer some basic questions BEFORE beginning to implement the change. Two of these questions are:

DISCflex™

- "What good will come of this change?" and
- "What do we expect to happen because of the change?"

The statement of expectations can begin with these types of words and phrases:

- We are making this decision because we anticipate...
- We are looking forward and need to accomplish...

Establish an effective statement of expectations and others will respect you more and will ask you less questions about the new change. Delivering a statement of expectations will help you dial down your accuracy because it puts you into a more influential and persuading role.

3. Explain Expectations For Deliverables in RA² Interface Documents.

Once you put the RA² Document in place, set the people loose with periodic benchmarking and feedback periods. Having an elevated Accuracy Sub-factor can cause you to unfairly micromanage people and padlock them. People will not respect you if you continuously put then through accuracy standards without having a good explanation of the expectations upfront.

All you need to do is put the RA² Document together and explain the responsibilities, accountability metrics, and the authority parameters associated with each of your team members. This has the added benefit of giving you accuracy standards while still allowing your coworkers to have their own independence and process for achieving those goals. If you can do this, you will dial down your accuracy without sacrificing results.

4. Make a List of Key Points.

When checking over your work, make a list of key things that need to be checked and leave minute details, such as the size of the margin, out. Give your people some latitude to be creative and to do work the way they have been hired to do it. If you made the right selection for employees they will rarely disappoint you in their deliverables. For example, if you are delegating a report that must be written, list only the important things such as: length, content, correct calculations, and other important information. When you keep reminding yourself of the important things in the overall project, you won't be so focused on the tiny details that no one else will notice.

"If you allow team members to own a project, you must trust in their professionalism that they will get the job done. Stepping back is the hardest thing to do sometimes. But to grow people you have to avoid micromanagement. It doesn't mean turning away. Keep an open door. Explain the parameters of when they should come to you. Be there to provide support when needed, but don't unduly influence or insert yourself into everything. If you let them, they'll usually exceed your expectations. Rarely will they disappoint you. If you don't let them do things on their own, there are dire consequences. When employees feel micromanaged, they feel minimized as professionals."

~Hellen Davis

5. Resist Micromanagement.

Micromanagement is the curse of directing a knowledge-based workforce. Nit picking, obsessive managers who insist on getting everything done precisely the way they want it done will result in a very unproductive workforce. The best will leave and the others will be resentful. Dialing down the preciseness - the amount of Compliance - that you require from your people will make for a happier, self-directed, and more cohesive workforce. People pull away from people they think are overbearing and overly controlling. Resist this tendency.

The Management Gates principle is the best way to understand this principle and its effect on an organization. Companies that have a high organizational accuracy Sub-factor tend to have a closed gate system. This means that they start out by giving little instruction at the beginning, instead correcting their employees as they make mistakes, highlighting those mistakes more and more as the individual continues his career with the organization. Contrasting that is an open gate system. This management gate usually starts with an RA^2 Interface Document, showing the individual what they need to accomplish and what their authority guidelines are. In the open gate system, the individual is given more autonomy and latitude as he or she progresses in their career. This has proven to work better in employee development. Incorporating an open gate management style will help you dial down your accuracy Sub-factor.

Secondary Steps:

After completing the immediate steps to help dial down your accuracy Sub-factor, some secondary steps can help you further your development of this skill. Keep practicing these steps until you are comfortable with them and can dial down your accuracy whenever you feel it is necessary.

1. Talk To Your Supervisor to Ratify RA^2 Interface Documents Before You Deploy.

There may be times when you want to talk to your supervisor to ask how quickly you need to accomplish tasks and how perfect they need to be. Your boss may have a plan to get the first draft done and then have a meeting on it to improve it. If you don't ask about this, you may end up taking more time than necessary and miss the meeting, or deciding that you should take extra time to fix it even more.

If you know that this is the first draft, you know you have wiggle room and it does not need to be perfect the first time. Make sure you know exactly what your expectations are. This will help you dial down your own accuracy because you won't need to continuously come back to your supervisor to ask if you are completing the task the way they want. You will already know what they expect of you.

2. Negotiate With the Person Assigning Your Taskers.

Negotiate deliverables and deadlines to keep yourself and the organization out of trouble. One of the most important leadership lessons I learned was that not everything you want to accomplish can get done. Be clear when going through the RA^2 Document what you believe you can accomplish in the given timeframe. Do not try and abide by the first expectations set if you know the project will not be completed effectively. This is one of those points where you have to dial down your accuracy so that your Dominance and Influence Sub-factors can come out to negotiate realistic accountability metrics for the deadline.

3. **Think About Return on Investment and Focused Effort.**

   You have to prioritize and think in terms of ROI on the investment of people's time, energy and of the organization's resources. Whenever you assign a new deliverable, if you come up with another great idea you run the risk of de-focusing employees. Even though you may be trying to keep ahead of your team members to ensure accuracy, this can have fatal effects on a team's focus.

   The ROI should ask for the appropriate level of accuracy for the task required. I had this experience before with my team when I assigned a new team member with the task of researching and coming up with initial outlines for a new course we were writing. I did not specify the ROI and the individual spent an inordinate amount of time doing research when I just wanted an initial outline to look over. This caused me to become more accurate with this team member, whereas I could have dialed down my accuracy if I would have just specified what the ROI should have been for the project.

4. **Hold-Fast to Deadlines.**

   This may be a hard concept to grasp and practice, but you must hold yourself to your deadlines. You may think that deadlines are just guidelines, especially when you are in an industry that is forced to hold to accurate standards, and that you can't turn in the project until the accuracy standards are fully met and checked over multiple times. This is not true, especially when others are depending on you to get your work done by a certain time. Remember to go back to secondary step two and negotiate the RA^2 deadlines if you believe the project will take longer than the quoted expectations.

"Without deadlines and restrictions I just tend to become preoccupied with other things."

~Val Kilmer

46 Sensitivity Generic Profile

Definition

When Compliance is greater than Steadiness, you have the Sensitivity Sub-factor. Sensitive people are very aware of their environment. People with this Sub-factor are also sensitive to change, they can sense when it is coming, and they see the benefits and consequences of it. Sensitive people have a strong care and understanding of their requirements and of their needs. This type of person is sensitive to details and sees the little nuances that others might not see.

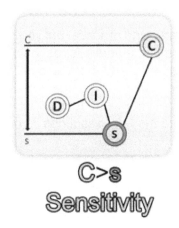

C>s
Sensitivity

Descriptors

Words that describe the Sensitivity Sub-factor are:

- Compassion
- Understanding
- Awareness
- Delicacy
- Keenness

- Sympathy
- Acuteness
- Consciousness
- Reactive
- Perceptive

Strengths

The strengths of the Sensitivity Sub-factor are an enhanced perception and awareness, a great deal of empathy and understanding, and the ability to be conscious of the benefits and consequences of any choice and how it affects them.

Sensitive people have the ability to recognize minor and subtle details of anything. Sensitive people make great managers and inspectors because they can see where a project might go wrong or how something small that can drastically affect a product.

Sensitive people have a great deal of empathy and understanding which allows them to build rapport and gain trust with others. They can see where others are having problems and understand why they are having those problems. Sensitive people are able to make quick assessments of risks in order to determine whether or not to take them.

Weaknesses

The weaknesses of the Sensitivity Sub-factor are a low attention span and a tendency to take things personally, especially feedback. This can lead people with this Sub-factor to have negative energy exerted from feedback, instead of taking it positively as a way to improve. Sensitive people are easily distracted and can change what they are thinking about on a moment's notice. This happens because they notice everything happening in their environment. This can lead to miscommunication in a fast-paced work environment if not watched carefully.

The Space Shuttle Challenger disaster is an example of sensitivity being ignored and ultimately leading to catastrophe. The Challenger was originally scheduled to liftoff on January 22, 1986 but a series of problems pushed back the launch date. Scientists and engineers at NASA were eager to get the mission underway as soon as possible. The day before the launch, an engineer noticed and brought up his concern about the material used to create the O-rings in the booster rockets. Several conference calls were held to discuss the issue and the group decided to go ahead with the launch despite the engineers concerns. The Challenger exploded shortly after liftoff on January 28. Ultimately, the engineer's concerns about the questionable O-rings were found to be the cause of the Challenger's explosion.

While coaching, I have met many people who are too sensitive in their workplace. After working with them and coaching them on how to change their habits, selling techniques, or decision making, I give them feedback. There have been times when they have taken my constructive criticism and help too personally and considered it an attack. There have also been instances where I've moved people around on projects to try a different approach and they have taken it personally. Although sensitivity is oftentimes a good trait, it can become negative when people are too sensitive to the situations around them and personalize them.

Situational Adaptation - Dial Up or Dial Down

"Wallow too much in sensitivity and you can't deal with life, or the truth."

~Neal Boortz

You have to dial down your sensitivity when getting feedback. It's important to use your sensitivity to gain understanding as to why you are getting the feedback. You're getting feedback in order to improve yourself and make adjustments to your working skills and abilities.

It is just as important to dial up your sensitivity whenever you are thinking about the benefits or consequences of a situation. You have to be able to hone your sensitivity to all the details that affect the situation and how they will affect you personally. This is a great skill to have. The Sensitivity Sub-factor can help you take the best opportunities and avoid the worst threats.

> *"Writing a really general parser is a major but different undertaking, by far the hardest points being sensitivity to context and resolution of ambiguity."*
>
> *~Graham Nelson*

Imagine for a moment the highly sensitive employee who is speaking with a customer about paying their invoice in a timely manner. It is important to be sensitive to the client's situation, and sometimes it is right to make exceptions to the rule, especially when the client may be dealing with financial difficulties. Making an exception for a dire circumstance is different than making exceptions all the time. Feeling high sensitivity for every client could be detrimental to the life of the business. The company will go under if their clients fail to pay their bills. This 'sensitive' individual needs to tap into their persistence Sub-factor and work diligently toward a satisfactory resolution. Rather than being too sensitive, they need to show their sensitivity while continuously seeking a positive resolution.

If this individual learns how to use their persistence Sub-factor while being a sensitive individual, they can be more effective when working on a team project. They need to be sensitive, but persistent, in an effort to get the team's job completed on time. What if the team's members aren't working effectively on their individual contributions? They are missing deadlines and causing others to fall behind also. The project will be lagging behind. Pushing their persistence will help cause other team members to stay on track, so they won't hold up progress. On the flip side, persistence can also have negative effects. If this individual is too persistent and not sensitive to others, this person could cause the team to lose their motivation. The team will get annoyed at the persistence and may continue their pace and avoid the employee. They need to draw on the Sensitivity Sub-factor while still being persistent.

There have been times when I have been ready to take a risk and have not thought through the consequences. Sometimes people think that if the consequences are not apparent, they must not be that important. In these cases I must dial up my sensitivity and look at the details to see what I may have missed. This is especially important when I prepare a contract for a client. I may think that the contract looks perfect and is ready to go, but I must dial up my sensitivity to notice the details that may be missing.

In coaching inexperienced sales people, I've noticed they make a typical flaw if a deal does not work out: they take it personally. Although they may have put in a lot of hard work with a client, if something comes up and they choose not to do business with them, they must not take it personally and instead look at what went wrong. Chances are, they changed their minds not because of who the sales person is personally, but because they found a better deal, they were not offered the best possible option, or the sales person was not strong or confident enough in their delivery. If a deal does not work out, they shouldn't take it personally, but instead stop to look at what happened and ensure that it does not happen again the next time.

Next Steps

Next, you will explore the benefits and consequences of the Sensitivity Sub-factor. If you think that this Sub-factor is important for your success, you can target your knowledge by investigating various ways to dial up or dial down your Sensitivity Sub-factor in our 'How to' sessions.

"But I think that sensitivity is also a good counselor when it comes to enforcing one's interests."

~Johannes Rau

47 How to Dial Up Sensitivity

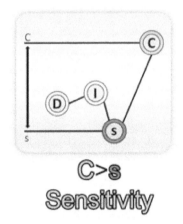

Many people think that being told they are being sensitive is not desirable. People are often told to be less sensitive and to grow thicker skin; rather than to be too sensitive. However, being sensitive isn't always a bad thing. There are situations when being sensitive is the best approach and skill to have. Think about major changes in the workplace. While everyone else is gung-ho and excited about the 'what ifs' that are about to happen, a sensitive person may notice a fatal flaw that could ruin everything. When they bring their observations to the table, raise their concerns, or surface the issue early, things can be quickly resolved before any damage ensues or problems develop. Having someone tuned in and sensitive to subtle nuances is important; because when turbulent times occur, most people find it difficult to do much more than just get through what they need to do. They rarely have extra bandwidth for being sensitive.

So, what exactly does being sensitive indicate? Being sensitive may mean that you notice changes and problems before others will. Being aware of your surroundings and the implications of changes or issues in the workplace is a benefit to any organization. Be sensitive to the changes in relationships in time to make course corrections or being tuned in to the issues confronting friends or family members helps you build trust. People with high sensitivity are aware in general of market conditions, changes in circumstances, and having the ability to be perceptive is a fabulous skill to acquire. What being sensitive doesn't mean is being easily upset, thin-skinned, hypersensitive, touchy-feeling, or vulnerable. Think of appropriate sensitivity as being receptive, aware, perceptive, insightful, and ultimately responsive to your surroundings and in your relationships.

Immediate Steps:

Individuals with the sensitivity Sub-factor tend to have a great deal of empathy and understanding. This characteristic helps them establish rapport and gain trust. Being able to be sensitive helps an individual examine the benefits and consequences of choices in order to determine how it would affect them. This makes it easier for the individual to make quick assessments of risks to see if they should follow through with them. Like any Sub-factor, it will take practice and dedication to learn to dial up your sensitivity to an appropriate level for the situation you are facing; or, if you decide that you need to be more sensitive in nature, you can choose to dial sensitivity up and make it a habit through long-term behavioral morphing. No matter what your goals are for the short or long term: Here are some immediate steps you can take to help you dial up your sensitivity.

1. **Tune in Your Primary Senses: Look, Listen, Feel**

   People who are highly sensitive are very aware of their surroundings. To become more aware, make an effort to lock into the present moment and tune in your primary senses: Look, Listen, and Feel. Seeing what is happening around you on a more finely tuned basis will let you notice your environment on a different level. When you tune in visually, it also opens the window to your other senses. So, first start with concentrating on seeing more of what is going on around you.

2. **Up Your Hearing.**

   Learning to listen will help you become more aware of the people and needs around you. When a person is truly listening to someone, they usually concentrate more and are able to retain more. They become increasingly aware of the person they are talking to and are able to gain an insight into their life to understand who that person is and why they do things. Being able to truly listen to someone will help you slow your thoughts down in order to retain more information and will provide a way for you to gain their trust and establish rapport with them. Next time you want to say something while someone else is talking to you, try being patient and continue to listen. If you practice your listening skills, you may be surprised at how quickly people will open up to you. Now, crank up your emotional involvement. Sensitive individuals are keenly aware of how their actions affect other people. Notice the subtle signals that people give off when their emotional involvement kicks in. Use mirroring and matching to adjust your body language to theirs and see how you become better at feeling and sensing other people's emotional involvement.

3. **Take a Moment to Take It In.**

   It can be so easy for us to walk through our days on auto pilot; rarely being aware of our surroundings and the people that cross our paths in our busy lives. Learn to push pause on your day every so often to just look around you and become aware of what is going on. Take notice of your work space, your colleagues and how they interact. Tune into yourself, your place in the world and really see the people and places around you. By making this a habit, you can learn to become more aware and perceptive.

4. **Maintain a Healthy Lifestyle.**

   When we're dehydrated, fatigued, hungry, or stressed in any number of ways, it's harder for our minds and bodies to function and work. To be fully aware of your surroundings, you need to stay healthy, alert and tuned in. Let's look at how something as simple as dehydration can affect your ability to be sensitive. Think about that 3 o'clock afternoon hour when you're dragging and counting the time down until the end of the business day. Most people are not aware, however studies show, that people usually get dehydrated around this time of the day.

When this happens, it contributes to making us less mindful of our surroundings, less able to listen effectively, and less capable of concentrating. Keep drinking fluids steadily throughout the day and you'll find that you can fight that mid-afternoon tired feeling and as a result you'll be more aware to your surroundings. This is true of other components that make up a healthy lifestyle, too. Try to make time to eat at least three healthy meals a day and participate in some type of exercise throughout the week. This will help you maintain your energy and focus during the day - which will help your overall awareness and perception.

One of the strengths of the Sensitivity Sub-factor is the ability to be perceptive and aware of minor and subtle details. Individuals that are C>s are able to understand more throughly their perception - which allows them to make more accurate decisions. Having the ability to perceive details and be aware of other Factors helps an individual become more successful and achieve more. An example of this is the Super Soaker, a toy water gun created by Larami Toy Corporation. In the toy industry a great run for the marketability of a popular toy is 18 months. Most toy companies expect a toy to be a fad for a period of two to three months at best. When it happens during the holiday season this is an added bonus! Past clients of mine, the Larami Toy Corporation, produced the Super Soaker Squirt Gun but in the late 1980s. When I first met the owners of Larami, their best products were the Koosh Ball and the Sea Monkeys.

Most people don't even remember those toys, but the vast majority of people still remember the Super Soakers and many of us had one or two in our homes. The first year the Super Soaker came out, it received an enormous amount of press because it was a particularly hot summer and TV stations aired people running around the neighborhood squirting each other to cool down.

In many cities, people compared the Super Soakers to violent weapons that had the potential of corrupting children. Pundits brought up the controversy surrounding toy guns and actively debated whether or not they should be banned. The free publicity the Super Soaker was receiving drove sales through the roof! When I spoke to the owners during the initial product launch, they only hoped for it to be the fad toy of the summer. Then they were hopeful that it would be a steady seller over the next few years, much like their Koosh Ball and Sea Monkeys. Little did they know that it would run for three consecutive summers and still be a hit toy today, many years later. You can just imagine the revenue stream that the Super Soaker has produced for the Larami Corporation and now after selling the company to Hasbro Toys. They did not however make the mistake of assuming that the trend pattern would continue. They looked at every year as a bonus year for that toy and continue to put out Lego Block, Sea Monkey's, Koosh Balls and toy guns. Their perception and awareness of the market helped the Larami Corporation establish a new product as well as prepare for the future through their other products.

"I believe that we are all born with certain characteristics – the ability to sense the world around us and tune into a deep level of sensitivity, the ability to love deeply, the capacity to strive for what we believe in and to overcome impossible odds, and perhaps the most important, the power in our soul to feel the intensity of profound passion. We make the choice to give each other the gift of communication and understanding. All these are marvelous attributes. The degree to which we capitalize on these characteristics sets us apart – and brings like-minded souls together. At the beginning of our journey we don't understand how important these are, but as we grow, we learn how terribly important these are."

~Hellen Davis

Secondary Steps:

Here are some secondary steps you can take to help dial up your sensitivity. Take the time to concentrate on these steps and you can see your sensitivity in different situations increase, helping you establish rapport and gain the trust of those around you.

1. Put Yourself in Someone Else's Shoes.

Occasionally, it may be hard to empathize with others and understand where they're coming from, perhaps making you seem cold and uncaring. It may take some practice, but start thinking about where they're coming from. After sitting in traffic all morning, spilling coffee on your tie, and running late to work, you may have a hard time empathizing with your coworker's complaints about the broken copier. Although you may think that your day has been harder than theirs, put yourself in their shoes. Perhaps the copier being broken ruins their whole day, will make them late and miss deadlines, and disappoint others they're working with. Always try to think about how someone else deals with problems. Although a flat tire may not seem like a big deal to you, it may be to someone else. Empathize with others and be sensitive to their needs.

2. Listen to Your Emotions.

Sometimes, we have gut instincts and feelings and can brush them off. When it comes to making an important decision, we sometimes decide to side with our logic and the facts. Sensitivity, however, is ruled by emotions. Have you ever been in a situation where you thought "I like this, but I don't know why…" and then ignore your feelings because you didn't know why you liked it? Side with your emotions. Stop to think about why you felt that way. We have instincts for a reason. The key is stopping to listen to those instincts. Sensitive people follow their gut feeling and make decisions off of their emotions.

3. Simply Give.

The simple act of giving someone something of value, whether it is a card, a small gift they can use around the house, or something they really wanted, takes sensitivity and awareness. An excellent way to dial up your sensitivity is to get someone a gift. Your gift could be a material gift or it might just be your time, but by giving, you show that you are aware of the other person and sensitive to their thoughts and needs. An example of this in my own life is a gift I received from now retired, NBA star Charles Barkley.

The gift itself was nice but the part that made an impression on me was the act. It was the day after my birthday and some friends and my husband and I were going out to dinner. The dinner wasn't to celebrate my birthday, just a casual dinner and Charles and his wife were coming. To my surprise when I got there, I found a gift waiting for me at the restaurant from the Barkley's. I asked his wife how she even managed to remember that my birthday was yesterday and she replied that she had no idea and that it was Charles who had remembered. I was completely shocked by his consideration and thoughtfulness. I remembered that six weeks prior to the dinner, in a meeting with Charles, the topic of birthdays had come up and we had mentioned when our birthdays were. We weren't best friends but six weeks later he still remembered my birthday and made it a point to get me a gift. This completely unexpected gift was a profound example of his sensitivity and attention to detail and made a lasting impression on me.

48 How to Dial Down Sensitivity

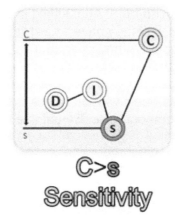

C>s
Sensitivity

In some cases, you must learn to dial down your sensitivity. This may come in situations when you must get things done immediately. If you are too sensitive, you may hinder yourself by dwelling on your hurt feelings rather than getting the job done quickly. Or, during a performance review, you may take things too personally and get upset. You must remember, however, that your boss is doing their job and the goal is for you to perform better after receiving constructive criticism. Also, in workplace relations, when you're passed over for a group project you may take it personally. You need to understand that you aren't being personally attacked, but that you may be on a more important project that demands attention and cannot take part in a group project right now.

In these situations, you need to learn how to dial down your Sensitivity. There are a few steps that you can take immediately and a few steps that will take longer to accomplish and perfect.

Immediate Steps:

These next few steps can be taken immediately, but do require practice.

1. **Think Noble Intent.**

   One of the foundations of Noble Intent is that people are inherently good and will do what is right or noble. Two facets of Noble Intent are acting and assuming. Acting with Noble Intent is relatively effortless compared to assuming Noble Intent because we are able to control our own actions. Assuming Noble Intent is a little more difficult because you have to consciously trust that the people you are dealing with believe in, and are motivated by, some kind of Noble Intent. If you assume Noble Intent in others, they will often match and exceed your expectations. Conversely, if you believe people are not acting with Noble Intent, chances are they will live down to your expectations. If you feel like someone is taking advantage of you or in some extreme cases, out to get you, confront them and have the conversation with them if you are in any doubt. If you act and assume with Noble Intent you will be well respected, perceived as fair and someone who works for the common good. This will allow them to place their trust in you. Acting and assuming Noble Intent will help dial down your sensitivity and will help you become more successful in the workplace.

2. Remember That Not Everything is a Personal Attack.

If your boss or coworker is giving you constructive criticism, don't take it personally. They are helping you to work towards your full potential. If you understand that your boss is trying to help you be more successful, you will be able to take what they say and apply it to your work performance. Taking things personally will only hinder you in the long run. Be aware of your strengths, but also know that your weaknesses are things you can work on, not things that will drag you down.

"Don't listen to those who say, you are taking too big a chance. Michelangelo would have painted the Sistine floor, and it would surely be rubbed out by today. Most important, don't listen when the little voice of fear inside you rears its ugly head and says: 'They are all smarter than you out there. They're more talented, they're taller, blonder, prettier, luckier, and they have connections.' I firmly believe that if you follow a path that interests you, not to the exclusion of love, sensitivity, and cooperation with others, but with the strength of conviction that you can move others by your own efforts, and do not make success or failure the criteria by which you live, the chances are you'll be a person worthy of your own respects."

~ Neil Simon

3. Are You Being Reasonable?

If you find yourself taking something personally, stop and ask yourself, "Am I being reasonable? Is Deena REALLY attacking me for how I did the last project?"

Taking a 3rd person point of view will help you to analyze the situation and decide if you really are being reasonable or not. Sometimes, sensitivity is due to assuming an unreasonable position and reacting from there.

4. Study The Perceptual Position Model and Practice Getting Out of Your 'Me, me, me' Mode

The Perceptual Prisms Model is a model that deals exclusively with our sensory input, and how we process the information we receive from our senses. Sensory input is how you perceive things through your senses. The model also references how to process our own, as well as other people's distinct point of view through three different perceptual positions.

The first position is the Ego position. It is the 'me, myself, and I' position and is based entirely on the self and on the ego. When an individual has an Elevated Sensitivity Sub-factor, they typically see things from this position the majority of the time, especially when criticized. If a person with an elevated Sensitivity Factor is able to move from this position to the second or third position, they can better understand what reality really is.

The second position is called the Alliance position and is the 'walk a mile in the other person's shoes' attitude. This position puts you in another person's place when viewing a situation and allows you to see how they perceive the situation. Being in this position will dial down your sensitivity because you are able to see a situation from both sides.

The third and last perceptual position is called the observer or 'fly on the wall' position. This position is devoid of intimacy and only looks at a situation from a detached and objective viewpoint. Acting with Noble Intent typically means you are in this position. In looking through all three positions at home, you might be a huge sports fan that loves to spend your Sunday afternoon watching football; however your loving spouse would rather enjoy a relaxing walk on the beach. At this point both you and your spouse are looking at the situation from the first, ego, position. Imagine if you both looked at the situation from your partner's point of view. You could spend a beautiful, sunny day on the beach and agree to watch the game after sunset. Then, your spouse could agree to take on all family responsibilities on Sunday evening for a few hours to give you uninterrupted time to watch your game. Now, if you both looked at it from the third position and looked at their family as a whole unit, both you and your spouse might come to understand that by spending quality time together and giving up a little bit of what you both value, you could possibly ensure that your relationship remains stronger than it would have. It is important to look at situations from each of the three perceptual positions in order make the right decision and dial down your sensitivity. For more information on the Perceptual Prisms Model, look at session #3 in the Change Course.

Secondary Steps:

1. Visualize

If you foresee a situation arising where you feel you will overreact and get upset, visualize exactly what you will do to stay calm and not get upset. If you are getting ready to walk into a performance review and you know that you may get upset, take a deep breath and visualize. Tell yourself: "I am calm, cool, and collected" and "I will not take things personally." Doing this can give you confidence and the belief that you are what you tell yourself. Self-talk and visualization is extremely important in every aspect of your life and will help you dial down your sensitivity. For an example of vision and how powerful visualizing can be, let's look at the story of Fred Smith.

Fred Smith has eagle vision. In the mid 1960's, he was writing a term paper for his economics class at Yale University. Smith envisioned an overnight, nationwide, air express delivery system for urgent packages. Unfortunately, his professor didn't share the same excitement of Smith's idea and gave him a "C" on the term paper. Smith, however, took the ideas from this "average work" paper and created an exceptional, international company -- Federal Express.

Today Federal Express enjoys a well-earned reputation as one of the finest companies in the world and has captured a healthy percentage of the air express market in the United States. In addition, Federal Express is consistently ranked in the top ten of the best places to work in America.

Fred Smith saw an opportunity others were missing. He didn't allow the discouragement of a college professor to thwart his vision. Rather, he used the setback as a springboard to make his idea a 'flying' success.

Vision is an extremely powerful tool that should be tapped into. Fred Smith and countless others utilized their vision and let it drive them to success. If you feel that you need to dial down your sensitivity, visualize how you will do it and when. This will help prepare you to succeed when a situation arises.

2. Identify Your Triggers.

Look at the times that you've felt the most sensitive and have become upset. Was it something someone said specifically? Statements such as "You don't know what you're talking about" or "You don't know anything, do you?" can trigger us to shut down and be upset. If you know what triggers your sensitivity, you can prepare for it and remind yourself to remain calm. Make sure and complete the Emotions Trigger Activity in the Activity section of the website.

49 Elevated D Generic Profile

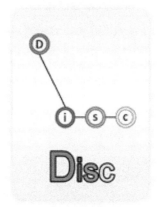

Individuals who have an elevated score in Dominance generally exhibit extrovert and controlling types of tendencies:

They are usually a combination of independence, efficiency, and self-motivation characteristics. Elevated D Personalities are driven to achieve, love getting results, and are determined to find success. Often, the Elevated D individual will break established rules and guidelines if they feel those rules are counter-productive to their goals. This is particularly true of people who also have comparatively lower Compliance scores. Elevated Ds typically like to set their own rules.

A famous example of an Elevated D is Donald Trump. His empire was raised from his self-motivation and his desire to succeed. If you have ever watched his TV show, The Apprentice, you can tell that Mr. Trump is an Elevated D by how he judges each team's performance. He loves when the teams give him the expected results, while being as efficient as possible.

The Elevated D person is oftentimes the leader, although this personality can also be the Devil's Advocate in the room. This individual will not simply agree with the group, but will be strong-willed and outspoken about their opinions. In public sector organizations, the Elevated D personalities rise through the ranks because they like authority and control. They love to be passionately involved in attaining mission-based results and are driven by purposeful determination.

In life, the Elevated D individual is ambitious and aggressive. With extremely Elevated Dominance scores this can be off-putting to those they interact with. They need to see their actions come to a conclusion or else they will push the issue. They are usually self-confident, decisive, and are able to initiate activity. Elevated Ds are pioneers and visionaries. They bring a new way of thinking to the organization or create new ventures.

Entrepreneurs are generally Elevated Ds. They like to be in control and use their own ideas to produce results. This is the process by which new businesses and even new marketplaces, missions, or in some cases whole new industries are created. The Elevated D personality is associated with individuality. Even in the workplace, employees or bosses with this personality can bring great ideas to the table that other people in the organization have not thought of.

In times of crisis or conflict, Elevated Ds are forward-looking, have a big picture focus, and are able to be the voice to take action to counter the conflict. They are quick to react to the situation and are generally optimistic in getting to a good end result.

Elevated Ds are also known as risk-takers. They are more likely than any other personality profile to make quick decisions without all the facts. They are confident in their intuition and generally believe they are lucky.

Motivated By:

Elevated Ds are motivated by results. They get bored easily by routine or mundane tasks and need to see results coming from their efforts to continue their motivation. They live for a challenging and innovative environment where they can put their visions to work.

Obstacles are another source of motivation for the Elevated D personality. They are the type of people that love putting out fires because they love the challenge it provides. They also like the high level of authority required to put out fires and solve problems. They are 'fixers' and problem solvers.

Margaret Thatcher is an excellent example of this personality type. She had a clear vision of what the United Kingdom needed to stop what she perceived as a national decline. Even when her approval ratings were lowering, she continued to push her ideas, and ended up being a strong leader in history. Her Elevated Dominance showed when dealing with Soviet Union as well. She was given the nickname of the "Iron Lady" for her tough rhetoric.

In any endeavor, Elevated Ds need freedom from routine. They like a variety of activities that they can choose from with their own decision making prowess. As they achieve their goals, Elevated Ds like the recognition and rewards that come from their good results.

Possible Weaknesses:

There are also some possible weaknesses that the Elevated D individual might have. First of all, Elevated Ds typically will overstep or challenge authority when they believe they are right. This can cause conflicts to occur. When these conflicts occur, Elevated Ds can be argumentative and combative, which could lead to real problems in the workplace.

Another weakness that might be exhibited by the Elevated D personality is poor time management. Because Elevated Ds dislike routine and can often take on too much work at once, they can let their over ambitious and optimistic attitude give them deadlines they can't possibly meet. This can be a problem when deadlines need to be met.

Elevated Ds also tend to get 'set in their ways'. It's usually 'my way or the highway' with the Elevated D individual, even if they don't openly say it. This can cause the Elevated D person to ignore other people's views or twist the situation to look favorably upon themselves.

Dominant individuals appear in all of our lives. Usually this type of personality is the one that we remember from previous bosses. Sometimes the Dominance Factor can make a boss forget that their employees can provide brilliant insight into projects and tasks.

Whenever I get into this mode where I am set on an idea, I make sure to take a step back and listen to my employees' feedback and concerns. I find that they are able to give me good suggestions and sometimes they can build off my ideas and help make them better.

Be sure to look at the suggestions provided for Elevated D profiles. Use your strengths as an Elevated D to be successful in your life, but don't let your weaknesses stop you from getting there. Know how to use the other DISC Factors when they will help you achieve your goals.

"Conflict is inevitable. If you are brainstorming, getting things accomplished and driving forward at the pace business demands, people will want to be in control and have it done their way. These are elevated Dominance traits. But, to achieve the best results and provide customers with solutions, a variety of ideas and approaches are needed. These are the spices and ingredients of a great business. Throw them in the mix; and it's a recipe for conflict. You have to dial that D down, take a breath, and listen!"

~Hellen Davis

50 Elevated I Generic Profile

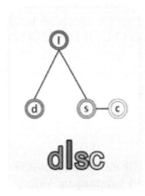

Individuals who have an elevated score in Steadiness generally exhibit these types of tendencies:

They tend to have a magnetic, charismatic personality. They make friends easily and love the social atmosphere. Generally, they are trusted by their friends. And, they rarely if ever break that trust because they hate to erode or destroy relationships. Usually the Elevated I individual is described as political, convincing, and warm. Because of the Elevated I's advanced level of social expertise, they are typically entertaining and motivating in their social circles.

Former President Bill Clinton is an example of the Elevated I individual. He is often seen as the elder statesman and as a special motivating force behind the Democrat Party in the United States. Whenever he gives a speech to a group of supporters, he can get them enthused to vote, support his initiatives, donate in substantial amounts or anything else that he or the party sees as necessary to promote the cause. He is an excellent communicator who has garnered substantial influence in the world.

"Man's main task in life is to give birth to himself, to become what he potentially is. The most important product of his effort is his own personality."

~Erich Fromm

Elevated Is are social by nature. They are talkative and replenish their energy through social interactions with others. Known to have a great sense of humor, Elevated Is are well liked by others. They are instinctive influencers and communicators. Elevated Is are enthusiastic problem solvers, preferring to work in team-oriented situations. They love to share information with other people on the team.

Elevated Is are generally demonstrative in their communication with others. They are talkative, but are usually seen by others as persuasive. Elevated Is make excellent negotiators, knowing how to make peace between different parties.

Motivated By:

The Elevated I individual is motivated when others express acceptance or praise of their performance at work. They perform well when they are popular in the office, and take very well to flattery from their bosses or employees. Elevated Is are best motivated in a peaceful and friendly environment. This is an environment where they are free to comment and build on the ideas of others, they are free from nitpicking and pettiness, and where there is open debate and dialogue. Elevated Is like to get everything out in the open to deal with it. They are generally extroverts in that they want to deal externally with issues instead of holding them back.

President Clinton was always at his best when he was able to give a speech or have open debates with the members of Congress and his Executive Board. He was able to use his Influential nature to work together with the Republican-controlled Congress. This allowed more ideas to come into the political atmosphere, which is always healthy. The Influence Factor allows for speech to be encouraged instead of limited, which is a great asset for any organization.

Possible Weaknesses:

The possible weaknesses of the Elevated I individual involve relying on gut instinct, preferring intuition and a sixth sense over logic when relating to others. When in decision making teams, the Elevated I individual may choose form over substance. They may want to gain acceptance from their boss instead of doing what is necessary to make something work. Because the Elevated I often strives to be liked, they will sometimes let deadlines slip rather than hold others accountable. When dealing with conflict, the Elevated I individual can be overly emotional or may be more concerned with popularity than rendering a solution. At times, Elevated Is listen only when convenient for a self-serving interest. This can cause Elevated Is to have a lack of attention to detail when they don't have a vested interest in the work they are doing.

"Instinct must be thwarted just as one prunes the branches of a tree so that it will grow better."

~ Henri Matisse

51 Elevated S Generic Profile

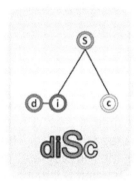

Individuals who have an elevated score in Steadiness generally exhibit these types of tendencies:

Elevated S individuals are thoughtful, attentive, and considerate. They are instinctively good at relating to others. They accomplish goals through personal relationships with other team members and employees, but are also able to complete tasks reliably. Elevated S individuals make others in the organization feel like they belong because they are able to listen attentively and think deeply about other people's concerns. Generally, they show sincerity and are trustworthy individuals. This is truly the personality type that has a high degree of common sense, and they are often pragmatic and see simpler or easier ways of doing things.

> *"Being considerate of others will take you further in life than a college degree."*
>
> *~Marian Wright Edelman*

Elevated S individuals identify strongly with working together in harmony with others in the team. They are good listeners, team players, and they strive to build relationships. Often, the Elevated S person will be the most diplomatic in the organization and is often counted on to reconcile conflicts between disparate parties.

Elevated S individuals are usually truthful, authentic, honorable, loyal, and dedicated. They are usually predictable in their behavior and therefore are more stable individuals. They are likely to be more even-tempered than most, as they are typically more calm, relaxed, and patient. They tend to be good facilitators, even though they are not necessarily good at influencing. Elevated S individuals can be understanding, empathetic, and supportive of others. They are easily assimilated into team goals and are usually compliant to authority standards.

One person who used their Elevated S Factor to their advantage is Rosa Parks. Her thoughtful qualities led her to make a stand and refuse to give up her seat to a white man on a segregated bus. Although others had done this before her, her actions sparked the Montgomery Bus Boycott.

Her act of civil disobedience became an important symbol of the modern Civil Rights Movement.

Parks was predictable and consistent in her values. At the time of her actions, she was the secretary of the Montgomery Chapter of the NAACP, the National Association for the Advancement of Colored People.

She had also recently attended the Highlander Folk School, a center for workers' rights and racial equality. She was very loyal and dedicated to the cause but when she took action, she did so as a private citizen. When she acted, she was calm and patient, very typical of an S personality.

Motivated By:

Elevated S individuals are motivated by a clear definition of responsibilities, accountabilities, and authority parameters. They like to work at a steady pace with no sudden changes to their duties. They want to be in an environment that allows them to work behind the scenes, but still get rewarded for their efforts. People with a Elevated S want safety and security in their workplace. They are very motivated by any recognition given for their loyalty and dependability. When working on a task or activity, the Elevated S individual likes to be lead

"One key to successful leadership is continuous personal change. Personal change is a reflection of our inner growth and empowerment."

~Robert E. Quinn

logically from start to finish. They want to work in a team atmosphere that is fair and balanced with regard to rewards and recognition for all team players. They prefer the cooperative environment without conflict or unnecessary arguments, but will stick to their principles or responsibilities if they find themselves to be in conflict with other team members. All in all, the Elevated S individual likes to have a respectful debate rather than an environment where unstructured brainstorming, boisterous debate, and conflict are the norm.

Rosa Parks, though a peaceful woman, stuck to her principles and responsibilities to herself and other African Americans. Working with other activists, she was in a cooperative environment and being the secretary of the NAACP, she had her own responsibilities and accountabilities for that as well.

Possible Weaknesses:

Possible weaknesses of the Elevated S individual are that they can be resistant to change and if they do deal with the change, it can typically take a long time for them to adjust to it. Because they are so thoughtful, their introspective can turn to the dark side and become brooding and self-absorbed. In professional relationships, Elevated S's dislike receiving or giving harsh feedback, even when it is necessary. Sometimes, they can exhibit difficulty in establishing priorities. This is particularly true when dealing with paradoxical, competing imperatives. Another possible weakness is that the Elevated S individual may exhibit passive aggressive behavior when they don't agree with something, such as being openly agreeable, but inwardly unyielding. They want to get along with the other person or people in the conflict, but they don't want to change their approach, principles, or values. Being thoughtful, they might have a tendency to slow down the implementation part of a project.

Rosa Parks participated in Civil Disobedience, which could be seen as passive aggressive behavior. She did not act in anger or in huge forms, but did so subtly and her actions sparked the

Bus Boycott in Montgomery. Although she did not like conflict, she did not change her principles or values about desegregation.

Another person who used his Elevated S Factor to his advantage was Jimmy Carter. His values shaped his Presidency and caused the development of new departments, specifically the Department of Education. He also established a national energy policy that included conservation. He also strongly emphasized human rights and after leaving office, he founded the Carter Center, a nongovernmental not-for-profit organization that works to advance human rights. He is also a key figure in the Habitat for Humanity project. He uses his thoughtfulness and dedicated to change the lives of others, especially those in Third World countries.

On the flip side, President Carter exhibited some of the weaknesses of the Elevated S personality. He was sometimes viewed as ineffective because his detractors deemed that he did not take charge of the American international policy appropriately. Many thought that he took far too long to make decisions and they he looked indecisive because he asked too many people their opinions. Thoughtful people are often agreeable peacemakers, but when you are attempting to make peace with those who do not want to participate in the peace process, a leader can be seen as unsuccessful and ineffective. This is especially true when many believe that they are too persistent in pursuing futile paths of action as happened with Carter's position in the Middle East in the early 1980s.

52 Elevated C Generic Profile

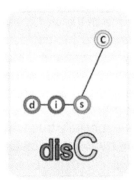

> "Surround yourself with the best people you can find, delegate authority, and don't interfere as long as the policy you've decided upon is being carried out."
>
> ~**Ronald Reagan**

Individuals who have an elevated score in Compliance generally exhibit these types of tendencies:

The Elevated C individual requires structure and organization for peak performance. They are conscientious, careful, and have high standards for themselves and their work. Typically, Elevated Cs are referred to as analytical, methodical, or systematic. They are the types of people who seem to have a plan and contingency plan for any task or project they take on. Elevated C individuals are fact-finders with cautious focus on the details and quality of a responsibility. They love planning and contingency planning.

Cass Sunstein is a person who uses his Elevated C in everyday life. He is an American scholar, focused on constitutional law, administrative law, environmental law, and the law of behavioral economics. He is the administrator of the White House Office of Information and Regulatory Affairs in the Obama administration. Sunstein's works requires him to be very focused and meticulous.

The Elevated C individual constantly checks for accuracy, usually wanting to know the 'how' and the 'why' before stimulating debate, locking down ideas and most certainly well prior to taking any action. They are often seen as the 'anchor of reality' to other team members because they will consistently refer back to guidelines or regulations - especially when dealing with people who are permission-takers by nature. In fact, most Elevated Cs are permission-askers even when suggesting how to change the rules. Elevated Cs are even-tempered and typically can remain objective as they gather information and engage with others. This can change if they have a vested interest in a project or task however and might try to get their way by quoting rules and regulations that support their positions.

The vast majority of Elevated Cs are careful planners and work hard to keep their team organized. They like to define a situation and delve into the important situational assessment questions up front, before making decisions or gathering data. These are questions like: What is the problem we are trying to solve? What are we trying to figure out? And what are the expected outcomes?

Ruth Bader Ginsberg is another example of an Elevated Compliance individual. Since taking the oath of office in 1993, Ginsberg follows the rule of law and applies every case that she takes on to the laws set forth. The weakness in this is that she follows the rule of law as she understands it, which can possibly be different than others understand it. Her Elevated Compliance puts her on a strict path with rules and regulations, but doesn't necessarily mean that you will agree with her.

Motivated By:

Elevated C individuals are motivated by high quality standards and organizational effectiveness. They like tasks and projects that are scoped and defined. They work best when there are clear-cut expectations of and boundaries for actions and relationships. Elevated Cs like rewards and recognition for individual work efforts even though they are motivated by team commitment to a project. They prefer practical work procedures and routines that lead to enhanced efficiencies. Typically, they like a work environment without conflicts or arguments. They like to have instructions and reassurance that the work they are doing is adhering to the standards expected of them.

"The most difficult thing is the decision to act, the rest is merely tenacity. The fears are paper tigers. You can do anything you decide to do. You can act to change and control your life; and the procedure, the process is its own reward."

~Amelia Earhart

Possible Weaknesses:

Some possible weaknesses of the Elevated C individual can be stress when they do not understand precisely how the task fits into the big picture. They can become agitated when surprises or sudden changes occur, and can become uncomfortable when ideas and statements are not fully supported with a comprehensive proven set of data.

Sometimes, the Elevated C individual is constrained by procedures and methods, which can cut back on their creativity. Rather than argue or openly go head-to-head with colleagues for what they believe in, they can become mired in resistance or sabotage when they do not agree with the goals or methodologies being employed. Occasionally, the Elevated C person will cave into authority and can become bogged down by their inability to grant exceptions to their coworkers. Sometimes, the Elevated C person can be viewed as stubborn by other team members or peers because of their unwillingness to budge from their thinking of what the proper or appropriate way to complete a project is. They are often viewed as 'stoppers', pen pushers, or bureaucrats because of their tendency to quote rules to make others fall in line with the current way of doing things.

"The one who adapts his policy to the times prospers, and likewise that the one whose policy clashes with the demands of the times does not."

~Niccolo Machiavelli

In examining how Sunstein has to operate, he must be very set in his ways and very sure of the rules and procedures and probably does not like to deviate from them. For him and the country, the stakes are high. As an Elevated C person, he may believe that there is one right way of doing things and he may be tempted to lock out other ideas and suggestions. Sunstein is sometimes viewed as getting frustrated when his team is working on a regulation and it is called off, seemingly on a whim from elected officials. He thinks that once he has set his team in motion and they are working their plan it is a waste of valuable expended time and efforts to change direction.

Another person who is had Elevated C tendencies is Albert Einstein. He used his knowledge of physics and the rules of how the universe operates to develop his Theory of Relativity and the $E=MC^2$ equation. Although he did not participate directly in the invention of the atomic bomb, his research and theories were instrumental in its development.

He also discovered the theory of general relativity, revolutionizing physics. Although he changed the rules, he had to use his knowledge of the general rules of scientific discovery to put forth new theories and laws.

"The important thing is not to stop questioning. Curiosity has its own reason for existing."

~Albert Einstein

53 Elevated DI Generic Profile

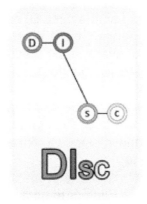

Individuals who rank Elevated Dominance with Elevated Influence generally exhibit these tendencies:

Elevated Dominance and Influence individuals generally exhibit a blend of assertiveness, political astuteness, independence, and sociability. These individuals have a tendency to be direct and dynamic, tempered with an enthusiastic and self-confident manner. They can be charming, while at the same time being extremely action oriented and self-motivated. Most often, individuals with this type of personality will attempt to work toward decisive goals that often involve teamwork or those that are dependent on the work of others to get them accomplished. Fortunately, the Elevated D and I individual will most often try to achieve their goals by working closely with those around them, creating a highly motivated team. A word of caution, however, that if their team members do not have a high energy level or the ability to move at a fast pace, they might be quickly burnt out working for this type of person or they may be frustrated at the pace of change that is likely to occur in a team led by an Elevated D, Elevated I type.

Rush Limbaugh is a person who uses his DI to his advantage. Limbaugh is an American Talk Show Host, a conservative political commentator, and an opinion leader in conservative politics in the United States. Using his on-air popularity and domineering personality, he criticizes liberal policies and accuses the American mainstream media of being too strongly liberal. Limbaugh is very enthusiastic and, as such, attracts attention from across the United States. It also causes him to be polarizing, often pitting the rest of the media against him.

The Elevated D and I individual will be more than willing to sacrifice their assertiveness and tendency to be domineering because they often have a burning desire to be respected, while at the same time having people like and approve of them. DISC instructors typically point out this type of profile shape as the classic profile for a salesperson, who is required to work independently, to think and react quickly, and to adapt to changing situations that require them to use a subtle combination of persuasion and influence as well as driving to get others to accept their points of view or proposals.

They look for continuous improvement, so that the situation does not repeat itself, and they are capable of propelling people toward decisions, but they will seek adequate time to either work behind the scenes or build buy in and consensus with other team members.

Many salespeople are good examples of the Elevated D and I personality, as are radio-personalities. For radio-personalities, there is just audio and the power of voice, which is the only one method of persuasion.

> *"One important key to success is self-confidence. An important key to self- confidence is preparation."*
>
> *~Arthur Ashe*

Another example of an Elevated DI person was John F. Kennedy. JFK is still one of America's most revered public figures. He consistently knew how to leverage the media to drive his agenda. His famous Nixon debate will go down in the history books as an excellent example of influence tactics (using the Law of Image and the Law of Status) winning out over a far more prepared elder statesman. JFK knew how to use his good looks and a subtle combination of persuasion and influence to drive his points home to win the highest office in the land.

JFK also used his Dominance and Influence Factors to accomplish many things during his short presidency by sending out clear messages about his vision of America's future. He was the youngest president ever elected and he and his family were regarded more like movie stars than politicians. Theodore White's December 1963 essay, based on an interview with Jacqueline Kennedy, established the analogy of King Arthur and Camelot with John F. Kennedy's presidency. It was this essay that created the association of Camelot with JFK's 1000-day presidency. White wrote these words describing what JFK's Camelot represented, "a magic moment in American history, when gallant men danced with beautiful women, when great deeds were done, when artists, writers, and poets met at the White House, and the barbarians beyond the walls held back". But it wasn't just music and laughter at the White House. This was a time when an Elevated Dominance and Influence personality was essential for the country. Events during his short two year presidency included the Bay of Pigs Invasion, the Cuban Missile Crisis, the building of the Berlin Wall, the Space Race, the African-American Civil Rights Movement, and the early stages of the Vietnam War. During his Presidency and even today, JFK ranks highly in public opinion ratings. JFK came in third, after Martin Luther King and Mother Theresa, in Gallup's List of Widely Admired People.

> *"My main job was developing talent. I was a gardener providing water and other nourishment to our top 750 people. Of course, I had to pull out some weeds, too."*
>
> *~Jack Welch*

Associated Sub-Factors:
D>s - Self-motivation
D>c - Independence
I>s - Enthusiasm
I>c - Self-confidence

Opposing Sub-Factors Necessary for Adaptation:
S>d - Patience
C>d- Cooperativeness
S>i - Thoughtfulness
C>i - Accuracy

Motivated By:

The Elevated DI individual is motivated by an emphasis on results through working with teams and through others in challenging and innovative team environments. They seek out new challenges and often do extremely well in highly stressful situations and professions that many others would find much too harrowing or difficult to deal with. They love overcoming obstacles in a collaborative atmosphere, and they also love putting out fires in team situations! Their need for achievement and success will insist that they find the root cause and influence of situations.

"If you pick the right people and give them the opportunity to spread their wings and put compensation as a carrier behind it, you almost don't have to manage them."

~Jack Welch

They are often fully capable of a high level of authority because their influencing skills are matched by their drive to complete goals, and although competitive, they will not stomp on others to achieve goals at times, achieve success or recognition. They tend to be good motivators who will 'egg the team on' to better the last best. They are highly motivated by friendly competition.

Rush Limbaugh uses his authority and influencing skills to drive his goals and compete with other radio stations and opinions. In his line of work, you have to be the best. If ratings drop and not as many people are listening, the radio station will find someone else whose opinions will generate audience support. Competition is key in the radio world and Limbaugh uses his Dominance and Influence to his advantage when presenting on air.

The necessity for successful achievement means that they are predisposed to undertake almost any challenge as long as the challenge has associated rewards and recognition tagged to it. The Elevated Dominance individual is usually willing to take calculated risks, but the Elevated Influence Factor associated with this type of individual will temper that same risk-taking. It is important to grant the appropriate level of authority to these individuals for them to make decisions, however, this authority may be swayed by personal relationships or other subjective persuasion Factors. This type of individual has their batteries renewed by other people and therefore they exhibit a high energy level that is rarely seen in other types of profiles. But be warned: Unfortunately, this energy level can burn out those around them!

When Limbaugh presents on air, he must have high energy. A boring radio presentation would turn away listeners and they would choose another station. High energy entices people and makes them sit up and pay attention. When you have high energy and confidence when you speak, people automatically regard you as informative and knowledgeable.

"Nothing builds self-esteem and self-confidence like accomplishment."

~Thomas Carlyle

They are motivated by professional and personal growth for themselves as well as other team members on a consistent basis. These individuals will do extremely well with more authority and less supervision in a collaborative team environment, where they can be free to express themselves and have significant freedom from rules, strict processes, and set methodologies. Elevated Dominance and Influence individuals often see the big picture or overall vision of what should occur in order to achieve success. However, it is important for other team members around them to make sure that someone else fills in the details and maps out the steps necessary to implement plans and ideas.

Possible Weaknesses:

A possible weakness of the Elevated DI individual is that their desire for freedom from routine and outside influence of others can make them seem mercurial in nature to other team members. Although they are focused on bottom-line results, their judgment can be swayed depending on what interests or intrigues them at the moment.

Their desire for recognition, rewards, prestige, or status is often seen as a weakness as they climb the leadership ladder. In addition, these individuals can be highly adaptive, and if they don't see the team moving along in the direction they deem appropriate, they can revert to an overbearing or aggressive behavior style, especially when under pressure.

This type of personality does not fear confrontation, and confront their superiors and upper-level management without trepidation.

In extreme cases, the Elevated D Elevated I individual can be difficult to work with because of their refusal to step away from conflict. When they are dealing with less assertive or less confrontational team members, they may steamroll over them to drive home their points, or get their way. Because of this, others may find it difficult to work with them for extended periods of time.

"Successful entrepreneurs may hate hierarchies and structures and try to destroy them. They may garner the disapproval of MBAs for their creativity and wildness. But they have antennae in their heads. When they walk down the street anywhere in the world, they have their antennae out, evaluating how what they see can relate back to what they are doing. It might be packaging, a word, a poem, or even something in a completely different business."

~Anita Roddick

54 Elevated DS Generic Profile

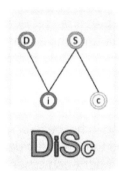

"I hire people brighter than me and I get out of their way."

~Lee Iacocca

Individuals who have Elevated Dominance and Steadiness Factors (and comparatively lower I and C) generally exhibit these tendencies:

Anyone well versed in DISC methodologies - especially DISC practitioners - will find that the Elevated Dominance and Steadiness profile is fairly uncommon in the general population. When it does occur, it is important to understand that the competing Factors of Dominance and Steadiness are behavioral opposites. Additionally, Dominance and Steadiness imply fundamentally dissimilar values and behavior tendencies that in most individuals are polar opposite. These strong characteristics involving trust are in direct competition and this will undoubtedly cause conflict. This is because an Elevated Steadiness Factor is an extremely open characteristic. Elevated Steadiness levels indicate someone who likes to have rapport and trust when dealing with others and they tend to work openly. On the other end of the spectrum, individuals with the Elevated Dominance characteristics most often represent people who are controlling in nature - because they like to control the situation. Elevated D tendencies will temper how much information this type of individual will willingly share with others. To compound this, they like things done their way and therefore can be cynical or suspicious of others ability to get the job done. Additionally, because of these two competing Factors, it is often extremely difficult for Elevated Dominance and Elevated Steadiness Factors to coexist without causing an inordinate amount of stress in an individual. As such, people are less likely to trust Elevated D Elevated S types because others sense the internal battle - this often comes across as a sensed cognitive dissonance - of something not quite right. This doesn't mean that people can't have these two elevated Factors and be stress-free. It is simply a low probability of occurrence in human personalities.

George Washington is an example of an Elevated DS personality. Although it is rare to see, Washington displayed his two Factors - Dominance and Steadiness - equally and used them to his advantage when being the dominant military and political leader of the United States of America. He

"Always be vigilant, but never be suspicious."

~Hellen Davis

led the Americans to victory over Britain in the American Revolutionary War as Commander in Chief of the Continental Army.

Associated Sub-Factors:	Opposing Sub-Factors Necessary for Adaptation:
D>i - Efficiency	I>d - Friendliness
D>c - Independence	C>d - Cooperativeness
S>i - Thoughtfulness	I>s - Enthusiasm
S>c - Persistence	C>s - Sensitivity

"I have no special talents. I am only passionately curious."

~Albert Einstein

Motivated by:

Individuals who have successfully found a balance between Elevated Dominance and Elevated Steadiness will exhibit tendencies that will make it difficult for others to successfully predict the direction that they're most likely to take when interacting with others. Elevated Dominance and Elevated Steadiness are competing Factors that create cognitive dissonance in others.

Washington was a quiet man, but was very strong in his beliefs. After presiding over the writing of the Constitution, he was voted in unanimously as the first President of the United States. He used his competing Dominance and Steadiness to temper each other to develop the forms and rituals of government to lay the foundation for the leadership of the new-found United States. As the first President, Washington was considerably thoughtful about the impact he would have on the new nation. He thought long and hard about how he wanted to lead and after deep thought, adhered strictly to the tenets he prescribed. This was because of his Elevated Steadiness Factor. However, his Elevated Dominance also sought to govern his actions. And Steadiness was in direct contrast to the Elevated Dominance Factor competing for supremacy in his profile. Washington lamented to friends that he was often frustrated at the pace that people took to make decisions and on more than one occasion left the city rather than participate in prolonged debate. As President, he was a strong, determined leader and as such, he built a strong, well-financed, disciplined, and well-managed government. This was the direct result of his highly Elevated Dominance Factor. Most important, Washington was mature in handling his competing Dominance and Steadiness Factors. He successfully let each govern to bring about the best results for the situations and challenges he faced.

Successful coexistence of the paradoxical Elevated D, Elevated S therefore depends on the person's ability to adapt to each situation. For example, the Elevated DS individual might show a highly open and friendly side of their personality if a high level of trust occurs between them and the others with whom they are interacting. On the other hand, they might show a high degree of assertiveness, and provide a calming influence during chaotic times by insisting on a methodical approach. These actions may slow the team down when others want to charge ahead before adequate planning is accomplished. When he was the Commander in Chief of the Continental Army, Washington had to use his Elevated D to be a leader and to develop plans of action. Upon changing roles, and becoming President, he had to help design and lead the new nation, and had to utilize his Elevated S. He was exceedingly thoughtful, political, and diplomatic. He used his Factors to his advantage for his own

"The suspicious mind doubts more than it trusts. The curious mind wonders and questions with delight – it wants to believe in the fabulousness of the world. It's through curiosity and looking at opportunities with inquisitiveness and interest that we thrive and grow."

~Hellen Davis

DISCflex™

advancement and for the good of the nation.

*"Two wrongs
don't make a right,
but don't three lefts make
a right? Two wrongs don't
make a right, but don't two
negatives make a positive?"*

~Andrew Clements

The Elevated DS profile will exhibit a single-mindedness typically displayed by the person insisting on a particular plan being seen through till the end. Once they think about the best course of action, it is almost impossible to sway their thinking. Washington was very concentrated in his efforts to lead people forward. He exhibited a high energy level and high levels of determination in being the leader of the Continental Army. He was very results-oriented and persistent in his goals. In fact, sometimes these Elevated DS folks can become doggedly focused to the point of belligerent stubbornness. This is not always a bad thing when things just have to be done - especially tough things that no one else has the stomach for. In leadership positions, this profile will employ concentrated effort and high levels of determination to achieve their objectives placing a high emphasis on the planning and deliberation processes. With the practical nature of this profile, they will attempt to successfully complete their responsibilities within realistic constraints and timelines. One word of warning - because of the competing Dominance and Steadiness Factors, when this individual is under very little stress, the more thoughtful or contemplative aspects of the behavior will tend to overshadow the more controlling or assertive aspects of their personality. If the they start to feel pressure when timelines become tight, or when urgent or demanding forces appear, this person's behavior will reveal a more dominant or overbearing personality. Their thoughtfulness might disappear, surprising some. When allowed to operate at a comfortable pace, these individuals are very results-oriented, persistent, efficient, independent, and thoughtful in nature.

Possible Weaknesses:

Duality is inherent in this pattern or behavior type, wherein Dominance seeks power and control and Steadiness seeks out a stable and unchanging environment with adequate time to make decisions and mull over options. Remember the most important thing about this profile is that the competing Factors of Steadiness and Dominance mean that fundamentally dissimilar values and behavioral tendencies are competing with each other; these in most individuals are polar opposite. This may cause the individual to be perceived as stressed or duplicitous, treacherous, tricky, or untrustworthy to those who do not adequately understand the nature of their underlying paradoxical and seemingly contradictory value system. Another person who exhibited Elevated D and Elevated S Factors was Carl Jung. He was a Swiss psychiatrist and the father of Transpersonal Psychology. He also founded Analytical Psychology and was one of the most well known pioneers in the field of dream analysis. Jung had to be very thoughtful in his works, displaying his Elevated Steadiness tendencies. He also used his Elevated Dominance to further the advancement of his theories, debate with his detractors, and spread his ideas. Jung often described himself as "dignified, authoritative, and influential".

*"He was a
thundering paradox of
a man, noble and ignoble,
inspiring and outrageous,
arrogant and shy, the best of men
and the worst of men, the most
protean, most ridiculous, and most
sublime. No more baffling, exasperating
soldier ever wore a uniform. Flamboyant,
imperious, and apocalyptic, he carried
the plumage of a flamingo, could not
acknowledge errors, and tried to cover up
his mistakes with sly, childish tricks. Yet he
was also endowed with great personal
charm, a will of iron, and a soaring
intellect. Unquestionably he was the
most gifted man-at arms this nation
has produced."*

**~William Manchester on
Douglas MacArthur**

DISCflex™

55 Elevated DC Generic Profile

This predominantly U-shaped profile of individuals who have Elevated Dominance and Compliance Factors, and comparatively lower Influence and Steadiness Factors, is not especially rare or unusual to find in people. It is the typical profile of a highly disciplined and well-prepared individual with a direct and sometimes frank, honest, no-nonsense communication style. This type of individual prefers compartmentalization between their business and personal life. A person with this type of profile will often be extremely private, preferring to keep personal matters to themselves. This personality tendency might be perceived by others as being distant, unfeeling, overly private, or not sharing in the typical way team members often do.

"One must not think slightingly of the paradoxical...for the paradox is the source of the thinker's passion, and the thinker without a paradox is like a lover without feeling: a paltry mediocrity."

~Søren Kierkegaard

Charles Barkley is a person whom I have met who has the Elevated D and Elevated C personality. He was very driven and disciplined in his NBA career while playing basketball. In his personal life, he is very organized and focused. When he returns from trips, the first thing he does is unpack his suitcase. He notices when people set drinks down on the coffee table without a coaster underneath it. He likes everything a certain way and is very dominant about his views on how things should be done. He has opinions on a wide range of issues and toyed with the idea of going into politics so that he could be instrumental in changing the rules that govern how he thinks elected officials should behave and how the country should move forward.

For the Elevated D, Elevated C individual, they tend to be private individuals and guard their privacy as a matter of course. It is extremely important for them to safeguard what they consider personal information from those they work with until levels of trust between them and the other person is extremely high. They don't like information to get out about how they think and the rules they prescribe to so that others will not turn this information into tactics to their detriment. They might be reluctant to share even to the detriment of team spirit and camaraderie unless someone explains the consequences of doing so. They will prefer to keep their own counsel, rather than confiding in others, and even when others share such information, they will refrain from revealing their personal information. As such, they will avoid situations where they will be forced to communicate with other people about private information and they will tend to avoid mixing business with pleasure. Barkley keeps his personal life and professional life separate. He often leaves work at work and home issues at home. Crossing over either of the two worlds would most likely cause him stress and make him uncomfortable. There is a time and place for everything and he likes them to be separate.

Associated Sub-Factors:
D>i – Efficiency
D>s - Self-motivation
C>i – Accuracy
C>s - Sensitivity

Opposing Sub-Factors Necessary for Adaptation:
I>d - Friendliness
S>d - Patience
I>c - Self-confidence
S>c - Persistence

Motivated By:

An Elevated D, Elevated C individual doesn't consider it necessary to relate to people on a personal level unless there is a purpose for such communication. They just don't see this as a high priority or beneficial in any form. Therefore, when they communicate it will primarily be when it is essential. Furthermore, such communication will tend to be specific, brief, well thought out, with a particular focus on getting the job done, and concisely to the point. Elevated D, Elevated C individuals are highly motivated by efficiencies, personal achievement, and are results oriented, just as are all Elevated D personalities.

"The love of their country is with them only a mode of flattering its master; as soon as they think that master can no longer hear, they speak of everything with a frankness which is the more startling because those who listen to it become responsible."

~Marquis De Custine

Most of Barkley's public relations are NBA based. After he retired from playing basketball, he chose to become a sports announcer for major games. His communications are specific and brief, mostly on what he knows, specifically sports tactics and how to best win the game.

The Elevated Dominance aspect of their personality can be toned down or mitigated by the Elevated Compliance Factor, since Compliance traits will compete for attention to detail and necessity for preciseness. If you've ever seen a team member who insists on correcting other people's errors or pointing out flaws in other's proposals, this is most likely an Elevated D, Elevated C individual.

So, how would you motivate an Elevated D, Elevated C individual? As in common with all Elevated Dominance individuals, these individuals have a burning desire for results, personal achievement, and success. Combine this with the fact that they also must be of the opinion that the tasks being completed have relevance, value, and will provide a return on investment for their time and effort. Unfortunately, for managers leading these people, it can be extremely difficult to determine whether they are motivated or not by your leadership. Although you might be tempted, don't take this personally. It is difficult to tell whether or not these individuals become motivated for any particular set of circumstances, because they hold so much of their personality in - often not willing to share any of their personal feelings - especially about whether they are emotionally engaged or not; motivated or not.

It will take an astute manager to read the subtle signs which these individuals will display. In particular, look for a willingness to open up about their thoughts and their feelings of success, and when this occurs, take advantage of the moment to delve a little bit deeper. And don't forget to give an 'Atta boy!', or 'Atta girl!' whenever warranted - especially in writing. When people they respect show gratitude, they will respond with a warm feeling - even if they don't immediately show it. They will reward you with extra effort if you take the time to say "Thank you!" recognizing their efforts. As an Elevated D, they will most certainly appreciate the recognition even if they hide their pleasure when receiving it.

Like other athletes, Barkley enjoys good press and recognition for his efforts during major games. Being an athlete, it proves that all his hard work and training paid off and he was successful. Barkley was very popular with fans and media, when he was recognized for his good game day skills, his drive to be the best, and to play for the best team, as well as his winning attitude.

Possible Weaknesses:

Unfortunately, the combination of Elevated D, Elevated C Factors in this profile can manifest itself as the individual being perceived as highly skeptical or distrustful of other people. If this person is in a situation where they are skeptical or distrusting, they might not share their personal information too easily. Unless this tendency can be curtailed, it often erodes other people's confidence in the individual and creates a division within a team.

In a world filled with hate, we must still dare to hope. In a world filled with anger, we must still dare to comfort. In a world filled with despair, we must still dare to dream. And in a world filled with distrust, we must still dare to believe."

~Michael Jackson

Barkley is very organized in his own home and knows exactly where everything goes. He can get annoyed when he sees that something has moved and gets frustrated when no one owns up to it or puts it right. He has a hawk's eye for things no longer in their place as not where he put it the last time. He intensely dislikes asymmetry and easily notices that something is not right or out of balance. I have seen him move many things unconsciously to just the right distance apart or to put them in a more harmonious placement. If he doesn't he is not at peace in his surroundings.

People with this profile will also have the tendency to correct others, no matter how inconsequential, trivial, or unimportant the error or oversight might appear. If this behavior is seen as a petty habit, others might discount the person's ideas even if they have merit. On the flipside, an effective melding of meticulousness and accuracy with effectiveness, good organizational skill, and competence, can prove to be highly effective, especially if the person's assertive an forthright communication style enables them to overcome obstacles and persuade others to do the right thing. The consistency and forthrightness of their personality can be a formidable asset - especially when combined with expertise or proficiency. In other words, when they are right, they are right; and when they used this communication style effectively, people sit up and take notice when they speak.

Another example of a person who displayed Elevated D and Elevated C Factors was Franklin D. Roosevelt. FDR made his own rules to how he thought America should be run. His goal was to make American the "Arsenal of Democracy". He launched the "New Deal" to produce relief, recovery, and reform after the Stock Market Crash. This was done how he wanted it done because of his Elevated Dominance and Compliance Factors. He wanted to change the way that America lived.

He created 'The Coalition', which united labor unions, city machines, white ethnics, African Americans, and rural white Southerners. He also launched the Federal Deposit Insurance Corporation and Social Security. He strove to make huge changes in the United States and created more of his own rules about how the country should be run, all due to his Elevated Dominance and Compliance Factors.

56 Elevated IS Generic Profile

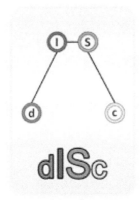

Individuals who tally up an Elevated Influence and Steadiness score (and comparatively lower Dominance & Compliance) generally are indicative of an individual who is geared toward emotional involvement and feelings rather than data, facts, and objectivity. The inverted U-shaped pattern depicted by the combination of the Elevated I & S Factors of this profile, will generally spend an inordinate amount of time trying to understand people. These individuals enjoy getting involved at a deeper level in relationships than most would consider comfortable. This pattern is often labeled the 'counselor' or 'advisor' profile. These individuals seek knowledge about other people's feelings, emotions, thoughts, view points, perceptions, and ways of behaving to make sense of the world. These people are open and confident in their dealings with others. They have a high level of empathy and a willingness to be helpful, especially when others are suffering or in pain, which is the mark of this pattern.

When the U-shaped pattern is highly elevated - and there is a big difference in the elevated IS and lower DC Factors - the individual will tend to be extremely outgoing, persuasive, charming, charismatic, and sometimes described as having a magnetic personality. Their friends and co-workers tend to find them alluring, easy to be around, and fascinating. When Elevated I & S speak, because of their depth of knowledge of emotions and their ability to influence people, others find them easy to be around and enjoy their company. Because of their ability to be thoughtful as well as have a high degree of influence and empathy, they're often described as kind and captivating.

Benjamin Franklin is an excellent example someone with an elevated I & S personality. Throughout his life he was known as charming, witty, and charismatic. While serving as the American ambassador to the Court of Louis XVI, he was able to use his popularity and captivating personality to help influence France into signing The Treaty of Alliance with America in 1778. By signing the treaty, France acknowledged that America was an independent nation and promised to aid militarily if attacked by England. Franklin's personality helped bring about America's victory in the Revolutionary War through the signing of this treaty.

Franklin, as is often with people who have elevated I & S, had honed his communication abilities and was able to read people well. He was the consummate elder statesman helping his peers come together for the good of the fledgling nation.

During the First Continental Congress, he assisted the crafters of the Declaration of Independence think through the impact of their statements; and was the cooler head reining in Adams and Jefferson by prompting them to be mindful of their actions and words as they debated.

Co-workers will regard these types of people as leaders in the classic sense of the word, and many will naturally trust them and follow their advice because they tend to have put a lot of thoughtfulness into their recommendations so they make sense. In addition, they will be looked to for vision, direction, or strategy. When this occurs, people are most often looking for validation of ideas already put forward by a leader, rather than looking to this individual to provide the actual direction.

The Elevated I & S will tend to thrive in a leadership supporting role because of their communication and empathy, but their dislike of antagonism and conflict may keep them from taking on a more dominant role. In the team environment, they are often considered the peacemakers and generally seek a win-win situation for all involved. An example of this would be Mahatma Gandhi, one of the most influential people in the last one hundred years. His belief in civil disobedience and influence helped India gain independence and inspired civil rights and freedom around the world. He is known for his belief in peaceful resistance and strong nonviolence stance, which he used to form hunger strikes and peaceful protests that helped bring freedom and equality to India. However, this personality type will frustrate an Elevated D-type individual because Elevated Dominance personalities will perceive this person as too wrapped up in the emotions, talking for the sake of talking, and having feelings for the situation, rather than focusing on results and efficiencies.

> *"The remarkable thing is we have a choice every day regarding the attitude we will embrace for that day. We cannot change our past . . . we cannot change the fact that people will act in a certain way. We cannot change the inevitable. The only thing we can do is play on the one string we have, and that is our attitude. . . . I am convinced that life is 10% what happens to me and 90% how I react to it."*
>
> *~Charles Swindoll*

Associated Sub-Factors:
I>d - Friendliness
I>c - Self-confidence
S>d - Patience
S>c - Persistence

Opposing Sub-Factors Necessary for Adaptation:
D>i - Efficiency
C>i - Accuracy
D>s - Self-Motivation
C>s - Sensitivity

Motivated By:

When a person has an elevated I & S, they have the classic profile of a people pleaser. The law of people pleasing is a powerful Factor in their human relationships. The elevated I & S individual will go out of their way to please people, because of their desire to be liked by everyone. They will shun antagonism, conflict and will avoid rejection and confrontation whenever possible. In teams, where conflict may occur frequently, this person serves a vital function. They need to feel that they are adding value by helping others work through their problems on a personal level.

The Elevated I & S individuals work most effectively in environments where cooperation, communication, and open debate are deemed valuable. If this environment does not exist, they will strive to make it so. Because of this, elevated I & S's are often best suited in a supporting role for a more dominant leader. When the partnership of a dominant leader and this inverted U-shaped profile exist, the organization can benefit enormously.

The balance between these two different individuals causes enough stress to propel and drive a team forward; while at the same time making sure that the individuals in the team are listened to and respected as integral parts of the organization. This individual's Elevated I Factor, complete with high level of communication abilities, will offset a more domineering leader for the betterment of the team. For this partnership to work, this individual must feel that they are appreciated and respected in their own right. They must be allowed enough latitude to socialize and communicate within a team environment without being labeled as too touchy-feely or ineffective.

Possible Weaknesses:

The individual displaying an Elevated I & S, should make sure that they are not overly involved in personal matters with other employees. This can cause frustration and the perception that the individual is inefficient and ineffective. They should strive to balance emotional involvement with appropriate facts and data. In a business setting, they must ensure that they add sufficient value in achieving goals as well as communicating effectively, and the balance between the two is important. In a family setting, they have to make sure that they don't take on the responsibility of solving everyone's problem and always being the peacemaker. Another problem in families is that this individual might become the hub of conflict when all family members gravitate to them whenever conflict arises.

Another example of someone with a elevated I & S would be the American astrophysicist Carl Sagan. Sagan was extremely influential through his 1980's television series Cosmos: A Personal Voyage and through over six hundred scientific papers and articles. His charismatic personality and thoughtfulness allowed him to be a pioneer for space exploration and natural sciences. Christiane Amanpour is another great example of an Elevated IS individual. Working for CNN, CBS, and ABC, she has covered numerous stories, mainly international issues, which have awarded her much recognition. She is persistent and friendly in her approach and works hard to get the most from the news. The Influence and Steadiness Factors blend together well to produce great news reporting.

"We need to be in control of ourselves - our appetites, our passions - to do right by others. It takes will to keep emotion under the control of reason."

~Thomas Lickona

57 Elevated IC Generic Profile

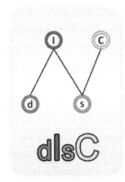

Individuals that have both Elevated Influence & Compliance Factors (and comparatively lower Dominance & Steadiness Factors) will generally exhibit these types of tendencies:

Depending upon the actual circumstance, the hallmark of this profile pattern, where Influence and Compliance are nearly equally highly elevated when compared to the two D&S scores on the chart, is that this individual might exhibit either influencing or Compliance related behaviors depending on the Factor that governs the situation. On one hand, the highly Elevated Influence Factor means that the individual has a high need for relationships, and will seek other people's approval; and will be flexible in dealing with different people and is more than able to change influencing tactics when required. While on the other hand, due to the elevated Compliance Factor, that same person will need to know what is expected of them, what rules govern them, and how the pieces of the puzzle fit together.

These two Factors are constantly competing for governorship of the individual's behavior asking questions like: Should I try to make the situation better by persuading them to do the right thing, or should I simply state the rules? Should I set up guidelines in how we should tackle this, or is it best to let everyone do what comes naturally so that they feel comfortable? Questions like these constantly play in the head of a person as the Influence and Compliance Factors constantly compete. As they maneuver through relationships, this can cause significant internal stress as well as external stress on those they interact with as they flip-flop from one to the other.

> *"A noble man compares and estimates himself by an idea which is higher than himself; and a mean man, by one lower than himself. The one produces aspiration; the other ambition, which is the way in which a vulgar man aspires."*
>
> **~Marcus Aurelius**

One person who displays his Elevated I and C Factors is Al Gore. He uses his Elevated C to study and research global warming and other policies for the express purpose of setting rules and guidelines for organizations and government entities to follow. He understands that Compliance is a powerful tool so he put himself in the position to further his agenda through his role as the Founder and current chair of the Alliance for Climate Protection. He uses his elevated I to influence others and to speak on the issue of Global Warming and Climate Protection and to convince others of his information.

The two elevated Factors, Influence and Compliance, rarely meld together in complete harmony. One will always compete with the other for supremacy. Because these two Factors are so vastly different, they are not easily separated, resulting in the person having to pick one behavioral type over another for every situation. This poses a problem for those that work with the Elevated I & C individual, because an Elevated IC's behavior is not predictable since it is so changeable and so dependent on the situation at hand. For example, when faced with a highly social situation, the high influencing abilities of the person will come to the forefront. When policies and procedures need to be followed, the person will become more compliant, based on the situation. The more trusting and open the environment, the more relaxed and open the person will tend to be. For example, a person with Elevated I & C Factors will most likely become very friendly and animated in a more social and casual circumstance.

"Talkers have always ruled. They will continue to rule. The smart thing is to join them."

~Bruce Barton

This may change in a closely regulated and formal setting. The more structured or organizationally constrained the situation, the more the person will try to fit into the rules and expectations, leaving their influential side parked on the sidelines. During a formal situation, this person's ambition and drive may become more apparent and they will tend to become more blunt and plain speaking. This type of profile does not do well in situations where stress factors are high because they feel the need for everyone to get along and approve of each other, much like their personal need for approval. They may look for group approval rather than a solid solution to conflict when it arises. Fortunately, this pattern (when it occurs) tends to have the Influence Factor slightly more elevated than Compliance, meaning that the person will try to communicate and influence in a situation rather than simply comply with rules and regulations like that of a robot. Additionally, this type of individual might have learned how to change the rules to their benefit by using their influencing tactics to their full advantage.

Al Gore must use both of his Factors in tandem. Although one usually wins out over another in specific situations, he must be able to utilize both to further his career and his goals. As Vice President of the United States he initially took a back seat to the more outgoing Clinton. However, as time went on, Gore honed his presentation and influencing skills and became one of the most highly paid orators on the speakers' circuit after leaving public service. Al Gore, contrary to the typical I and C profile, however, does not wait for group approval. Although he does not do anything too extreme, he challenges the status quo and strives to introduce unknown information.

"Developing excellent communication skills is absolutely essential to effective leadership. The leader must be able to share knowledge and ideas to transmit a sense of urgency and enthusiasm to others. If a leader can't get a message across clearly and motivate others to act on it, then having a message doesn't even matter."

~Gilbert Amelio

DISCflex™

Associated Sub-Factors:
I>d – Friendliness
I>s – Enthusiasm
C>d – Cooperativeness
C>s - Sensitivity

Opposing Sub-Factors Necessary for adaptation:
D>i - Efficiency
S>i - Thoughtfulness
D>c - Independence
S>c - Persistence

Motivated by:

People with an Elevated I & C discreetly want and seek the attention of others. They typically need approval from others, especially their superiors. Certainty and knowing the plan is a necessary motivation for their persona. Finding a clear idea of their position and what their job is supposed to accomplish is a highly motivating Factor in their lives and work performance.

Elevated I & C's will strive to discover the expectations of others to know where their expectations lie. People with elevated I & C tend to need directions and instructions, but often don't ask for them directly.

Gore's main goal is to draw attention to his major issues such as Global Warming and Climate Protection. Receiving attention and approval of others furthers his campaign, especially receiving notable awards such as the Nobel Peace Prize and a Grammy Award.

Possible Weaknesses:

I & C's might have the tendency to display an unwillingness to speak up and challenge the rules. This is especially true if their Compliance Factor is more elevated than their Influence Factor. But, as we said before, in most instances, the profiles show that this profile tends to place I higher than C. If this does occur, it is most certainly a weakness that can make them perceived to be changeable unpredictable and fickle, and in extreme circumstances, even unreliable, depending on the conditions. People will think that the person who behaves in this way simply takes direction on how they should behave by putting his finger in the wind or takes a straw poll before making decisions. As such, they can appear indecisive.

"I am not going to give you a destination. I can only give you a direction - awake, throbbing with life, unknown, always surprising, unpredictable."

~Bhagwan Shree Rajneesh

Another person who uses their Elevated I and C is Martha Stewart. She is an American businesswoman, media personality, author, magazine publisher, and the founder of Martha Stewart Living Omnimedia. Stewart is very organized, utilizing her Elevated C and promoting her organization in her magazine and shows, fully capitalizing on her Elevated Influence Factor. She is the epitome of a brilliant media personality. In this regard, she uses her Elevated Influence to promote and expand her business empire.

58 Elevated SC Generic Profile

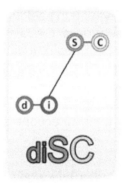

Individuals whose assessment results show a ranking Elevated in both Steadiness and Compliance Factors; and also indicate comparatively lower scores in Dominance & Influence; will generally exhibit these sorts of tendencies:

Individuals that have an Elevated Steadiness & Compliance profile tend to have a combination of accuracy and patience that leads them to be very practical, procedural, methodological, and/or technical in nature. They are more than able to work on a project thoroughly until its conclusion. Rather than just producing work, this personality type is interested in producing high quality work and they will often work overtime to make sure that their projects are completely accurate and devoid of mistakes. Albert Einstein is an example of an Elevated S & C. He spent years on his Theory of Relativity and ended up winning a Nobel Prize in Physics in 1921. His need for accuracy and the patience he had to attain it provides an excellent example of someone with an Elevated Steadiness & Compliance profile.

> *"Patience strengthens the spirit, sweetens the temper, stifles anger, extinguishes envy, subdues pride, bridles the tongue."*
>
> *~George Horne*

Elevated Steadiness & Compliance individuals are calm and logical in their approach to any issue. Even though they may sometimes appear detached because they are thinking deeply, they are extremely sensitive to other people's personal or emotional issues and know how to work with those facing adverse situations. They are often deeply thinking about how best to relate to people. These individuals value strong friendships and good relationships with others but because their Influence Factor is relatively low, in other words they appear to be introverted in comparison to someone with an Elevated I, they won't necessarily be perceived as valuing relationships too much. And unfortunately, this type of misperception - that they are not thoughtful of others - that they are rather thoughtful and reserved can result in people thinking they are aloof and that they have a rather standoffish personality. In fact, this might be true. Over time, because that is what people think of them, that is precisely what they become.

Their self-talk might sound like this: "If you think that I am reserved, that is what I will be in your company." Think about the concept of self-fulfilling prophecies. They live up to the perceptions and expectations that people have of them. This is unfortunate and can result in a skewing of who they really are inside versus what they show the world.

"Successful salesmen, authors, executives and workmen of every sort need patience. The great liability of youth is not inexperience but impatience."

~William Feather

To compound this, this reserved or passive style can make it hard for Elevated S & C's to relate to people, especially in unfamiliar settings because of their need to know exactly where to stand in order to act. So they'll tend to sit back, get the lay of the land, before they engage with the group. This again will make them appear to be standoffish though this is not their intent.

"What was previously perceived as nerdy is now viewed as original. What I like about nerdiness, geekiness, is it doesn't really matter what you're into - it just means you're not a follower."

~Kristen Bell

An example of someone, who through their actions, demonstrated Elevated Steadiness and Compliance Factors is Abraham Lincoln. His persistency and determination with abolishing slavery shows the Steadiness, while his lack of charisma and aloofness can be seen through his Elevated Compliance Factor. He doggedly pursued his goal of abolishing slavery and keeping the United States intact after the secession of the Confederate States. The question is what if his focus and willpower had been turned the other way? How would that have changed the way we live today? The Elevated Steadiness and Compliance Factors can be both helpful and dangerous to the world.

Whenever dealing with interpersonal issues, this individual is usually very direct even though they have a low Dominance Factor and outgoing even though they have a low Influence Factor. This may be a result of the logical approach taken to reach the best solutions.

Associated Sub-Factors:
S>d - Patience
S>i - Thoughtfulness
C>d - Cooperativeness
C>i - Accuracy

Opposing Sub-Factors Necessary for Adaption:
D>s - Self-Motivation
I>s - Enthusiasm
D>c - Independence
I>c - Self-Confidence

Motivated By:

Individuals with an Elevated S & C personality type must have a plan or direction in order to act as well as having the necessary time to accomplish goals and tasks. Not feeling rushed is an important Factor needed by this personality type. This individual is patient and they expect others to be patient with them. An Elevated S & C will work persistently, which means that they don't like to be interrupted by others. Although Elevated Steadiness individuals can get distracted rather easily, combining the Elevated Steadiness profile with the Elevated Compliance Factor means that these individuals do not like distractions and are completely focused on the task at hand. They can be seen as doggedly persistent in getting things done according to the schedule.

Elevated S & C individuals absolutely hate slipped deadlines and have no patience for people who think that punctuality and deadlines are not important. Einstein worked for over nine years tirelessly on his "General Theory of Relativity". His personality motivated his focus and patience and he was also the stereotypical "absent-minded professor"; he frequently became so absorbed in his work that he would become oblivious to his surroundings. If you know that you have this trait or work with someone who does, always make sure to avoid this absentmindedness about time by assigning deadlines and schedules. Doing this will make sure that you stay on track. It will bother the Elevated S & C personality if this is not the case.

People with Elevated S & C also need to be certain that they are conforming to the expectations and rules of the work environment they are in. These individuals like warm relations with others even though they don't necessarily show it which can be a great motivational Factor for group and team projects. Another important consideration of the Elevated S & C personality is that they tend to be rock solid in their value system. They think long and hard about who they are and what they stand for, then, because of their desire to have priorities and guidelines - governed by their Elevated Compliance Factor, once they are set in their value hierarchy, they rarely are swayed from it.

Possible Weaknesses:

These individuals are not typically assertive - unless they are backed into a corner by rules and regulations - and are typically introverted because they are such deep thinkers. They are typically not impressive in group situations because they won't offer input in team situations or act independently unless and until the level of trust in that group is extremely high. This means that people with this profile typically never attain leadership roles without making an effort to dial up the other DISC factors of Dominance or Influence. This describes Einstein well. He was utterly independent which could be seen through his approach to scientific problems and his aloofness from university and governmental politics.

Elevated S & C personalities have to follow the rules and regulations - if they don't it truly bothers them and causes them discomfort - and most are more than content in staying with their status quo. They will rarely if ever ask for a promotion or even a raise though these individuals may go far beyond the norm in going the extra mile. If they do not set deadlines or a schedule or when tasks are not defined in terms of time constraints, they may take more time than others would in completing assignments because of their thoughtful nature. This might sound wonderful because they will get it right and be thorough but it could also result in it costing the business more money in overtime pay. Although they produce high quality work, they might not be able to make instinctive, quick, and necessary decisions at times, which can slow down production and hurt efficiency. Many also cannot handle risk situations adeptly and are often too reserved or cautious in leadership roles.

Ben Bernanke is another example of an Elevated S & C. His methodical, anti-climatic personality is seen through his work as Chairman of the Federal Reserve. He is known as being shy and unassuming, accurate and grounded in data. He is the leading authority on the Great Depression and he used this knowledge to help not only save America's economy, but the world's as well, during the United States housing market crash.

> *"Leadership consists not in degrees of technique but in traits of character; it requires moral rather than athletic or intellectual effort, and it imposes on both leader and follower alike the burdens of self-restraint."*
>
> *~Lewis H. Lapham*

59 Elevated DIS Generic Profile

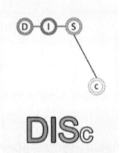

DISc

> *"Remember that feelings or emotions emanate from the more ancient, less evolved, lower part of the human brain, while thoughts are a product of our highly evolved, uniquely human, outer part of the brain."*
>
> *~Laura Schlessinger*

Individuals whose assessment grading indicates an Elevated score in three of the Factors - D, I & S (and comparatively lower Compliance) generally exhibit these tendencies:

The prevailing Factor in the Elevated Dominance, Influence, and Steadiness profile is that the Compliance ranking is low. People with this profile have specific ideas about their goals and they will drive hard to achieve them. These individuals will be fiercely independent and willing to break rules or make new rules that are better suited for their means.

One such example of this kind of person is Oprah Winfrey. Oprah was born into poverty, but strove to accomplish great things. She became a millionaire at age 32 when her talk show went national. She changed talk shows and reinvented hers to include literature, self-improvement, and spirituality. All of this was on her own terms; sometimes directly in defiance of what the studio executives thought she should be doing. But because she is so driven, thoughtful, and influential with her audience, Oprah prevailed and produced television shows that she wanted to be proud of - ones that gave her audience what she thought was important.

Fortunately, because of their Elevated Steadiness Factor, people with this profile will tend to be more thoughtful rather than impulsive which will be to their advantage. They will consider and choose their preference more wisely, thoroughly considering the best option for each individual situation. This was definitely the case for Oprah when she thought about her programming content. In interviews she said she thought long and hard about the consequences of her decision to go against the grain and produce more positively oriented talk shows rather than shocking, or sensationalist shows like Jerry Springer's. She also changed direction and refused to create programs that were scandalous or melodramatic like those produced in the 1980s by controversial and influential American television talk show legendary host, Morton Downey Jr., who pioneered the 'trash talk show' format.

While being very thoughtful and taking a considerable amount of time in the planning stage and sometimes scheming around the rules to get to the result they want might be a great strategy in completing goals faster, to some it may seem that the individual will go to any means to achieve their objectives. Skirting rules at times might be ok if they are ineffective rules but remember, Elevated Compliance people will not appreciate this at all and will work hard to stop you. This might erode all the time you thought you were saving. Elevated DIS people are also fond of ramming home points using thoughtfulness and a high level of logic - even if it flies in the face of current policies and procedures. They constantly question the rules, making sure that existing rules won't stand in their way by using their high level of influencing skills.

> *"There is no substitute for knowledge. To this day, I read three newspapers a day. It is impossible to read a paper without being exposed to ideas. And ideas....more than money... are the real currency for success."*
>
> *~Eli Broad*

Oprah is known for being thoughtful and sensitive. She has donated millions of dollars to causes and people all over the world. As her successes continue, she continues to give back to the community and to the world. Even on her shows, she brings up sensitive topics and discusses them. Oprah is a classic combination of the Elevated Dominance, Influence, and Steadiness Factors.

Associated Sub-Factors:	Opposing Sub-Factors Necessary for adaptation:
D>c - Independence	C>d - Cooperativeness
I>c - Self-confidence	C>i - Accuracy
S>c - Persistence	C>s - Sensitivity

Motivated By:

Individuals with the Elevated DIS profile are fiercely independent, driven to succeed, and persistent. Therefore, these individuals will always want a significant degree of independence when given the freedom over their work responsibilities and job requirements. They will look for ways to excel, and for opportunities to help their team achieve success, but, having the Elevated D will cause them to be highly motivated toward their own ambitions and goals. They like the recognition and rewards for their efforts, but because of their Elevated Influence Factor and its associated need for building and maintaining relationships, they will not try to steamroll over other people in order to achieve personal success at the cost of peers, teammates, or the organization. In this regard, they are prudent, considerate, and thoughtful.

Oprah is a very modest woman who has obviously tempered her strong Dominance Factor by having it exert itself in being fiercely independent rather than domineering or bossy. She runs her talk show and, now, her own network. Although she is very independent, she is also very loyal specifically an attribute of people with an Elevated Influence Factor. She has been known to take her entire staff on vacation to places like Hawaii to say "Thank you!" She is a very modest and thoughtful woman and uses her success and popularity to help others. This is a typical quality of Elevated Steadiness individuals.

The Elevated Steadiness Factor is glaringly apparent in Oprah's exceptionally thoughtful efforts in South Africa where she built the Oprah Winfrey Leadership Academy for Girls. Winfrey dreamt of building a first-class school to nurture, educate and turn gifted South African girls from impoverished backgrounds into the country's future leaders. Her dream became a reality in 2007, when this school opened its doors. This type of effort is abundantly probable coming from an Elevated DIS personality like Oprah. Most Elevated Steadiness Factor individuals place a high value on education because of their thoughtfulness characteristic.

People with this type of profile will most likely work long hours, even over long periods of time to get the assignment or job completed. Due to their Elevated I, these people will tend to be fairly open and trusting, affable and outgoing. They mix well with other people and are naturally curious and they have an interesting combination of assertiveness and patience that works particularly well in a corporate environment. Most of the time, they will appear easy-going, but be warned, their river of determination runs deep. On the positive front, the strong undercurrents of assertiveness will sweep teams along, but in a friendly, jovial manner. Individuals with this profile are often thought of as good facilitators; however, they have to make sure that they actually taking on the role of a true facilitator, rather than centrally masking their determination to get things done their way in the aura of facilitation. In a team environment, they will tend to be sociable by communicating and cooperating easily and skillfully with teammates, even in a highly political environment. This doesn't mean that they are group thinkers, however. They know what they like and do not like, and have a strong sense of independence and direction. Although they won't go into conflict for conflict's sake, they will not shy away from it to standing up for what they believe by defending their views, team, or turf when pushed.

> *"Understand that you need to sell you and your ideas in order to advance in your career, gain more respect, and increase your success, influence and income."*
>
> *~Jay Abraham*

Oprah is very social and loves talking to new people. She is very friendly, personable, and an excellent facilitator. She usually is not aggressive but it is clear to all that she is self-assured and confident. Oprah is bold and she stands for what she believes in. A good sense of responsibility is a primary strength for people with this personality type. Family, friends, and co-workers look to Elevated D, I, S individuals for direction and they can wear the mantle of leadership well. These individuals can be the bedrock of most organizations, because they have a strong willingness to be proactive and take initiative while still being team players.

Possible Weaknesses:

> *"When I am under the gun and I've got pressure on me, I don't panic.*
>
> *I look for the right solution, and then I go for it."*
>
> *~Magic Johnson*

Unfortunately, as with all profiles that contain three elevated Factors, internal stressors and the circumstances the individual is currently dealing with determine to a large extent, what characteristics and behaviors the individual will exhibit at any particular moment. What is lost in this type of profile (with the comparatively low Compliance Factor) from an influencing and trust building standpoint, is someone who demonstrates stable, consistent behavior. The Law of Consistency states that: "People are more willing to trust those who behave in a stable and predictable manner. A person who exhibits a high degree of consistency is often perceived as trustworthy, powerful, and intelligent. Consistency has the effect of lowering the person's defenses in favor of your ability to influence them." Although they are well-liked by most people, they have to be warned how true and powerful the Law of Consistency can be. When this law is ignored, it has the potential to instantly destroy an inordinate amount of leadership currency that the person might have gathered. With their high capacity for influence and a drive to get things done, combined with the need for people to like them, this type of individual might be tempted to break the rules or be overly influenced by the last person who walks into their office - managers who have this type of profile should especially be wary of this tendency.

Although they are usually able to make rational decisions in an objective manner, the low Compliance Factor in this profile suggests that they might tend to overlook policies and procedures, rules and regulations, which may get in the way of achieving their goals. They might frustrate and seriously aggravate an Elevated Compliance person - especially if this person is forced to work with them.

"Concentration can be cultivated. One can learn to exercise will power, discipline one's body and train one's mind."

~Anil Ambani

If the Elevated Compliance individual also has Elevated Dominance - watch out - the fireworks will explode in team meetings causing the rest of the team members to back away from the conflict. Fortunately, the elevated Steadiness Factor balances out this tendency. That said, individuals with this type of pattern should always remember to consider their options carefully in the decision-making process before taking action or making decisions.

Another example of a person who used their DIS traits to the advantage is Nelson Mandela. He was an anti-apartheid activist and broke the rules for what he believed in. He was arrested and sentenced to life in prison. Four years after serving twenty-seven years in prison, showing his Steadiness and using his Influence and Dominance, he was elected President of South Africa. He led his party to negotiations that led to a multi-racial democracy. As president, he gave priority to reconciliation. He had to fight an uphill battle to achieve what he believed in, including breaking rules to get there.

Sigmund Freud is another example of a person who used his DIS Factors to his benefit. He was a very thoughtful man who brought new ideas to the world of psychology and neurology. He was very in tune with people and developed his theories of psychoanalysis from them. Freud was very sure of his theories and did not waiver from them. He modified them as he saw fit, but he stuck to his original ideas.

"A successful life is one that is lived through understanding and pursuing one's own path, not chasing after the dream of others."

~Chin-Ning Chu

60 Elevated DIC Generic Profile

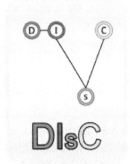

Individuals whose assessment shows rankings of three Factors: Elevated in D, I, & C (and comparatively lower S) generally exhibit these tendencies:

People that have a high sense of urgency, understand time constraints and how to deal with them, are usually Elevated D, I, & C's. Their speed of response and impatient style make them efficient and willing to do anything to meet the deadlines put on their work. Due to their comparatively lower Steadiness Factor, people with this profile are more likely to be impatient and ambitious. They will also tend to act quickly and sometimes not think things through from beginning to end prior to making announcements.

Mark Zuckerberg, the creator and founder of Facebook.com, is an example of how someone can use the elevated DIC profile successfully to build a company but still have the problems associated with leaders with this profile. Mark Zuckerberg first created a website called Facemash while he was attending college at Harvard. When the site had to be shut down after a few days because its popularity overloaded the Harvard servers, students began requesting that Harvard create a similar site. When Harvard did not act, Zuckerberg did - and he did so extremely quickly. He launched Facebook out of his Harvard dormitory room and it first began with the notion of linking only people at that one university. Soon, with help from his roommate, it spread virally to other colleges, across the country, and now, has tens of millions of users across the world. Facebook has grown primarily organically tacking into wind when changes are made to the site. In fact, many people complain that Facebook lacks foresight and planning when it launches changes - even major ones! This is type of behavior is typical in teams where the leaders have this profile.

Facebook has made it no secret that it would like to go public, and one of the things that it lacks is the discipline of thoughtfulness in is strategic direction and planning. In this regard many analysts think that Zuckerberg needs to learn if he wants to take his company

"I like to tell people that all of our products and business will go through three phases. There's vision, patience, and execution".

~Steve Ballmer

> *"I have been impressed with the urgency of doing. Knowing is not enough; we must apply. Being willing is not enough; we must do."*
>
> *~Leonardo da Vinci*

public that investors do not like turmoil. The revolving door of executives at Facebook make investors uneasy, and reluctant to invest in the company. An example of what hurts Facebook occurred early 2009 with the launch Facebook's Terms of Service. Because the Terms of Service were not well thought through, they created a storm of controversy.

They were quickly forced to do damage control at an ordinate level and had to cut its Terms of Service from 15 pages to 5 pages. Plus by explaining its actions Facebook admitted that it made some serious mistakes. This looked bad to investors and users. The issue was that users alleged that Facebook's new Terms claimed ownership over their photos, videos and other content posted to the site. This was shocking to most people who used Facebook. In the face of indignation from users, Facebook quickly backtracked and said again today that "users, not Facebook, own the content on the site". No slight intended at the young CEO, but I think this is where his youth comes as a major negative plus the fact that he was exhibiting the tendencies of an Elevated DI&C profile - a dominant predisposition to influence the rules combined with a severe lack of thoughtfulness created a firestorm of outrage. Knowing what we now know about this profile we can determine that individuals like this sometimes make announcements and judgments more based out of emotion and dominance rather than thinking them through first.

Elevated D, I, & C's have a good sense of self-control thanks to their Elevated Compliance Factor. They understand rules and regulations, but also have the drive to go around them and the influencing ability to talk through them and get them changed if necessary. The Elevated Compliance Factor makes this personality type far less impulsive than other extrovert types and therefore far more predictable. This is an important distinction. Individuals with this profile inherently have empathy and a deeper understanding of causal effects, the complexities of paradoxes, and the dynamics of relationships between people. Even if they do not know the model, they naturally understand the perceptual prisms model and how it works. For

> *"Without a sense of urgency, desire loses its value."*
>
> *~Jim Rohn*

example, they know that the organization has requirements that must be fulfilled, employees must be satisfied, customers must perceive value, and the individual's own needs should be met on some level for everyone to be happy. These Elevated D, I, & C's possess great social abilities in informal settings, having an open and enthusiastic approach, which provides them with a friendly and animated style. Their Elevated Compliance can however get in the way during formal settings. Elevated D, I, & C's will be more direct and determined during formal or closely regulated settings and will show less of the sociable, outgoing side than during casual circumstances.

Associated Sub-Factors:	Opposing Sub-Factors Necessary for Adaption:
D>s - Self-Motivation	S>d - Patience
I>s - Enthusiasm	S>i - Thoughtfulness
C>s - Sensitivity	S>c - Persistence

Motivated by:

Although Elevated D, I, & C's understand the needs of an organization, these individuals need to know that they can achieve personal success from their ambitions and they will not continue to work somewhere where they know they cannot advance. Acceptance from others is also very important to these individuals because the Elevated Compliance Factor needs acceptance to fuel their sense of doing right and being relevant. Certainty is also a motivating Factor for this personality type because they need to know their expectations and understand that they can achieve them. If your scores indicate that you have this profile I suggest that you review the 'Analyze Options' stage of the Decision making Course. In particular take note of the segments on dealing with uncertainty and probabilities.

"I listen and give input only if somebody asks."

~Barbara Bush

When Mark Zuckerberg created websites, he quickly realized which ones would not work and what aspects of each were successful. He then quickly regrouped to put the best of each website into one. Zuckerberg also refused to sell Facebook to major corporations, insisting that it wasn't about the money. As he built up the user base he wanted an open flow of information, and realized that in the early days of establishing Facebook that being owned by a major conglomerate would curtail this objective.

Possible Weaknesses:

The Elevated Compliance Factor in the Elevated D, I, & C's profile means that these individuals are likely to be too self-controlled in formal situations, to the point where they will not be as charming and enthusiastic as they would be in an informal situation. Depending on where their Compliance Factor is, they may not be willing to take risks necessary to further their career, or they may wait too long and let the window of opportunity close. The Dominance and Influence Factors can cancel this out, but beware that the Compliance Factor may cause you to spend too much time in the analysis stage. It is best to be aware of this and monitor its potential effects. Elevated D, I, & C's individuals can be impatient and often need to have their projects done right quickly, which causes stress on them and those around them.

When creating Facebook Mark Zuckerberg was very focused and driven, leading to frustration and loss of some of his friendships. During this time period, people just didn't want to deal with him. As he strove to create the network, his charming and enthusiastic characteristics took a backseat towards his goals. Zuckerberg was very impatient at getting Facebook launched and working because during that time, he thought that if he didn't create it fast, someone else would, leading him to stress over the potential lost window of opportunity. As Facebook launched and became successful, he decided not to return to Harvard to finish his degree. Had Facebook failed and dropped off in popularity, Zuckerberg would have been in a tough situation after letting his goals become more important than his education.

Another example of a person who used their DIC qualities to their advantage was Walt Disney. He started as a cartoonist and after a rough start with his companies and characters, he and his brother finally worked their way to success. He took risks and kept changing as he needed to. When a company collapsed or a character did not work out, he regrouped and changed direction. He assured his workers, that even when he couldn't afford to pay them, they would attain great benefits if they stuck with him. This highlighted his Compliance and Influence Factors, knowing that he had to give his workers some reason to stick around. His Dominance Factor was then able to drive the way to success.

Ronald Reagan, who used the Elevated DIC traits to his advantage, had great self-control and humility. He was very enthusiastic and outgoing with people, having honed his influencing skill when he was in the entertainment business as a successful leading man and actor. Reagan however also had dominant traits; exhibited by his desire to lead the union as the President of the Actor's Guild and later as he launched his political career.

When he entered the political arena, he combined his charming influence qualities with a dominant stance on conservative values. As President of the United States, he made hard decisions and forced Russia's hand in the Cold War, leading the way to its conclusion.

61 Elevated DSC Generic Profile

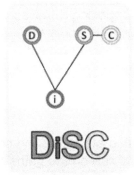

Individuals whose DISC assessment results point toward a ranking with three elevated Factors - Elevated D, S, & C (and comparatively lower Influence) will generally exhibit these types of tendencies:

The combination of three elevated Factors - Dominance, Steadiness, and Compliance - can be a fairly complex pattern. The three elevated Factors overshadow Influence, which causes individuals with this shape pattern to generally place a high value on data, facts, and rational decision-making - rather than using intuitive decision-making and persuasion Factors. They base very little weight on emotions, preferring to deal in the logical realm.

"To feel valued, to know, even if only once in a while, that you can do a job well is an absolutely marvelous feeling."

~Barbara Walters

An example of a person who uses the DSC Factors to their advantage is Barbara Walters. She was the first female co-anchor of network evening news. She strove to be a successful, powerful, and influential woman in the male dominated powerhouse of TV news. Walters began her career before the Women's Movement, one in which women were not taken seriously reporting the 'hard news'. She worked her way to the top by proving that she was a top-rate interviewer by following the rules and not wavering when tough questions needed to be asked.

"Success can make you go one of two ways. It can make you a prima donna - or it can smooth the edges, take away the insecurities, let the nice things come out."

~Barbara Walters

Walters is renowned for her preparation and the thoughtfulness she puts into her interviews about what the audience might like to learn from the people she was interviewing. Even more important, Walters is persistent in her desire to interview the most captivating, powerful and interesting people in the world - a characteristic of this profile is the desire for excellence in their chosen endeavors.

In this profile, when the individual becomes stressed, the Elevated D Factor might have the tendency to become overbearing, domineering, or antagonistic. Without the balance of the influencing Factor, people with this profile might be at odds with those around them during brainstorming sessions or when conflict arises. The further apart the patterns of D and I are, the more this could become problematic.

Walters struggled with surviving in the news world as a powerful woman. She was often the odd person out, but her persistence and Steadiness helped her stay on track and on her way to being successful in the news world.

Associated Sub-Factors:	Opposing Sub-Factors Necessary for Adaption:
D>i - Efficiency	I>d - Friendliness
S>i - Thoughtfulness	I>s - Enthusiasm
C>i - Accuracy	I>c – Self-confidence

Motivated By:

Individuals with this pattern tend to value efficiency and competence, and might have a problem with perfectionism. They place a high value on the gains made from the investment of their time and efforts in concrete terms. They like to be appreciated and recognized for their efforts but this recognition must be as something akin to professional respect not just platitudes and flattery. When working in teams or on complex projects, Elevated D, S, & C type individuals often insist that appropriate strategy and planning be completed before starting actions leading to the final goal. They believe this is prudent and necessary in order to gain a competitive edge and to preserve their valuable resources. Not doing so makes them anxious and stressed which might in turn be detrimental to their relationship with their teammates. Because of this required 'strategy and planning phase', these individuals should map out and pay adequate attention to the transitional timeline phases. This would be especially valuable in the first four phases of the Transitional Time Line. These individuals like to have a comprehensive understanding of the risks and rewards, consequences, costs and penalties for failure to reach goals before going into implementation phases. In addition, these individuals are willing to be held accountable, and will insist that others around them be held to the same standard.

Walters knew how difficult her road to becoming accepted and successful in the news world would be. She knew that if she wanted to make it happen, however, she had to stay on the path and deal with the obstacles people put in her path and difficulties that being the first woman on a male-dominated field brought her. She had a strategy and it was to be a consummate professional in everything she did, to persevere no matter what, work harder than anyone in her field, make connections, and continually work her way to the top. Her strategy and dogged persistence eventually paid off when she finally got her break and became the first female co-anchor on NBC in 1974.

Possible Weaknesses:

People with an Elevated D, S, & C profile tend to communicate sporadically, and will provide input only when they feel pressured to do so or to satisfy the requirement of some measure of control. Because of this, these individuals tend to keep their own counsel, especially when things go awry.

This may frustrate team members, even more so if this individual also exhibits a hindsight bias. In some instances, it might seem like they have a hidden agenda because they tend to play things so close to the vest. Fortunately though, because of the Sub-factors of efficiency, accuracy, and thoughtfulness, their steadfast and patient approach in getting things done will be welcomed as a valuable asset on most teams. In a team environment or in a social group, they will be seen as the bedrock or foundation that the group depends on. In a business setting this means that they will keep the team out of trouble because of their logical ways and thoughtfulness and abilities to strategize and plan for contingencies. In this way they help to avoid risk and to capitalize effectively on opportunities. In a family situation, they keep the family goals on track and are often the ones who make sure that financial plans stay on track and make certain that plans are in place for emergencies. Furthermore, because this type of individual constantly evaluates contingency plans, always considering best and worst case scenario and thinking of exit plans in case things do not go as planned, they are a calming influence for any group.

Others look to them in times of change and during emergency situations. Because of these qualities, many think of Elevated D, S & C individuals as being comfortable with the 'systems approach' to project management. They are highly efficient and effective administrators and are highly adept at understanding complex systems at the micro and macro levels. Most important, this profile shows a high level of loyalty and patience - both highly desirable in the workplace.

Through her Elevated Steadiness Factor, Walters used an incredible amount of patience in her quest for accomplishment in the news world. Although she could have been successful in any number of arenas and could have quit the news business and decided to pursue a different career that would have been far less stressful and challenging, she remained persistent and accomplished her goals. She was highly efficient in her work and did what she had to do to get ahead in her field.

Because of their low influencing Factors, this type of DISC pattern may result in someone being resistant to change. Their Elevated Dominance Factor might overshadow situations where their instinct should be followed. In this regard, they may be open to manipulation, because they are not able to read when people are using confirmation biases to sway the influencing process.

Because they place a relatively low value on influencing abilities, their willingness to facilitate or engage in critical discussions in a political manner will also be low.

This could hamper cooperativeness in team discussions, and it could potentially hurt their ability to be promoted into team leadership positions. The individual with this profile should be careful not to spend too much time in strategic development or be overly focused on the planning stages.

They must understand that as circumstances change, plans will have to be adjusted, and being overly concerned with perfectionism will be the enemy of getting some things done in a timely manner. Sometimes they just have to bite the bullet and move ahead even if plans aren't picture perfect or even remotely finalized.

Another person who used their Elevated DS&C Factors to their benefit was John Quincy Adams. He was President of the United States from 1825-1829. He was deeply conservative and shaped America's foreign policy on his beliefs, following his compliant nature. John Quincy Adams was also ardently committed to his Republican Party's principles and core values. He mentored Abraham Lincoln and correctly predicted that the President could use his war powers to abolish slavery, just as Lincoln did with the Emancipation Proclamation.

Jonas Salk is another person who used his DSC Factors to his advantage. When he was inventing the polio vaccine, polio was the United States' most rampant disease. He strove to find a vaccine and worked tirelessly to do so. He used his medical knowledge to go into medical research rather than becoming a physician, which shocked his peers at Medical School. He had to persevere through seven years of using his scientific and medical knowledge to find a vaccine for polio. Discovering the vaccine is a perfect example of someone using their Steadiness and Compliance Factors to their benefit to achieve something great.

62 Elevated ISC Generic Profile

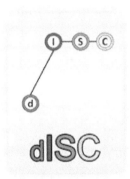

Individuals whose assessment results depict an Elevated I, S & C ranking (and comparatively lower D) generally exhibit these tendencies:

Individuals with Elevated I, S & C Factors exhibit a low Dominance Factor, which means that they are not very likely to be assertive or demanding. Rather, these individuals try to influence others through communication and thoughtful persuasion, especially using rational discussion and logical reasoning. Individuals with this profile pattern are very persuasive because they are social, thoughtful, and know the rules of engagement and how people in their social and professional life expect them to behave. Building strong relationships with others is essential to this personality type and they work well on teams or in group settings. This individual relates easily with others because they are friendly, social, and outgoing.

In a social setting this is the type of individual who will try hard to make sure everyone is happy and will listen attentively to all. In a family, think of someone who everyone loves because they are thoughtful, kind, patient and considerate. They have a way about them with words and always know just what to say to make people be the best they can be. Also, teamwork and cooperation are very high on the value list of this individual, because of their Elevated Influence Factor. In family and social situations, this is the type of individual who organizes the reunions and spends time going over the implications of the seating arrangements at weddings.

Individuals with Elevated I, S & C Factors are thoughtful about relationships at an extremely deep level. The combination of these three Factors allows for a rational view of

"But if thought is to become the possession of many, not the privilege of the few, we must have done with fear. It is fear that holds men back — fear lest their cherished beliefs should prove delusions, fear lest the institutions by which they live should prove harmful, fear lest they themselves should prove less worthy of respect than they have supposed themselves to be."

~Bertrand Russell

how to influence in most situations and allows the individual to be very aware of how others are responding to their ideas. The Steadiness Factor allows the individual to maintain active listening skills and the patience necessary for dealing with group matters.

As I said before, Elevated IS&C individuals try to influence others through communication and thoughtful persuasion which means that they are not very likely to be assertive or demanding. Unfortunately, the lower Dominance Factor ranking also means that they will not push when conflict arises. They will tend to back off when temperatures rise, preferring to let things settle down. Once settled, they will try to remind people to let cooler heads prevail. Sometimes this type of reconciliation comes too late because stronger personalities, those with much more Elevated Dominance Factors, win out. When this happens, they take relevant options away from the group or this individual.

Over time, if a more dominant person consistently overrides the Elevated IS&C's views, this will have three potential effects:

1. It might erode the person's confidence in their abilities to move a team along in a logical fashion. They might become frustrated at having to constantly reiterate a logical and rational path forward. Because of their lower Dominance score they tend not to like the leadership role so this will cause stress.

2. If they are constantly thwarted by a team member with elevated Dominance characteristics, they may choose to disengage or in extreme circumstances, leave the team altogether rather than constantly battling with the Elevated Dominance personality.

3   And finally, if their Steadiness Factor is much greater than their Dominance Factor - where the spreads are the most significant of their associated Sub-factors - then their patience will ensure that they take adequate time to sort through the situation and they will be patient and make sure that a satisfactory conclusion is reached. Not doing so would cause them more stress than not dealing effectively with the issue.

One such person who demonstrated his use of Elevated I, S, and C Factors working in harmony for the greater good is Dr. Martin Luther King, Jr. Dr. King persuaded people through his thoughtfulness and his exemplary oratory skills. In his 'I Have a Dream' speech King spoke to end racial segregation and racial discrimination. Most people only know the words that came at the end of the speech.

The memorable words that said: "I have a dream that my four children will one day live in a nation where they will not be judged by the color of their skin but by the content of their character." These words are indeed beautiful and memorable but Dr. King's entire speech was thoughtful and was a call to action to end injustice. He knew that his words could carry an enormous amount of weight if he chose them well. He did not do this by being a demanding tyrant; he used his inherent behavioral characteristics and was authentic in the delivery of his message. He used reasoning and wanted to stimulate action and discussion across the nation.

Dr. King spent a tremendous amount of time thinking of the precise words he would use making certain his speeches hit their mark. He gained support and called for civil disobedience and nonviolent means of ending racial segregation.

> *"The trouble with the world is that the stupid are cocksure and the intelligent are full of doubt."*
>
> **~Bertrand Russell**

Dr. King was highly effective because he aligned with all aspects of his governing Sub-factors - patience, friendliness, and cooperativeness. He called up the influencing tactics, diplomatic means, and policies he believed would prevail. Plus, Dr. King realized that he was weak in certain areas - one being the fact that he was not elevated in the Dominance Factor.

"Great minds discuss ideas; Average minds discuss events; Small minds discuss people"
~Eleanor Roosevelt

This meant Dr. King had to dial up his sense of urgency and find a way to bring people together but in one where he felt comfortable. In this regard he used these words to insist that people take action immediately: "It would be fatal for the nation to overlook the urgency of the moment…" and these words to make sure that his Elevated Compliance - his need to make sure his followers stayed within society's rules and norms were met: "But there is something that I must say to my people who stand on the warm threshold which leads into the palace of justice. In the process of gaining our rightful place we must not be guilty of wrongful deeds. Let us not seek to satisfy our thirst for freedom by drinking from the cup of bitterness and hatred. We must forever conduct our struggle on the high plane of dignity and discipline. We must not allow our creative protest to degenerate into physical violence. Again and again we must rise to the majestic heights of meeting physical force with soul force."

And finally, Dr. Martin Luther King used these words to make sure that people had patience and fortitude for the long haul: "And as we walk, we must make the pledge that we shall march ahead. We cannot turn back."

Associated Sub-Factors:
I>d - Friendliness
S>d - Patience
C>d - Cooperativeness

Opposing Sub-Factors Necessary for Adaption:
D>i - Efficiency
D>s – Self-motivation
D>c – Independence

Motivated By:

Elevated ISC Profiles are motivated most by furthering personal interests that are in line with what they care about and in making sure they maintain good relationships with others who share their interests and those who think deeply about issues. Motivation should be developed around keeping this person content and happy by placing them in team or social environments to get their work done. In ideal situations, this type of individual will shine in a highly cooperative and collaborative team environment. When working, this individual needs certainty about their position and what they are trying to accomplish. Often people with this profile will look at the expectations set for others in comparison to themselves. This profile pattern does not appreciate others being held to different standards and will not work effectively if they find this out. Sureness about the social aspects of their job is one of the most important motivating Factors for this individual.

King did not want justice and desegregation for just himself and his family, he wanted it for all African Americans and all people in the United States of America. Although King was very ambitious, his goals were not for himself, but for the country and its citizens as a whole. King knew that if he could gain support and affect America socially, a change would happen. He knew that if he impacted people and held fast to his beliefs and acts, he could achieve his goals.

"Ethics and equity and the principles of justice do not change with the calendar."
~D.H. Lawrence

Possible Weaknesses:

Being low in the dominant Factor, this individual may have a hard time asserting themselves in their career and advancing into higher positions of authority. People with this profile typically remain steady, lack the ambition to advance in their career and rarely set specific goals for themselves. Without setting goals, this person will find it hard to further their career. This individual finds it hard to get tasks done without any communication with other people and they can sometimes be morphed by a more dominant boss and made to do their boss' work. Plus, as we mentioned, these individuals, because of their lower Dominance Factor, might choose to walk away from conflict or not fight for their ideas or go up against more dominant individuals.

Another individual who uses her ISC Factors is Audrey Hepburn. She used her war-time experiences growing up and her fame to become a humanitarian and attempted to help disadvantaged communities after her film career. She was appointed the Goodwill Ambassador to the United Nations Children's Fund (UNICEF) where she had the platform to speak out as an agent of transformation to help legislatures across the world adjust their laws to help those in need. In this regard she took advantage of her Elevated Compliance Factor and used its strength to change policies worldwide. Audrey Hepburn spent many years volunteering her time in impoverished countries. She used her Steadiness and Influence to push through the difficult times in order to help others.

"You are the embodiment of the information you choose to accept and act upon. To change your circumstances you need to change your thinking and subsequent actions."

~Adlin Sinclair

63 Compressed Profile

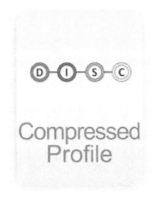

When a profile is produced where all four Factors are within 15 points of each other, it represents a special case and is labeled as a 'Compressed Profile.' When the scores are within that range, it indicates that none of the DISC Factors are significantly higher or lower in comparison to the others, meaning that the profile cannot be interpreted with any level of authority and cannot be discussed for distinct or governing attributes. Although this profile is a result of the test, it cannot be used the same way as the other profiles. It cannot be characterized by specific qualities, but certain inferences can be made. This unusual profile usually results as one of five possibilities:

1. The candidate completed the DISC questionnaire incorrectly or

2. The profile represents a person's perceived behavioral style, a fixed and fairly narrow view of how they see themselves.

3. This person behaves according to what other people expect of them all the time; shifting their behavior for the person they are with and for the situation they are facing - much like a behavior chameleon.

4. The participant took the assessment with a view to making them appear to be different than what they are inside.

5. The results depict an individual who is under a severe amount of stress at the moment in time when they took the assessment tool.

A Compressed Profile is usually an outcome of a mistake or misunderstanding on the part of the participant. When the DISC questionnaire result is a Compressed Profile, it typically is not dependable realistic with regard to how someone might behave. This can be a bona fide representation of your answers and how you selected them, but these cannot be reliably interpreted because of their compacted baseline scores. This result could have happened because the participant misunderstood some of the questions on the questionnaire or deliberately attempted to answer the results according to what they think the test results should be; rather than being brutally honest in their self assessment. You could have answered evasively and changed your answers to fit a style you think you rather want to be or you think would be a good outcome for someone else - for example if you knew an executive coach was going to read the results you might have skewed the results to appear different than what you feel inside in an effort to look better in your coach's eyes. Fortunately, the comprehensiveness of the assessment will not allow this to occur. It will flag instances like this because it checks for inconsistencies and incongruencies.

If you have received a Compressed Profile result after taking the DISC questionnaire, this can mean a few things. It can represent a real aspect of your behavior. The interpretation of 'true' Compressed Profiles will depend on two areas: External and Internal.

Externally, the Compressed Profile usually means that you were confused while taking the questionnaire. You may be unsure of the type of behavior that you should be showing in your current life situation. An example of this is during an interview situation, where you may be unsure of the behavioral needs necessary of the role or job. In an attempt to be the best possible candidate, you may answer depending on what you think the interviewer wants to see.

The external issues of the Compressed Profile usually are short term pressures in your life, such as moving, a new job, loss of a loved one, illness in the family, being ill yourself or fatigued, working on a project that is all-consuming and draining, working with someone on a day-to-day basis with whom you have a less than desirable relationship, or because of the strain of financial problems. If you are changing locations or under stress, you may not be answering as you would if you were calm and relaxed.

Internally, you may be involved with events or circumstances that are placing you under pressure or stress, such as long term events. In this case, your life situation will likely have a more distinct effect on your behavior and how you answer the DISC questionnaire.

If you have received a Compressed Profile and are absolutely certain that this directly reflects your personality, then you could be a 'jack of all trades' or have the behavioral flexibility of a 'chameleon on a rainbow.' Let's look at this Compressed Profile from another perspective: Imagine you are introduced to a new person at a social gathering. The person is humorous, intelligent, and adventurous. They are sensitive, authoritative, understanding, and confident, yet also very careful. As you get to know this person more closely, you start seeing that he represents every aspect of DISC and is Dominant, Influential, Steady, and Compliant. You keep waiting for one Factor to become more apparent...and it doesn't. As you get to know him, you start to feel uneasy; trying to figure out their governing Factor; knowing that there is no way that he doesn't have one!

The truth is, we all know that people have their strong points and weaknesses. When you fail to display a governing Factor in your life to define who you are, people begin to become wonder why you don't display a behavior compass, pointing one way or another. When this happens they become wary of your motives or distrustful because they can't figure you out. They may believe that you are either faking it or are being manipulative for some reason.

Most of us can generalize our friends' behavioral tendencies and say what Factor or Factors are most distinct in their behavior and personality. After getting to know someone, I can sum them up as a result of a combination of Factors that I have witnessed based on their work ethic, likes and dislikes, and from conversations we've had. That helps me to know what I can expect from them. My friends with Elevated Compliance will always have things done on time by the book; while my Steadiness Factor friends may take longer, but will likely be more creative. Then again, my more

Dominant friends might change the original idea from top to bottom, making it more of their goal instead of anyone else's! But you can take it to the bank that it will get accomplished! My Influence based friends will talk it through; making sure that everyone is as comfortable as possible. So you can see, I look for patterns and try to assess what people will do based on how I view their governing behavior Factors. When someone has a Compressed Profile, expected behavior is hard to determine. If all of your Factors are equal, there is no way to predict how you will act or what you will do, which makes people uncomfortable. You may react differently at every single situation, making people nervous that you're so fickle and unpredictable. Most people like things to be consistent; rather than mercurial. If you are always changing, you will make people nervous and they will not know what to expect.

Although we all want to appear as the perfect combination of all Factors, the truth is that we all have preferences to how we like things and how we want them to be. If you have no preferences, you must realize that people will be distrustful and suspicious of you.

And remember, there are no right or wrong answers according to DISC assessments - there are just the governing behaviors in the moment.

The bottom line: If your results point to a Compressed Profile, I suggest that you take the DISC questionnaire again and answer the questions to the best of your ability based on your candid views of what your genuine preferences are. Although you may wish to answer in order to get 'the best profile,' you must answer honestly or else it will not be an accurate portrayal of your preferred behavior.

Contact & Sales & Marketing Information

Indaba Global, Inc. has been in business since 1989. We have the world's most comprehensive blended eLearning solution for small, medium, and large organizations. We take pride in providing assessments, blended learning solutions, as well as certification in a variety of products and services.

Years ago, we recognized a trend in the DISC Assessment industry. After receiving and reading an assessment, participants generally arrive at the same question, "Now What?" We have solved the perennial problem of the assessment and training and development worlds and have provided the answer in a low cost, mass market based solution. DISCflex™ participants learn how to enhance their productivity and communication flexibility. DISCflex™ provides a total comprehensive solution to employee training and development. No longer are solutions based on behavior assessments only available to the privileged few. With DISCflex™ anyone can learn and grow to their full potential.

Imagine your employees having the confidence to enter any meeting or business setting fully equipped with the vital communication skills needed to achieve your firm's overall objectives. In the past, the knowledge necessary to accomplish this - the assessment and hours of instruction and training - have been expensive to deliver. DISCflex™ answers the "Now What?" question efficiently and affordably. By providing participants access to targeted eLearning materials with an emphasis on building a person's behavioral flexibility, a participant will learn the critical skills required to become 'a chameleon on a rainbow'. They will be well positioned in life no matter what situations they face; no matter what challenges they take on.

Another issue the DISCflex™ solution targets: Most assessment tools are based on self-perception only. DISCflex™ offers participants the unique ability to invite their co-workers, family members, and friends to participate and provide their viewpoints on the participant's Business Behaviors. This is invaluable feedback for the participant to adjust behaviors as needed or desired for self-improvement or self-awareness. Comparing the results of self-awareness versus perception from others is one of the most profound experiences in personal and professional development. Making these comparisons over an extended period (after eLearning and applying targeted knowledge) provides the participant with invaluable feedback on their progress and makes certain the organization can prove a substantial return on investment. The DISCflex™ Business Behavior Reporting System allows for this.

Visit our websites: www.DISCflex.com or www.Indaba1.com for additional DISCflex™ supplementary information, FREE whitepapers, and certification information.

Email us at: info@DISCflex.com
Call us at: (727) 327-8777 to learn how to become a DISCflex™ Independent Distributor or to find a DISCflex™ Coach for your organization.

DISCflex™

CPSIA information can be obtained
at www.ICGtesting.com
Printed in the USA
BVHW010607160222
629144BV00009B/244